The Tongue Is Fire

The shadows of memory. Xhosa women at dusk.

The Tongue Is Fire

South African Storytellers and Apartheid

Harold Scheub

For Mark —
With greatest respect
and my best wishes,
Harold Scheub
12 February 1997

The University of Wisconsin Press

The University of Wisconsin Press
114 North Murray Street
Madison, Wisconsin 53715

3 Henrietta Street
London WC2E 8LU, England

"Chakijana, the Trickster" is reprinted from Harold Scheub, *The African Storyteller* (1990) by permission of Kendall/Hunt Publishing Company.

Library of Congress Cataloging-in-Publication Data
Scheub, Harold.
The tongue is fire : South African storytellers and apartheid /
Harold Scheub.
476 p.   cm.
Includes bibliographical references and index.
ISBN 0-299-15090-9 (cloth: alk. paper).
ISBN 0-299-15094-1 (pbk.: alk. paper).
1. Storytelling—South Africa.   2. Oral tradition—South Africa.
3. Folklore—Political aspects—South Africa.   4. Apartheid—South Africa.
5. South Africa—Social life and customs.   I. Title.
GR359.S34   1996
398'.0968—dc20   96-17774

I remember a girl from Soweto, a young high school girl, an African, determinedly marching in that urban ghetto in June of 1976, with a group of fellow students, a combination in her of fear and bravado, of daring to do something that she thought her parents should have done, taking her young life and fiercely thrusting it forward, her coin for the future.

Did she survive the horrors of that year of youthful death in South Africa? I was present at a glorious quest for freedom.

I knew her briefly. We spoke as I stood watching on a shabby street in Soweto, fifteen miles outside Johannesburg. Her name was Thembeka, she was a Zulu, fifteen years old, and I had met her briefly at a home in Soweto the week before, at a poetry performance: poetry was one of the weapons in the struggle against apartheid. Now she was in the streets, her life her weapon, determined, as she had told me, to make a land worth the fulfillment of her life. Without such a land, she said, life was empty and not worth the effort.

How could such a young and fragile person make such awesome decisions at such a time in her life? In this dreadful place that race hatred had created, this Soweto, home of three million Africans living in squalor and despair, this fragile tendril rose and, for a splendid moment, made the world shine.

Who was she? What happened to her during those dread months when over five hundred young teenagers would die, destroyed by the bullets of the stormtroopers of apartheid? Where is she now?

That image affected my destiny as surely as the events of 1976 affected this splendid young girl, who may never have grown into womanhood, whose body may have been one of those fallen children the world saw on the front pages of its newspapers at the time.

This volume is dedicated to her, to Thembeka, and all of the other Thembekas who struggled for freedom during three hundred and fifty years of efforts to enslave them.

Yes, this is God's place, but God is not here right now.
He shall arrive in his own time,
I don't know when because he tells no one that.
He may arrive today, or tomorrow. . . .
I watch over the homestead when God is not here.

—from "The Endless Mountain,"
by Nongenile Masithathu Zenani

Contents

Illustrations   xiii
Preface   xv
Note   xxvii

Introduction: *Some Moments, Figures, and Themes in South African History*   3

PROLOGUE
FOUNDERS OF THE INHERITANCE: "LET ME GO BACK"
Introduction   21
Ndumiso Bhotomane, *Origins of the Xhosa*   31
    The Development of the Kingdom   31
    The State of the Kingdom   43

PART 1   CULTIVATING THE PAST: "THIS IS GOD'S PLACE"
Introduction   51
Nongenile Masithathu Zenani, *"The Necessary Clown"*   61
Nongenile Masithathu Zenani, *"The Endless Mountain"*   78
    Hayibo, Mityi's Stepbrother   78
    Mityi, the Neglected   97
    Mityi, the Creator   119
    Mityi, the Queen   133

PART 2   AMBIGUOUS PROMISE: "IT KEEPS ON HAPPENING, IT KEEPS ON HAPPENING"
Introduction   149
Noplani Gxavu, *Malikophu's Daughter*   163
Emily Ntsobane, *The Deadly Pumpkin*   187

PART 3   THE THREATENED DREAM: "THE LAND WAS SEIZED"
Introduction   205
Mdukiswa Tyabashe, *So Tall He Touched the Heavens*   223

Mdukiswa Tyabashe, *All the Land of the
Mpondomise*   227
   From the Blue Region   227
   The Hunter and Master of Magic   229
   The Dreamer   231
   Struggle for the Throne   236
   The Sacred Snake   243
   The Woman Who Would Be King   245
   Shaka Invades the Mpondomise   250
   A Land Divided   253
   Conflict with the Thembu   257
   Like a Woman Carrying Children on Her Back   260
   Freedom-fighter   262
   Flight   268
Mtshophane Mamba, *Snapping at the Water's Foam*   275
Ndumiso Bhotomane, *The Land Was Seized:
The Ngcayechibi War of 1877*   279
Ashton Ngcama, *The Land Has Grown Old*   282
Ashton Ngcama, *Tears in Your Stomach*   287

PART 4 UNCERTAIN HOPE: LIGHTING
"AN UNCONTROLLABLE FIRE"
Introduction   293
Ndumiso Bhotomane, *She Spoke about the
Resurrection: Nongqawuse and the Cattle
Killing of 1857*   304
Nongenile Masithathu Zenani, *No Person Arose*   307
Sondoda Ngcobo, *Chakijana, the Trickster*   314
Sondoda Ngcobo, *Chakijana, Zulu
Freedom-fighter*   334
Frederick William Calverley, *So Everybody
Was After Chakijana*   346
P. W. van Niekerk, *The Whites Were to Be Killed*   358

EPILOGUE
SEIZERS OF THE INHERITANCE:
"THE STORY IS PAINFUL"
Introduction   361
Nomusa Makhoba, *Jabulani Alone*   369
   Death of the Father   369
   Destitute   377
   Seizers of the Inheritance   379
   Coming of Age   381
   Death of the Mother   385
   Independence   387
   Return   389
   Jabulani Alone   392

Magagamela Koko, *Age and Death*   395
    When You Are Grey   395
    Now I Am Spent   396

Notes   401
Sources   421
Index   429

Illustrations

Xhosa women at dusk	*frontispiece*
A gathering of Xhosa storytellers	xxii
Map of South Africa	4
A Xhosa storyteller	23
A young Xhosa storyteller	29
Xhosa men going to a conference	41
A Zulu performer	56
Nongenile Masithathu Zenani, during a storytelling performance	79
A Xhosa teenaged girl	106
A Xhosa woman	127
Nohatyula Miyeki, a Xhosa storyteller, and her grandchildren	151
A Xhosa storyteller	154
Noplani Gxavu, a Gcaleka storyteller	164
Emily Ntsobane, a Xhosa storyteller	188
Xhosa homes	206
Nombhonjo Zungu, a Zulu poet	212
Mdukiswa Tyabashe, a Mpondomise poet and historian	224
Xhosa children	237
A young Xhosa man	239
Four Xhosa youth	255
Herdboys at sunset	274
Ashton Ngcama, a Xesibe poet	288
Nongenile Masithathu Zenani, Xhosa storyteller, historian, poet	309
Three boys	327
A Zulu storyteller	363
Dancing at dusk	371
Going to the market	380

Preface

"But the tongue," said the apostle, James, "can no man tame. . . ."[1] He might well have been writing of the storyteller, the bard, the historian, who, in the world's oral traditions, breathe life and meaning into the past, and vividly draw its connections with the present.

Political rulers and others have throughout history sought to tame the tongue of the storyteller, but success in such endeavors is only sporadically successful, is never long-lasting. Storytellers, and this includes the poets and the historians in the oral tradition, fuse idea and emotion into story, and in that interchange audience members are wedded to the past, as a significant exchange occurs: the past influences and shapes the experience of the present, at the same time that the experience of the present determines what of the past is useful and meaningful today. Because it is the storyteller who makes the choices, it is the storyteller who most persuasively provides the insights and the contexts that give the lives of audience members meaning. And that is what gives political rulers and others pause. At the same time, the storyteller works within a tradition that assures he does not become an apostate . . . until the times call for that more radical posture.

Writing about African nationalism in apartheid South Africa, Z. Pallo Jordan, later a minister in Nelson Mandela's government, wrote, ". . . the 'folk' can be a revolutionary concept employed for the reaffirmation of a national identity." His father, the Xhosa writer, A. C. Jordan, he asserted, selected the oral tale "as the medium through which to express his protest against the existing order. He sought to transform the tale into a great collective symbol around which the African people could be mobilized for social and political change."[2]

This is a study that gives voice to the observers and commentators, the storytellers and poets and historians who are seldom heard from outside their immediate environs. The collection of stories, histories, and poems that comprise this volume was begun in 1968 and continued into the middle of the 1970s. That period seemed to be the height of apartheid in South Africa, but, in retrospect, occurring as it did between two events that were to precipitate a major change in that country, the Sharpeville Massacre of 1960 and the Soweto Uprising of 1976, it was a time when the end of the racist regime might have been forecast.

The volume has its origins in two experiences that I had in 1968. The first was a visit that I made to friends in Soweto, the vast sprawling township fifteen miles outside Johannesburg, and the abysmal symbol of South African apartheid. I had been playing tapes of some of the stories that I had collected in the South African rural countryside, and doubting young Africans argued that the lack of any clear statements about apartheid revealed that these traditions were antiquated and not relevant to contemporary issues and history in that country. When I returned to the countryside, I told some of the storytellers what the youthful Africans had said. One storyteller said, "Our traditions were here long before apartheid came to South Africa, and our traditions will be here long after apartheid is gone. How do you think we have survived these three hundred and fifty years? It is the truths embodied in the images of the stories that helped us to endure. The stories deal with eternal truths, not with the exigencies of the moment." Other raconteurs agreed.

The second experience occurred while I was working among the Zulu, in Mahlabatini District in southeastern Africa. I was walking alone at dusk that day, in a densely hushed valley. The heat of the day was palpable in the listless mist that touched the tall grass and browsed along the dirt paths. I encountered a solitary Zulu man—his name was Mandla Madlala, and I was to come to know him well in the months and years that followed. As we walked along the path on the floor of the vast valley, dusk became dark and the old man told me of his experiences working in the gold mines, of his early separation from his family because of the system of apartheid, of the misery that system brought to the people of South Africa. His final words that evening, which still echo in my memory, were these: "*Inkululeko!* Freedom! The word is beautiful, the word is precious. We have struggled against this political system from the beginning, we have nothing to be ashamed of. Our young people and our old have died striving for a better world. Our struggle will be successful, but it must never be forgotten." Then he touched my arm, and, knowing what my purpose was here in South Africa, gave me instructions: "You must preserve our words, carry them to the wider world, but preserve them too for our own posterity, that our children never forget what we struggled for, what we lost, what we sought to gain. Freedom," the old man said quietly as we parted that evening. "*Inkululeko.*"

From that moment, I was determined that people who were not normally heard from would be heard. This would be a unique opportunity to document South African traditions and institutions from the inside, a documentation provided by those who have lived and experienced those traditions and institutions, the Africans themselves. And it would be an opportunity to register first-hand and without intermediaries their reactions to the fearful institution that threatened their traditions, apartheid. Mandla Madlala made it clear to me that these thinkers, infrequently heard and rarely heeded, needed and deserved a wider audience.

But the youth in Soweto had insisted that such people were out of touch. These were the country people, the folk: What relevant comments, some wondered, could they make about what was transpiring in Pretoria?

In his novel, *One Hundred Years of Solitude*, Gabriel García Márquez wrote, ". . . in the southern extremes of Africa there were men so intelligent and peaceful that their only pastime was to sit and think. . . ."[3] Intelligent and peaceful, yes, and a pastime of thoughtfulness, yes. But there was a fearful context for this activity of musing and reflection, and these commentaries, poems, histories, and stories reveal that.

This book is an effort to give these unheard people their voices. I have purposely kept out of the way, providing clearly marked introductions and relegating other observers to footnotes. The book belongs to the storytellers of the oral tradition: the historians, the poets, the epic-performers, the myth-makers. Nongenile Masithathu Zenani, Ndumiso Bhotomane, Emily Ntsobane, Noplani Gxavu, Mdukiswa Tyabashe, Mtshophane Mamba, Ashton Ngcama, Magagamela Koko, Sondoda Ngcobo, Nomusa Makhoba: these Swati, Xhosa, and Zulu storytellers and poets provide their own commentaries about their land and their experiences. They would have agreed with the character in Masithathu Zenani's epic: "This is God's place," so let now those entrusted by God to watch over the homestead when he is not here speak, clearly and without the filter of writers, historians, and novelists who can only guess at the sensibilities of those who most desperately experienced apartheid's shackles. Ringing through the histories is the voice of the ancestor, and the harsh and clear warning of Eva Ndlovu, a Ndebele storyteller from neighboring Zimbabwe: "You see what happens when you go against the tradition of the ancients. People who do not heed custom are consumed, they have not followed patterns of behavior prescribed in ancient times. Nothing goes well for those who do not listen to the values of the people of old."[4]

I wandered the southeastern coast of Africa, seeking out the intellectuals in the Xhosa, Zulu, Swati, and Ndebele oral traditions. One of the themes that ran through the works of art and my discussions was the reaction to the brutal repression that all in some way experienced, no matter how remote their homes. With the words of Mandla Madlala and the young people of Soweto ringing a challenge, I became determined that one day I would give voice to these artists and historians.

This volume could not have been published earlier, because of commitments that I made to my sources. While some of them had no objection to their work being published under their names, others requested that pseudonyms be used; still others insisted that their materials not be published until freedom came to South Africa. I have been faithful to my word and only now, in 1995, five years into the new South

Africa, do I publish the words of those too seldom heard from: the folk, the people outside the cities. White writers like Nadine Gordimer, Alan Paton, and J. M. Coetzee by and large told the world of apartheid, and, with smaller international audiences, so did Africans like Sipho Sepamla, Es'kia Mphahlele, and Miriam Tlali.[5] Now, here are the views of the people, of farmers who lived in the distant rural reaches of apartheid South Africa.

I am deeply sensitive to my own inadequacies when it comes to interpreting and analyzing these materials of the oral tradition. It was during my first research trip to South Africa, when I was working among the Zulu in 1968, that I received this epiphany. After a particularly complex story had been performed one evening, the members of the audience were discussing its implications. Feeling somewhat certain of myself, I launched into a symbolic analysis of the story, waxing heroic about internal meanings and the like. Midway through my peroration, the Zulu performer who had created the story stopped me: "If I am to tell you what my story means," she said, "I must tell it again." For her, it was not possible to come to the end of the story, and then, Aesop's fable-like, find a neat philosophical statement to summarize it. Stories are performances, she said, and can only be understood in their fullness.

Smartly and sharply put in my place, I became more modest in my analytical pretensions, preferring instead to allow the interpretations and analyses of the storytellers and their audiences to shape my own perceptions of these works of art. I know that anything of value that I have to say about these works has little to do with my own approaches, everything to do with the schemes of those who became my most devoted teachers, the storytellers of southern Africa. In my efforts to decode the ideas woven into the images and patterns of these poems, stories, and histories, I have largely depended on the performers themselves and their audiences. They enlightened me as to the meanings of their works, and of the way thought and imagination interweave.

"All art is metaphor and form,"[6] wrote Jan Vansina. And, he might have added, so is history.

In discussions that I had with Xhosa and Zulu historians, including Ndumiso Bhotomane, Sondoda Ngcobo, and Mdukiswa Tyabashe, I developed a definition of history that informs the works and the commentaries in this volume. Tyabashe was especially helpful to me in defining history and examining its effects and its ends. He did not hesitate, when relating the history of the Mpondomise people, to include in that history Xhosa stories clearly seen as fictional, working all, history and fiction, into a seamless narrative. The purpose of history, he insisted, was not simply to reconstruct the past, but to place that past into a contemporary context. To do that, to order the past in terms of the present, and to order the present in terms of the past, took the skills of a storyteller. It was not simply a narrative of the past that interested Tyabashe, but the devising of a narrative that contained strands of the past interwoven with threads of the present: the rich combination was the fabric of his society. Past and present have a reciprocal relationship, he averred, each influencing and shaping the audience's experience of the other. For him, there was no such thing as an objective history, nor was there an accounting of the past for its own sake. He echoed the words of another poet, Robert Lowell: "History has to live with what was here, / clutching and close to fumbling all we had. . . ."[7] Tyabashe had no difficulty building history into narrative. Such narratives, as Simon Schama has argued, may be artificial, but "they often correspond to ways in which historical actors construct events. That is to say, many, if not most, public men see their conduct as in part situated between role models from an historic past and expectations of the judgement of posterity."[8]

"Stories," objects Hayden White, "are not lived but told." He argues, "Life has no beginnings, middles and ends. . . . Narrative qualities are transferred from art to life."[9] And David Carr suggests, ". . . we are constantly striving, with more or less success, to occupy the story-tellers' position with respect to our own lives." He continues, "When asked, 'What are you doing?' we may be expected to come up with a story, complete with beginning, middle, and end, an accounting which is descriptive and justification all at once." Carr concludes, "The fact that we often need to tell such a story even to ourselves in order to become clear on what we are about brings to light two important things. The first is that such narrative activity, even apart from its social role, is a constitutive part of action, and not just an embellishment, commentary, or other incidental accompaniment. The second is that we sometimes assume, in a sense, the point of view of audience to whom the story is told, even with regard to our own action, as well as the two points of view . . . of agent or character and of story-teller."[10] It was Tyabashe's contention that the aim of history, the art of the historian, is to illuminate the present. He knew, as a storyteller, the power of story to move an audience to the essence of human and cultural experience; he knew that story is a means to truth. In fact, he argued, story moves to truth as mere chronology, mere memoir, mere memory cannot. And the historian's quest is for a truth that goes beyond linearity. History is a means of organizing experience, but it does more than sift and sort. Always, the past is a conduit to the present. "The past," Immanuel Wallerstein has famously observed, "can only be told as it truly *is*, not *was*."[11]

Tyabashe agreed that the stuff of history is chronology, but that is only the beginning. "History," Paul Veyne has noted, "is an account of events:

all else flows from that. Since it is a direct account, it does not revive, any more than the novel does. The actual experience, as it comes from the hands of the historian, is not that of the actors; it is a narration, so it can eliminate certain erroneous problems. Like the novel, history sorts, simplifies, organizes, fits a century into a page."[12] It is this kind of narration that fascinated and, when he was contemplating his work as a historian, seemed to obsess Tyabashe. Historical narrative, he insisted, has at its center the mythic experience of the people. Whenever a history is related, there is a ritualistic move to the mythic core of the society, to its essential truths. Entrusted to the historian are the keys to these truths, keys that have to do with story and with form.

Writing of myth, Steven Feierman finds that it combines, "in a single neat form, both the historical and the timeless symbolic elements." Considering this "interplay between symbolic and historical statements which is so often found in oral tradition," he observes, "What is in question here . . . is the historical intent of the teller."[13] This "historical intent," said Tyabashe, depends upon the moment, depends upon the mood of the historian, depends upon the events of the day, because the present, he was fond of emphasizing, always influences the historian's conception of the past. Felipe Fernández-Armesto agrees: History, he contends, "is like *Rashomon,* the well-known story by Akutagawa Ryunosuke in which seven witnesses describe a husband's murder from their respective standpoints. Mutually contradictory confessions are made by the wife in the case and the robber who raped her. . . . The objective truth—though there is a sense in which it certainly exists—is indistinguishable, and the evidence is evidence only of the witnesses' states of mind. All historical sources are rays from equally glistening prisms. . . ."[14] Jacob Burckhardt noted, "In the wide ocean upon which we venture, the possible ways and directions are many; and the same studies which served for this work might easily, in other hands, not only receive a wholly different treatment and application, but lead also to essentially different conclusions."[15]

The historian, said Tyabashe, has a repertory of images, both historical and folkloric, but that by itself is not enough. The historian must be a poet, an artist, at the same time that he is a source of remembrance. The past comes to life in the words of the historian, he said, because the past is always experienced within the figures, images, and events of the present. Fernández-Armesto argues that "history is a creative art, best produced with an imagination disciplined by knowledge of and respect for the sources." For him, "the best of a good history book is not so much whether the past is verifiably constructed and cogently expounded as whether it is convincingly imagined and vividly evoked."[16] He quotes a fourteen-year-old girl: "What's important about history," she said, "is that you can sort of be alive when you weren't really alive."[17] It is the past, masquerading as the present, that gives our contemporary experiences meaning and resonance, Tyabashe concluded.

History, then, is at once cultural memory and folkloric motif; the historian is a master of metaphor and form, a deft manipulator of symbol and history. The oral traditions help "a people to explain the mysteries of nature and the universe," commented Isidore Okpewho, "in a way that makes sense to them and reflects their peculiar culture."[18] And Philip D. Curtin has noted, "It is well known that history serves many purposes, not least of which is to influence present action by inculcating appropriate beliefs about the past."[19] For Tyabashe, images are selective, experience is managed into history. These images, writes Donald Cosentino, "act more like reflections from a telescope than a mirror, vastly enlarging some areas and leaving others dark."[20] So it is that history is coaxed into metaphor and given artistic form: "Narrative form organizes a life *into* greatness," concludes Eileen Julien, "ushers it *into* heroism."[21] Let Tyabashe have the last word in this galaxy of comments by historians and critics: It is not by accident that many historians in oral societies are also poets. The historian who is not a poet can only deal with surface chronologies, he insisted; the historian who is a poet takes us to essential history, to the meaning of human experience—as perceived then, yes, but especially as it is perceived now.

The storytellers of South Africa—tale-tellers, historians, poets—are the repositories of remembered images, of the shadows of memory, of wraiths at once unambiguous and Delphic, shimmering between certainty and irresolution, a set of images that quaver in time, now lending confident insight, now posing unanswerable questions. The material of the storyteller is a compound of images sometimes brilliantly designed, often vaguely conceived, always dependent on the vagaries of memory; these images of memory and their organization by storytellers provide, in the end, the only means of shaping reality.

Central themes in the oral traditions of southern Africa—in the tales, histories, heroic poetry, and songs—have to do with tradition and freedom, and the implicit dilemma created by the conflict between the two concepts. In stories having to do with cultural heroes, these two themes merge in the character of a single person, struggling between loyalties to his traditional society and the vision of a new, unfettered community. The tale tradition, by and large, is supportive of the traditions of the society, and the historical tradition documents the tradition-freedom struggle. In the unique history that is South Africa's, because of the relationship between Africans and Europeans, blacks and whites, and the abrasive sys-

Examining tradition, exploring the past, commenting on the present. A gathering of Xhosa storytellers.

tem of apartheid, these themes are given impetus and urgency, and are driven by an extraordinary set of emotions that have their roots in the ancient motifs, the evocative tropes, of the people.

There is a double hero in southern African tradition: the hero who embodies change at the expense of tradition, and the hero who stands for tradition with no chance of change. Freedom is the cause of the first, it is sacrificed in the second.

Tradition, when strong, provides the basis for change: within the context of tradition, the revolutionary hero can thrive, this visionary who moves the traditions and the society into a new dispensation. But when the impetus for change comes from the outside, and would forcibly alter the society and its tradition, the society does not move toward change and the freedom that is the concomitant quality of change, but reverses its movement and seeks harbor in its traditions. It is then that tradition and nationalism and culture-centerness take control. This double-movement occurs in the oral traditions of southern Africa, where the hero regularly pulls the society into new definitions and shapes of tradition, at the same time that apartheid acts as the agent pushing the society back on its traditional foundation. External threats obviate the role of the hero as a visionary, and the militant hero as a protector of tradition emerges.

While apartheid is not always an obvious theme in the oral tales, it nevertheless looms ominously in the function of those stories, occurring as they do in the space between the realm of the imagination and memory, on the one hand, and the real world on the other. When the tales move towards heroic epic, the strain and stresses become evident, and would be so even without the injection of direct references to racist apartheid. The themes of apartheid and racism have the effect of sharpening the conflict, however. In the heroic poetry, the songs, and the histories, the themes of freedom and tradition, of racism and apartheid, appear on the surface of the stories, and an interesting thing occurs at this stage, as the two themes become one: freedom, when one lives under the alien and inhuman system of apartheid, can only be discovered in a return to roots, to tradition. Whereas freedom seems antithetical to tradition under normal cultural conditions, in the context of alien rule the two merge.

When the society is under attack, its myths become more vital. Such myths require subtle alterations in the hands of the visionary hero, but they become a crucial weapon when the society is confronted by unwelcome outsiders. "Myth," wrote Mircea Eliade, "narrates a sacred history; it relates an event that took place in primordial time, the fabled time of the 'beginnings.' In other words, myth tells how, through the deeds of supernatural beings, a reality came into existence, be it the whole reality, the cosmos, or only a fragment of reality—an island, a species of plant, a particular kind of human behavior, an institution. Myth, then, is always an account of a 'creation'; it relates how something was produced, began to *be*."[22] When pressed and subjugated, people turn to their myths, to their heroes, to the truths of their past, and their storytellers, historians, and poets become decisive leaders in the ensuing struggle.

"[T]he tongue is a little member," said James, "and boasteth great things. Behold, how great a matter a little fire kindleth! . . . And the tongue is a fire . . . ; the tongue among our members . . . setteth on fire the course of nature. . . ."[23]

"You must preserve our words," said Mandla Madlala. This book is a beginning. . . .

THE ARGUMENT

The reaction of storytellers, historians, and bards to apartheid in South Africa took a variety of forms, and understandably so, given the idiosyncratic nature of artists and their intent. Generally, the response can be organized into three categories: the pre-apartheid ideal, as reflected in the ancient traditions and stories; the threats to that tradition, present from the beginning, with apartheid being one virulent form of such threats; and the responses to the threats, the emergence of heroes, but with the melancholy sense that accompanies such a life-and-death struggle.

TRADITION

Tradition and the manipulation of tradition to shape the present: that is the crucial quest of the storyteller, the bard, the historian. This grounding in tradition is most clearly seen in such histories as that created by the Xhosa historian, Ndumiso Bhotomane, composed as it is of genealogies that reassuringly locate present society within a rich ordering of person and place of the past.

This quest to link tradition and the contemporary world is revealed in Nongenile Masithathu Zenani's depiction of the traditional master of ceremonies' role at a Xhosa marriage. A contemporary person dons a mask, plays an unwonted role, and, in his duality and his ambiguity, he orchestrates the relationship between past and present, in this case the acculturation process continuing as two beings become culturally married. In this, he plays the role of storyteller, poet, and historian.

The struggle between tradition and freedom, as seen in the tales and histories that deal solely with the society itself, is felt in "The Endless Mountain," a Xhosa epic performance by Masithathu Zenani. The horns of a fabulous ox become, in the language of storytelling, a symbolic connection to the past. But Mityi, the hero, even as she maintains her ties to the past, is moving the society into a new dispensation. The storyteller is creating the most ancient of histories, the founding of tradition. To do so, she mingles tale, history, and poetic metaphor. Tale provides the mythic ideals, history provides the grounding in time, and metaphor serves as the connective and the conduit to the imaginations and emotions of the members of the audience.

Storytellers and historians argue that their histories and narratives, even when they do not contain themes directly pertinent to apartheid, confront apartheid by championing the ancient truths embodied in their works. "We have the only workable antidote to apartheid," they insisted, "the eternal truths embodied in our stories." In the first three sections of this collection, then, the lack of clear anti-apartheid sentiment in no way suggests that the stories do not contain images, patterns, and experiences that are essential weapons in the struggle against racism and ethnocentrism.

THREATS TO TRADITION

Tales like "The Deadly Pumpkin" and "Malikophu's Daughter," both Xhosa narratives, reveal the ideal society, a disruption of the ideal, and the recovery of equilibrium by means of an appeal to tradition. That is the proper use of the tale, connecting the present and the past, shaping the present largely although not wholly by reference to the images of the past. In these two cases, the focus is on the transition of human beings from one state of being to another. This is a dangerous period, because during the transformation process the humans are moved to the boundaries of society, where tradition holds no sway. These dangers are generic and unnamed here, but they are no less historical for that: storytellers knew that their audiences would integrate their own contemporary experiences, with the forces of apartheid, for example, into these potent cultural forms.

From this point, the disruptive historical forces become less subtle. In Tyabashe's history of the Mpondomise, a Xhosa people, a society is contending with the disruptions caused by various external forces: the armies of Shaka, those of the Thembu, and the heavily armed white government forces from Pretoria. Tradition in the end is no effective means of struggling against these forces, and the result is the rending of the polity, with a consequent shriveling of the Mpondomise kingdom and the ideal of the Mpondomise nation. This divergence between present and past is graphically drawn in the poetry of the Xhosa bards, Tyabashe and Ashton Ngcama, in which current African leaders, puppets of the white apartheid regime, are contrasted with the great mythic leaders and representatives of the people of the past.

Bhotomane's history of the Ngcayechibi War also reveals the pulling of the weave of tradition by external forces. The movement of this Xhosa history is suffused with tradition, with the rich lineages providing a clear structural underpinning for a story of the growth of the Xhosa political system to its destruction with the coming of the whites. This is suggested when the Mfengu are allied with the whites, and is moved to its tragic end in the depiction of the Ngcayechibi War.

In Mtshophane Mamba's heroic poem about Sobhuza II, Swati tradition is being subsumed into a larger world context; while that larger context is not represented as the disruption and destruction of the tradition, the tradition is nevertheless under attack.

RESPONSES TO THE THREATS

The disorientation felt by the incursion of aliens, and the resulting shaking of traditional foundations, can be seen in the saga of Nongqawuse, a tale in which tradition is re-invented. The people seek to live the tale rather than see it as a metaphorical insight into culture. The poets lament the passing of tradition, when the society was whole and its leaders represented the people rather than the foreign rulers in Pretoria. Despair results in the emergence of a hero, an unlikely hero, who points the way to tradition, to a release from captivity.

That melancholia and a consequent quest for freedom, that quest embodied in a champion of rights and tradition, are also evident in Sondoda Ngcobo's story of the Zulu trickster, Chakijana. But with the coming of the whites, that society is endangered, as we see in the stories having to do with the freedom-fighter Bambatha, who is aligned in his aggressive need to defend tradition with Mahlangeni in Tyabashe's story.

Nomusa Makhoba's Zulu story, "Jabulani Alone," is a dolorous tale of a youth who, in his move to manhood, becomes progressively more and more alone. In stories that celebrate such transformations, that aloneness is a necessary prelude to newness. But in this case, and Makhoba made plain in discussions about the story that she was treating the contemporary atmosphere of apartheid South Africa, the aloneness means a dangerous movement away from tradition.

The lament of the Xhosa poet, Magagamela Koko, becomes the plaint of a society that has moved into a cheerless relationship with an unyielding and repressive regime.

The introductions to each of the six sections that follow are comprised of three parts. Generally, the first part introduces the section and the genres being considered, the second provides theoretical discussions, and the third presents analyses of the stories, histories, and poems in that section.

Note

Unless otherwise indicated, all of the oral materials in this volume are from collections that I made in southern Africa.

The difficulties of translation are manifestly evident to anyone who has attempted that challenging task; those difficulties are multipled when one seeks to translate from an oral to a literary tradition: How does one translate the nuances of the body? the subtleties of the voice?[1] Considering that oral performance—whether of poetry, tale, history, or epic—is a rich and complex combination of the word, of dance, and of music, the perils involved in translation are endless. Within the limitations imposed by these complexities, I have sought to keep my translations as close to the original performances as possible.

In some cases, interjections or comments by members of audiences are included in the text. When such comments seem less relevant, the comments are relegated to the notes.

A. C. Jordan was my language teacher. I was assisted in some of these translations by Wandile Kuse, Gideon Mangoaela, and Durward Ntusi.

Sondoda Ngcobo, Mdukiswa Tyabashe, and Nongenile Masithathu Zenani provided me with countless invaluable insights into their works, their ideas, and into the histories and cultures of southern Africa. They were my friends and my teachers, and they are present in many ways in all parts of this study.

The Tongue Is Fire

INTRODUCTION

SOME MOMENTS, FIGURES, AND THEMES IN SOUTH AFRICAN HISTORY

Wandering through the rural countryside of South Africa, I came upon a rocky outcrop, undistinguished from a distance: grass and bushes, and a few isolated trees marked the spot, and rondavel-style homes punctuated the farmlands that ringed the area. A sparse grove of stunted trees cloaked the slate of rock, but as I ventured around the trees, I could see shadowed behind them a concave wall of smooth rock. Then I knew where I was: here was an ancient art trove, a magisterial museum containing representations imagined an eon ago. Here, painted and engraved on dusky walls, were works of art ten thousand years old and more, mute testimony to one of the most venerable aesthetic traditions known to man, creations of the San, the first inhabitants of this refulgent, tormented country.

The paintings that I saw were luminous red and yellow figures, with animals shaded in whites and blacks, artists' renderings of hunters and their quarry of sleek elands and fleet antelopes. And hovering in the background, often masked, were the distant but not uninterested figures of the gods: human activities unfolded within a mythic context, with gods and humans and animals decisively bonded in a cosmic unity frozen along the walls of this outdoor museum for all time by masterful San painters and engravers.

BEGINNINGS: THE KHOI AND THE SAN

The story of South Africa[1] is a story of the land—for hundreds of years, that story centered on the cultivation of the surface of the land; then, in the past one hundred years, there was a frenzied, rapacious focus on the excavation of what was under the land. The story of South Africa has to do with that land, luxuriated in for hundreds of years by Africans, then controlled for generations by whites. A romance of the sharing of the land shifted to a story of conquest, and the working of that land by a black underclass.

Before Western conquest, the San were farmers, hunters, and fishers, and their fellow South Africans were the Khoi, pastoralists. Together, they shared the agrarian plenitude of the southwestern part of the continent. The San and the Khoi, called Bushmen and Hottentots by those whose predatory history required that they impugn those whom they enslaved,

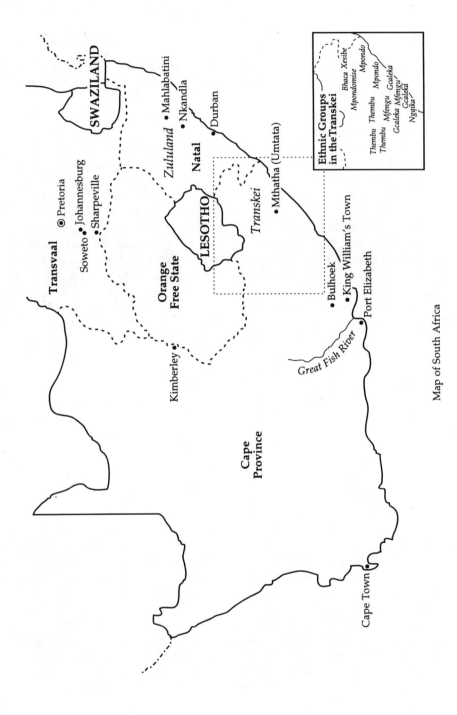

Map of South Africa

were the creators of the first known civilizations of what was to become South Africa, and they were to be the first Africans to experience the pillaging drives of the West.

In the meantime, moving south in leaps and starts from the great lakes area of the eastern part of the continent, Africans who spoke Bantu languages settled in southeastern Africa as early as 300 A.D. These were the Nguni and the Sotho people, along with the Venda and Tsonga. Among the Nguni were people who would become known as the Bomvana, Gcaleka, Mfengu, Mpondo, Mpondomise, Thembu, Xesibe, Xhosa, and further north, the Zulu. These were farming people, cattle-raisers, seeking land for planting and pastures for grazing, and they shared the land and intermarried with the Khoi and the San.

Then, in 1652, the Dutch intruded. A Dutch East India Company fleet arrived, headed by the Dutch merchant, Jan van Riebeeck. He sailed on the ship *Drommedaris,* reaching Table Mountain at the lowest reaches of the African continent on April 5, 1652. His people built a fortress, the Fort of Good Hope, in fulfillment of their charge by the Company to establish a refreshment station to provide Company ships on their way to Indian Ocean countries with fresh vegetables and livestock. Immediately, the Dutch set about to dispossess the original inhabitants, the Khoi, of their land.

There had been earlier European arrivals. "In 1626 a very large number of Dutch ships had visited Table Bay, and during that year the Khoi-khoi traded generously with the English but not with the Dutch, because of 'their ill euill useadge of the blackes.' "[2] And from the start, race was on the minds of the interlopers. From the beginning, an immorality act was in place. "By the *Dutch* laws it is *Death* for a *Dutchman* to lie with a *Hottentot-Woman:* tho' I think they need not have laid that Restriction upon them, the very Smell and Looks of such hideous Creatures being a sufficient Antidote against Lechery."[3]

In 1659, the Khoi and the Dutch were at war. The Dutch told the Khoi, "Your people have now once for all lost the land around the Cape through war, and you must accordingly never dwell on the idea of getting it back again through peace or through war."[4] But the Khoi were equally determined, and so began an unending series of efforts to cause the whites to leave. "We . . . will not leave the Dutch in peace," said a Khoi after a commando of Dutch had raided his community.[5] But the Dutch were victorious, and now more of them, along with French Huguenots, came to the Cape from Europe. These European farmers expanded their herds and their farms, and so drove the Khoi into extinction. In the end, their societies broken, the Khoi were forced to seek work with the whites. In fact, any Khoi not in the employment of a Dutch farmer could be shot.

Land and cheap labor to work the land: these are the themes of human relations in the first two hundred years of black-white relations in South Africa. The Khoi and the San were only the first to become involved in the struggle: South African history resonates with heroic names and tragic places, as represented by the art in the San museum and engraved in historical memory: Shaka, Nongqawuse, Bambatha, Mgijima, Biko, Mandela . . . Bulhoek, Sharpeville, Soweto. In this brief space, let these figures and these places become the symbols for the history of a monumental struggle between contending groups for land, a struggle that moved bloodily to the end of a millennium as a world watched in fascination . . . and did nothing.

REACTION TO CONQUEST, I: SHAKA AND NONGQAWUSE

Now the Dutch, later to be called "Boers," and still later "Afrikaners,"[6] began to move north in quest of farming land. They considered themselves rugged individualists, were intensely religious, kept slaves, and resented any interference from the government in Cape Town. Some, called *trekboere*, trekking farmers, became cattle farmers. They established huge farms and, with their harsh religion as their guide, moved further and further away from the Cape. They drove the San off their land, often killing the adults and forcing the children to work for them as herdsmen. In time, as they continued their relentless move to the north and the east, they came into contact with the Xhosa people at the Great Fish River in the eastern Cape. This collision between the Afrikaners and the Xhosa occurred during the last quarter of the eighteenth century; the consequent struggle over land led to one hundred years of sporadic wars.

At the end of the eighteenth century, the Cape had grown to about thirty thousand Dutch and Huguenots. In the Cape Colony, slaves imported from other parts of Africa, along with Malaysians, began to form what would become known as the Cape Colored people.

In 1795, because of wars in Europe, the British occupied the Cape. It was restored to the Dutch in 1802 in accordance with the Treaty of Amiens. Then, to keep their trade with the Indian Ocean countries within their control, the British reoccupied the Cape in 1806, and this time they did not return it. They reorganized the government of the Cape. Circuit courts were established, angering the Afrikaners because of court rulings having to do with Khoi servants and slaves. The slave trade was abolished, but to combat the labor shortage the government instituted a pass law to restrict the movement of the Khoi.

Further north in the southeastern region, from 1820 to 1828, the Zulu nation was forged by a gifted military leader, Shaka, son of Senzangakhona who led a small group of people called the Zulu. Shaka grew to manhood among fellow Zulu who contested his claim to the throne. He became a soldier in the army of Dingiswayo and so impressed that military ruler that, when Senzangakhona died, Dingiswayo championed his accession to his father's chieftaincy. At once, Shaka set about to organize his people, to modernize the army. He commenced a series of wars of territorial acquisition, deliberately, brilliantly, bloodily consolidating his power militarily and politically. He instituted the *imfecane*, wars of conquest that had the result of unifying parts of the Nguni population of Natal and dispersing others. By the time he was assassinated in 1828, he had welded a group of disparate peoples into the Zulu nation, and had thrown much of the subcontinent of Africa into upheaval.

It was also in 1820 that five thousand British citizens, suffering unemployment at home, settled in the eastern Cape, providing a buffer between the warring Afrikaners and Xhosa. In the meantime, further reforms were instituted in Cape Town, including, in 1827, freedom of the press. A Charter of Justice made the judiciary independent, and in 1834 slavery was abolished. New towns were built, the road infrastructure of the country developed. But the Afrikaners were increasingly unhappy with the economic expansion and administrative reform instituted by the British. They were further incensed when English became the only official language. This law was reversed thirty years later, but the Afrikaners would never forget these efforts to suppress the Dutch language. Then, in 1828, the government repealed the pass laws and instituted equality for "all free persons of color." The Afrikaner frontiersmen seethed.

And the frontier wars, called "Kaffir Wars," continued. The Afrikaner farmers, clamoring for more and more land, fiercely, continuously annexed African territory. From 1836 to 1846, some ten thousand Afrikaner men, women, and children, seeking new land cheaply, trekked west of the African territories. They believed that the government in the Cape was opposed to them, and they were disheartened by the restraints on their language and institutions, angry because of the lack of protection on the frontier, infuriated by the liberation of the slaves, and indignant at having no voice in the government that taxed them. Thus, they journeyed to escape the reach of the British government. These Voortrekkers sought an independent state, a land where white and black would not be equal. The Zulu fought these acquisitive aliens, but, in 1838, at the Battle of Blood River, they were defeated, and their lands were confiscated by the Afrikaners. The Cape government, refusing to allow the Afrikaners to set up a rival shipping depot at Durban, annexed Natal in 1843. The Trekkers, wrathful, again journeyed, over the Drakensberg Mountains into what is now the Orange Free State and Transvaal. But the British followed, in 1848 proclaiming the Orange River Sovereignty.

Finally, in 1852, the British, who vacillated regularly in their relations with the determined Afrikaners, withdrew claims to authority beyond the Vaal River. So it was that two Boer republics independent of British control were born, the Orange Free State and the South African Republic (Transvaal). Many of the Africans in these republics, now having lost their rights to occupy land, struggled against this dispossession. While Afrikaner farms became enormous, up to a hundred thousand acres, Africans were placed in reserves. The Great Trek brought huge tracts of land and millions of Africans under European control.

The constitutions of the new republics provided democratic institutions, but for whites only, while in the Cape responsible government would come for all races. Two diverse European policies regarding Africans had come into being. For the Afrikaners, the Great Trek was a signal spiritual, cultural, and political event: it gave birth to the Afrikaner nation, and led to the rise of Afrikaner nationalism and the Nationalist Party. The Cape was granted representative government in 1853, and in 1872 it achieved full governmental responsibility. There was no color bar, but franchise qualifications kept the number of non-European voters small.

The hundred years of frontier wars dispirited many Africans. After the eighth war, the Xhosa, suffering and despairing, sought hope where they could. In 1856 a Xhosa girl, Nongqawuse, whose home was near the Kei River, claimed that her ancestors had spoken to her, that the community of ancestors would rise from the dead. For this to happen, the cattle had to be slaughtered, the granaries had to be emptied, no farming could take place. King Sarhili believed her story, and ordered his subordinates to follow Nongqawuse's instructions. The resurrection from the dead would occur on August 11, 1856. When that did not happen, it was argued that the reason was that people had not killed their cattle. And so the tragedy lengthened, a shadow of death heavy on the land. When the episode finally ended in July, 1857, many Xhosa had died. Starvation and death were everywhere. Some Xhosa argued that the cattle-killing was a sad delusion. Others insisted that it was a plot by the Europeans to get Xhosa land and drive the Xhosa to work in the Cape.

REACTION TO CONQUEST, II: BAMBATHA AND MGIJIMA

Then, in 1870, everything changed: diamonds were discovered in Kimberley. Now there was a struggle for that land: an African group called the Griquas claimed it, and so did the Afrikaners of both the Transvaal and the Orange Free State. Now South Africa was no longer a purely agricultural country, and hundreds of migrants came into the country to make their fortunes in the diamond diggings. Cecil Rhodes and Barney

Barnato got control of the mines and made fortunes. In 1886, gold was discovered on the Witwatersrand, and more foreigners came into South Africa, and predatory Randlords made their fortunes. The Afrikaners in the Transvaal feared the influence of the many new forces, and this turned them against Britain and against any idea of a federation in South Africa. In 1899, predictably, the Boers and the British went to war. The Anglo-Boer War was a difficult and brutal conflict, a war of attrition, of burning farms, concentration camps and typhoid fever epidemics in which twenty-six thousand Afrikaner women and children died. In 1902, the treaty of Vereeniging was signed, and eight years later the Union of South Africa came into being, and racial segregation became official policy of a new South Africa. In the Union constitution, it was decided to allow the Cape to keep its franchise with no color bar, and to allow the Transvaal and Orange Free State to refuse to grant the vote to non-Europeans. Africans at this time were concerned about the Union's preoccupation with "native problems," and African leaders began to meet to assess their situation. The South African Native Convention met in March, 1909, and the Cape Native Convention met in April of that year. Other meetings followed, and in January, 1912, the South African Native National Congress was formed; in 1923, it would become the African National Congress.

Land and cheap labor to work the land had been defining characteristics of relations between Africans and Europeans to this point: now, add to those the issues of mining and cheap labor to extract minerals from the bowels of the earth, and the themes of the next hundred and fifty years of black-white relations in South Africa were set. And if, until this point, Africans did not know what their place in the scheme of things would be, they began to learn quickly.

As it was in the beginning, whites continued to force Africans from the land to work cheaply on white lands, and now also in white-owned mines. When Africans refused to work, ways were found to force them from their homes to white-owned lands, and white-operated mines. In 1905, white authorities in Natal instituted a £1 poll tax which, when added to "hut" and dog taxes, was intolerable for many Zulu. These authorities knew that the only way Africans could earn the money to pay the taxes was to work for white farmers and the mining industry, which were always looking for cheap black labor. The first taxes were to be paid on January 1, 1906. Africans, resenting these new impositions on their freedom, rebelled. The Africans killed a white farmer in January, then also killed their white animals and destroyed their European tools. Whites panicked. In February, two policemen were killed during a struggle resulting from Africans' refusal to pay the tax. Hysteria among the whites ensued, so that the British army was sent in. Under Colonel Duncan McKenzie, brutal efforts to put down the insurrection occurred. Then a

Zulu local leader named Bambatha, deposed by his uncle, Magwababa, went into the Zulu countryside and began a war of liberation. Also involved in the insurrection was the wily trickster, Chakijana. Before the battles were over and the uprising put down, three thousand Africans had been killed, five hundred of them in a massacre at Mome Gorge where Bambatha was killed and beheaded by the British. The Zulu king, Dinuzulu, was arrested by white authorities because he was supposed to be involved: he was convicted of high treason and imprisoned for four years.

African struggles against white domination continued. Enoch Mgijima was a prophet who led a religious group with about three thousand members called the Israelites. Following instructions that Mgijima received in a vision in 1919, the group built a "refuge from oppression" at Ntabelanga, the mountain of the sun, near a place called Bulhoek, a location near Queenstown. This was to be a refuge from taxes, from white oppression, a place where Africans would be given land. Mgijima assured his followers that on the Day of Judgement, the Israelites would go to heaven in wagons. African farmers in this area had fallen on bad times; the locations in which they lived were overcrowded, and soil erosion made farming increasingly difficult. Droughts and rinderpest exacerbated their distress. And white farmers and white mine owners, who needed cheap labor, contributed greatly to their plight. The white government therefore passed laws, including higher tax laws and pass laws, to force the blacks off their land. The Natives' Land Act of 1913 forced many African sharecroppers off white farms, and divided South Africa into white and black areas. The whites had the best land, while Africans could not make a living off of the land they had. Mgijima's message, therefore, had an appeal.

When government representatives attempted to get them to move away, Mgijima's son Charles said, "God has sent us to this place. We shall let you know when it is necessary that we go."[7] Converts continued to move in, and government officials became more and more uneasy. There were rumors that the Israelites were planning an uprising. When, in 1921, the government offered free rail tickets and rations to those who would leave, no one accepted. Then eight hundred policemen were assembled in Queenstown. On May 21, the police commander, Colonel Theo Truter, sent an ultimatum to Mgijima: Israelites would be arrested, would be deported, and their homes would be razed. Mgijima responded, "The whole world is going to sink in blood. I am not the cause of it, but God is going to cause it. The time of Jehovah has now arrived."[8] On May 24, the police took up their positions, and the Israelites were sent to defend their settlement. When the police gave them an ultimatum, the Israelites said, "Jehovah will fight with us and for us." Dressed in white robes, they ran towards the police. Now the police opened fire, and in just twenty minutes, 183 Israelites were killed, with another hundred injured. Mgijima went to the tabernacle and said, "Look up to your God. The Israelites are finished." Enoch Mgijima, his sons, and one hundred followers were jailed. Mgijima was released from prison in 1924; he died on May 16, 1929. This was the Bulhoek Massacre. On the tombstone of the mass grave of the fallen Israelites at Bulhoek are the words, "Because they chose the plan of God so the world did not have a place for them."[9]

Nelson Mandela has said, "South Africa is known throughout the world as a country where the most fierce forms of color discrimination are practiced, and where peaceful struggles of the African people for freedom are violently suppressed. It is a country torn from top to bottom by fierce racial strife and where the blood of African patriots frequently flows. Almost every African household in South Africa knows about the massacre at Bulhoek. . . ."[10] Z. K. Matthews, an African intellectual and political leader, said, "The Bulhoek massacre . . . is talked about to children and so on as an incident that has passed into what we might call the political history of the people."[11] The then prime minister of South Africa, Jan Smuts, commented, "These miserable, deluded people defied the Government and invited death. They were a crazy little band of religious fanatics and passive resisters, such as will arise at times in all country and among all peoples. . . ."[12]

At this time, British and Afrikaners could not agree on participation in the First World War, with some Afrikaners openly siding with the Germans. Between the two wars, rapid industrialization occurred, and Europeans moved to the towns. The Nationalist party came to power with the aid of the Labor Party in 1924.

In the 1920s, mass political action swept through rural South Africa.[13] Africans, in association with liberal politicians, were seeking to change and reshape the "native policy" that moved Africans into increasingly entrenched poverty and servitude. Africans, supported by communists, trade unionists, and independent churches, engaged in various forms of resistance. Clements Kadalie, from Nyasaland (Malawi) organized African workers into unions, and Africans, voicing the cry, "*Mayibuye iAfrika!*" (Let Africa return), opposed taxation, and fees for cattle-dipping and dog licenses. Many were influenced by Marcus Garvey, who founded the Universal Negro Improvement Association in 1914, with an argument for black unity. In the Transkei, Wellington Buthelezi created a mass movement. In Herschel District, an African district in the Cape, there was deep poverty and dissatisfaction. Women urged a boycott of white shops because of high prices. The Amafelandawonye (the Die-hards) movement initially sought to protect African rights in society as a whole, and later attempted to maintain local authority. They had an anti-white ideology and wanted a political system based on a popular chieftaincy. Under the influence of the Wellington Movement, some believed that American blacks would relieve their misery and, arriving in airplanes, would bomb whites and African non-believers.[14]

In 1930, South Africa became an independent member of the British Commonwealth. In 1939, the Afrikaners again opposed South Africa's entry into the war. But South Africa did participate, and some Afrikaners went to jail because of their open support of Germany.

Jan Smuts, the leader of South Africa, enjoyed a positive world reputation as a liberal visionary and fair-minded statesman. In 1945, as the Second World War drew to a close, he travelled to the United States to take part in the international San Francisco Conference, where he hoped to see his plans for a new order crystallized. It was his preamble to the Charter of the United Nations that was adopted by the Conference. Yet, like so many white South Africans, liberalism abroad was one thing, liberalism at home another. In a speech in London in 1917, Smuts said, "Natives have the simplest minds, understand only the simplest ideas or ideals, and are almost animal-like in the simplicity of their minds and ways." For Smuts, "the easiest, most natural and obvious way to civilize the African native is to give him decent white employment. White employment is his best school; the gospel of labor is the most salutary gospel for him." But Smuts' Afrikaner adversaries were even further to the right.

In the general election in 1948, the Nationalist and Afrikaner parties won, merging into the Nationalist Party in 1951. For the first time since Union, a purely Afrikaans-speaking party was in power, and over the next decade and a half the Afrikaners, mainly under the leadership of Hendrik Verwoerd, brought into existence the several hundred laws of apartheid,[15] including the immorality act (decreeing whom one could marry), the group areas act (decreeing where people could live), the Bantu education act (dictating the extent of education available to Africans), and the population registration act (determining one's race, and therefore the limits of one's options in life).

Then, in 1960, white voters decided that South Africa should become a republic.

BEGINNING OF THE END: SHARPEVILLE AND SOWETO

African resistance continued and intensified,[16] and an uneasy peace between the races smoldered across the land. In March, 1960, the Pan Africanist Congress sponsored a demonstration against the pass laws, and sixty-nine Africans were killed by the police. On March 21, several thousand Africans moved to the police station at Sharpeville, an African location near the industrial city, Vereeniging. They had been urged to leave their passes at home, to go to the nearest police station, and to offer themselves for arrest, as an act of non-violent civil disobedience. The police had Saracen armored cars. No apparent order was given to fire, but the police panicked, and began to shoot into the crowd, and did so for thirty seconds. An assistant editor of *Drum* magazine, Humphrey Tyler, wrote, "We went into Sharpeville the back way, behind a grey police car, and three Saracens. As we drove through fringes of the township many people shouted the Pan-Africanist slogan, 'Izwe Lethu,' which means 'Our Land,' or gave the thumbs up freedom salute and shouted 'Afrika!' . . . Then the shooting started. A gun opened up toc-toc-toc-toc and another and another. . . . There were hundreds of women. Some of these people were laughing, probably thinking the police were firing blanks. But they were not. Bodies were falling behind them and among them. One woman was hit about ten yards from our car. Her companion, a young man, went back when she fell. He thought she had stumbled. He turned her over in the grass. Then he saw that her chest was shot away. He looked at his hand. There was blood on it. He said: 'My God, she's gone.' There were hundreds of kids running too. One had on an old black coat and he held it behind his head as he ran, to save his head from bullets, I suppose. Some of the children were leaping like rabbits, hardly as tall as the grass. Some of them were hit too. Still there was shooting. One policeman was standing on top of a Saracen and it looked as if he was firing his Sten gun into the fleeing crowd. . . . Most of the bodies were strewn in the road which runs alongside the field we were in. . . . There was no crowd any more. It was very quiet."[17]

"Even in this turbulent country," a Johannesburg correspondent wrote, "there had never been such an upheaval as there was during the ten days that shook South Africa. When housewives in the comfortable suburbs had to fetch the family's daily bread and milk because African delivery 'boys' stayed away from work, the taste of complete *apartheid* began to be appreciated. The stay-at-home strike was an impressive protest, 90 percent successful in Johannesburg. . . . Nearly all African leaders are now in prison, for how long no one can tell. Yet African protest is not extinguished and unfamiliar new voices are being heard as the A.N.C. and P.A.C. are outlawed. . . . South Africa now lies at the mercy of its Afrikaner rulers, whose tyranny has become harsher and more efficient."[18]

All of this occurred within the context of the rise of the Black Consciousness movement, a program that instituted a renewed sense of pride in Africans and in blackness. Then, in June, 1976, Soweto exploded,[19] as did urban ghettoes throughout South Africa. Twenty thousand pupils in Soweto went on a protest march, refusing to learn Afrikaans, considering it a language of oppression.[20] On June 16, the Soweto Students' Representative Council called for a demonstration to protest the use of that language in the schools. Over ten thousand pupils gathered, marching from school to school. They were confronted by armed policemen. Teargas and gunfire followed, and the children stoned the police. Whites were evacuated from nearby areas, and the area was sealed off. By the end of the day, twenty-five people were dead. "Flaming night," headlined the *Rand Daily Mail* on June 17: "Troops were on standby outside Soweto last night while thousands of angry Africans set fire to buildings and cars after a day of violence and death." The rioting continued, and unrest spread to Dobsonville and Kliptown, then to the campuses of the Universities of Turfloop and Zululand. The press was banned from Soweto. University students and black workers who marched in support in Johannesburg were attacked by whites. On June 18, the minister of justice invoked the Riotous Assemblies Act, the death toll was over ninety, police guarded the white suburbs, the Citizen Force was placed on standby, and *The Rand Daily Mail* headlined, "Violence spreads," noting that "[e]scalating violence in Soweto spread to neighboring townships and Johannesburg itself." On June 19, the headline read, "Police guard White homes," adding, "Violence spread from Soweto to townships along the entire Reef yesterday and the estimated death toll rose to at least 90. The number of injured reached the 1000 mark and included children with bullet wounds." The *South African Outlook* wondered, "Will we whites choose to concede the humanity of our neighbors? Or will we, in our frightened clinging to power, choose the way of greater repression which leads ultimately to self-destruction? The moment of choice is upon us."[21]

Over five hundred children would lose their lives during the year of upheaval following the Soweto Massacre.

THE END AND THE BEGINNING: BIKO AND MANDELA

On August 18, 1977, Steve Biko, the charismatic leader of the Black Consciousness movement, was arrested. He was born in King William's Town in 1947. When he was attending the University of Natal, he helped to organize the South African Students' Organization (July, 1969), and became its first president. It was an organization committed to the ideal of black consciousness, for which he became an eloquent spokesman. "What is Black Consciousness?" he asked. "In essence this is an attitude of mind and a way of life. . . . Its unadulterated quintessence is the realization by the Black man of the need to rally together with his brothers around the cause of their oppression—the blackness of their skin—and to operate as a group to rid themselves of the shackles that bind them to perpetual servitude."[22] Within a month he was dead, killed because of head injuries sustained during interrogation at police headquarters in Port Elizabeth. Donald Woods, the editor of the East London *Daily Dispatch*, wrote, "On

Tuesday, September 6, 1977, a close friend of mine named Bantu Stephen Biko was taken by South African political police to Room 619 of the Sanlam Building in Strand Street, Port Elizabeth, Cape Province, where he was handcuffed, put into leg irons, chained to a grille and subjected to twenty-two house of interrogation in the course of which he was tortured and beaten, sustaining several blows to the head which damaged his brain fatally, causing him to lapse into a coma and die six days later."[23] Justice Minister J. Kruger said on the day after Biko's death, "I am not glad and I am not sorry about Mr. Biko. . . . He leaves me cold."[24] Biko had been held, naked, and in September, still unclothed and in irons, he was interrogated by a five-man team that insisted that Biko had bumped his head against a wall during a struggle. When the police decided he should be taken to a hospital, he was put, naked, in the back of a Land Rover, and driven 700 miles to Pretoria where he died. "Steve Biko," wrote Adam Small in *Drum*, "is dead. We who dream of freedom felt outraged by his death. And we were angered. He was a man haunted under this regime. Haunted because his pride was indestructible, because as a black man he walked tall. And many white men in this country do not like a black man walking tall."[25]

"Who is not concerned about his people's destiny," wrote the Xhosa poet, John Solilo, "Not proud of his people's uniqueness?"[26]

When Rolilahlahla Nelson Dalibhunga Mandela, born on July 18, 1918, in the Transkei, was a student at Fort Hare, he was travelling on a bus with three Indian student friends. When the conductor ordered them to get off the bus, they refused. They had to appear on a charge under a municipal by-law, but all were acquitted. So began the career of one of the world's notable statesmen. Unlike many South Africans, Mandela refused to seek sanctuary outside his country. "As for myself," he said in 1961, "I have made my decision. I am not quitting South Africa. This is my country and my homeland. The freedom movement is my life, and I shall strive side by side with the brave sons and daughters of Africa until the end of my days."

In December of 1956, Mandela was among 156 political leaders seized by the police and charged with high treason. Four and one-half years later, on March 26, 1961, the accused were found not guilty. When the African National Congress and the Pan Africanist Congress were banned after the Sharpeville Massacre on March 21, 1960, Mandela was arrested and accused of incitement. He went underground, and he and Walter Sisulu travelled about the country, organizing such protests as a three-day stay-at-home strike in May, 1961. Mandela remained a fugitive for seventeen months, and became known as "the Black Pimpernel," recalling Emmuska Orczy's *The Scarlet Pimpernel*[27]: "Is he in heaven or is he in hell, / That damned elusive Pimpernel." Mandela remained underground, and continued leading his movement, defying the vast South African police force, the army, and the security police. He seemed to be everywhere, engaged in the struggle against apartheid. He gave telephone interviews, now appearing, and as suddenly disappearing. He attended a meeting of the Pan-African Freedom Movement of East and Central Africa in Addis Ababa.[28] He was everywhere and nowhere. A month before he was arrested, his wife, Winnie Mandela, celebrated her fourth wedding anniversary in the absence of her husband. About forty close friends were invited; two hundred showed up. And the police were there also, as a toast to the absent host was proposed by one of his friends.

The security force did catch up with him in 1962. By that time, he was the most wanted man in the country, and he had played hide and seek with the police until that day, when, dressed as a chauffeur, on the road to Pietermaritzburg, he was finally caught in their net. Mandela was tried, and in November, 1962, convicted for incitement and illegally leaving the country. He was sentenced to five years imprisonment in Pretoria Central Prison. While he was in jail, in October, 1963, there was a treason trial, and Mandela was accused of sabotage and conspiracy to overthrow the government. On June 12, 1964, Mandela, the leader of Umkhonto weSizwe, Spear of the Nation, the military arm of the African National Congress, was sentenced, with eight others, to life imprisonment. He was held on Robben Island until 1982, then was transferred to Polsmoor Prison outside Cape Town.

In the mid 1980s, there was general revolution: South Africa was ungovernable. In 1989, Mandela had secret meetings with President P. W. Botha.[29] On September 20, 1989, F. W. De Klerk became president, and the movement towards a free South Africa quickened. On February 11, 1990, Mandela was released from prison, and the banning of various African organizations was lifted. Africans living in the so-called homelands had their South African citizenship restored on January 1, 1994. April 27, 1994, was the date of the first free election, and the African National Congress won with 62.65 percent of the vote, with a plurality in seven of the nine provinces. On May 10, 1994, Mandela was inaugurated as president.

Nelson Mandela gave a speech on the Grand Parade in Cape Town. Concluding his address, he said, "I wish to quote my own words during my trial in 1964. They are as true today as they were then. . . . 'I have fought against white domination and I have fought against black domination. I have carried the ideal of a democratic and free society in which all persons live together in harmony and with equal opportunity. It is an ideal which I hope to live for and to achieve. But, if needs be, it is an ideal for which I am prepared to die.'" Later, in New York, he said, "We are now closer to the goal [of a free South Africa] than at any time in our history. In the words of the prophet Isaiah, we have risen up on the wings of eagles. We have run and not grown weary . . . and finally our destination is in sight."[30]

South African poet John Matshikiza wrote, "It has been for this man's life / To paint the new light in the sky."[31]

FOUNDERS OF THE INHERITANCE

"LET ME GO BACK"

Let us now praise famous men,
and our fathers that begat us. . . .
Such as did bear rule in their kingdoms,
men renowned for their power,
giving counsel by their understanding,
and declaring prophecies:
Leaders of the people by their counsels,
and by their knowledge of learning
meet for the people,
wise and eloquent in their instructions . . . :
All these were honored in their generations,
and were the glory of their times.
           —*Ecclesisasticus*[1]

INTRODUCTION

The storyteller and the historian strengthened the will of the people to withstand apartheid's onslaught by firmly weaving images from the past into the experience of the present. We therefore launch this odyssey into the world of the storyteller with a set of genealogies, "Origins of the Xhosa," created by a respected Xhosa historian, Ndumiso Bhotomane, in 1967. A number of Xhosa elders were in attendance the day that I heard Mr. Bhotomane recall the history of the Xhosa people.

The historian, Bhotomane told me, remembers the past in order to give meaning to the present. So it is that he recalls the significant rulers of tradition, those whose wisdom and activities contributed to the cultural heritage of the people. He begins with a bare list of memorable leaders, the shapers of the Xhosa inheritance.

Other storytellers, including Bhotomane himself, would give flesh and dimension to this regal register by developing associated stories meant to illuminate and to make comprehensible, meant, as the storytellers routinely insisted, to move to truth.

ONE

A Zulu poet-historian worked in a broad space, garbed in the pelts of wild animals, addressing an audience that formed an arc around poet and subject. The bodies of members of the audience were sometimes in motion, held and controlled by the calculated movements of the poet's body and the music of his voice. The presence of both the leader, when the leader is the subject of the poem, and a portion of his people constitutes an event ripe with aesthetic and social tension. The artist catches in his artistically organized images both ruler and ruled in a combination that ties them to past cultural and historical experiences, which are vividly expressed and symbolized, and blended with realistic images selected from the contemporary world. But these realistic shards are placed within settings in which the uses to which body and voice are put are rhythmical reorderings of their routine functions—the cadence of delivery, for example, the sound of the voice—and within patterns of imagery that have no apparent relationship to reality. Meaning is expressed in the defining of the relationship, largely by the poetic line and its patterning, between the two worlds.

Deneys Reitz described the Zulu bard and historian, Mankulumane. In the winter of 1923, Reitz and General Jan Smuts "stumped Natal in connection with the proposal for closer union between South Africa and

Rhodesia." But, he wrote, "The people of Rhodesia were unwilling to be dragged into our race and language squabbles and our ideal of a greater South Africa found little support. We spoke in many towns and villages, but it all came to nothing in the end. A plebiscite was taken in Rhodesia and the result was overwhelmingly against us. Having said our say, we proceeded to Zululand, for General Smuts wished to examine the prospects of building a harbor on the coast. . . ."[2]

At Nongoma they were met by some ten thousand warriors who were assembled to meet them, and Smuts received the royal salute from the assembled Zulu. Then the royal bard, Mankulumane, spoke. According to Reitz, he "was a magnificent savage of over ninety years, tall and erect, and every line of his heavy jowl spoke of strength and character. He had been chief counsellor to Cetewayo [Cetshwayo] and Dinuzulu as he was now to Solomon, and the Zulus look on him as the greatest orator of all time. He spoke in court Zulu, a more involved language than is in everyday use but with some knowledge of their tongue and with the help of an interpreter I was able to follow him. He played upon his audience in masterly fashion. One moment he worked them into a rage and whole batches of warriors sprang to their feet to glower at their hereditary foes across the common border; then by a dexterous turn he sent them rocking with laughter at some witty tale of cattle or the chase. Next, in lowered tones, he spoke of the former glories of the Zulu people, of the spirits of the dead and of great battles of the past, and when he chided them for their quarrels they sank their heads between their knees and rocked and moaned in unison."[3]

Nelson Mandela writes of the storytellers of his youth, "[T]he chiefs and headmen . . . came to the Great Place to settle disputes and try cases. . . . Some days, they would finish early and sit around telling stories. I hovered silently and listened. They spoke in an idiom that I'd never heard before. Their speech was formal and lofty, their manner slow and unhurried, and the traditional clicks of our language were long and dramatic." He told of how "The most ancient of chiefs [Zwelibhangile Joyi] . . . railed against the white man, who he believed had deliberately sundered the Xhosa tribe, dividing brother from brother," how "the African people lived in relative peace until the coming of the *abelungu,* the white people, who arrived from across the sea with fire-breaking weapons. . . . The white man shattered the . . . fellowship, of the various tribes. The white man was hungry and greedy for land, and the black man shared the land with him as they shared the air and water; land was not for man to possess. But the white man took the land as you might seize another man's horse."[4]

The bard inevitably deals with the past, a kind of dream time of mythic feats, utopian community, and extravagantly triumphant achievements.

Connecting the present and the past. A Xhosa storyteller.

Historical persons and events are placed in this fabulous antiquity, and are themselves made myth. The poetry requires such a past perfection as a measure for the present: it embodies the truths vital and precious to the people. It turns men into demigods and routine affairs into times of precious moment. This heroic art is no less real for all the fabrication. During the period of the performance, the ideal past and the flawed present world come into conjunction.

I worked with oral historians and bards, becoming something of an apprentice to Mdukiswa Tyabashe of the Mpondomise, listening to the performances of hundreds of poets and historians among the Xhosa, Zulu, and Swati people. They were the most forthright of the oral performers as far as apartheid was concerned. Poets and historians worked with metaphors, but their images of violence and brutality frequently burst through metaphorical contexts and glistened, burning in the full light of historical reality. "Freedom!" thundered one Zulu historian, having related the history of the Zulu king, Shaka: "Shaka is the symbol of our struggles for our freedom." He made it clear that any contemporary rendering of the story of the historical Shaka was as much a comment on the contemporary state of apartheid South Africa as it was a description of early nineteenth-century life among the Zulu.

TWO

We begin at the mythic beginning, with the historical fact: "Xhosa fathered Malangana." The lists that follow are king lists, lists of the major (or great) royal houses, the minor and supporting houses, lists of the burial places of the kings, and lists also of the favorite cattle of the kings. These catalogues provide the grid for the storytellers, the historians, the poets: they will build on it, develop it, embroider and embellish it, give it direction and dimension. The historian's craft begins with the genealogical time-line, argued Bhotomane, and he then cultivates that.

A contemporary historian, comparing history to a machine, sees it as "clicking out colliding perceptions of the same events. It mutates according to a law of relativity: just as space and time shrink or expand relative to the speed of the observer, so our impression of the past seems to warp into different shapes according to the angle of approach." He continues, "[H]istory, after all, happened to people who experienced it variously at the time, registered it mentally in contrasting patterns and recorded it in mutually contradictory ways. The onlooker is part of the event." He observes, "From time to time, a paradise gets mislaid or regained, as each period debunks the golden age myths of others and substitutes its own."[5]

It was to Ndumiso Bhotomane to remember the past, never to let it go. His memory was the link to the past, and it was the artistry of poets and storytellers that gave his king-lists their context and meaning. Within the oral tradition, a rich and important relationship exists between the genealogist and the storyteller and poet: history is compounded of chronology, narrative, and poetic metaphor.

Consider the genealogy of the Biyela people of Zululand. The list develops, in part, as follows:

> Ndaba[6] was the father of Xhoko,
> Founder of the Biyela people;
> Xhoko, in turn, sired Menziwa,
> Prominent among the people of Ngwabalanda;
> Didi was the son of Menziwa,
> He of the Hlayizeni people. . . .

It is poets like the Zulu bard Umhle Biyela[7] who give dimension to the genealogical lists, by developing them within an inherited set of metaphors and formulas:

> I will start with our common ancestor, Xhoko, son of Ndaba, who is the one who founded the Biyela people:

> Ngcengcezi, son of Mqulakazi,
> Boy with ticks as a blanket.
> We thought we were piecing together
> What was falling apart,
> Even though we did not have much thread
> That would sew, sewing a person together.
> Ndaba stepped hard, and a lake appeared.
> Restless one,
> Bird weighed down by its tail.
> Lake that was pulled down by elephants.
> Xhoko, son of Ndaba
> Of the Biyela people: his heroic poem.

> His son, whom he sired, the prince Menziwa, son of Xhoko:

> Scion of Xhoko,
> He who when he set up house became prominent,
> Became great among the people of Ngwabalanda.
> Mother's enclosure shines,
> It spells trouble to anyone who looks threateningly at it.
> Axe to those who took refuge at Qaphela-bazozela.[8]

Rope of the cabbage tree of Sikhakha's household,
I fear it because it has an ear like an elephant.
Ndaba's eagle was born and immediately started walking,
And said it was going to Maziyane,
When he began to spring.
Beauty as revealed in houses:
They are beautiful, including the one at Mbuyeni,
Because they are beautiful and black.
Precipices!
One-who-is-put-on,
Put on by men,
Who devours diviners
Of kwaNkweleni
So that they stopped doctoring.
He devoured Nomvula, born at kwaNzuza.
He said he had no bile,
He said he had no paunch,
He said his paunch
Is actually a tough cushion.
That is Menziwa, son of Xhoko,
The prince, Son of Xhoko.

Menziwa was followed in the order of birth by our Didi, of the
Hlayizeni people:

Milk that curdles without foam,
Builder and deserter of outposts:
That is Didi.
He comes after Xhoko,
A younger chief, prince, son of Menziwa.
Small-rabbit,
Our Millet-grain, Khabeni,
Awesome Cliffs-of-the-wilderness:
I called them, they echoed.
Phunga responded, so did Mageba
Who was dispossessed of a whisk by Dlungwana at Mbelembele;
Then he was given one by Macingwane of Ngonyama.
Repeater-like-a-sinner,
Sudden-appearer-with-the-Ndwandwe-braves,
Stabber-into-the-mist,
Gatherer, like the one of Zwide,
Tail-whisk of a white cow —
White one, like that of kwaNandi.

Stabber-into-the-mist,
He tied them and could not join them,
The children will join together by the thousand.
Little hare, run away,
And the land too will run away.
Cliffs, come back,
And the land too will come back.
One whose cattle have not built Ndonga,
They did no good for Mthweli,
They did no good to Nkayishana,
They did no good to Nqaqa, son of Mandamela.

It is the richness of the poetic language, the combination of image and pattern, that provides the social memory that makes of history a connective between past and present. Beyond this are tale and epic.

THREE

Bhotomane's history provides the foundation: the historian remembers the great kings, even to the point of remembering their graves and their favorite oxen. He provides the drop against which history can be told. What is lacking here is story: this will be provided by Bhotomane himself, and by his fellows, the storytellers, poets, and epic-performers.

This historian starts with the formative details: it is the task of oral archivists like Ndumiso Bhotomane to remember the names of the forebears, those who embody the inheritance of the people. It is to the poets, storytellers, and epic performers to provide the mythic context that will give meaning to the acts of those sovereigns. Bhotomane dealt in facts: he was careful to correct himself when facts fell out of place. Others are not so particular about the facts: they are more interested in poetic, or complete, truth. We have moved into the realm of story. In his historical account of the Ngcayechibi War of 1877, Bhotomane continues his use of genealogical lists ("Mxoli is the son of Mbune," "He came with Nkuzana," etc.), but he now gives these lists a context, and that context is a story.

How is the moment made historical, given historical depth? Why is it important to make the moment historical? The storyteller's art is an art of illusion, a mnemonic sleight of hand, a matter of historical smoke and poetic shadows. She deals in words and images, drawn together into patterns, worked into art by means of performance. The illusory product of the storyteller's activities is history, is a perception of the real. It is not for nothing that one of the major repertories of imagery for the storyteller is the world of experience, the real world, the world that is daily and routinely known to the audience. This is the central part of the great and beautiful hoax being perpetrated by the orchestrator of history. But these shards, this flotsam and jetsam of human experience, are given form by means of art. The storyteller takes the audience on an excursion: history deals with change, and the storyteller moves the audience to the boundaries, and then begins the journey to the center—to wholeness, to essence and unity. This movement is achieved by placing realistic images within a patterned context that includes images that are not realistic. The audience is not viewing this activity from a distance; rather, the effect is achieved because of its active participation. The story is constructed on the emotions that are elicited in performance from the members of that audience.

In order to give meaning to experience, that is, to render experience history, the storyteller must first dissect it, and then, through art, reorder it. History thus created is theatrical: it is not reality, but it contains reality; it is not fantasy, but it partakes of fantasy. It is truth, it is meaning, in the sense that the storyteller convinces us that her wonder-making is truth, is meaning. It is one grand charade, and the audience thirsts after more, for the illusionary activity gives form and meaning to an existence that lacks form and meaning.

It is to the storyteller that the society entrusts this activity of making the real seem historic, of making experience resonate with the rich, reassuring sounds of tradition. So it is that storytellers argue that apartheid in South Africa was a moment in history. The storytellers do not document the horrors of apartheid; rather, they give it a context that renders it historical, and thereby endows it with meaning. Chinua Achebe, the Nigerian writer, says, "It is the storyteller . . . that makes us what we are, that creates history."[9]

The strength of story, because of its mythic content, is that it enables us to grow and develop with the years. Questions more easily answered as a child become more complex: we demand more complete answers as we mature, and so we return to the myths, and we recover new layers, new dimensions of meaning. The ambiguity of mythological discourse enables us to move more deeply into our history, our social experience, and our traditions, and so our truths and meanings have deeper dimensions with each encounter with our mythic system.

Performance is the crucial element in making the moment historical. In the epic, as in the much shorter performances, the experience is of forms, and combinations of forms. The body, in those narratives in which movement is engaged in by the artist and her audience, assists in revealing the forms and their interrelationships. The significance of the non-verbal aspects of such narratives was emphasized for me in August, 1972, when, attending performances among the Xesibe people of the Transkei in South Africa, I experienced another extraordinary production. Manya-

Mastering the language of storytelling. A young Xhosa storyteller.

wusa Sodidi, a performer whom I knew well, was creating narratives for her friends. It was the 23rd of August, in Mrs. Sodidi's home, late afternoon, with an audience, besides myself, of some fifteen women, one man, about ten children. While Mrs. Sodidi was performing, her close friend, Manto Matshezi, was sitting on a stool nearby. Mrs. Sodidi sat and knelt on a mat, depending on the animation with which she was evoking the images of the narrative; the mat was in the center of her home. Her performances were generally lively ones, involving much use of the body and hands, her face constantly shifting expressions. And during such performances, the audience was also actively engaged in the narrative actions, and none more than Mrs. Matshezi (she was then about thirty-five years old, Mrs. Sodidi about sixty). As Mrs. Sodidi continued her narrative, Mrs. Matshezi was miming everything that the performer was doing. The audience was entranced, as Mrs. Matshezi abstracted and stylized Mrs. Sodidi's actions, and herself became a part of the performance. She anticipated the actions of her friend with precise timing and surprising accuracy. And her body reflected keenly the shattering of the patterns. Her body and actions became a separate work of art, a moving comment on the tradition and on the narrative that the artist in front of her was performing. Mrs. Matshezi was abstracting the basic aspects of the performance and the system: her body was rhythmic motion, with new movements emerging out of the regular movements, miming the actions of the narrative. These movements were heavily symbolized, almost dance, and Mrs. Sodidi was in fact doing the same thing, symbolizing and abstracting the mimed movements into something less directly connected with the words. The bodies moved in harmony, the words, sounds, and movements establishing Mrs. Sodidi's actions, and these actions, already symbolizing, condensing, and displacing, were taken by Mrs. Matshezi and converted to ballet.

And where was meaning in this performance? The levels of activity created a performance of such density and layers of metaphor spoken and unspoken, of words and movement, music and emotion, that the members of the audience could only allow these performers to have their way with them, as they were shuttled into history, as they experienced the rich nexus between present experience and the fertile world of the past.

Ndumiso Bhotomane

ORIGINS OF THE XHOSA

(XHOSA)

Chief Ndumiso Bhotomane, a Gcaleka, was eighty-four years old when he related this historical account. The date was September 10, 1967; the place was outside, in his kraal in Rwantsana Location, Centane District, in the Transkei. The audience varied, with Gcaleka men and women attending for different lengths of time; three Gcaleka elders remained in attendance throughout. (No. 589; tape 10, side 2)

The Xhosa are a nation that came down from the north, from the north of Africa. Xhosa, the one after whom the Xhosa people are named, descended, and during his emergence from the north he fathered Malangana:

> Malangana then fathered Malandela,
> Malandela fathered Nkosiyamntu,
> Nkosiyamntu fathered Tshawe,
> Tshawe fathered Sikhomo,
> Sikhomo fathered Togu,
> Togu fathered Ngconde,
> Ngconde fathered Tshiwo,
> Tshiwo fathered Phalo.

The Xhosa kingship separated when the line got to Phalo because of what happened when he married.

THE DEVELOPMENT OF THE KINGDOM

ONE

Two daughters of kings, one of them of the Ndayeni clan, the other a Gqubushe-mpulomsini clanswoman, arrived on the same day to be married to Phalo. That had never occurred before. Because this matter regarding the acquiring of a wife for Phalo concerned the entire kingdom, the fates of those two young women were decided by a gathering of all the Xhosa people, including Tshiwo's councillors. The decision was made by Majeke, a Nkabana clansman and a man already old: it was determined that the one who would bear the heir was the Ndayeni woman; the Gqubushe clanswoman would bear the right-hand house.

It was further concluded that, because of these uncommon events, the right-hand house should be moved to a distant place, to become a kingdom in its own right. It would still represent and be ruled by the great house[1] because that house had established this right-hand house. Those at the meeting agreed to this. That is how the chiefs' homesteads came to be designated "great house" and "right-hand house."

These events took place at Gcuwa, in the village of Monakali. It was not called Monakali's village in those days; then it was the homestead of the king, from which the country was ruled. The right-hand house was shifted; it was established here at Nyila's place, by that hill. The other house, the great house, was established below there, at the hill where Gqongqo's homestead is now located. Fesi's homestead is just below. The right-hand house, then, was established in the village of Nyila. That is where they were made into two houses.

When this apportioning was complete, when the homesteads were moved, Phalo's great house moved here. The great house was moved first; it was the house that gave birth to the heir; the wife of the great house, the mother of Gcaleka, bore the heir. This house was established at Khwenxura, in the neighborhood of Monti.[2] After that, the right-hand house moved, and was established at Qonce,[3] where, at that time, the Thwa,[4] the original inhabitants, were living. When the Xhosa got there, they found the Thwa, and Rharhabe fought with them. Certain clans went with Rharhabe from Gcuwa; they were with him when he fought those Thwa. The clans that had been given to him, to go with him to establish the right-hand house—the clans that were taken out of the Xhosa nation and given to Rharhabe from the royal residence were the Dange, the Hleke, the Mbalu, and the Ntinde.[5] Mngqalasi was Phalo's minor house. These, then, are the clans with which Rharhabe departed on the day that he left for Qonce, when he arrived there to find the Thwa. He fought the Thwa. In keeping with the instructions which had been given to him, that even when he was over there in Qonce he was still to be ruled by the great house here—when Rharhabe got there, he reported the war; he reported that when he arrived there, the Thwa were there, and he fought with them and scattered them.

Then Rharhabe married a Thembu woman, a Gcina clanswoman, and

He fathered Mlawu,
He fathered Ndlambe,
He fathered Ntsusa,
He fathered Gasela,
He fathered Nukwa.

I made an error—these are the children whom Rharhabe fathered: they were Mlawu, and Ndlambe, and Ntsusa, and Nukwa. There were four of them in the great house of the right-hand house. And in the right-hand house of the right-hand house, he fathered Cebo. As for Cebo, he fathered no children. Councillors decided that he should be given a child, and he was therefore given Ndlambe's oldest son, Mdushane.

> Mdushane fathered Siwani, then,
> Siwani fathered Menziwa,
> Menziwa fathered Gushiphela,
> Gushiphela fathered Zimlindile,
> the current chief of the Dushane.
> Nukwa fathered Gasela,
> Gasela fathered Toyise,
> Toyise fathered Dom,
> Dom fathered Kadeni.

Kadeni is the one who is ruling at Qonce at Bulembu right now, as I speak.

When Mlawu married, he had two important wives: one was the mother of Ngqika, the other was Ntimbo's mother. Ntimbo was the right-hand house; he did not father any children. As for Ngqika, he fathered Sandile. But the first-born was not the heir; he became the regent for Sandile. That was Maqoma, the son of Ngqika of the right-hand house, who was born first. Maqoma is the right-hand house; the first son born to Ngqika was Maqoma, in the right-hand house. Maqoma was the regent, Sandile's regent.

> Sandile then fathered Gonya,
> Gonya fathered Faku,
> Faku fathered Archie.

It is Archie who is in Qonce now. Sandile's right-hand house is Gumna.

I shall shift, now, to the line of the great house. I have been speaking of Rharhabe's line. Sandile, as I have said, fathered Gonya, Gonya fathered Faku, Faku fathered Archie. And that's how the great line stands; Archie is the one who is living now.

I shall put aside the line of the right-hand house, and go to the paramount line of the Xhosa. Phalo, by his great wife, the daughter of Ndayeni, fathered Gcaleka; he fathered Gcaleka. Phalo's eldest son was Gcaleka.

> Gcaleka then fathered Khawuta,
> Khawuta fathered Hintsa,

Hintsa fathered Sarhili,
Sarhili fathered Sigcawu,
Sigcawu fathered Gwebinkumbi,
Gwebinkumbi fathered Mpisekhaya then.

And Mpisekhaya died, not having fathered anyone. Because Mpisekhaya had not sired a son, the Xhosa, after they had discussed the matter, established in the line Zwelidumile, Mpisekhaya's younger brother who follows him in birth in his mother's womb. Zwelidumile became king, then, when Mpisekhaya died. Zwelidumile fathered Xolilizwe, who is living now. He has not yet married; he does have wives whom he has just taken, and he will soon be gotten a great wife, the one who will be created to preside over the kingdom of the Xhosa. That is the way the clans of the Xhosa, the Xhosa kingdom, are constructed. The paramount chief is Xolilizwe, the one who was fathered by Zwelidumile.

Zwelidumile was fathered by Gwebinkumbi,
Gwebinkumbi was fathered by Sigcawu,
Sigcawu was fathered by Sarhili,
Sarhili was fathered by Hintsa,
Hintsa was fathered by Khawuta,
Khawuta was fathered by Gcaleka,
Gcaleka was fathered by Phalo,
Phalo was fathered by Tshiwo,
Tshiwo was fathered by Ngconde,
Ngconde was fathered by Togu,
Togu was fathered by Sikhomo,
Sikhomo was fathered by Tshawe,
Tshawe was fathered by Nkosiyamntu,
Nkosiyamntu was fathered by Malandela,
Malandela was fathered by Malangana,
Malangana was fathered by Xhosa.

These are the clans in the line of Gcaleka.

The right-hand house of the Xhosa is Rharhabe; and Gcaleka, when he fathered children, had his own right-hand house:

Gcaleka fathered Velelo,
Velelo fathered Gxaba,
Gxaba fathered Dalasile,
Dalasile fathered Mdabuka,
Mdabuka fathered Daluhlanga.

This is Gxaba's right-hand house:

Gxaba fathered Ncamba,
Ncamba fathered Ngxito,
Ngxito fathered Sitata,
Sitata fathered Soya.

This is the right-hand house of Gcaleka.

When Khawuta, the first son of Gcaleka, had established his right-hand house, it developed in this way:

Khawuta fathered Bhuru,
Bhuru fathered Mapasa,
Mapasa fathered Xhoxho,
Xhoxho fathered Mabobothi,

the one who is living now.

The right-hand house that follows is that of the Jingqi clan: it is Hintsa's right-hand house, the home of Jingqi. The right-hand house of Hintsa is Ngcaphayi, the calf of a Thembu woman, of Thembuland, at Tshatshu's place:

Ngcaphayi then fathered Dumalisile,
Dumalisile fathered Dwayi,

and Dwayi is the one who is living now. Dwayi has a son who is also living now—what is his name?

The right-hand house that follows that one is that of Sarhili (the one I have just given is Hintsa's right-hand house). The right-hand house of Sarhili is Mcothama. The heir of Mcothama was Krazukile, and Krazukile also fathered sons: his heir was Bhota, but he died. The one who is living now, Bhota having died, the eldest son of Krazukile, became Gawusha. It was Gawusha who was condemned to hang, having been found guilty of killing Ngubezulu. His chieftainship was left with Zanelanga, whom they call Selele. It is he who is ruling now. That is the right-hand house of Sarhili.

Sigcawu's right-hand house is as follows: it is Xhelinkunzi. Xhelinkunzi fathered Thabathile, and Thabathile is the one who is presently ruling at Bhojini. I'll leave it there, and note that Zwelidumile also has a right-hand house that is called Madodendlini; he is the son, the founder of this house. The son of Zwelidumile in the right-hand house is Madodendlini, who is living now. He is a raw young man—he has been recently circumcised. His mother is a Kwayi clanswoman there at Nqadu. I think I have finished the account of the right-hand house of Gcaleka now.

TWO

I shall comment briefly on the "supporting houses."[6] The first supporting house, that of Ngconde, is Ntinde—the Ntinde clan, the ones that you see at Qonce to this day, that is the supporting house of Ngconde.

Here is Gcaleka's major supporting house: it is Faku,

> Faku fathered Raba then,
> Raba fathered Mdlabela,
> Mdlabela fathered Sibhozo,
> Sibhozo fathered Dimanda,
> Dimanda fathered Griffiths.

He is the one who is ruling in the supporting house now. Those supporting houses are Gcaleka's.

The supporting house that is under that one was founded by Mneke:

> Mneke fathered Mdushane,
> Mdushane fathered Sitokwe,
> Sitokwe fathered Ngcweleshe,
> Ngcweleshe fathered Fundakubi,

and there Fundakubi is, at Idutywa.

The supporting house that is under that one in turn: this supporting house had sons, it bore Cende,

> Cende fathered Jojo,
> Jojo fathered Mgengo,
> Mgengo fathered Vena,
> Vena fathered Veldtman,

and he is at Sebeni now, where he has settled in the land of Gatyana at the sea. I am finished now with the major supporting houses of Gcaleka.

I shall go on to Khawuta's supporting houses. The supporting house of Khawuta is Nkani:

> Nkani then fathered Mthini,
> Mthini fathered Bhotomane,
> Bhotomane then fathered Ngqongongqongo,
> Ngqongongqongo fathered Ndumiso,

and it is Ndumiso who is speaking into this machine.

I pass on from these supporting houses of Khawuta, and move to

Hintsa's supporting houses. The major supporting house of Hintsa is Mthirara; the one that follows that one is Ludidi, Ludidi Hintsa. The one that follows that is Ndima. And the one that follows that one—no, let me stop there.

THREE

The "minor house" of Hintsa is Manxiwa. During the Ngcayechibi war, when Sarhili was at odds with the European government, Sarhili ordered that his stock and his family be looked after by this Manxiwa. He said that Manxiwa should remain neutral, in case the king were defeated, because this war was a big one, this war of Ngcayechibi. If he were defeated, let his stock be watched by Manxiwa as befits a minor house. The stock would provide Manxiwa—and, therefore, Sarhili's family—with a livelihood. The stock should be kept by Manxiwa at his place, and he should remain neutral in the hostilities lest Sarhili be defeated, for this war of Ngcayechibi was a great one. If he were defeated, then his cattle should be kept by Manxiwa in his role as minor house. He would nourish himself on them. Now Manxiwa was a son of Hintsa in the minor house.

Sarhili has a supporting house: Mtoto. Mtoto was a son of Sarhili in the supporting house, and he fathered Ntlakomzi, the present chief of Chafutweni.

Now then, let me start with the minor houses here. One minor house, I said, was Manxiwa; another was Mgwebi,

> Mgwebi, then, is the son of Ngxito,
> Ngxito is the son of Lutshaba,
> Lutshaba is the son of Gcaleka.

Lutshaba, a son of Gcaleka, comes after a girl whose name is Vukela. That girl comes after Nqoko; Nqoko, then, follows Khawuta directly.

> Mgwebi, then, is the son of Ngxito,
> Ngxito is the son of Ncamba—
> Ngxito is the son of Lutshaba,
> Lutshaba is the son of Gcaleka in the minor house.

This, then, is the household of Mgwebi, for

> Mgwebi himself fathered Zwelinzima,
> Zwelinzima, then, fathered Ngangolwandle;

he is the son at Mtshayelweni in Qwaninga. That one is a foremost minor house, but the primary minor house is Mngqalasi, that of Tshiwo:

It begot Lutshaba,
And begot Xhonxa,
And begot Mrawuzeli. . . .[7]

FOUR

Let me go now to Ngqikaland, and leave Gcalekaland for a while. We'll go to Ngqikaland now.[8]

I had said,

Archie is the son of Faku,
Faku is the son of Gonya,
Gonya is the son of Sandile,
Sandile is the son of Ngqika,
Ngqika is the son of Mlawu,
Mlawu is the son of Rharhabe,
Rharhabe is the son of Phalo

in the right-hand house.

I said that in the first right-hand house was Mdushane. It was Cebo, a son of Ndlambe, who was taken and given to Mdushane; Mdushane did not actually father Cebo. Yes, a son of Ndlambe, Mdushane, was taken and given to Cebo because there was no child in the right-hand house:

Mdushane, then, fathered Siwani,
Siwani, then, fathered Menziwa,
Menziwa, then, fathered Gushiphela,
Gushiphela, then, fathered Zimlindile,

the one now at Qonce.

I spoke of the Toyise clan: Gasela is the younger brother of Ndlambe; he comes directly after Ndlambe. This Gasela follows Ndlambe directly. I said—however, let me start in that house.

When he brought forth in the great house,

Rharhabe fathered Mlawu,
And he fathered Ndlambe,
And he fathered Ntsusa,
And he fathered Gasela, the last born.

As for Ndlambe, the first born were Dyan and Mqhayi. But they were later "smelled out"[9] because their father became ill; and they were then chased out. They ran, they were driven from their heirship which then remained with Mhala. The heir of Mhala, then, was Makinana:

> Makinana fathered Silimela,
> Silimela, then, begot Ngwenyenyathi,

the one who is ruling now. He is at Mncotsho, as I speak. The bull of the Ndlambe is that one.

Now, the right-hand of Ndlambe is Smith:

> Smith has fathered Hlathikhulu,
> Hlathikhulu has fathered Zenzile,

and Zenzile is here at Idutywa now.

Now, let me go to Mdushane. He is the right-hand of Rharhabe. He fathered Menziwa—rather,

> He fathered Siwani,
> Siwani fathered Menziwa,
> Menziwa fathered Gushiphela,
> Gushiphela fathered Zimlindile,

and he is at Qonce.

As for the Gasela clan, the juniors in Ndlambe's household, according to the way their fathers come, one after the other: Nukwa comes after Ndlambe,

> Nukwa, then, has fathered Gasela,
> Gasela fathered Toyise,
> Toyise fathered Dom,
> Dom fathered Kadeni,

and he is at Bulembu—that is where he is now, as I speak. That is the Toyise clan.

Now, I come to the right-hand house of Mlawu, Mlawu's right-hand house. Mlawu's heir was Ngqika.

The right-hand was Ntimbo. Ntimbo never had children. Ngqika's younger brother, Anta, was taken then to the right-hand:

> Anta, then, fathered Bhobhozayo,
> Bhobhozayo fathered Velaphi,
> Velaphi fathered Siwabese,

the one who is still there now. There he is, at Nsintsana. That is the right-hand house of Mlawu.

Ngqika's right-hand house is as follows: it is Maqoma, the one first in order of birth of all of Ngqika's sons. Maqoma was born first, and then Khawuta set him up to be Sandile's regent, for Sandile was still young. Maqoma's eldest son, his heir, was Namba:

> Namba, then, fathered Jamangile,
> Jamangile fathered Velenzima,

and here he is now, at Gqungqe, but he is not reigning. The person who reigns there at Gqungqe is Jongizulu, and he was fathered by Mhlabeni:

> Mhlabeni was fathered by Ndamase,
> Ndamase was fathered by Kona,
> And Kona was Maqoma's son

of the right-hand house. Kona's mother was a Gwashu clanswoman. He is the right-hand, this one, the heir. The reason the older one, the heir, did not reign was the dispersions of war, the Xhosa constantly being engaged in warfare. Namba was born during the hostilities. He was born at his mother's home, borne by a Thembu woman, a Tshatshu clanswoman, Maqoma's heir. Then this Jongizulu, Mhlabeni's son, was born. Mhlabeni is of Kona, is of Maqoma, in the right-hand house. That is how the right-hand house of Mlawu of Ngqika stands.

I shall discuss Sandile's right-hand house. I have finished Ngqika's right-hand house; I said it is

> Velenzima, fathered by Jamangile,
> Jamangile was fathered by Namba,
> Namba was the heir to Maqoma.

This Kona fathered Mhlabeni; he is the right-hand house:

> Kona, then, fathered Ndamase,
> Ndamase fathered Mhlabeni,
> Mhlabeni fathered Jongizulu,

and Jongizulu is the one reigning; he is the right-hand to Jingqi's home.

This is Sandile's right-hand house. Sandile's great wife is Noposi; her grave is here at Qombolo. She never had children—let me say, she bore only one girl, and she married among the Mpondo at Mzimkhulu; she married Mdlangazi, a Mpondo minor chief, not really a king even with

Xhosa men going to a conference

the Mpondo. Their daughter was Fitoyi, that daughter of Noposi, an only child. Then Gonya was taken from the supporting house; he was taken to the side of the great house. Gonya then is followed by Mathanzima, the one they call "the hairy one of Bholo," the one who commanded the forces of the Ngqika. Gonya was born of a Ngqosini woman; his mother was Nolenti, a daughter of the Ngqosini clan, the wife of Sandile in the supporting house. Gonya, then, was born, and so was Mathanzima. Gonya was taken and grafted onto that great house of Noposi, and he thereby became the son of Noposi. Gonya, then, in this royal house of the Ngqika,

> Gonya fathered Faku,
> Faku fathered Archie.

Mathanzima remained in the supporting house,

> and fathered Bonisani,
> Bonisani, then, fathered his son,

the present ruler, this youngster—I don't recall his name right now, it escapes my memory, he is—he is—But in the supporting house, it is Bonisani, that one born to Mathanzima. It is Lindile, the son of—I recall now. In the minor house,

> Mathanzima fathered Bonisani,
> Bonisani fathered Lindile,

Lindile, the present chief.

Now then, Faku had no right-hand house; he had one wife. Gonya was educated, he was educated in Cape Town; he was the magistrate's assistant at Qonce. When the Ngcayechibi war broke out, the Ngqika forces were commanded by Mathanzima, "the hairy one of Bholo," as the Ngqika say. Faku did not have a right-hand house. Archie did not have a right-hand house, for Archie's son was Mxolisi, who they say is Bazindlovu; he married the daughter of Poto of Mpondoland. That's the way the royal houses stand.[10]

Ngqika, when he married, fathered Maqoma in his right-hand house. Maqoma precedes all the sons of Ngqika in the order of birth; he is the son of a Ngqosini woman, Nothonto, the mother of Maqoma in the right-hand house; she bore Maqoma.

The minor house—yes: Tyhali is the son of Ngqika in the minor house; his mother is a Qocwa woman, a woman from here. She bore Tyhali in the minor house. Tyhali, then, fathered Feni, and in the right-hand house he fathered Ngonyama. Yet, according to age, it is Ngonyama who was born first, that is, before Feni, but still in the right-hand house. When he married, Feni married Ngubezulu, whom they call Ntlikithi:

> Ntlikithi, then, fathered Dike,
> Dike fathered the one called Qala-indawo.

Tyhali, then, fathered Ngonyama and Nombanjana in the right-hand house. Nombanjana fathered Bomvu. Bomvu is exactly my equal in age. Nombanjana is followed by Sibango, and Sibango is reigning at Godidi. He was pensioned by the [European] government while reigning. Nombanjana fathered Bomvu. Bomvu has fathered this youngster now reigning over there at the mouth of the Khobonqaba. That is the household of Ngqika in the minor house. This is the first minor house in Ngqikaland. It is Mnyaluza who fathered Mgodeli, and he fathered these youngsters now present. That is the first minor house.

Let me now go to the peoples who arrived; let me go to the Xhosa clans now. I have finished with the royal houses.[11]

FIVE

Now then, here are the names of the favorite oxen of the kings, an institution established during the time of Ngconde. Tshiwo's favorite ox was Mnqalazi.

Tshiwo's ox was Mnqalazi,
Gcaleka's ox was Mtshayelo,
Khawuta's ox was Gojela,
Hintsa's ox was Mali,
Sarhili's ox was Thiso,
Sigcawu's ox was Zulu,
Gwebinkumbi's ox was Holela,
Zwelidumile's ox was Ngqaqini.

That is the order of the oxen of the royal houses; according to Xhosa custom, the royal houses used to be named after oxen.

THE STATE OF THE KINGDOM

I shall continue by commenting on the state of the kingdom; it was a realm that would stop for a time in a certain area, then move on. Consider the burial places of the kings:

Nkosiyamntu's grave is in Zululand,
Sikhomo's is in Ntabankulu,
Togu's is at Qhokama in Ngqeleni,
Ngconde's is at Cumngce,

the place called Badzir, where today the seminary is located: that is Ngconde's grave.

Tshiwo's grave is at Ngcwanguba,
Gcaleka's is at Nxaruni,
Phalo's is over there at Thongwana,

over there at the boundary, by the big road that goes from Ndabakazi and passes through the land of Dyosini, dividing Mthulu and Dyosini—on the boundary: Phalo's grave is there. Phalo died in two supporting houses; he died in the home of Mbiko, and he died in the home of Bhayi—Phalo died at the houses of the women who bore these men. Gcaleka died in the supporting houses at the house of Faku and the house of Mneke. [Member of audience: Where was he buried?]

Gcaleka was buried at Msuze,
Phalo was buried at Thongwana,
Khawuta was buried at Mnyameni,

in the land of Ndiyalwa, in a forest called Mbubhuzile, at its head. Khawuta's grave is there.

> Hintsa's grave is at Mbangcolo, at Gatyana,
> Sarhili's is at Tyholora, across the Mbashe River,
> Sigcawu's is at Mngazana, beyond the Mbashe.

The Tyholora and the Mngazana are near each other. Sigcawu's grave is at Mngazana.

> Gwebinkumbi's grave is at Nqadu,
> Mpisekhaya's is at Nqadu,
> Zwelidumile's is at Nqadu.

I should note something about Ngcwanguba. The Tshomane, the Nqabe, the Hegebe, and the Tshezi—these are clans. Because the European government did not get along well with the Xhosa, because of Xhosa hardiness and bravery, the European government impounded those clans and gave them to the Thembu. Then the Thembu came under the European government, and they also fought against the Xhosa. And, because it now ruled, the European government was the bull: it had defeated Sarhili. The Nqabe joined the Thembu, the Hegebe joined the Thembu, the Tshomane joined the Thembu, the Tshezi joined the Thembu. Those are clans from here. Remember that Tshiwo's grave is over there at Ngcwanguba.

You see, the Bomvana had also come at that time. The Bomvana and the Tshezi are really one people. It happened in the course of time, as the Bomvana served the Xhosa at the place of their forebears, that Hintsa married Ntshunqe's daughter, Nomse, who gave birth to Sarhili. She bore Sarhili and Mqoloza only, no more. So it was that Hintsa elevated this group, this segment of the Bomvana; its status became higher than that of the Tshomane, as far as he was concerned. This group appears more important because Sarhili has elevated it.

Now, those clans over there—the Nqabe, the Tshomane, the Hegebe [Member of audience: The districts of Mqanduli]—all of the Mqanduli area belongs to the Gcaleka. And that is the way it happened. Because of the obstreperousness of the Xhosa, the European government decided to cede the land of the Thembu to people who were subservient to the European government, who obeyed the European government in the same way that I would treat a person who served me. The Thembu had not to that time had access to the sea—not at all. They were driven to the north, up this way, by Tshiwo, by Togu, by Ngconde. They were confined to the north. The sea enters this discussion with the graves of Xhosa kings, of Sikhomo, Togu, Ngconde, Tshiwo, Phalo. I mean those clans over there.

The Mqanduli area is *the* area of the Gcaleka. But because the land belongs to the European government, it did as it pleased, and the Thembu
got favored treatment because they were clients.

Look at what has happened. Sabatha, the present one, was even claiming the Xhosa. The Bomvana refused, "*We* were never clients to your
people! *We* were never subservient to the Thembu kingdom! *We* served
the Xhosa. Never have we served in your line!" In refusing, the Bomvana
were motivated by one thing—by Nomse, the mother of Sarhili, because
she is their paternal aunt. Nomse is the daughter of Ntshunqe:

> Ntshunqe fathered Gabushe,
> Gabushe fathered Moni,
> Moni fathered Ngonyama,
> Ngonyama fathered Gweb'indlala,
> Gweb'indlala fathered Ngubezulu,
> Ngubezulu fathered Zelenqaba,

the one who is presently king. Other clans that came and served were the
Maya—they were being scattered by Ngubencuka.[12]

They are here at Gcara, at the place of Mbuyazwe, son of Stokwe. Their
chief is the one now at Gatyana, at Nqadu, also called Mgudlwa; he is
the son of Mgudlwa, of Sobhini.

Let me go back. The household of Mboland arrived in 1818. It came
upon King Hintsa. The Mbo were being pursued by the Shaka,[13] having
quarrelled with them. They descended on Gcuwa. At that time, Hintsa's
site was where the Methodist minister's house now is, where the church
is. When the Mfengu arrived, hungry, with the Shaka in close pursuit,
Hintsa embraced them and kept them safe. It was during the second year
after the Mfengu had got there that the Shaka arrived, following them.
Hintsa declined to have anything to do with them. He drove the Shaka
back, and did not let them cross the Mbashe. So the Shaka fled, pursued
by Hintsa because they had been following the Mfengu. Then Hintsa kept
the Mfengu as his clients.

Hintsa inquired about the Mfengu chieftaincy. He would give the one
who was identified as the chief fifty head of cattle. Among the Hlubi
chiefs, Mhlambiso is the one who was circumcised by Hintsa. And Hintsa
apportioned the Mfengu throughout his kingdom, so that they could
maintain themselves. Nyila, the one who lives across here, is Mvelelo, because he was given to Velelo's place. The chieftaincy of my home here is
Nkatha at Zingqayi. The clan names of the Gcaleka were given to some
of them, clan names derived from the names of people here.

And so it went. Veldtman Bhikitshi belongs to the Giqwa clan at
Ngxala's household. The father of the lawyer, Charlie, who just died,

who had been an interpreter here at Gcuwa, used to sleep overnight at Nzima's place, beyond this hill here, at the home of a board member from our homestead, a councillor from our homestead, by reason of that Giqwa-ness which he achieved because Hintsa had assigned him to the Giqwa clan.

We are not the same as the Mfengu, as the Mbo people. The name "Mfengu" means "dispersion." These Mfengu people are really Mbo people. "Mfengu" means "diaspora" or "dispersion." These people are Mbo people. Yes, yes sir, you understand me, this word "Mfengu" is not a clan name. It is the name of a refugee. Whoever goes about begging, no matter what his clan, he used the word, *"Ndiyamfenguza,"* "I am begging, I am begging." These are Mbo, and they come from Shaka's land. Even now, they have clan names that point to Shaka's land over there— the Dlamini, the Radebe, the Hlubi. Yes, and the Dlambulo. These clans I have just named also exist over there, among the Zulu. When those Mbo people arrived here, Hintsa adopted them. He was friendly to them, and assigned them land to live on, land reaching up to the Ngqamakhwe and Tsomo areas. Hintsa mixed them in with his own people in the villages.

Then the first missionaries came to preach, Methodist missionaries, the John Wesleys, and they went on preaching. Hintsa gave them permission to go about preaching about God. Then came Ayliff,[14] a missionary who caused a division to develop between the Mfengu and the Xhosa. This was the Reverend Ayliff. There is a building in Gcuwa, the Methodist Church, with the inscription, "Ayliff Memorial Church." That is his memorial. When Ayliff came to Hintsa, the king gave the missionary permission to preach as he had given permission to those who had come before him, and so they evangelized. As it turned out, Ayliff got together with this Mbo group, and told the Mbo that the European government would treat them better than Hintsa did. Ayliff continued to evangelize, telling the Mfengu this same thing, until finally they came to be of the same mind. They agreed to do what Ayliff suggested. When, in 1834, the European government came to fetch the Mfengu, it did so without telling Hintsa, and it brought its armies along. Hintsa had heard nothing about this, so that when the European government arrived, he was surprised. That is how Hintsa came to die at Nqabara. He had gone to reclaim the Mfengu.

The European government had taken the Mfengu to the Nxuba River at Mqhwashu.[15] At Ngqushwa. This Mqhwashu is at Ngqushwa, where the European government caused the Mfengu to take oaths. Here are the oaths that they were made to take:

The European government said, "Will you serve me?"
The Mfengu said, "Sir, we will serve you."
The government said, "Will you go to school?"

They said, "We will."

The government said, "Will you be subject to me?"

They said, "We will be subject to you."

The government said, "Will you convert?"[16]

They said, "We will convert."

The government said, "Should a war be declared against me, will you fight it on my side?"

They said, "We will fight it."

Those are the vows that the Mfengu made at Mqhwashu. They thereby became the European government's people in that land from 1818 to 1834. They departed from Hintsa's territory in 1834.

And so time passed.

Part One

CULTIVATING THE PAST

"THIS IS GOD'S PLACE"

Great history, like great literature in other genres, is written along the fault-line where experience meets imagination.
—*Felipe Fernández-Armesto*[1]

History is the recital of facts presented as true. Fable, on the contrary, is the recital of facts presented as fiction.
—*Voltaire*[2]

"We must separate reality from image."
—*Charles G. Boyd*[3]

INTRODUCTION

Storyteller, historian, epic-performer, poet: all create their works in much the same way, in the sense that each manipulates and patterns relations between images of the past and those of present time.

Nongenile Masithathu Zenani, a Xhosa storyteller,[4] reveals this function of the storyteller when she describes the role played by the ritual master of ceremonies in real life, as he orders and shapes the actions of those involved in a Xhosa wedding ceremony. This vivid description will become a metaphor for the craft of storytellers, historians, and poets, as they move their characters and events on imaginative, historical, and poetic stages, theatrical events in the same way as is the wedding ritual.

Masithathu Zenani then shows how she plays this role of artistic master of ceremonies, as she creates the first day of a seventeen-day Xhosa epic: she develops her characters and events in such a way that she gives insight and meaning to the origins of the Xhosa. If Bhotomane provides the names, it is left to the imagination of the storytellers to bring history and story into an effective union, to cultivate the past. The theme weaving through her epic is as straightforward as it is potent: This is God's place, but God is not here: he has left his place in the care of the people.

This is God's place: The storyteller communicates an urgent message to members of her audience who daily inhabit a world which, they are reminded by their white masters, is anything but their place. The storyteller reminds them that this land is their land, that this place is God's place, that their presence here has mythic sanction.

ONE

When Masithathu Zenani set about to recreate an epic that emphasized the role played by women in the origins of Xhosa society, she used the names of the fantasy tradition: Nomehlomathathu, Nomehlomane, Hayibo, and the names of her kings and queens—Mityi, Mandla, Noma-cecembisa—are not discoverable in Bhotomane's lists.

The world is renewed routinely, because of the artistic ministrations of the storyteller. The genealogist gives all the illusion of fact: but truth is embodied in the less-than-factual renderings of the storyteller. The storyteller assures that historical time occurs within cosmic time,[5] so that linear history and the circularity of cosmic time are unified in story. Masithathu Zenani moves the time linearity of Bhotomane into mythic non-time. It is this crucial activity of the storyteller that enables a people to see contemporary history within a context that gives meaning to its experiences. So it is that apartheid loses its linear edge when set within the cosmic context of the storyteller.

Bhotomane and Zenani show two ways of recalling the past, that of the oral historian, and that of an oral storyteller. The one gives dimension to the other. Story, history, myth; Ndumiso Bhotomane, Nongenile Masithathu Zenani: What is the relationship? The one deals in facts, the other gives facts their contexts and so converts them to truth. Ndumiso Bhotomane remembered the past; crucial names and places were locked in his memory. It was the artistry of Nongenile Masithathu Zenani that gave his king-lists their context and meaning. In these two works, we see the rich relationship that exists between the genealogist and the storyteller, and the history that is the result.

Both are engaged in giving Xhosa society its roots, in providing conduits to the ancient past, to give the contemporary society its foundation. Neither of the two storytellers addresses apartheid in any concrete, obvious way, but each is giving the lie to the tenets of apartheid by providing the substance of African civilization. This begins the exposure of apartheid; it is their account that the architects and purveyors of the racist system rigorously denied. But the storytellers remained constant.

Deep within the images related by both Bhotomane and Masithathu Zenani are the undercurrents of myth, that which gives the genealogies of the former their significance, that which provides the fictional images of the latter with their resonance. History, myth, and fiction are the essential elements here, a mixture as controversial and explosive as it is fraught with the potential for meaning and truth. Masithathu Zenani's story is at once an origin myth and a myth of renewal. Running through it is the linear time-line of Bhotomane: Mityi's shade ramifies, shapes, and informs the magisterial remembrances of the oral historian. And Masithathu Zenani's myth is also a story.

The astonishing epic performance, which the artist sees as an imaginative history of the onset of Xhosa civilization, took place on three occasions, in July and November of 1975 and January and February of 1976, a total of some five hundred hours. The performer had last experienced the narratives as a unified work some fifty or sixty years before, when her grandmother performed them for her and her peers. She recalled that the performances occurred when she was a young teenager, and took place in the evenings and late afternoons, over long periods of time. The narratives as she was developing them in 1975 were not, of course, precisely like those her grandmother had created—"We're living in different times," she said, but the images and the movements of characters were substantially the same. And the formal relationships were little altered. This is the real tradition, she emphasized, not those "little children's tales" that her neighbors told. She had herself more recently performed many of the separate narratives that comprise the vast epics, but only as individual twenty- or thirty-minute stories.

The three epic performances are quite different in many ways, but the artist sees the second and third building thematically and culturally on the first, focusing on Xhosa traditional doctors and medicine (Mrs. Zenani is herself a doctor of some renown), as she moves her history away from magical, supernatural activities characteristic of the Mityi narrative. Like the earlier work, the second and third depend on imaginative narratives and a complex of emotionally experienced forms to communicate their message.

TWO

Now fact is joined to image, and the audience watches as this is accomplished by the astute manipulator of images. The work of the storyteller parallels that of the master of ceremonies at the Xhosa marriage ceremony. The storyteller similarly orchestrates images, joining the imaginative image of the storytelling tradition and the imagination of the performer to the fact of the historian. In epic is seen the triumphant merging of historical fact and imaginative story.

Storytellers have taught me this about the construction of stories: that image, the basic material of oral narrative art forms, mediates between audience and reality. It is so constructed and manipulated in performance that it shapes the audience's perception of the real. Image is composed of words that are given a unique framework by means of rhythm, intonation, and gesture, by body movement, which tends to dance, and by verbal drama, which inclines to song. Image is a visualized action or set of actions evoked in the minds of the audience by verbal and nonverbal elements arranged by the performer, in an interchange that, to carry meaning, requires that a common experience of images be held by both artist and audience, with the artist seeking by a judicious and artistic use of images to shape that experience and give it meaning.

The performer can have little effect on his audience if its members do not share with him certain experiences of traditional images; he depends on those common experiences, for the oral narrative is a communion between artist and audience on the one hand and the contemporary external reality on the other, with the artist and the audience involved in a kind of conspiracy to come to terms with reality within a context which does no damage to the society's links with its past. They seek to capture the real in the work of art, trapping, as Lu Chi says, "heaven and earth in the cage of form."[6] If artist and audience are alien to one another, if there is no shared experience which makes it possible for images to blossom, then there is no work of art—and, in the oral society, no educational system. Because images are evoked rather than created by the performer, the participation of the audience is critical: the artist requires the active assistance of the members of the audience in the transformation of plot clichés into vivid images.

Words do not have the malleability that sound has in music, for example, or that stone has in sculpture. Experiences cling to words; their sounds, moreover, cannot be altered in any dramatic way without a consequent loss of sense. But it is not the combination of *words* that composes the material to be shaped by the artist. It is the experience of the audience of a variety of images, a repertory of ancient images.[7] Words are the vehicles which call up and control the various image experiences of the members of the audience, the means whereby the images are evoked, arranged, and manipulated. When the artist objectifies an image, the audience gives it life in deep and colorful ways; it not only brings the surface narrative to life, it introduces into the performance its many experiences involving that surface narrative in hundreds of varied contexts. Image thus becomes far more than a single visualized action; it evokes the visualized actions of countless performances, actions which have been provided with many shades of meaning by many artists in their separate struggles to bring their audiences into harmony with their own conception of the real. These connotations obviously cannot be discounted during the performance. The sound of the word and the referents of the images refuse to allow word and image to be twisted into fantastic shapes; nevertheless, those associations are many, and the artist must seek to channel and govern the audience's experiences of the images if those images are to have any particularity. This imposes upon the performer the need for a special kind of artistic method; to manipulate the word into image, and to liberate the image from its many connotations at the same time that those connotations are exploited to reveal and enrich theme, the oral performer must bring that image into contact with yet others, altering the effect of the first image by means of those others. He cannot substantially change them simply by evoking them, and he cannot diminish the values that the members of the audience almost instinctively bring to those freshly recalled images. The surface narratives cannot be altered; they are the language of the tradition. It is the audience's experiences of the images that are progressively narrowed and sharpened. The artist must introduce other images into the work of art in order to contain and direct the potential meaning of the initial images, and thereby shape the audience's view of the real. The raw material of the oral performance, then, includes the experiences that the members of the audience have had with the images in past evocations—in a sense, the experiences that the audience has had with reality. The performer controls his audience by the very plot of the narrative, with its suspense, its chase, its dynamic move from conflict to resolution. Another means of control is achieved through securing and sustaining the participation of the audience in the nonverbal and verbal aspects of production. Thus, the artist encourages his audience to clap its hands, to sing when appropriate. The artist evokes image in this mesmerizing and poetic way, and the audience responds by also creating image, but always under the control of the artist who so shapes the narrative surfaces as to reduce ambiguity regarding what he is seeking to communicate. The repertory of images is the only material possessed by the artist, and hence his view of the real is circumscribed by that repertory and his ability to manipulate the images in the repertory to respond to his own vision of reality.

Among Xhosa and Zulu performers of oral imaginative narratives, there are no professionals. Everyone is a potential creator of the vivid images, and most do at some time attempt to objectify them, usually before an audience that is composed of family members and intimate friends. These narrative images, taken as a group, form the educational system of these oral societies, and in such communities the artist is the intellectual, the teacher. The Xhosa and Zulu audiences are caught up emotionally and psychologically in the enveloping images, and the ideals of the society are thereby communicated in an aesthetically compelling fashion. But this does not mean that every member of the society accepts without analysis the themes of the narratives, for, in a society in which everyone is a potential performer, everyone is also a potential teacher, and each has the opportunity to analyze and comment upon his society through the system of narrative images.[8]

The storyteller is an orchestrator, organizing events and characters on his stage, the space within arm's reach of his body, taking the real and rendering it theatrical. In the process, he takes the members of his audience into the essence of the real, allowing them to experience it according to his terms and those of the tradition in which he operates. His artistry is to be discovered in the way he takes the diverse elements of his craft and integrates these with images that he selects from the real world, or from history.

The storyteller is a shaper, forging links between the real and the imaginative, then working the audience into that combination. The result is a metaphorical relationship built to a large extent on the imaginations and experiences of the members of the audience. The storyteller discovers relationships between the worlds of history and imagination: His artistry is revealed in the effectiveness with which he weaves the audience into those relationships.

The artist is a teacher, a moralizer, finding truth in the conjunction of the real and the imaginative, and imbuing the audience with that

The storyteller is a shaper. A Zulu performer.

truth. Truth, meaning, occurs in the nexus of history and the imaginative tradition. Historians will create time lines, genealogical listings, cause-and-effect movements: the storyteller, and this includes the storyteller-historian, gives dimension and a new order to those lines and listings and movements. But most of all, the artist is a performer, organizing the three worlds of history, imagination, and audience into a semblance of unity, an ordering that is fraught with tension and fragile beauty, its existence short-lived, its impact lasting.

The storyteller gives meaning and dimension to a moment in history. Three hundred and fifty years of apartheid is such a moment, and the storyteller enfolds that violent and ugly moment in the images of his craft and tradition, and so gives it a meaning that transcends the moment, providing it with its meaning and also giving what appears to be hopelessness a modicum of hope.

THREE

The storyteller is a creator, then, taking the events of the real and casting them within a framework of his imagination. This role is seen most obviously when, in the evening and around the hearth fire, the raconteur dazzles audiences with images of fantasy from the oral tradition of the people. It is also evident in the rituals of the society. The master of ceremonies, during the marriage ceremony of Xhosa tradition, provides an example of the storyteller's art in a theatrical setting. He is the necessary clown, but he must also be recognizable as a respected member of the community. When he steps out of his respectable role, and into the guise of the clown, he has not been transformed, but is clearly playing a role. It is important to the onlookers and participants that all recognize that a role is being played, that a respected person is playing the role of a fop. It is the tension of this dual character that gives the activity its humor, its ceremony, its meaning.

He is truly a master of ceremonies: He plays a role, involved in the complexity of his storytelling activities. He coordinates the various means whereby the bride is moved from the outside to the inside. This is done theatrically and also in concrete ways. One of the symbolic means whereby the bride is integrated into the home and family of the groom is achieved monetarily: "We left a shilling at the place at which I [i.e., the bride] had been sitting. . . ." These symbols reveal the progressive movement of the bride into the center of the groom's homestead. Parallel to her movement is that of the master of ceremonies, a "flamboyant fellow" who makes faces at the members of the groom's home, and who is insulted by them in outrageous and frequently sexual ways, in phrases such as "you bony, awkward thing!" Slowly and elaborately, and hilariously, he unveils the bride to the members of her new home. He is the facilitator, but he is more: he is the storyteller, the organizer, and his actions move him to the periphery of the society, suggesting rampant, deviant, deformed sexuality. He moves the bride and her retinue, within the context of the audience composed of members of the groom's home, to the boundaries, making possible the movement into a new identity. He becomes the symbol of the bride's duality, her dual state of singleness and marriage: he is her betwixt-and-between state, the dramatic storytelling embodiment of her inner condition. He is doing what storytellers do as a matter of course, moving us, through his peripheral characters, into the mental states of the central characters, and all the while providing linkages, such as money and the ceremonial beast, that tie her to her new family. He orchestrates the activities of women no longer married, women who are considered peripheral characters in real life, until finally "the actual marriage ceremony took place," with the ceremonial drinking of the milk, the presentation of the dowry, and the return of the members of the bridal party to their own homes: "When they departed, I remained behind in this homestead of the groom as a married woman." In this complex image of transition—and, at least by implication, of the life course—the woman who is no longer married, who also participates in the organizing of the ceremony, is certainly appropriate.

The master of ceremonies is an apt symbol of the role of the storyteller, the historian, the poet, the epic-performer, and so he deserves to be placed at the commencement of this study. That he is a clown is clear, but one that is ambiguous, both respectable and outrageous: a respectable person at the heart of the culture, an outrageous person at the boundaries of the culture. That he is necessary should also be clear: he personifies and dramatizes the movements that the central character, the bride, is undergoing. In this latter sense, he is the storyteller, the facilitator, and the historian giving historical depth to the moment, a depth that is realized and achieved by means of the ceremony that he engages in and organizes. The master of ceremonies is at once the moment and its history. And that is what the storyteller, the bard, the historian are.

The opening of a basic pattern and the inclusion of new, usually subsidiary patterns is a central aesthetic experience of the narrative. As the patterns organize the separate images, so the fundamental formal relationships organize all subsidiary forms. On July 1, 1975, the Gcaleka artist, Nongenile Masithathu Zenani, began an oral narrative that was to become a unique experience for those in her small audience. Before a group of eight or nine Gcaleka intimates, she started her extraordinary work of art at ten that morning, sketching in the spaces and the characters that would occupy her for the next weeks. Mrs. Zenani was beginning an epic account of a Xhosa heroine, Mityi ("Isn't she beautiful, Child of my father?" asks one of the characters in the story. "She is the daughter of God . . ."), which would not be completed for seventeen days. Performing an average of six or seven hours each day, this great performer produced a unified narrative that ultimately totalled a staggering one hundred hours, a narrative that imaginatively incorporates Xhosa origins, with such ethnographic data as fully detailed marriages, circumcision ceremonies, and women's purification rituals, but with imaginative narratives forming the basis of the performance. She introduced images from the ancient art tradition, exploring three generations of characters, each with a woman at the center, developing their activities against a single traditional narrative which she boldly and competently incised, so that a large number of other Xhosa narratives and narrative segments could be worked in and locked to the basic core of images. The performance was never allowed to become a mere series of loosely connected stories.

The basic narrative is the Xhosa Cinderella story. Mityi is badly treated by her stepmother, who had earlier, jealously, killed the child's mother. With her two daughters, Three Eyes and Four Eyes, this stepmother attempts to kill Mityi also, to starve her. Mityi's father, one of the many rudderless men who people Masithathu Zenani's narratives, is helpless to do anything to preserve his daughter. When he attempts to give Mityi some of her dead mother's clothes to wear, the father is stopped by the stepmother, who tears the clothes to shreds. The father takes the torn pieces of cloth, mixes them with salt and water, and feeds them to a magnificent ox in his herd. That is the first of the ox's symbolic ties to the dead mother. When Mityi, in desperation, visits her mother's grave, she is told by the mother, "That ox is me." The daughter must go to that beast when she requires anything; she has but to strike its horn, and what she needs will magically appear.

This familiar image-sequence, the striking of the horns of a beast so that all good things appear, becomes the controlling image, the thematic generator of this vast epic narrative. The symbolic relationship between the mother and the ox becomes a significant spiritual link between the living and the dead, between Mityi and her ancestors. It is that relationship which is activated every time she goes to the horn and chants the formula, "Horn of the ox of my mother, it was said that you would provide for me."

Mityi and the ox escape the stepmother, and move miles from this homestead. Many months later, after encountering and struggling with scores of threatening beasts and overcoming them, the old ox dies, having instructed Mityi to cut off its horns and to carry on with them. In the middle of the veld, with the assistance of the horns, Mityi establishes a splendid homestead overnight. At the same time, far off in a remote village, a king has died, leaving no male progeny. The people of that village, thrown into disorder because of the lack of a royal heir, have been anxiously seeking a solution. They conclude that the homestead in the distance, the one that had sprung into existence in a single night, must surely be the homestead of God. They therefore send a delegation to go to "God's homestead" to ask for advice. Mityi meets the delegation, and when its members ask her if this is in fact God's homestead, the canny young woman tells them that it is, but that God is not in just now, he has gone off somewhere. But she will give God their message, then will come with his advice when she has it. The delegation returns to that far-off village, then a few days later Mityi follows. She informs them that God has returned, and that his advice to them is that his daughter, Mityi, should become their ruler. This has never occurred before, a woman as king, but since it is God's will, the people agree. Mityi becomes their leader, and, with the assistance of the horn, she supplies the people with their cattle, their homes, their rituals and forms of justice, everything that is of significance to the Xhosa way of life. The origins of all of these things are in the horns, the symbolic link between the present and the ancestral past. After a time, Mityi marries, then she slowly gives power to her husband, training him, and with the help of the horns, making it possible for a tongue-tied, reluctant male to confront crises and to handle them successfully, within Xhosa custom and law.

An ambiguous character in the early part of this epic is Hayibo, an incompletely shaped being who becomes symbolic of the untutored, unformed material that Mityi works with as she molds Xhosa civilization. Hayibo, the early being, represents the dawn of civilization, and Mityi will now move beyond this, working the world into a higher state.

These are the early images in a narrative that stretches on for many hours. The performance depends on the manipulation of a single narrative, which dominates the work, by interlocking imaginative narratives and cultural data. It is a daring and grand development of the patterning principle on which the narrative system is built.

Performance, whether of tale, history, epic, or poetry, involves this movement to the boundaries, followed by renewal and rebirth, a return to essence. Like the master of ceremonies, the storyteller is guide and facilitator, artist and historian. One cannot, therefore, stop with his words alone, as central as they may seem to be for meaning. Performance involves the word, but it includes such unspoken elements as the music of the word, the rhythm of the human body, and the complex web of relationships between performer and audience. And always, always, with the storyteller fully in charge.

Nongenile Masithathu Zenani

THE NECESSARY CLOWN

(XHOSA)

Nongenile Masithathu Zenani related a version of her autobiography, from which this excerpt is taken, on August 12, 1972, in Nkanga, Gatyana District, in the Transkei. Her performance took place outside, in an abandoned, roofless, rondavel-style house near her own home, along the side of a hill. In the audience were five women (among them, her sister, who was visiting at the time), two men, two teenagers, and three children—all Xhosa. (NS-156; tape 8, side 1)

She[1] was taken to be married to her homestead by marriage. The bridal party consisted of two young women, one being her sister who came directly after her in age. The other was also from the village. Also in the bridal retinue were two older women, an older woman together with an *inkazana*[2] who, in comparison with the other, was still young. And there were two men, an older man together with a younger.

As they travelled to the homestead of marriage, they crossed the Qwaninga River, then followed a wagon road. These guests continued to travel, going to the wedding ceremony at Nkanga, at a place called Ngqaqini, the headman being Mabala. As they were going there, they moved along a certain path—the roads being what they are, with various curves, there is usually a foot path that one can take as a short cut. They took such a foot path, leaving the wagon road behind, moving in the direction of a certain little valley, because it happened to be a valley that had no water in it. As they were travelling, they were driving a ceremonial beast: this animal is driven by the bride when she is travelling to her new homestead by marriage. Then, when she gets to that homestead, this ox is slaughtered on the morning following the evening of the arrival of the bridal party. Now that ox, the one they were driving, a yellow beast whose name was Selani, ran off. It was being driven in front while the family of the bridal party followed behind. It was being driven by this second man, it was evening, and Selani began to run wildly, bucking. It was evening, and this area had trees and thickets and long grass, as well as many ditches, so that a thing might easily disappear. And so it was that this ox got lost in the high grass of this area. That man pursued Selani, attempting to bring it back to the road, but he was unable to find it. The beast was lost.

The man returned to the group with which he was travelling, and he said, "I cannot find this ox! Perhaps it has turned back. It doesn't know

61

the place we're going to. Besides, this ox is an old one, and it is in the nature of the beast not to like being driven alone, without other oxen."

The members of the bridal party agreed with him.

"Yes, this is the kind of thing that might happen when the ox is travelling alone. When it becomes dark, then the eyes cannot see, and it might just decide to go back. It's very likely that it has just gone back home."

The bridal party stopped.

"What is to be done, now that the ox is gone?"

They reasoned together, and concluded that they should go on, because a bridal party cannot turn back once it has started. It was necessary that it go on, and then, when it arrived at that homestead which was their destination, the negotiators of the bridal party should leave early in the morning, and go back home to see if the ox is there. The ox would miss the day on which it was to be slaughtered, and it would have to be killed on the second day.

After they had taken counsel in this way, they proceeded on the path that went in the direction of the homestead by marriage. They went over the first hill, called Ngangana. There was a quarry on the left side of the path; when they got to the quarry, they rested. They sat there, smoking their pipes, and it was getting very dark by then. Then, after some time, it was said, "Let's go." And they travelled on. They took a curving, ascending road, and when they were fairly near the homestead that was their destination, it became clear that no one knew which juncture in the road they should take.

But I, the bride who was going to this homestead of the groom, knew the right path to take. An older woman in the bridal party asked me, "But how could you just allow us to wander around like this? It is for your marriage that we are travelling. Why didn't you tell us the way? Why did you just let us wander about at night? Do you think that it will help you to go back home?"

I, the one who was being taken to be married, was silent, I did not say a word.

They went on, but I could see that they were taking the wrong road. They were moving towards a shop, the Nkanga shop. That shop was beyond a ridge, at a place that was at a bend. When one goes over the ridge, when one is moving to the shop, one keeps close, as if one is going down. The name of the white man who operated the shop in those days, in those years of my marriage long ago, was Ben Blaudin.

I watched this group of people as they headed towards the shop. There was a homestead just above the shop, to the north of it; the name of this homestead was Gomomo[3] of the Qwambi clan. As the bridal party came to a certain curve in the road, just before going over the hill at Nkanga, they stopped and said, "Well, the homestead does not seem to be in this direction."

Others said, "Isn't this the place?" referring to Gomomo's homestead. "That homestead overlooking the shop?"

And another person came up and said, "The homestead that we're looking for is down below, it's a big homestead, it has wagons and a lot of livestock." In those days, it was considered a very large homestead.

Another person said, "Why don't we turn back?"

"We should just go over that hill."

They went over the hill, travelling along the wagon road. If you look at that road today, it is something else entirely, compared to the way it was in these days that we are speaking of. In those days, it was not the way it is today. Today, in these days when we have tractors, it is made of gravel that has been dug up in a quarry, then piled up. Such things were not present in those days, at the time of my marriage. There was nothing like that then. In those days, a road on which cars would drive was still being made in this way: men would be employed, and they would dig the road with picks, all the while singing a work song. Keeping in time, they would raise their arms, singing a joyful, languid song. They would not hurry themselves, singing, steadily,

"You're heaving it!
I'm heaving it!
This arm of mine—*nka!*"[4]

So the picks would follow that pattern, that is the way they did it. It was before there were any buses, before there were all these myriad kinds of things crawling over and mixing with each other, all this congestion which is visible before our eyes these days. In those days, there were little motorcars, not like the ones that we see now. And when we did see such a thing, it was rare: we called it a "motorcar." What was more common at that time was a cart drawn by two horses.

We were sitting there next to that road that is there now but was not there then—there was only grass in that place then. Then we saw a fire that glowed, it was blinking at some distance from us.

It was said to the young man who was the master of ceremonies[5] that he should go to that homestead where there was a light, and ask anyone[6] there about the location of the homestead to which we were going.

That young man, the master of ceremonies, went then, he went to this homestead, and we all sat down and waited.

He arrived there, and, when he had knocked, he was told to enter.

He said, "Come outside. I am a traveller, I want to ask something."

A young man appeared in the doorway, then; his name was Ngodwana.

Ngodwana said, "Where do you come from?"

This master of ceremonies said, "I am a person who comes from afar. I am seeking a homestead that I intend to visit." So he said.

This young man said, "Where is this homestead?"

The other one answered, "It is in this Nkanga area, at the Ntlane clan."

This young man said, "Oh, you must be the guests we are expecting! The homestead is just near here. But it's already early evening, deep dusk. It's meal-time for those who eat early.[7] You won't be able to see the homestead because there's no moon." He added, "The homestead you're looking for is really quite near. If I shouted, they would hear me. But it would be far for you, because you're a visitor. Where are those with whom you're travelling?"

The young man said, "They're here, those whom I'm travelling with. There they are, up there. I told them to remain there while I came here to inquire."

So he said, and the other young man said, "We should go to them, then I'll accompany all of you here."

This young man walked with the master of ceremonies then, that representative of the bridal party, conversing with him: "You are the guests of our home. This place you're going to is also our home, it's the same homestead really. And this bride whom you're taking there is going to be married to my older brother. I'm his younger brother, we belong to the Ntlane clan. I'll accompany all of you to that place."

The master of ceremonies came then and found us sitting as he had left us. He approached with this person, and we could hear them as they were coming, conversing pleasantly. They were laughing.

When they arrived, the master of ceremonies said, "Get up, bring your things."

Now these goods that we were carrying included pots, billycans, dishes, that sort of thing, everything that had to do with marriage in those days. There were no boxes then, nor anything that resembles a chest. All the goods were carried in shoulder bags and in pails. Some would be wrapped in mats, some would be carried in kerchiefs.

We travelled now with this young man. They turned around on the road, because the road cut below the hill at Nkanga, then they went below Nkanga and crossed a stream bed, then another stream bed. They were more or less like stream beds—the way the land was shaped, they only resembled stream beds. When someone said "across," the meaning was not "across a river," the meaning was "across this depression of land." Because it was now dark, and because we might get hurt as we moved along these depressions, it seemed as if we were travelling over cliffs.

I was wrapped in my new cape, the one that had been wrapped around me at home—it is this one that I am still wearing now.

We walked on there, and as we were skirting that place, as we neared the homestead to which I was being taken, we encountered bushes and copses—apple trees and cabbage trees, and there were also thickets on either side of the road. Beyond the thickets were peach trees, which we realized belonged to the orchard of this homestead of mine, this homestead of marriage, the orchard of my father-in-law.

We travelled there. We women were treated with care, because in the bridal party was the person who would marry, and she was the one who was especially cared for. They took care that she did not stumble and fall and thereby have a blemish at the place where she got hurt. She was taken care of especially. Repeatedly, someone would come near to me, holding me so that I would not get hurt.

We walked to this homestead, coming down from above that place. We arrived, then sat at a spot overlooking the homestead. Dogs came out and barked. When we had settled down, this young man who had accompanied us, the youth of the Ntlane clan, went ahead to the house, because it was also his home. When he was in his home, he explained that I was coming with some visitors. By then, the dogs—and this homestead had many of them—were barking at this group of people who were sitting above the homestead.

Then a young woman who had already been married, called an *inkazana*—according to Xhosa custom, a married woman who returns to her home of birth, for whatever reason, is called an *inkazana* here at her home of birth. This young woman came out of the house, she walked up to us and asked, "Where have you people come from?"

They told her that we had come from across the Mbashe River and were going to the Nciba River,[8] "and we've been benighted. We have a child with us who is not too well, and we're asking for a place to spend the night."

The young woman casually hopped about in her response—this exchange was customary: the bridal party always made up an exaggerated and false excuse, to invent a reason for spending the night at the groom's homestead. Even though everyone knows what is going on, including the young woman, the *inkazana,* the game must be played through to its end.

She said, "But why did you choose this particular homestead, of all the homesteads around here?"[9]

It was said, in answer, "Well, really, it's not because of that, it's just that it happens to be this time of day and the health of this child is a problem. You see, she is limping. And when one is limping, it's difficult to travel in the dark. More than the darkness, it's these cliffs. And we've been carrying her on our backs for a long time now, and she's heavy."

That woman, the *inkazana*, said, "Well, I'll report this to those in the house." So she said, and she departed.

She was gone for a while, and in the meantime we sat there. I had my head veiled with a new cape that was being used for the first time. In fact, all of us had our heads covered, including these women who were accompanying me. One of them was my sister, coming after me in age. They were on either side of me, my sister was next to me on the one side, and the other, from another village, sat on the other side. She also had her head covered. And so we sat there in that way.

After a time, that *inkazana* returned. She said, "Please get up. It is said that you should go to that house."

We got up as one, that entire group of people, and we went to that house. When we entered the house, we found that everything had been removed from it, because the house had just been coated with cow dung. Firewood had been put into a corner, by the doorway. Some had been chopped, some had not been chopped. And some had been kindled, probably by this *inkazana*, here in the hearth.

When we arrived, mats were spread out for us. We sat, and an old cape belonging to one of the men with whom we were travelling was tied and made into a curtain. We sat over there, out of sight, on the other side of this curtain.

After a short time, there was a knock at the door, and some food was brought in, stamped maize that was cooked together with beans. Then we ate here in this house.

This fellow who was the master of ceremonies told our hosts that we had a request concerning a thing that we had lost, a thing that we had been carrying with us. He said that we had a small request, that our hosts might permit the master of ceremonies to go out in the morning and be gone a brief time, so that he might go to the place from which we had come to get information about the loss of that thing that we had been carrying with us on our travels. He was referring to the ox that had been lost at the fork in the wagon road, as we were leaving the Qwaninga River area.

In those days, both homesteads had respect for each other, so there was no undue concern about this request; it was not suspect. Under these circumstances, this request was agreed to.

The master of ceremonies went and explained that matter in the house, while the bride's party waited. But the hosts had an inkling that this request, that had the urgency of a demand, might possibly have to do with the ceremonial beast—that thing that had been lost to the bridal party. Because they had come and made that urgent request, it meant that they thought that it was time that the proceedings should focus on the ceremonial beast, so the bridal party remained patient, waiting for that thing.

Then, before it was time to go to bed, another person of the groom's home came there and knocked. He was told by the bridal party to enter. They asked, "Is this person of this homestead bringing us any word?"

He said, "Yes, I have been sent from over there at that house. It was said that a man should come out of this house for a time, that he should come out briefly and identify something, because there is a thing that we do not know, it might be the thing that you say was lost as you travelled. We do not even know what thing it is that you lost, what it looked like, but there is something here that we're trying to identify. It arrived here before it was dark, early in the evening. It arrived after our livestock had been penned up. Please look."

Immediately, a member of the bridal party got up, and this young fellow and the old man of the bridal party ran over each other, going to look. When they had gone to look, they arrived and found that beast that the bridal party had been driving, its name being Selani, the yellow ox. The members of the bridal party were amazed that it should have preceded them here, that it had already been here for a long time.

They said, "This is the one about which we have been speaking."

It was then said at the Ntlane homestead, "This ox has been here a long time. It was here already by the time you arrived. It came as we were shutting in our stock. It lay down in the kraal, in the middle, between the posts, in front of the entrance. It faced the entrance to the kraal. I tell you, it lay there between the posts! At first, we thought it was an ox from this area," because in those days this homestead had a lot of stock—it had cattle, it had horses, it had sheep, it had wagons, it had all the things of those days. If any ox should stay around here, no one would take notice or raise the question of where it came from.

After a short time, the people returned from the kraal.

"It's amazing! This ox turned out to be ours. As we lost our way, going over to Nkanga, desiring to cut by the shop, the ox knew the way to this homestead. And so it was that it parted company with us over there at Ndlambe's place. It did this because we were going the wrong way, and were therefore going to mislead it and drive it to a place where it was not intended to go. So it left us, deciding to come and rest here, leaving us to wander aimlessly alone."

The members of the bridal party laughed, and, as time passed, they would come back to this subject and laugh again. They chatted about it until the next morning.

Eventually, as morning was approaching and before dawn, the master of ceremonies arose and asked those of the homestead of the groom to assist him, to help him to slaughter that ceremonial ox. It was fat now, amazingly fat. This is not just a subjective comment that I am making: that ox *was* remarkably fat! surpassingly fat! its fat would fill billycans!

When everything was in readiness, then, there came the various occasions for doing things according to schedule—things like "Bring down from the mountains,"[10] getting water for the bridal party, things like that. And beer was prepared for the celebration, much beer was prepared for the celebration. Maize for this beer would be brought to the house of the bridal party, and grinding stones would be brought there as well. And the members of the bridal party would rough-grind the maize. The initial stages of brewing the beer would follow, then the dough would be transported. It was the women in the bridal party who did the grinding, and I also ground maize, along with my companions who were in this house of the bridal party, so that the dough could be transported by this young man who was also a member of the bridal party. When we finished grinding, he transported it to the main house.

It was dusk then, and we went to sleep.

Then there was a knock at the door again. If it was not the *inkazana* who was knocking, it would be a young recently married woman.

When she knocked, it was said, "Come in," and they asked where she had come from.

She said, "I have come to borrow the bridal party—the women, especially the bride."[11]

And when she had said that she had come to borrow the bridal party, the women and especially the bride, it was said, "*We* cannot produce the bridal party, the girls and especially the bride. We don't have a custom like that—a custom that, before they are viewed formally, they already sleep with the men."

Because this matter of sleeping with the men was a Xhosa custom in itself, it was necessary that it be done. It was necessary that the master of ceremonies come out with a mat, and go with these women, the bridal party, taking them to the house in which the groom and his companions would be. Having arrived there, the groom would sleep with his bride on his own mat, and the companions would sleep on their mats.

If they were still sleeping when daylight appeared, if they overslept and it was very light outside, it was necessary that, when the glimmering on the horns at dawn appeared,[12] the bridal party, the women and especially the bride, should come out, and the bride and her party should go and enter the house of the bridal party. Then, with the master of ceremonies with them, they would come out with buckets, and go and wash their bodies. Then they would return and sit. If they overslept and what has just been described did not occur, if they did not get up at the crack of dawn and be ahead of the time, then the groom's party would be fined. The groom's party would have to produce money for sleeping with people beyond the appropriate time. The master of ceremonies had a financial interest in this, because this is where he received his money.

If the members of the bridal party, the women and especially the bride, overslept, the fine that was paid by the groom's party went to him. It was said to us as we were leaving, "You *should* oversleep![13] Don't keep saying, 'We want to go now!' It is necessary that you oversleep! Otherwise this master of ceremonies will leave having gotten no money!" We went then.

Now, when we were over there with the groom's party, my groom and I did not trouble each other, we just slept there.[14] But our companions were causing each other grief, they were rowdy, they *were* grappling with each other because there was an amorous interest there among them.

One of the members of the groom's party said, "Oh, this woman! I wish she would not go home! I wish she'd be mine!"

And that resulted in a lot of commotion here in the house, with the groom repeatedly warning, "Don't be unruly over there!"

That went on, time passed, that went on and at last things fell into place. And we did oversleep. My groom and I were wide awake, but the others were fast asleep. Remember that they were giving each other trouble all night. The night went on like that, and eventually, when it was almost daybreak, they did go to sleep.

When I said to my groom, "Well, let's go now. Wake up the others," he said, "No, leave it alone. Where do you think the master of ceremonies will get his money?"

I said, "Well then, it's all right."

The bigger share of the fine would come from the groom, even though he himself had done nothing to deserve that fine, he had just let things happen, had just let the others oversleep.

The master of ceremonies arrived, and he knocked on the door. When he entered, he said, "Ho! Got you! Who gave you these women?"

And they rushed to get up.

"Oh! No!"

"Pardon, pardon!"

"Really!"

He said, "I told you! Pour! Pour! Pour!"[15] he said, insisting that money be poured into his hand.

And the groom's party begged, "No, really! You'll get the money when we go to the house."

They went to that house then. And we did not wash that day when we went back to the bridal party's house.

The master of ceremonies said, "Well done, my woman! Do that again when night comes!" He had his eye on more money.

Then the money arrived: the fine for the companions was a half crown each, the fine of the groom was six shillings. The money of the master of ceremonies was uncontested,[16] and he had his eye on getting more.

Time passed in that way.

As the celebration of the marriage went on, it became necessary that the bridal party should come outside, to be formally seen.

The wind that day was very strong, Friend. The wind of the Ntlane clan—I can comment on the wind because I now belong to them, to the Ntlane clan. Now this wind of the Ntlane clan was beautiful, a good omen: there was no lightning, there were no overcast skies, no thundering. Nothing like thunder. It was a wind on a clear day. As they were observing it here in this homestead, they took calabashes and faced them into the wind. The mouths of the calabashes were closed, so that musical notes would be produced there.

The bridal party watched and whispered critically about these activities.

It was said, "This wind has some significance here." But the wind had no such significance for the bridal party, it was alien to them.

You see, they would take calabashes and face them into the wind.

Now the ceremony was moving towards the cattle kraal, but it was repeatedly delayed.

Someone was sent from the house, asking, "When will the bridal party come out?"

And the answer was, "No, no, no, we'll be there! We'll be there!"

This happened again and again, and a person would come: "When will this bridal party here at home come out? Don't you want us to see this wife of yours?"

"No no no, we'll be there, sir!"

And the fellow returned.

What was delaying them was the washing of the entire body, that it be clean. Then there was the combing of the hair, that it be flat.[17] Then they put on a knot of a monkey on the head, an object that has been plaited and made into a rope. Sometimes, there were three of those ropes inside, sometimes four ropes made up this bun or knot in the hair. Each woman chose her own style, decided how her own hair should be prepared.

Then, on the neck, there would be shells that had been picked up along the shore. A shell would be found on the seashore, and it was then smoothed on rocks. Two strings were made for it. It was worn around the neck and hung with a chain in front, so that it came down to the breast. Those shells looked marvelous.

Another item was a necklace of green beads that are sometimes called "dove beads." These beads were arranged into a pattern, a coil was run through them, and this coil was rolled. It was a long coil that had a loop that reached to the thighs when a person was kneeling. Then those beads would be looped around the neck.

The bride would not have a breast-covering, she would wear nothing. She would simply stand naked in the kraal, girded with a little loin cover, it did not matter which shape or form, there were varieties of them. She would emerge with her head covered with a turban that had been unrolled, just put on the head with no knots or anything. This turban would be held in place by a cape that was just thrown over her shoulders. She caught hold of it in front, and that kept the turban in place so that the wind would not blow it off.

Friend, I tell you, that is how it was in those days of my marriage.

This is the way the procession was ordered: The master of ceremonies was to be in front—that young man, not the old man here in the bridal party. It was to be the young man who would be in front, and he was to be followed by an *inkazana*. This *inkazana*, glancing about, whispered from time to time to the master of ceremonies when she saw that there was something that ought to be put right, because *we* had our heads covered, all three of us: I was in the middle, between my sister who was in front and the other young woman who was behind me. As we walked along, our capes trailed on the ground, and there was the danger that we might step on them. This *inkazana* would tell us to stop, and then the woman in front would stop, and she would turn around to put right whatever was to be put right—either she or the master of ceremonies would adjust our capes, pulling them here over the feet and shaking them off, pulling them back a little. Then the *inkazana* would whisper when she got up, telling us, "Shuffle your feet along the ground, don't just stomp. Don't raise your feet: that way, you step on the capes and pull them off. Shuffle your feet so that you do not step on the capes." Then she would notice something, and say, "What's this? Are we going to have to keep putting this thing right?"

As she spoke in that way, she could not be heard by the groom's party that was sitting over there in the kraal. What she was saying to us, she was saying softly.

Meanwhile, those people over there were chiding them, criticizing what they were doing over there. At this point, the women of the groom's side were sitting in the cattle fold, and the men were in the courtyard.

Now the bridal party was coming in a procession, slowly, with the *inkazana* and the master of ceremonies attending to their chores, helping them along, pulling up the capes, as the procession moved across the courtyard to the kraal where the groom's party was waiting. The bridal party was in the middle of the courtyard, and the groom's party was also in order, coming out of the house, also composed of three people. The women and men of the groom's home were sitting in the kraal, as the bridal party walked in procession from one side and the groom's party from the other.

That groom of mine, like me, was in the middle. When I looked at them, I observed that their order was a mirror image of ours. His party was led by an Ntlane clansman, and that clansman was also followed by someone from the village, with the groom in the middle as I was in the middle

in our party. They came into the kraal and sat on the right hand side—
there were special places for the various parties to sit, one did not just sit
anywhere; even the seating arrangements were carried out according to
Xhosa custom. It was necessary that, when they came in, they turn to the
right and sit on that side. All the men in the house sat on that right-hand
side. Whenever we were being put right, our garments or whatever, we
walked very slowly. I tell you, if you were watching it, you would have
become dizzy with boredom, it was a *slow* process. The bridal party did
not advance very rapidly, each member of the party stepping in the same
place as the person who came before, and after a very long time we arrived at our destination.

And, I tell you! as this was happening, the master of ceremonies was
being insulted about all of this. The *inkazana* was being insulted more
casually. The ones who did the most insulting were the women.

They said to the master of ceremonies, "You with these hipbones!
Don't get in our way as we gaze at those children in the bridal party!"

"Why do you keep looking at them, you bony, awkward thing!"

"We don't want *you!*"

"We see how you busybody around them with those scaly feet of
yours!"

"Hurry up with those children!"

"Really, we wonder where they found this fool!"

"This thing suddenly looks like The-one-who-peers-in-there-nosily!"

The master of ceremonies paid no attention to these comments. A flamboyant fellow, he merely stared at those who spoke. Sometimes, when he
felt like it, he made faces at them. But this matter of their deriding him
was not really serious, no one took it seriously. It was custom that he be
insulted in that way; Xhosa custom was thereby being observed.

In the end, the two processions arrived at the cattle kraal, the cattle
fold. The master of ceremonies went in front of the bridal party, remov-
ing every bit of dried cow dung. And he was even scolded by the men,
who said, "Go on! Go on, you young man!"

"What is all this?"

"When will you finally get there?"

"You waste too much time being an exhibitionist!"

"You nobody, you don't even have a wife! And now, you come to be
an exhibitionist before these women!"

"Is that your mistress[18] whose eyes you keeping looking into so intently?"

"Acting so familiar with her!"

So the men said, but the master of ceremonies did not care.

Then, when all were in the cattle fold, in the middle of the kraal, attention was again paid to seating arrangements. People did not just sit anywhere. When the master of ceremonies got there, he spread things out, preparing our places, so that we could properly take our positions.

Then the master of ceremonies covered us. As he busily moved about, his penis cover was bouncing about, and, as he hastened about, his inner groin and his hips faced the people, and the small of the tail. He was naked because he was stepping on his cape with his feet, his legs spread wide, covering us so that we should be inside the covering with him. He was hiding the bridal party from the groom's people.

Then the *inkazana* caused us to sit down, to go to our knees. The garments were taken and put over our thighs, and our bodies were exposed from the navel up—all the area down to the navel. It was necessary that the body, from the navel up, be exposed, that it be clearly observed along with the breasts—all the form of the top portion of the body, how it stands.

Those black kerchiefs on our heads were removed and put on the ground. We kept our heads low, reverentially, towards the people that day. Yes, I bowed my head, being a young woman who was something great, perfect in my time, and my sister, too, was something special, having a good complexion, a complexion that was better than mine.

So we were on our knees, facing the men of the groom's place.

And the men burst out and said, "Yu yu yu yu yu!"[19]

There was a man who went further, and said, "My daughter-in-law, we loved her even before we saw her!"

Meanwhile, the master of ceremonies was thrusting out his buttocks and hanging his testicles in our direction, as he delicately closed the capes about us so that the groom's party could not see us. And when he did that, he was insulted.

It was said, "Open up again! Let us see her again!"

But he did not altogether unveil us for the men.

The members of the groom's party were similar to us in the sense that they also had these knots in their hair, they also wore necklaces of beads, they also put on shells, and they also wore capes. They went bareheaded, while we had our heads covered with black turbans. On the feet, where the lower legs end entering the feet, we wore boots and a thing called "black beads" over the boots, rows of black beads on the inside and rows of white beads on the outside. These beads were worn by a bride when she was still young. At the time of my marriage, these boots and beads were worn by the bride until she stopped wearing her turban just over the eyes; she wore the boots all the time until she took off the cloth that was tied around her waist, wearing the boots all the time until she became a young married woman. And when these boots gave out,[20] they did so when she was a woman who attended beer-drinks. People would know her by those boots. She would also wear chains in those days, along with all the things that were worn as a person chose.

Nowadays, that is no more, the custom has fallen into disuse. Today, these boots are worn on the wedding day only, the day the bride is unveiled and viewed, and that is the only day: never again will she wear boots.

That is how it was, the manner of my getting married. . . .

When we had been viewed by the men of the groom's home, we went to the women. And the women also chided the master of ceremonies. We left a shilling in the place at which I had been sitting in the kraal among the men of the groom's party, and another shilling was being carried with us: it would be left under me among the women.[21]

Before the women, we went down on our knees in the same way as in the kraal, and once again there was the buttocks-thrusting activities of the master of ceremonies, and we were again exposed and caused to go naked, being shown to the women as we had earlier been shown to the men. We went down on our knees, and faced the women, and the master of ceremonies uncovered us, and when he uncovered us, it was said, "Oh oh oh! She is beautiful, friends!"

"Oh oh!"

So they would say, those who were being derisive as well as those who were in earnest.

Now the master of ceremonies, having covered us, caused us to stand because we were going to the house.

Then the women said, "The legs! Show us her legs, lest you bring a cripple to us!"

Then we were turned towards the east, being adjusted in that direction by the master of ceremonies, and the *inkazana* and the master of ceremonies helped each other to expose our legs for the women of the groom's home, and the garment was lifted.

"Oh oh oh oh!"

Then they observed me, to ascertain that I was not a cripple. Even that comment about cripples was a mere matter of form, so that both the top and bottom parts of the body should be exposed.

Then we went on very slowly again, moving now to the house. We arrived at the house of the bridal party, and we undressed. Our skirts were ready for us, we put on the skirts, the *amankazana* of the groom's house as well as their daughters. Weren't they naughty! Their naughtiness was legendary.

Now hoes and buckets were brought to the bridal house—there was such a racket! And the *amankazana* of the groom's house came, and said, "At this home here, the fields are cultivated." And they struck the ground.[22]

"At this home here, water is dipped."

And others chopped wood: "At this home here, wood is gathered."

As they said these words, they demonstrated everything, all these activities were mixed up. Things were noisy at this home.

Then, out of the door came the master of ceremonies. He took a strap, he took a billycan, and sat in front of them. Then he squatted and put the billycan between his thighs, and imitated the milk when it strikes the can.[23] Then he acted as if he were milking, going through the motions, all the while saying, "Before any milking is done at this home here, you have to produce cattle. Then we can milk and plough."[24]

Now, all of that is the procedure of custom, that is the way this portion of the marriage ceremony works.

Then the *amankazana* departed, and we put on our skirts and began to put on our breast-covers. These *amankazana* took off their breast-covers as we donned ours. Then we covered our heads to the eyes, and the turbans were knotted under our chins. Once again, we became those lumpy-headed ones, just like hammerheads.[25]

Now we went to the river. There we were, going to the river—lined up, shawled. Then we came back from the river, carrying those buckets in a circumspect manner, going around the homestead, avoiding the courtyard.

After that, the actual marriage ceremony took place.

"Master of ceremonies, the ceremony has already taken place!"

As the master of ceremonies came out of the house, a member of the groom's home put a bar across the entrance to the cattle kraal. The master of ceremonies put money there for the removal of the bar. When the bar had been removed, they delayed killing the beast, because they wanted the money of the spear from him. So the master of ceremonies produced the money of the spear. Then that ox was slaughtered: this part of the ceremony was called "The marrying of me." That is what they were saying, they were marrying me by means of this ox, whereby I became a wife of this homestead.

We ate that meat then, and portions went to the people of the groom's homestead, to the guests, and others, the meat of the home being helped along by appropriate payments of money.

After that, it was said that I should go through the ritual of drinking buttermilk made of the milk from this cow. Confusion occurred at that point of the day that I married and became a wife: my people said, "We will not allow it to happen, that a beast of marriage that has travelled all over the land should be the one with which this bride will go through the ritual of drinking buttermilk. The ritual of drinking buttermilk only happens by means of a goat that will have been suitable to this custom. An ox? Never! An ox is for celebration, not for this buttermilk-drinking ritual."

Oh! The members of the bridal party said, "This is the kind of thing they did when others in this groom's family got married. They got away with it with those others, but they won't get away with such cheap and uncustomary actions with us!"

Then a member of the bridal party said to the groom's party, "You did that to those people of Tsomo, but we're not like those people! This bride will have the correct buttermilk-drinking ritual! You won't deceive us with an ox! What you're doing is folly, it's certainly not the ceremony of drinking buttermilk!"

At length, my groom surrendered his goat, a gelding of a goat, and the ceremony of drinking buttermilk was performed. The ceremony was performed, they brought a strap along with a pail that had buttermilk in it. Then they roasted a slice of meat, and the strap was soaked in the buttermilk. A mouthful of the meat was soaked in buttermilk, and I was made to suck on the strap, and was given that mouthful of meat that had been soaked in buttermilk, a really disgusting thing to taste. But, because it was the custom, it was acceptable, and so I swallowed that thing. We ate the meat then, and then that meat was taken to the homestead of the groom's people.

This is the procedure: the skin of marriage, that is, the skin of the goat that was killed for the marriage ceremony, is the skin of the master of ceremonies.[26] These things are distributed; they are not things that are casually thrown this way and that, they are distributed here in the house according to the ordering of the people, according to protocol. The master of ceremonies is this young man who is sent to get everything required in this house of the bridal party.

Time passed then, and the money of the *amankazana* was demanded, and then the money of the homestead. On the occasion of my marriage, there was no money that was not made available.

Now the bridal party made plans to return home quickly, because my father was a Christian convert, and he simply wanted to produce twelve pounds on the spot. He said that it was necessary that his obligations be properly discharged according to their protocol, so it was necessary that money be available. He did not know if twelve pounds would be enough, if that amount of money would meet the demands.[27]

That money of the *amankazana* was distinct, it had its own name, it was said, "It is the money of the *amankazana*," and that was all; it could not be used for anything else, it was earmarked for that purpose. And the money that went to the women of this homestead of mine: they did not share it with any other group. It was distributed within that group, that three pounds. The smaller currency was distributed among the women, those who happened to be present in this homestead, each according to her status.[28] The daughter-in-law had no part in the share of the money of the mothers-in-law.[29] The older brother as well as the younger brother[30] are the ones who are privileged to have a share of the money. All the way, then, the money reached up to the aunts and whomever, except for the daughter-in-law.

That marriage ceremony ended in that way then, and at the end of the ceremony everyone went home. I was taken to the main house, along with all of my baggage which had been in the guest house and which was placed now in the main house of my new home. In the main house of my new home, I had no father-in-law nor mother-in-law, no older brother; the only person present there was the wife of my older brother[31] in the place of the parents.[32] She presided over the preparations, making them right. The bridal party came outside to the men, and was able to depart with four cattle—the six had already been sent, to make a total dowry of ten. When they departed, I remained behind in this homestead of the groom as a married woman.

Nongenile Masithathu Zenani

THE ENDLESS MOUNTAIN

(XHOSA)

This epical narrative, the beginning of what would become a seventeen-day performance, began in mid-morning on July 1, 1975, at Nongenile Masithathu Zenani's home in Nkanga, Gatyana District, the Transkei. In the audience were seven women and two men: they remained a constant audience throughout the performance. Other men and women joined them from time to time, as the audience waxed and waned during the seventeen days. Mrs. Zenani had heard this story as a teenager, and had told it in parts and had heard it in parts since then, but not in its entirety. She said that she wanted to perform it "once more before I die," and she wanted me there to tape it for posterity. But this was only one part of what she considered a three-part Xhosa epic. Later that year, in October, she performed part two; the third part she performed in January, 1976. This is a somewhat abridged version of that first day's performance. (3S-305; tape 11, side 2, and tape 12, side 1)

HAYIBO, MITYI'S STEP-BROTHER

"HE DID NOT KNOW HIS OWN MOTHER."

At a royal residence lived a king who ruled over all the villages in the land. He had one wife: she became pregnant, she grew large, and, in the ninth month of her pregnancy, when it came time, she gave birth. She bore a daughter.

Time passed for this child. She was beautiful; she grew up, doing all the normal things a child does: she crawled, she attempted to stand, she kept trying to walk. She was a child, and, in the course of time, she did walk.

She matured, and was weaned.

After a time, when the child had been weaned, the king's wife again became pregnant, and in the ninth month she bore a child, a boy. He also grew up.

He seemed an acceptable child, but it was clear that he was not really normal. The people endeavored to discover what kind of child he was.

He did not know his own mother. Everyone has a mother, but he did not know his. He would seek his mother in a man: he looked for kindness from him. Even a boy might be his mother: he looked for kindness from him. The parents of the boy began to scrutinize him carefully, as they attempted to understand this boy who did not resemble other chil-

"Horn of the ox of my mother, provide for me." Nongenile Masithathu Zenani, during a storytelling performance.

dren. Those who were his age-mates were not like him: they knew their mothers.

This child tried to stand up, and, finally, he learned to walk.

The people called him Hayibo, because no matter what he did, he was always told, *"Hayi bo!*[1] No! *Hayi bo!"*

Not far from his home was another child, a girl, his age-mate. The two played together until the time they were weaned.

At length, when their mothers became pregnant again, the two children knew one another well. But Hayibo's habits were not at all like those of the other child. This one knew her mother; she was able to separate her mother from other people. But Hayibo did not know who his mother was. No matter whom he encountered, that person was his mother; no matter whom he saw, it was his mother.

The days passed for these youngsters, and in time they were joined by other children who had been borne by their mothers.

Hayibo's mother bore yet another child, a boy. That child, even before he was crawling, knew who his mother was. If he happened to be taken by another person, as that person was walking away with him he would cry when he saw his mother, realizing that he was leaving her behind. Hayibo never did that.

As this other child grew up, he tried to stand; he walked, and, having been weaned, played with the others. He would frequently cry, complaining that he had been beaten by Hayibo.

Time passed for Hayibo and his age-mate, the girl who played with him. But now, because of the improper things that he did, she no longer wanted to be with Hayibo. Whenever he defecated, he would take the feces in his hands and bring it to his mouth. The other children would flee from him, saying, "Hayibo is defiling us!" Then they would beat him.

Hayibo had to be watched over by his mother. Whenever he went somewhere, he had to be minded by an older person who would continually have to turn him back from what he was doing. He insisted on going to the gatherings of other children, even when he was told not to go. When he arrived at the children's gathering place, he would say that he had been summoned there. "No," the others would say, "you haven't been summoned here!" Someone else would say, "There's nothing for you here!" But Hayibo would run to such places, saying that indeed he had been invited to come there. He would arrive there and ask, "Who called me?" They would say, "No, Hayibo! Go away!" Then he would depart.

The child was unloved; the things that he did were odious. The other children looked with disgust on the cloak that he wore. When he came to a pool of mud, even if pigs were sloshing there, he would frolic in the mire, becoming soiled along with his clothing. He would put his cloak into the mud, dragging it along the ground, then he would drape it on his shoulders. He did not feel cold, he did not know what coldness was.

Hayibo grew up in that way, and his mother felt unhappy about him. She concluded that this child should be taken to her mother, now an old woman, and live with her. Her own life was made miserable by this child. Whenever he went somewhere with others, he would return in tears. He did not even know his own house. He had to be brought home by the others. Whatever structure he saw, no matter how distant, was his home.

One day, Hayibo's sister said to him, "Let's go. We've been summoned, Hayibo." She was taking him to her mother's parents' place, to the mother of her mother.

Hayibo's sister travelled with him; they walked all day, and, because of Hayibo, the sun set while they were still walking. As they moved along, if he saw something to trifle with, he would simply sit down on the ground and play, scratching the earth with his fingernails. His sister would stop: "Hayibo, let's go!" He would stand briefly, then turn and go to toy with the leaves of a tree.

Finally, she took him gently by the arm, "because the sun is setting!" The sun set when they were still very far from their destination.

Hayibo's sister said, "What are we going to do now? The road we have to take winds about in a forest, it takes a long time to get through!" And that forest was dark, even in the daytime. "What can we do?" She sat down, sobbing. "Fool of my mother, you've done a terrible thing to me! Now I don't know where I'll sleep!"

While his sister cried, Hayibo did nothing. Even though he was an older boy, he just continued to dawdle.

When it had become very dark, Hayibo's sister saw, in the distance, the gleam of a light. She walked towards that glow. As she approached it, she saw the light—but it was puzzling, the shining came from *above*. After a time, there was no shining at all. Then a dwelling appeared.

She walked around until she came to a place through which she might enter, but it was small. Hayibo was quiet. Nor did his sister speak; she was wondering if there were a human being about—"because I see the light shining above, but I don't hear anyone speaking, I don't see anything moving."

But now, the glow—it was not clear, it appeared to be low, in the doorway.

Hayibo said, "I want to sleep, I want to sleep!"

His sister took him by the elbow, she tried to keep him from speaking.

Hayibo said, "I say, I want to sleep! Let's sleep! *I*'m going to sleep!"

His sister covered his mouth so that he could not speak. She wanted to discover exactly "what this thing is that I've encountered here. But it's night, it's dark. I can't see, there's no moon."

Hayibo said, "I'm cold! Look, here's a fire, here's a fire!"

Again, she covered his mouth.

Then, there suddenly appeared a thing that she had never seen before, a thing that emerged from the glow. It came out, creeping on its hands and knees, approaching them, crawling along the ground.

The thing asked the girl if she had anything to say.

She said, "Yes, I'm looking for a place to stay."

The thing said, "A place, a place! Where are you going?"

She said, "I'm going to my mother's parents' place. I've come from home, I'm bringing this child along."

The thing said, "The child, the child! Whose child?"

The girl said, "This child, my mother's child. I'm bringing him to my grandmother, the mother of my mother."

"The mother of my mother, the mother of my mother! Where is the mother of my mother?"

She said, "The mother of my mother is at my mother's parents' place."

The thing said, "Here? Here, here, here? Here is my mother's parents' place?"

"No, the sun set on me. It became dark, I couldn't even see the road. I'm asking for a place to sleep, then I can resume my journey in the morning."

"In the morning, in the morning! Do you know me?"

The girl said, "No, I don't know you. I only saw that glow, and thought that I might find a person here."

The thing said, "A person, a person! A person is who?"

She said, "Well, the person is *you*. When I got here, you were here, you're the person of this place."

"Here, here! Here, there is slept!"

"I'm only asking because I was benighted. I'm asking for a place to sleep."

"To sleep, to sleep! What will you give me?"

The girl said, "Let me sleep here, and I'll give you the child, Hayibo."

The thing said, "Hayibo, Hayibo! What shall I do with him?"

"Well, Hayibo will stay here with you. He'll gather firewood for you, he'll carry water for you, he'll wash things for you. He'll do everything for you."

"Everything, everything! What will you give me?"

The girl said, "I don't know what I must give you so that I might sleep here. I have nothing to give you. I've already said that I'll give you Hayibo."

"Hayibo, Hayibo! What's Hayibo?"

"Hayibo is a boy I'm travelling with."

"Travelling with, travelling with! I don't want that thing!"

The girl said, "All right, then, sir, what do you want? The only thing I have is Hayibo."

Hayibo spoke: "I'm going into the house! I'm going to sleep, *I* want to sleep!"

The girl again took him by the elbow, attempting to keep him quiet, trying to keep him from speaking, because she was fearful now—she was in difficulty.

Hayibo said, "Why are you beating me?" He spoke loudly, crying out: "Why are you beating me?"

The thing was quiet, silent. Then it said, "Sleep, sleep in the house!"

They went into the house. As they did so, they found that the entrance was small. The thing glowed above, this light that they saw did not shine in the doorway. It was not really a house, it had no frame, it was a hole in mud that had been mixed up.

As they entered, this thing threw down a sheepskin. When they had gone in, they saw that the entire side of the house had been constructed of the heads of people. Some of the heads were dry, others were wet. There was a row of teeth. There were many heads of people, but their bodies were not there. Old bones could be seen here, left after the bodies had been roasted by this thing.

It went to the other side, creeping on its hands and knees. It crept over there and took some meat, then put it on a plate. It brought the meat to them, saying, "Here it is, here it is! Take it."

The girl said, "I cannot eat meat. That is my custom."

The thing said, "Can't eat, can't eat! Can't eat meat?"

She said, "No, I have never eaten meat. *I* eat maize."

"Maize, maize! What is maize?"

The girl said, "I eat maize and corn. I do not eat meat."

"Corn, corn! What is corn? Eat meat!"

The girl trembled, she was afraid. In her fear, she hit Hayibo, she bent him over. She was shuddering.

Hayibo said, "You hit me! Yo yo yo yo!"

The thing got up then. It went to Hayibo and said, "Be silent! You're annoying!"

Then it took the meat and went to put it at the upper side of the house. It sat down, and said, "Sleep, sleep!"

The girl got into a reclining position, and Hayibo slept. He was fatigued; he fell asleep, snoring.

But the girl remained awake, she was afraid to sleep. This thing was there, the house was frightening, containing as it did the flesh of old people, some of it dry, some of it wet. The girl was distressed by this place.

Then the thing suddenly appeared above the heap of meat. It moved, parallel to the hearth.

The girl hit Hayibo, she dug her nails into his flesh so sharply that her nails disappeared.

Hayibo said, "Yo yo yo! She hit me!"

The thing went back and sat in a corner of the house. It said, "Yo yo, yo yo! What's that?"

Hayibo's sister said, "It's this child. I don't know him!"

"Know him, know him! What's that?"

The girl was silent.

Time passed then for this child, she did not sleep. But Hayibo again went to sleep. The night went on, and he slept, he continued to sleep.

Then that thing got up over there. They had no idea what the thing was, what it was among humankind. It had four hoofs, but in the face it resembled a human—an ugly and fearsome person.

Now it came again, it came to the hearth. And again, when it was parallel to the hearth, about to pass by, the girl hit Hayibo.

Hayibo said, "Yo yo yooo!"

Again, the thing went back and attached itself to the corner. It said, "Yo yo yo? What's that?"

The girl was silent. Except for some fowl, and except for them, there was nothing—other than this thing—that they could see in this house. The girl sat there, not sleeping.

Finally, it was dawn, and she was getting very tired. But whenever she became drowsy, she would take the lower edge of the blanket and put it into her mouth; then she would chew it and squeeze the water into her eyes—which itched painfully because of the dirt that had been poured into them. She twitched her eyes, and that finished any thought of sleep.

Then that thing got up, and said, "Hayiyi, it's morning! Hayiyi, it's morning! Hayiyi, it's morning! Hayiyi, it's morning!" It went over there to the girl and Hayibo.

When the girl realized that the thing was again coming towards them, she hit Hayibo.

Hayibo said, "Yooo! Yoo!"

And the thing went back to sit in its corner. When it got to the corner, it said, "Yooo! Yooo! Yooo! What's that?"

When it was dawn, when the morning light had appeared, the girl said, "Hayibo! Hayibo! Get up! Let's go and urinate."

They went outside to urinate.

"Oh, it's light!"

The girl wondered what would happen if she went away from there. She wanted to escape.

They went back into the house, and sat there. As they entered, Hayibo said, "I want some of this meat!"

His sister stared at him, she shook her head.

Hayibo also shook his head, then repeated, "I want some of this meat!"

That thing got up, took some of the meat, and gave it to Hayibo. But the girl took the meat from Hayibo.

He wailed, "Hey, my meat! Hey! My meat!"

The thing said, "Yeh, my meat! Yeh! My meat! What's that?"

The sister took the meat and put it down on the upper side of the house. Then the sun rose. And when the sun had arisen, the thing of this house took its dish and ate its meat, it ate the meat. This meat—oh, it was human flesh! Arms! And hands! And feet! The house was filled with heads, the entire side of the house was filled with heads!

The thing ate, it ate the flesh and finished it. Then it said, "You must remain outside. Gather some firewood so that I can cook! You don't want meat? What will you eat?"

The girl said, "Well, I'll eat maize and corn. I've brought some along with me."

"Eat then."

The girl at once brought the food out, and she ate.

The thing went away carrying a big thing—the girl did not know what it was. It was sharp on all sides. The thing was going off to get food with it—and the object was huge. The thing went away then, carrying what seemed to be a sharp spear, sharp on all sides.

The thing travelled, it travelled, and when it had disappeared, the girl concluded that she must now flee with Hayibo. But as she was about to do so, that thing suddenly appeared again. It came back, running hard, and it said, "Now, where's the firewood?"

The girl said, "I'm still eating my maize. I'll gather firewood when I've finished eating."

It said, "Gather! Gather! Gather firewood!"

And again it departed, again it disappeared in the same place.

The girl prepared to leave, saying to Hayibo, "Let's go!"

But Hayibo refused to go.

He remained there, playing, toying with those bones that were outside. The girl took the bones away forcibly; she threw them to one side, saying, "Hayibo, these are the bones of *people!* Don't handle such things!" She took a bone and threw it away.

That thing suddenly appeared again, running hard. The girl immediately sat down and brought out the maize, pretending to eat it.

The thing arrived, and said, "Gather! Gather! Gather firewood!"

The girl said, "I'll gather it soon, when I've finished eating."

The thing departed then, it disappeared in the same place. When it had gone, the girl looked carefully, standing on her toes, straining to see this thing—there it is! a cloud of dust, moving across that ridge!

The girl returned, and said, "Hayibo, get up!"

He refused, so she beat him, dragging him along. But he wanted to play.

The girl said, "We'll sleep with things that eat *people*, you fool! You're the one who caused me to be benighted yesterday, and now you refuse to leave the home of this thing that eats the flesh of humans! I'd rather die than stay with such things!"

She dragged this thing of her home then, this Hayibo. He was dragged by his sister, she dragged him, she dragged him. And when they were far off, his sister turned around. She tied Hayibo's hands, she tied them together with handkerchiefs, tying his hands behind his back. She tied him to a tree. Then she turned and went back to that thing's homestead. When she got to the homestead, she found that the thing had not yet returned.

She scattered locks of her hair all over the homestead: she put hair behind the house. She scattered locks of her hair. She put some on the upper side of the homestead. She scattered locks of her hair. She put some in the place where the thing had climbed.

Then she spoke to the hair: "You must answer at the end. Don't begin the conversation, you must answer in the end. Answer in the end."

Then she went and put some hair on that side on which the thing had appeared.

She went back to Hayibo.

She arrived. Hayibo had been struggling against his captivity, he was dirty and crying. She untied him, and they went on their way. Hayibo refused to walk, so she dragged him along.

Then they entered that great forest—the one that took so long to get out of that a person might forget where he had entered.

They walked, they walked in that forest. And everything in the forest was crying out—owls, jackals, there was nothing that did not cry out. But the girl determinedly travelled on.

Hayibo kept saying, "What's saying that?"

The girl said, "Please be quiet! It's a creepy creature that'll eat you!"

They walked on, they walked and walked.

An owl cried out.

When he was near the owl, Hayibo said, "What's saying that? It says, 'Hey, what's this?'"

The girl said, "Walk on, Hayibo! Now you're going to do something else to me! Please walk on! *Let's go!*"

Finally, they came to the end of the forest, to a precipice where baboons were crying out, "Yooo! Yooo!"

Hayibo said, "Who's speaking? It says, 'Yoo! Yoo!'"[2]

The girl said, "Go on, Hayibo! You're going to do something else to me!"

Finally, they emerged from that forest.

Time passed, time passed for Hayibo. He walked on, then turned around and went to play at the side of the road. The girl beat him, she dragged him along. He cried, but she continued to pull him along. This went on all day, and they visited no other place that day.

Meantime, the thing returned to its homestead. When it got there, it did not see the girl, nor did it see Hayibo. There was only silence.

The thing went outside, it walked about but did not see the firewood that the girl was supposed to have gathered.

It said, "The firewood! The firewood, where's the firewood?"

Silence.

It said, "Girl! Girl!"

The "girl" said, "Yo!" So this "girl" said, at the side of the house.

This thing came out then, it went round and round, but did not see the girl.

It said, "Girl! Girl! Girl! Yo, Girl!"

The "girl" said, "Yo!" So she said, at the upper side of the homestead.

It went there, but did not see her.

"Girl! Girl!" this thing repeated, "Girl!"

The "girl" spoke over there now, on the road on which they had appeared when they came there from their home. The thing went there, it ran. But it did not see the girl.

Again, it said, "Girl! Girl! Girl!"

The "girl" said, "Yooooo!" So she said, at the place where this thing had appeared, and where it disappeared. The thing ran, it went there and climbed. But there was no girl there.

"Girl! Girl! Girl!"

Silence.

The girl was not there. The thing turned, it went to enter the house.

"Girl!"

Silence.

"Girl!"

Silence. There was no girl.

This thing then did things for itself. It did its things in its own habitual way.

Now, back to the girl. The sun was setting, and she was waiting for Hayibo on the road. He had suddenly come to a pool, he ran to that little dam. When he got there, he played and smeared mud on his head; he even kneaded his cloak with mud. When the girl got there, Hayibo was already muddy, because he had left her behind when he had run off.

She scolded him: "What are you doing, Hayibo? You're always doing things like this to me!"

She washed the cloak, she wrung it out, and she washed him, too. Then she went on with him.

Time passed, time passed, and then the sun started to go down. It was late afternoon as they went on their way, and she was dragging him now. She was tired, she dragged him; she was tired, she dragged him; she was tired.

As for Hayibo, he did not neglect his work. If he saw anything on the road, he would sit down and play there. Then his sister would turn around and go back to him. She would scatter the things he was playing with, and throw them away. Then she would beat him, and they would travel on.

The sun set, and the girl was still travelling with Hayibo, her brother, going to their mother's parents' place. When the sun had set, they were in a deserted place that had no homestead at all. There was nobody there, not a person moved.

The girl travelled on, saying, "This is a difficult task that I was assigned by my mother! To go with Hayibo, to bring him to my grandmother! I've become a thing that does nothing but travel and sleep. When we were far off, we were beset by dangers. And today, there isn't even a homestead around, and now the sun is setting. We're in the middle of nowhere—because of Hayibo!"

Hayibo did not listen to what she was saying. He was playing with his things, he was dancing—whenever he wants to dance, he dances. He does whatever he chooses. Whenever he wants to defecate, he does so.

The girl took him and beat him, then sought water in the rivers that they were crossing so that she might wash him. And now it was dusk, and they were still travelling. It was night, and they were still travelling.

Finally, they came to a tree. It was in front of them, it was big, and near the road. When they got to the tree, the girl said, "Hayibo, there's no homestead around here, so let's climb this tree. But you must *sleep* here, you mustn't talk! Tomorrow, we'll go on to the home of Mother's parents."

Hayibo said, "Let's sleep."

They climbed the tree then, she dragged him up into the tree. They finally got into the tree, but it was not easy. She would get up into the tree, then have to return to pull him up. Finally, she got him up there, and Hayibo and his sister sat above, in the tree.

She again warned him not to speak.

Hayibo sat up there in the tree. Then, after a short time, he said, "No, *I* want to go down!"

His sister covered his mouth, and said, "What is this, Hayibo? I told you not to speak up here! What are you doing?"

Well, Hayibo was quiet.

After a time, various people arrived there. Some people were riding, others did not ride but travelled on foot. The girl was puzzled when she looked down at those people who were riding. The person who was riding: his face looked to the rear. And what is this? The girl stared: the person was riding on a baboon! As he rode this baboon, his legs and his face were turned in the direction of the baboon's tail! And the rear end of the person looked toward the head of the baboon! The baboon was moving forward, but the person was facing to the rear—and that is how he rode!

The girl said, "Mhmm! I have seen something!" But she did not speak.

The people filled the area beneath the tree. There were women and men—some of them were smaller than others, but there were no children there. There were girls here with the women and the men.

And in the tree, the girl sat.

As they sat in the tree, they could see the things that were being done down below—the people were eating something there, but those in the tree did not know what it was. And there was a person down there who gave a certain thing to all the others; they took this thing to this other person. And when they had given the thing to this person, they stood up.

Hayibo said then, "I want to go down!"

The girl struck him, and said, "Be quiet!"

He said, "Yoooo! Yo yo yo! She struck me! She struck me!"

When the people below heard noises above them in the tree, they rushed about, they ran. They ran, dispersing.

Then Hayibo said again, "No one hits me! Yo! Yo! Yo! Yo!"

The people ran, alarmed by something they had never before experienced in this place. Today, something had cried out above them! When they had run a distance, they reassembled. Now they wanted to understand who it was who had frightened them, who was riding above. They looked at each other, and found that their number was complete—no one was absent. And there was no stranger among them.

They concluded that four of them must be selected to go and find out what it was that had so startled them over there. They should just go quietly—perhaps it was only a bird or something.

Four of them, two women and two men, went. They went there, moving quietly.

And the girl saw them. Hayibo saw no one, he was playing there in the tree with his things. He was playing.

The four people arrived, walking, crouching silently—walking, stooping, looking intently above. When the girl saw that they were coming towards her, she broke off a small branch from the tree and placed it over them—so that those below would not know that they were there.

A man approached. He arrived, and looked around.

Then he said, "Come over here! I don't see anything!"

The girl in the tree heard him.

The other man came, and both of the women came as well. They looked about, going around the tree.

Then Hayibo defecated.

One of them felt Hayibo's feces fall on his head, and he said, "Oh, what is it that's feeding me?"

Now, when his sister saw that Hayibo was defecating, she struck him, and Hayibo said, "Yooo! Yo yo yo yo yo yo!"

Bo! These people on the ground ran again, one of them saying, "What was that thing that fed me here? I was fed by something I don't know!"

And when they were far off, one of them said, "Hey! *Hayi bo! I* won't go over there again! That's something! Now just look at this!" And he took the hand of the one who had been fed, and said, "Hey! Mhm! This thing smells! What is this? No, I don't know such a thing. It's a marvel! It seems to be something in that tree that was warning us not to remain under it. There's the tree's owner. There she is, crying up there. This is the business of evil people! We're being sent away."

Time passed there for Hayibo and his sister. They remained in the tree until morning. Then, when it was morning, Hayibo's sister wanted to descend so that they might continue on their way to their mother's parents' place.

They got down from the tree—a long business, because Hayibo did not know how to get down. The girl was under the tree, then she was climbing it again—it was impossible for Hayibo to get down. The boy was really quite old, but he was such a burden!

Finally, the girl had a plan. Hayibo must come down feet first, and she would fasten his feet to her waist. He could then hold on to the tree with his hands. So it was that they finally got to the ground.

Then the sister said, "Hayibo, let's go! You can see that we were almost dead! killed by something that would have eaten us when we were benighted. First, we slept with a thing that kept saying, 'Hayibo! Hayibo! Hayibo! What is Hayibo?' Then that thing gave us human flesh! Finally, we got moving again, but you kept going to the pools, doing that sort of thing. You would get dirty, and I would do the work! We were benighted again, and had to sleep in a tree. And you don't even know how to climb! I had to do the work—and it was difficult! Now I'm going to leave you here, and go on home!" That is what the girl said.

Hayibo did nothing, he just wanted to play. Whenever he saw a butterfly, he would say that it was a bird. He would chase it, throwing things at it all the day.

And the girl would keep shouting, "Hayibo! Please come back! That's a butterfly! Return, let's go!"

And finally, they would move on.

They walked on, they walked and walked, as she continued to restrain him.

Then one day they came to a village, a village of homesteads in which livestock was herded. Hayibo went off with the stock now, going with the child who was herding the livestock. And Hayibo turned them back. They were going to a certain place, but Hayibo turned them around and brought them back to the road.

The children who were herding said, "Where did this person come from?"

"We're taking the stock to the pasture, and he has turned them around!"

"Where do you come from?"

But Hayibo was quiet, he said nothing. He continued to turn the stock around.

Among the boys were some young men. They said to Hayibo, "Where do you come from?"

Little Hayibo said, "*I*'m Hayibo! I'm Hayibo! *I*'m Hayibo!"

"You're Hayibo?"

"Hayibo? From where?"

"From home! From home!"

They asked him where his home was, and Hayibo simply pointed to some houses. He said, "There's the home!"[3]

Then they heard the girl calling out to Hayibo, "You! Hayibo! Please come back here!"

One of the little ones said to him, "Go with her, Hayibo!"

Hayibo ran to his sister, and they again continued their journey. They went on, and finally appeared at the house of their mother's parents. As the sun set, they arrived at their mother's parents' place.

When they got there, the people were surprised, because they had never seen this child. They had only heard that their daughter had given birth to a child whose mind was not good.

They spoke to the older child, then—the girl.

In the meantime, Hayibo defecated here in the house. When they saw what he had done, he was already taking the feces in his hands.

Someone said, "What's he doing now?"

His sister said, "That's the way he is. My mother suggested that I bring him here, because she has had a difficult life, dealing with the things this child does. My mother told me to bring him here to my grandmother, and to leave him here with her. This child does whatever he pleases in all the homesteads that he comes to.[4] When he comes to a homestead, he goes to the upper side, opens the pot, and takes whatever is there. It's not that he steals things when no one is around—he doesn't see whether anyone is there or not."

The grandmother and Hayibo's uncle then began to wonder what could be done with the child. He had now been cleaned up after having defecated in the house.

The girl said, "I don't know. Mama and the people of the village are already annoyed with one another because of this child. He needs to be watched constantly. Now she says that I must bring him here to my grandmother; she says that he must remain here with my grandmother."

The old woman said, "Well, no matter what your mother said, Child of my child, I cannot live with such a child. I just don't have the strength.

Considering what you have just told us, it's clear that what is needed is a person who reacts quickly, a person who is still young. *I* must take care of myself. The things this child does would hang over me like a precipice, because this child is strong; he'll go on like this until he's quite old!

"He'll cross rivers, and who will go after him, I being as I am?

"He'll go to homesteads and open things up there and do whatever it is that he does, and who will pursue him, I being as I am?

"He'll spoil something with his hands, and who will stop him, I being as I am?

"Really, you must tell your mother that I'm not prepared to live with such a child. He's beyond my strength and ability."

The girl said that she had been sent by her mother, and now she would return with that message. She would bring the message to her mother. "But perhaps *you*, Uncle," the girl went on, "perhaps *you* can do something since my grandmother has no way of coping with this matter."

Her uncle answered, "No, Child of my sister, it is beyond me. I'm not prepared to live with such a child, either. You see, a person like this should remain at his own home, he should live at his own home because there's no one from any other homestead except his own who can care for a person who is such a creature. This creature must be taken care of by its own parents. It's proper, then, that you return with him to your home. I would be hated here because of this child. The things that he does are childish things, things that little boys do. But he is past that age. Really, he would cause me to be hated by the people. If I were to take such a child, he would defile all the people. Go, go with him."

They acted hospitably towards them now, Hayibo and his sister were treated hospitably, and a beast was slaughtered for them there at their mother's parents' place. They ate.

Then, at dawn the next day, the girl wanted to begin her journey. But she was tired of travelling with Hayibo. He was already on the road, and the girl asked her uncle, "Uncle, accompany us to our home. I've been almost injured by the various things that I've told you about, and now I'm afraid to travel alone."

Her uncle agreed, he went along with them.

As they passed by the first village, Hayibo refused to do what he had promised to do. He went along with the cattle that were being taken to the river by other people.

His uncle said, "Hayibo! Come back here! Come back!"

No, he ran!

He insisted that he would turn those cattle around, that he would turn them back to the road, that he would make them return to the place from which they had come.

His sister said to her uncle, "Stay, Uncle. He'll come back here with the cattle. And when he does so, tie him, restrain him with a rope."

When Hayibo returned, they tied him up, then dragged him along by means of a rope.

That day, the three of them journeyed, hoping to reach their home by sunset. Along the way, when Hayibo refused to move, they jerked him with the rope, and he walked on.

Finally, the uncle and the girl arrived at the house. The uncle greeted his sister and brother-in-law. He was received in a friendly way, but they could see that Hayibo had returned with them, that he had not been left behind.

The uncle asked them about their health, and they replied, explaining that they were all right. But the problem was that they saw that the girl had returned with the child.

About the child with whom she was travelling, the girl said, "My grandmother says that he must be cared for by his own mother."

"Well, we don't see any way to care for this child—"

They had just arrived, and already Hayibo had defecated in the house. He was now taking the feces in his hands. The mother leapt up, and so did his sister. They explained that this child must be tied up.

"Well," said the uncle, "I accompanied these children so that I might explain to you why we're not prepared to keep Hayibo. He'll cause us to be hated in our village. Because of his habits, he should not be given to anyone. Such a person can only live with his parents. Such a person should never be given to anyone else, he should be a problem at his own home. Now I must leave."

Hayibo's father said, "Yes, Friend, you're right. We're satisfied with what you have said. But it must be his mother who handles this. I'm not able to watch over him. She's the one who is always anxious about the child. Let him be taken to his mother; she has long cared for him."

These words were heard, and then Hayibo's sister said, "I'll tell you about Hayibo's activities on our trip. We almost died!

"On the first day, we got up and travelled. And the sun set on us because Hayibo would not walk along. He insisted on playing on the ground. Whenever he saw water or a dam, he would go there, running off, leaving me behind. When he got there, he would throw up the dust as he played, smearing his head with mud.

"Because of him, we were benighted. Then we saw a homestead glimmering in the distance, and we decided to head for that place. We got there, and found a marvel that I shall never forget. When we arrived, there was a fire shining above. We went around the place, but saw no one—not even a dog. We saw nothing at all. We heard nothing, it was utterly still. As we went around the place, we saw a little spot that was shining, close to the ground. It wasn't clear if this was a doorway or what. As we observed these things, Hayibo went off. He was talking, but I was afraid. I didn't know what we had come to. I didn't know what thing lived here, what kind of thing it was. I was still considering these matters when Hayibo said, '*I* want to sleep!' Then a thing came out of the house, it came out from below, through a small passage. This thing emerged, walking, walking on four hoofs—astonishing! I stared, but did not know what it was. This thing had four hoofs, but its *face* seemed human! And whatever we would say, it would imitate us. When, for example, I said that I wanted a place to sleep, it said, 'Place! Place! Place! Place! What is place?' When I said that we were tired and wanted to sleep, it said, 'Sleep! Sleep! Sleep! What is sleep?' No matter what I said, this thing would repeat it. I don't know why it spoke that way. It said nothing to Hayibo: 'Hayibo! Hayibo! What is Hayibo?'

"I continually had to restrain Hayibo, and whenever I did so, he would cry. Then this thing would get up—whenever Hayibo cried out—and it would go to the other side of the house. Finally, at dawn, this thing went away, after telling me that I should gather firewood in its absence. It went off, it travelled to the top of a ridge. It returned, and I assured it that 'We're going! We're going!' It returned to the house, and, when it arrived, it said, 'Firewood! Firewood! Firewood!' And *I* said, 'Yes, yes, I'm going! I'm still eating my corn!' Then the thing went off again, and disappeared. When I delayed, it again came running. I said, 'I'm going!' But I sat down and only pretended to eat. It came again and said, 'Firewood! Firewood! Firewood, firewood!' I said, 'No, I've not finished eating. I'm going shortly. I'll go to get the firewood shortly.' Then, when I saw that the thing had disappeared again, I scattered locks of my hair around the homestead—when I saw him going off, across a ridge. I put some hair at the side of the house, I put some above the house, I put some on the side on which we had appeared, I put some in the place where the thing had disappeared. That hair would answer for us in our absence. So we departed.

"But we had still not yet arrived at our mother's parents' place. During the day, whenever Hayibo saw something, he would go to it. If he saw a butterfly, he would take lumps of earth and throw them at it—running, chasing the butterfly, insisting that it was a bird. Then we went into that huge forest, the one that's far off, the one that takes a full day to get through. We walked there, and everything in that forest was crying out. And when things cried out there, Hayibo would imitate them. If an owl hooted—'Ooo! Ooo!'—Hayibo would say, 'What's that going "Ooo! Ooo!"?' We walked on, we walked and walked. Finally, a baboon cried out from a cliff, 'Yo! Yo!' And Hayibo said, 'What's that going "Yo! Yo!"?' We walked on, we walked and finally reached the top.

"We came to the first village. The livestock there was being driven by some children, and Hayibo went to them. He caused a disturbance because he was responsible for scattering the stock.

"The sun set, and we went to sleep in a tree that was in the middle of a desolate place—no one was around. But Hayibo did not know how to climb the tree, so I pulled him up by the arm. We finally got to the top of the tree, and Hayibo started to talk. But I had told him not to talk, that he must be completely silent up there. Now Hayibo kept insisting that he wanted to get down from the tree. I said, 'Sleep! Be quiet!' After a long time, during the night, many people arrived, some of them riding baboons. They rode these baboons backwards—the very baboons that we had seen on the road. A person riding a baboon was turned around, facing the tail. But the baboon was travelling in the opposite direction. The person faced backwards, the baboon moved forwards—but he was riding the creature all the same! We watched this, but Hayibo saw nothing, he was playing with the leaves in the tree. He wasn't concerned about the things that I saw. Many people now arrived below this tree, and they did things that I don't know—because we were above them, in the tree. I saw that they were eating something that they were given by one person. They were given something by a person, and when they had finished doing that, they stood around down there. Then Hayibo wanted to come down from the tree. I struck him, and he cried out, 'Yooooo! Why did she strike me? Yo! Yo yo yo!' The people below were startled by this noise, and they ran away and dispersed. Not one person was left behind there. I said to Hayibo, 'What are you doing?'

"Finally, dawn came. Then the sun set again, and we did not know where they had gone, where they had assembled. In the morning, four people returned. I broke some twigs from the tree, trying to conceal us, so that when they looked, they would not see us. One of the men then came forward, moving along, bending down, continuing to crouch down. He said, 'Approach, I don't see anyone.' They came along then—two of these people were men and two were women. And they talked beneath this tree, looking around, looking, then concluding, 'There's nothing here. It must have been a bird, there's nothing here.' Then Hayibo defecated, and the feces fell on the head of one of the men. This man said, 'What's this that is feeding me? What is feeding me?' I struck Hayibo again, and he said, 'Yooooo! Yoo! Yo!' And the people ran, speaking of the thing that had been fed to that man, a thing they did not know.

"Now, about Hayibo. When my uncle and grandmother speak about him, I know they are right." The sister of Hayibo continued, "I agree with my uncle, that Hayibo has no business in those places. When we got to my mother's parents' place, he defecated in the house. They were still asking where we had come from, and he was playing with his feces with his hands! No, my uncle is right."

Hayibo's mother and father were satisfied with this explanation. Then the uncle went home, and when he arrived at his home, he told of how he had taken the child home.

Hayibo now sat at his home. His age-mates were now men. It was said that Hayibo too should become a man, but his father did not agree.

He said, "No one like Hayibo is ever circumcised. Hayibo wouldn't know himself if he were circumcised. He'll stay with the children as he does now, he'll be a boy from the time he crawls until he has grown old."

Hayibo was a thing that imitated others.[5]

The girls, when they talked together, would say that whoever leapt in a certain place would become Hayibo's wife. A person feared to leap in that place, lest she should in fact become the wife of Hayibo.

Time passed in this way for Hayibo, and he and his sister remained in this homestead. Time passed, time passed, and Hayibo followed the people who accompanied his sister when she was to be married at their home. Hayibo heard that they were journeying—he was playing by himself in front of the house. He saw them when they moved off, and he got up and went along with them. They turned him around, and sent him home; they were afraid of what he might do over there. Hayibo refused to be turned around, he walked on. He would pretend to turn around, playing along the way. Then, when they were far off, he would chase them—and he would catch up to them, because he was a big boy.

So he came to arrive at the home of his sister. When he got there, his brother-in-law did not know who he was. Hayibo went into that house of strangers, and his sister was filled with disgust when she saw him come in. She said that the child must be taken back home by two young men, because he would do certain things here at this home. So the young men took him home.

When they arrived with him, they said, "We saw him when he entered the house over there. His sister told us to bring him home, because he would do his shameful things over there."

Time passed for Hayibo. After a long time, when he was older, his mother again gave birth. She bore twins, children born on the same day. One of them was Nomehlomane (Four Eyes), because she was a marvelous child: she had two eyes in the front, and two eyes behind, at the nape of the neck. The other child was Nomehlomathathu (Three Eyes): she had two eyes in the front, and the third was on the top of her head. Both of these children were girls, they were twins, and the mother nursed them. She actually had not yet given them names—the one with four eyes was called Nomehlomane, the one with three was called Nomehlomathathu, purely descriptive names.

Time passed for this woman and her children, and the children grew up well. When she had given birth to the twins, her husband said to her, "Wife, really, you create difficulties for yourself. Many things are in you, and now you have twins. But you've always had twins, because you have Hayibo—and Hayibo causes as much work as twins do. He must always be watched. A person like Hayibo must be watched even with dishes, or when he goes into the homes of other people, or when he plays in the mud, or when he returns to the house. Yes, you've always had twins. Now we must show each other another matter."

His wife explained, "As for Hayibo, I did not choose him. I didn't know that I would bear such a thing. And these twins too—I didn't choose them. I didn't know that I would give birth to two children. I've never seen children who look in many directions—these can look behind and in front! And now you want me to do what?"

The man said, "No, really, Wife, I said that because I must marry another wife, so that you might help one another in this house. She'll help you with these offspring of yours, she'll help you during this period when you must take care of another child."

The wife said, "Do you mean that she'll leave her own children to watch after mine?"

The husband said, "She has no child yet. So she can help you with yours."

His wife agreed then, this mother of Hayibo. And the man sought a wife. He sought her, and finally he found her. And when he had found her, she became a wife who came into his house—she was his junior wife.

MITYI, THE NEGLECTED

"MITYI WAS NAKED AND COLD."

This junior wife lived well, time passed for her. There was happiness in this house, nothing was amiss. The junior wife and Hayibo's mother helped one another. This junior wife also took the child and cared for him. It was good, the way they helped each other in that way.

After she had been there for quite a long time, the junior wife became pregnant. She grew large, the months passed, and when the ninth month arrived, she gave birth. She bore a child who was a girl.

Well, things went well for her after the birth. Nothing was wrong, there was happiness here.

Finally, this nursing mother emerged from her confinement.

Time passed, the child began to walk, and the husband built for his junior wife her own house—because she had been living in her sister's house, that of her husband's senior wife. Now the husband built a house for his junior wife.

The junior wife's house was a good one. It was finished, everything was in order, and the husband would go to sleep in one house, then he would go to sleep in the other, alternating between the two. When he slept in the house of the junior wife, he had to take something that the junior wife could eat. He left what he had been doing, and went to sleep in that house. Then, when it was morning, he came out and went to stay in his own house. He remained a short time sleeping, and when it was dawn, he was happy. Then, finally, the sun set again, and he was again happy in the house of the junior wife. And, little by little, he continued to call for his things there. Things began to change, until finally he spent all of his time in the dwelling of the junior wife. He wanted everything that was in that other house to be brought to this house of the junior wife. He called for his calabash first; he said that his calabash should be brought to his side. And so his calabash was taken and placed in the house of the junior wife.

So time passed for Hayibo's mother, the senior wife. She did not wholly understand the propriety of what was happening, whether or not it was proper. The things that her husband had habitually done for such a long time in her house, he now did in that other house. And so their relations became more and more disharmonious, but they did not speak about this.

The child, the girl, grew up. She grew up, the child grew and grew, this child of the beloved junior wife. The child was also loved very much by her father, in the same way that he loved her mother. But the children in that other house became diffident; it became difficult for them to communicate with their father. When they tried to speak to him, they were told that their father was not there, even though they knew that he was indeed present.

Time passed then, there at Hayibo's parents' place—time passed, time passed, time passed in that way.

Then this junior wife again became pregnant, having weaned her first child. She became pregnant, she again became large and gave birth. She was helped in her childbirth by that senior wife of her husband's.

This senior wife put a blanket into the mouth of the child of the junior wife. The child was suffocated by the blanket, and it died.

Then this senior wife went to tell her husband that there was nothing there: "Your wife had no child!"

The husband went out, he immediately went over there. He felt that something was wrong—the matter of giving birth, the fact that his wife had no child. Time passed, nothing happened. Time passed, nothing was spoken. The body of the child was taken away and hidden, and the matter was ended.

The wife continued to be loved, the husband continued to go to her house.

Then came the time for cultivating the fields, and everything necessary was done. When the time of the first fruits arrived, they continually went to the fields—the junior and senior wives of the husband went to examine the crops. When they returned, they would bring sugar cane. They would arrive at their homes carrying the cane, and the children would hurry to them, saying, "There's Mother and the others! There's Mother and the others!" They would run then, hurrying to them in that way. When a child would come to its mother, the mother would bring out a piece of cane from the pack on her head, and give it to her. The children would return then, walking with their mothers, walking and chewing the cane.

Time passed, and one day the two wives of the man went to the fields to examine the crops—Hayibo's mother, together with the junior wife. They went to examine the crops, and they began in the junior wife's field.

Hayibo's mother said, "Let's begin here. We'll begin here, and we'll finish with my field after we've carried the things that you'll want from yours."

The junior wife agreed. "All right."

So it was that they inspected the crops, they inspected them, going around the field, examining the various crops, looking to see if the corn had fallen, plucking the sugar cane.

When they had finished surveying these crops, the senior wife said, "There's some corn that I saw over there, above the sea. It should have kernels now. Let's go and see."

They walked over to that place. It was rather dizzying there, because the field was situated above a deep pool in a river, a precipitous site.

Hayibo's mother approached the junior wife, she turned around on the upper side and suddenly pushed her.

The junior wife fell into the pool below.

Then it was quiet.

Hayibo's mother went away with the things that had been found by the junior wife in her field, she walked with those things, then went to her own field. But there was nothing in her field to be carried.

She walked then, she walked and went home.

She arrived at home. Her husband was in the house. He looked at his wife as she appeared, he saw her as she came up, and he saw that she was travelling alone. The woman appeared at her house, and the children came running to her as usual, the child of the junior wife coming along with the children of Hayibo's mother. All the children rushed to her, saying, "Here's Mother and the others! Here's Mother and the others, they've arrived!"

She took some sugar cane from the pack on her head, and gave it to her children. The other girl arrived, not saying much because she did not see her mother. She wandered around, unsettled, and the mother of Hayibo said to her, "Go away! You're like your mother!"

The child was quiet, dejected. They had gone out to meet the woman, and now they went home. They arrived at the house, and Hayibo's mother went and unburdened herself in her house. The child went to her father, who was in the front of her mother's house.

Her father said, "Where is your mother?"

The child said, "I don't know. I do not see her."

Hayibo's father asked, "Where did you leave her?"

His senior wife said, "Well, I went to my field and she went to hers. Then I returned. Maybe she's still in the fields. I thought that she had already left."

Time passed for the girl then, she went into the house and was silent.

At length, the sun set, and the woman was still not seen. Her husband went to the fields, tracing her footsteps, looking for his wife who had not returned. He walked, he walked to the field, noticing that cane had been plucked in this place, that it had been picked here too, seeing a footprint, they had been here—but *she* was not to be seen. At dusk, he despaired, not seeing her, and he went home. He did not sleep: at dawn, he was sitting there.

In the morning, he went to his father-in-law's place, to seek his wife at her own home. He arrived there, he came to his father-in-law's place. He greeted them and asked about their health. The husband looked anxiously about, but he did not see his wife. He told them that his wife was not present at his home: "She departed from home yesterday, going to the fields. She went to examine the crops. But my wife did not return. At sunset, I went to the fields, going to look for her there. I found that she had indeed been there, that she had walked here and there, that she had picked cane there, but she herself was not to be seen. I have come to you to see if she is here."

The people were startled by what he said, because she was not there. They did not know where she was; she was not a child who enjoyed travelling.

"What can have happened?"

The husband was not able to stay long; he had to go on, hoping to get to his own home and find his wife there. He journeyed on in sorrow, going now to the home of his wife's mother's parents. He arrived there at the setting of the sun, because it was a distant place.

He knocked on the door, it was opened for him. He was greeted, and they asked him how things were. He explained the situation with his wife. "My wife departed the day before yesterday, and went to the fields. The day before yesterday, I went to my father-in-law's place, and I was told she was not there. I said that I must just come and look here, in this place. This wife had not travelled alone, she had gone to the fields together with her sister. Her child was very sorrowful, she was distressed, anguished. And when this sorrowing child went to the other children, those who had been borne by the senior mother, the senior mother had said to her, 'Get out! You're like your mother!' So this child told me. Well, I thought then that my wife, when she did not appear at home, might be in another place."

Her maternal uncle replied, "No, my child, she did not come here. You have told us a sad story, when you inform us that she is not there. This person went to the fields, but is there nothing in the fields that tells what happened to her? And this senior wife—where did she part from her?"

The husband said, "When I asked the senior wife, she said that she had gone to her own field, and that the other wife had gone to her field. She thought that the other wife had already gone home, she does not know what happened to her."

The junior wife's maternal uncle said, "Were these wives of yours harmonious?"

The husband answered, "I'm sure they were harmonious, because I've never heard them say anything antagonistic. When they speak, they don't say anything hostile." Then he was silent.

The other said, "Well, this matter of her absence is not good."

The husband asked permission to leave, and went on his way. He returned to his home.

He arrived at his home, then went to his house, the one in which he stayed—the house of the junior wife. When he arrived, he found the child, staying alone in that house. She herself prepared the things he must eat, she poured the food into her father's calabash, she fed him. The child also slept in that house, and so time passed for that husband. He ate food there, he did not want the food that was in the house of the woman who was Hayibo's mother.

After a long time, the crops were harvested in the fields, and he began to go to the home of Hayibo's people, to the house of the senior wife. He lived there now, and he was happy going with this child of his to that house.

Time passed, and they lived there, he and this child.

The child's name was Mityi.

Time passed in that way, and it became customary that the man would leave some food for this child, Mityi, whenever he ate.

One day, the senior wife said, "I don't grind corn for this child. I don't grind corn so that when I give *you* something to eat, you share it with this child! She must prepare it herself, I can't do all this work! She's old enough, this child! She should be eating with the other children."

The husband was silent, he did not respond. But he felt hurt. He satisfied this child by leaving her some food whenever he ate, because she had become accustomed to eating things that she liked, things that she was given by her mother. And now she had no mother.

Time passed, time passed in that way for this child. She became dirty, she would be washed by her father. Finally, it became obvious that her clothes were finished. And now her father no longer gave her food. He would eat, then give the rest to his senior wife.

Time passed, and the great bitch, the senior wife, again turned to her husband, and said, "What are you thinking of, Father of Hayibo? There is no boy here. My daughters are old now, and they have to herd the stock because Hayibo is a creature with no brains. He doesn't know his own home, he doesn't know the customs of his home. Now when you married a second time you said that you would help with such things. You can see what is the proper thing to do. Your daughters, who are older now, go off with the livestock—while here is this child who always stays at your side! How can this be?"

The man was silent, and after a short time he said, "What are you suggesting? After all, this child is really quite young, she has no understanding whatsoever of livestock—how they should be gathered together, or how they should not be gathered together."

The wife said, "Even if that is so, she can *look,* and when she sees that they are not there, then she must herd them! Let her go out and herd!"

The husband said, "Let the child go."

In the morning, when they awakened, the man said, "My child, go and herd with these sisters of yours. Look after the stock, because they also belong to your home."

The child went to herd there at her home. All the stock that the man had provided for the junior wife was there—cattle and sheep. So the child herded with the others. She continued to herd, and she was told, "Go! You'll be the leader of the younger children. We herd here. There's the stock!" She would run then, because she was afraid of the older children. And she would head off the animals that were running away. When the sun set, she would be tired. At that time, it would be said that she must turn the livestock back. "Let's go home!" So they would go home. And when she got home, she would be limping because of the thorns that had stabbed her feet when she was running around. And she would say to her father, "Father, please extract the thorn from my foot for me. I've been pricked by thorns." The man would then pull the thorns from the child's foot, feeling sorrow in his heart.

In the end, the child became accustomed to herding.

But she was ragged now, her clothes were worn out.

The father took some of her mother's things, the clothes of her mother, and cut out a covering for the child. He cut out a small dried skin for the upper part of the child's body.

The senior wife saw this, and said, "Now what are you doing? What are you doing? What is this? The property of that wife! What are you cutting out for the child? What are you making? What does she lack?"

The husband said, "This child is cold."

Hayibo's mother said, "No, that can't be. The property of my sister is *mine*, it does not belong to this child! She is not to be dressed in this material!" So she said, and Hayibo's mother took that property, she threw away every piece that had been cut out. She threw the pieces over there, and the father of the child got up and gathered the remnants that had been thrown away by his senior wife. He put them into the house from which he had taken them, the house of the senior wife. He put them there, and time passed.

Time passed for the child, and at dawn the next morning it rained.

It was said, "Let the livestock be brought out!"

She went out, clothed in skins that covered only a part of her body. One side of her body had no covering at all. They went out there to herd, the two children—one of them, the one who looked forward and behind, having remained at home. They herded all day in this rain, and Mityi was naked and cold. When it was time to change the course of movement of the livestock, it was said, "Mityi! Turn the stock around!" She did so, then returned to her home.

She now saw that her father no longer had much influence—he too would be scolded. If he tried to help her, then *he* would be reproved.

Time passed for her in that way, and when she got home, she was restored by food. But the food was cold when she ate it.

Her father watched her as she ate: she could not dip into the food very well because her hands had become hard and dry.

He asked her, "Mityi, what is the matter?"

The child said, "I am cold. My hands are hard."

Her father said, "Come, come here to the hearth."

But Hayibo's mother said, "No! Go on, go and sit in the corner! Why should *you* sit at the hearth? Oh! I despair of you! This child will become a soft and empty shell!"

So the child went to sit in the corner.

Her father said nothing, he was silent.

They ate their food, and finished it. But Mityi did not eat. She slept there, naked, the outward side of her body covered by the dried skin. The child was very dirty.

The next day, at dawn, the command was repeated: "Open up for the livestock! Let them be herded!"

Mityi travelled then, hungry. She went to herd again in the open field, constantly on the move, herding the stock. The older girl, the one with four eyes, stayed at home; she did not herd. The other one, the one with three eyes, taught Mityi how to herd, because she would in time be left alone with the stock.

So time passed for them.

In the meantime, her father took those small remnants of cloth that had been torn up and thrown away by the senior mother. He poured some water, he put salt into the water, then he placed these remnants into the water. He plucked some grass, and put it there as well.

Then, when he was awakened the next morning, he gave this mixture to an ox, the ox of this child's home. The ox ate that, a pleasant, salty, swallowable concoction. It ate it all, it finished it.

Hayibo's mother asked, "Mityi! What is that thing that ox is eating?"

The child said, "I don't know."

"Where did it get it from?"

The child said, "*I* don't know! I saw the ox chewing it over there."

Then she was quiet, and she watched the ox as it stood there alone, in the front of a house in the homestead, chewing.

She left it then, and time passed.

Then summer came, and the lands were cultivated. In time, the fields were plowed, and the field of Hayibo's people was prepared. The land of Mityi's people was cultivated only after the crops in the other field had sprouted. So this child had nothing from her own home to eat. She took in no crops of her own, there was nothing.

Everything from her own home was now in the house of the senior wife, and this girl was a nobody.

The hoeing was finished, and she was now a child who would sleep outside.

Hayibo's mother said, "This child smells bad! Her odor disgusts me! She has lice on her head, masses of them! I cannot live with such a thing in my house! Let her sleep outside, in the pig pen!"

The father had no response to the woman's complaint, he did not interfere with the decision to make the child sleep outside her own home. So it was that Mityi remained now at the side of the pig pen, that is where she slept.

At dawn, she would get up, and as time passed she was left alone after being given something to eat.

The child did everything. When she went out to herd, she had to gather firewood as well. When she had headed off the cattle and the sheep, she would gather firewood, putting it in places where she could pick it up and fasten it as she returned. She would drive the livestock, simultaneously carrying the firewood. If she failed to do that, she would be beaten.

Her father was unable to help her, he did not know what to say.

Time passed for the child in that way, she was in great pain. What really ached was her heart—nothing pained her physically, except for her dirtiness and the cold.

Time passed for her in that way, and one day, having taken it to the fields, she was herding the stock. She was moving slowly. She put the stock in a certain place, then went to the field of her home, the field of her mother.

She went to that field, walking, cutting the reaped corn stalks, eating them, stripping them of their coverings—because this field had been cultivated and was now sprouting. Its stalks were corn stalks. The child ate, she was hungry, she ate greedily.

Finally, she stopped—at a place just above the sea. She walked all around the field, looking for cane that was as ripe as the corn, but not seeing any.

She stayed there, walking slowly, and then she heard something saying, "Mityi! Mityi!"

She went in the direction of the voice, and when she got there, she found that the voice was that of her mother.

Mist cleared, and her mother appeared.

The child was astonished, she went around in a circle.

Her mother said, "Come down. There is nothing to be afraid of."

The child stopped resisting; she wanted to see her mother so badly that she would die if necessary. So she stopped resisting. She went down into the water and found herself in a house. She was sitting there with her mother.

The mother took the child, saying, "Oh, my child! In this condition? Like this? Oh!"

She washed her vigorously; she washed her, and Mityi was lovely again.

The mother took some white clay, and anointed her, then she gave her something to eat. The child dipped into the pumpkin four times, she dipped into the maize and milk four times, she dipped into the sugar four times, she dipped into the stamped maize four times—and finally she was satisfied.

Her mother asked, "Are you satisfied, Mityi?"

She said, "Yes, Mother, I'm satisfied now."

Then her mother said, "Now, you must not speak of me at home. I was killed by your senior mother—your senior mother pushed me, and I fell here. I am not able to come out, I now have my home here. Now, you must never again come to me, at any time! You will not be able to see me again. You must not come here, you must not try to see me, or *you* may be harmed, even killed.

"And you must help your father, you must find things for him. You must not be angry with your father, my child, because he knows nothing. He too is buying his life, and he must feel nothing that is bad. That which is painful will become pleasant, and that which is pleasant will become

A Xhosa teenaged girl

painful. I tell you then, my daughter, you must watch over your father—no matter what he does. He knows nothing. And the others—you must not be angry with them.

"Do you see that ox over there? Your father took my dresses and poured salt over them, then mixed them with grass and poured water into the mixture. This ox ate that, and that is now your food—the kind that a woman prepares and keeps for her absent husband.

"That ox is me.

"Now, this is what you must do. From today, when you are out herding, you will find that the ox will know what you are thinking even before you have spoken it. You must remain some distance from the others, and the ox will follow you. When it has followed you, you must say, 'I speak with this horn of the left side.' When you have said this, and when you have had enough of what the horn provides you, then you must say, 'Let it disappear.' But you must *never* do this when Nomehlomathathu and Nomehlomane are present!"

The child agreed, she was crying because of what her mother had said to her.

She cried, and her mother said, "No, Mityi, stop crying now. You'll make me weak if you cry. And I don't want to become weak. The time is finished when I might come out and be with you. We've been together now, but never again." Then she said, "Now go, my daughter. Go, you must go."

So the child travelled, she looked back as her mother cleared away like the mist.

"I tell you, go, my child. You must go."

The child walked on, then again looked back. But this time she did not see her mother.

Mityi returned to the place where her mother had disappeared, but she saw nothing at all—there was nothing there.

She said, "Oh, my mother!"

She knew now that her mother was dead.

She walked on, she went to the cattle. And she gathered firewood, she gathered the wood and then put it down. She put it down, all the while thinking in her heart, but not speaking, about what had been spoken by her mother. She wondered if it would come to be.

Then she walked over there, and disappeared.

The ox got up too, and followed her.

She stopped. The ox came up to her, and stopped in front of her. She looked at it, it looked at her.

She said to the left horn, "Please do it."

Suddenly, she saw all kinds of food in front of her! There was pumpkin, there was sugar, there was stamped maize. She dipped four times, she dipped four times into each of the three dishes.

When she was fully satisfied, she said, "Let them disappear."

And the food disappeared.

Water appeared then, and she took some of the water with a spoon and rinsed her mouth. She gargled, she drank, then put the spoon down. And the spoon also disappeared into the horn of this ox.

The girl travelled now, she walked on, and her heart was now free. She went to the cattle, and turned them all back. The ox now mingled with the others. The oxen looked at each other, and Mityi turned them back. They all came together with the sheep. She drove them all, she carried the firewood, and so she came to arrive at home. She drove them, drove them. She was dirty, very dirty, smeared with black mud.

When she got there, she shut up the stock, and put the firewood on the woodpile.

Her older sister, Nomehlomane, said, "Oh! You fool! Why is it, Mityi, that you're so dirty? You even put it on your head! What's the matter with you?"

She said, "No, I drank and did not see the mud."

"Oh."

Time passed for her.

"Oh! Hey hey hey hey! She's full of mud, this fool! She's nothing but a bundle of *rags!*"

Time passed for her, nothing more was said.

When she had finished putting the firewood on its stack, she went to the house. She arrived, and dipped some water and washed her hands. Then she began to wash the dishes, she washed them well. She did every-thing. Whenever she got home, she would be given everything to do, and the others would just sit around doing nothing. Now she gathered things together. She took a broom and swept the house thoroughly, until every-thing was in order. Food was dished out by the daughters of this home, and then they ate.

Mityi, however, sat over there in the doorway.

Night fell, it was night and she washed the dishes after the others had eaten. Then she poured the dirty water out.

She was told, "Go and drink with the hogs!"

She was left, then, to the care of the hogs and the dogs. She went, carrying the food for these beasts. She poured out the food for the dogs, she poured it out for the hogs.

The others watched her. What did she seem to be doing?

She explained, "I've eaten so much that I'm full, I can't breathe!"

"Why are you so full?"

She said, "Because I've been eating mimosa gum. That mimosa gum blows one up! It's a dark substance found in a tree. I eat a lot of it—some of it is dry, some is wet. That's why my stomach is so big and full."

They laughed.

"Mh! Did you know that she's blown up because of mimosa gum?"

Time passed, time passed, and she slept in her normal sleeping place, in the hog pen.

The next morning, when it was time to take the livestock out, she took the sheep and cattle, and went to herd them in the pasture. When she arrived in the pasture, she herded, and during the day she took the stock to drink. Then she returned, and walked away, not speaking. She went out of sight, and the ox of her mother pursued her. It came to her, and stopped in front of her. It stared at her, and she stared at it.

Then the girl said to the left horn, "Please do it then."

It brought out the food, all the dishes—corn came out, corn that was cooked and fresh. She took the fresh cooked ears of corn, and ate two of them. And she dipped four times into each of the dishes, and was satisfied.

She said, "Let them disappear."

The dishes disappeared, and water materialized. She rinsed her mouth, she drank, and then the spoon disappeared in the ox's horn.

Now she gathered firewood; she gathered it, she gathered this firewood and piled it up neatly. She bound it.

When the sun was setting, she assembled the livestock into one place, then went home. She put the firewood on the woodpile, then brought the livestock into the kraal and closed it.

Time passed, time passed in that way, then she got up and washed her hands. She washed the dishes, she put them away. Then she dished out the food, and it was eaten. When the others had finished eating, she washed the dishes, she scraped the pots so that they were clean, she mixed in that water.

Then she was told that she must go to the dogs and pigs, taking their food—that which stuck to the pots along with the water.

She went out and poured the food for the dogs, then went and did the same for the pigs.

So time passed for her, and when it was time she went to sleep. She slept in her place at the side of the pig pen, covered on one side by that little dried skin.

When she had slept, and it was dawn, she remained a person with hope. Even the frost at night was not much to her now, because she was satisfied in her stomach, she was not very cold.

Again that morning, she opened the kraal and let the livestock out. Then she took the stock to drink. She and the livestock travelled in that way, she and the cattle and the sheep.

Time passed, she went round the cattle frequently, herding them. And she brought them to the river at the appropriate time, then returned with them. She gathered firewood, she gathered it, she gathered the firewood and bound it.

Then she went and disappeared over there, away from the livestock. The ox of her mother immediately stood up, it went to her and stopped in front of her. They looked at each other, then the girl said, "Please do it," to the right horn.

When she had said "Please do it" to the right horn, many things appeared—blankets for sleeping, everything, everything, everything.

Then she said, "Let them disappear."

They disappeared.

She said to the left horn, "Please do it."

Four dishes of food appeared. She took some corn—today, two ears of corn that had been roasted appeared along with three dishes of food. Both of the ears of corn were roasted. She dipped into the various dishes, and when she had dipped into the fourth one, she was full.

Then she said, "Let them disappear."

They disappeared. Water then appeared, in a spoon. She took the water and rinsed her mouth. She finished, she drank, then got up and assembled the livestock. She was very happy to have seen what she had seen, she seemed to love to herd the stock. She was a ragged one, she did not go to meet the others dressed in the fine things she had been wearing, the things that had come from the ox's right horn. She took them off and put them to one side, and now she put on her rags again. She smiled, she laughed—while she was alone. And she walked on, she had no anxiety now. She had no thought of despair, her soul was exhilarated.

When she got home with the livestock, she put the firewood on the woodpile. Then she closed the stock in the kraal, and went into the house. When she had entered the house, she took water and washed her hands. She washed the dishes, she dished out the food. The others ate.

When they had finished eating, Mityi got up and washed the dishes; she also washed the pots.

Then it was said that she should go and stay with the dogs.

She said, "I'm left with them."

She went out, she went to pour out food for the dogs, she went to pour out food for the pigs.

Now, Nomehlomane saw that Mityi no longer ate those things of the pigs and dogs, the things that she poured out for those creatures.

She went back into the house, and said, "Have you noticed Mityi? She doesn't eat!"

"What can she be eating?"

"She's filled up with mimosa gum, that dark gum."

"And now, when I say that she should go out to the dogs and stay with them, she agrees. She pours the food for the dogs, she pours the food for the pigs, but she never puts anything into her own mouth!"

Her senior mother then said to her, "What did you eat, Mityi?"

Mityi said, "I've been eating mimosa gum."

"Did you eat so much?"

She said, "Yes, I've eaten a lot, because there is so much of it out there. I eat a lot of it, and now I'm full. I'm so full I'm in pain."

She said, "Are you full now?"

Mityi said, "Yes, I'm full."

She said, "Oh."

Time passed for them then, and their discussion about her eating habits ended.

One day, she had gone to herd in the fields.

"She's breaking ears of maize from the stalks and roasting them!"

"She must be watched!"

"We must find out what she's eating over there when she's with the cattle!"

So they decided to observe her.

That morning, she took the livestock out to the veld. Nomehlomane was told to follow her, to go along with Mityi. So she accompanied her, she walked with Mityi.

Mityi asked, "Where are *you* going today?"

She said, "I've come to help you. The livestock are getting so numerous, really, and you're only *one* person."

She said, "For such a long time, you haven't helped me. I'm accustomed to doing this now."

"Well, I'm going to help you, Child of my father," the other said.

Mityi did not pursue the subject, and they travelled together; they went to herd. They arrived, and herded. Nomehlomane continually walked about, but not looking directly at Mityi: she would look over there, away from Mityi, but the eyes that were in the back of her head watched Mityi.

Time passed, and Mityi said to her, "The cattle are grazing nicely, and I've finished gathering firewood. The cattle are feeding here, they're contented. Please come here, I'll crush lice for you."

Nomehlomane moved there, and Mityi crushed lice on her head, she crushed lice, she crushed, she crushed lice, she crushed lice, and finally Nomehlomane became drowsy. Mityi massaged her head, she massaged her, Nomehlomane continuing to watch with the eyes that were at the back of her head. She slept with these eyes in the front, she watched with these eyes in the back. Mityi massaged her, turning her, turning her over, and finally Nomehlomane dozed. When Mityi saw that she was asleep, she put her down gently—and she ran. She went off, and disappeared.

The ox of her home arrived, and she said to it, to the left horn, "Please do it." Two roasted ears of corn appeared, then the ox produced three dishes of food, pumpkin and samp and stamped maize. She ate both of the ears of corn, then dipped four times into the various dishes, she dipped four times, she dipped four times, and finally she was satisfied.

Then she said, "Let them disappear," and they disappeared.

Water appeared, and she gargled, she drank. The spoon that had contained the water disappeared.

Then Mityi got up and took the firewood; she piled it up and then fastened it to her head. She walked, singing a song, and she went to her sister.

Her sister was startled. "Oh! This thing has now gathered the firewood. What will be left for me?"

Mityi said, "I've never even seen you carry grass. And *I* gather firewood every day! I couldn't send you to do it."

So she said, and she put the firewood down.

Nomehlomane said, "Well, let's go home now. *I'm* hungry."

Mityi agreed. She carried her firewood, and they went home, driving the livestock.

Nomehlomane arrived and knocked at the door. She went into the house, and said, "Well, I haven't seen a thing! I saw her herding the stock. She herds, and when the cattle are grazing she does not sit down. She gets up and gathers firewood. I saw nothing!"

It seemed that, truly, she *was* filled with mimosa gum.

So time passed.

When Mityi had finished closing up the livestock, she entered the house. She washed her hands, she washed the dishes, then the food was dished out. The others ate, and finished their food. Mityi washed the dishes, she scraped the pot.

As usual, they said to her, "Don't forget the dogs. You'll stay with them."

She went there, she poured the food for the dogs, she poured the food for the pigs. Then she went to stay in her accustomed place.

Nomehlomathathu peeked at her, and said, "Oh! She's not eating! That thing pours food for the pigs, she pours it for the dogs, but she doesn't bring even a bit of it to her mouth! What can she be eating?" Well, *she* would go along with Mityi the next day.

Her mother said, "All right."

Her father said, "Look after her. Watch her. No person can live like that—not eating." The father knew nothing about this. He did not know the significance of his earlier actions, when he had fed that ox the remnants of the clothing belonging to Mityi's mother. He had just done it; he had given the material to the ox without realizing what he was doing. He knew nothing himself, he did not know what this child was eating.

The next morning, the livestock was released from the kraal; Mityi took the livestock out and travelled with it. Nomehlomathathu went along. When they were fairly far from home, Mityi said, "Nomehlomathathu, are *you* going to herd the cattle today?"

She said, "Yes."

"What happened to the one who came along yesterday?"

She said, "She's tired."

Mityi said, "Are you, aren't *you* tired?"

She said, "I'll sit down if I become tired."

Mityi said, "All right."

They travelled then, they arrived in the fields and herded the cattle, conversing there. Mityi was not disturbed, she simply conversed with the other.

Then Mityi realized that "Oh! I'm hungry!" Soon it would be time to go home. Mityi said, "Well, Friend, Nomehlomathathu, the cattle are filled now, and they're grazing well here. They're eating, they're happy. They'll go to sleep. Then they'll get up and be full again. Now we must just kill each other's lice. I'll crush your lice."

The other agreed. They crushed each other's lice then; Mityi crushed, she crushed, she crushed, running her fingers through Nomehlomathathu's hair, turning her, turning her over. Then Nomehlomathathu slept with those eyes that were in the front—but the other one was awake. Mityi crushed her lice, turning her over, turning her over, massaging her, crushing her lice. Finally, the eye that was on the top of her head was seen to go to sleep. Then Mityi gently put Nomehlomathathu down, and she herself got up and ran.

She began to gather firewood. She gathered it, she gathered it, then she bound it. And again, she looked at Nomehlomathathu to see if she was still sleeping.

She disappeared then, and the ox of her home came after her, and stopped in front of her. They stared at each other.

She said to the left horn, "Please do it."

Four dishes appeared. She took the two ears of corn, and ate them. She dipped four times into each of the three dishes, and then she was satisfied.

She said, "Let them disappear," and they disappeared.

Water appeared, and she gargled, and drank. Then she put the spoon down, and it disappeared into the horn.

She walked away. She took the firewood, and the ox merged with the others. Mityi walked along, singing, walking and singing her little songs.

Nomehlomathathu was surprised: "Oh! You've been gathering fire-wood!"

Mityi said, "Yes, I'm just coming back from gathering firewood. I must never go home without firewood."

"You did it quickly!"

Mityi said, "Well, there's a lot of it around. Really, it isn't scarce here."

The other girl said, "Let's go home. *I'm* hungry."

Mityi said, "All right. I'm hungry too."

The cattle were turned back then by Mityi, the one who always did it. They arrived at home, travelling with the cattle. She carried her firewood; she arrived, and put it on the woodpile. Then she went and closed the stock in the kraal.

Nomehlomathathu knocked, and entered the house. She said, "Mama! *Hayi bo!* I stayed with her all day. We crushed each other's lice. Mityi is eating nothing out there! I saw nothing! Nothing at all! I saw the fire-wood. She gathered the firewood, that's all."

"Is that all you have to report?"

"That's what I saw!"

"But what did she do?"

"She's just a person who eats."

"Where did she go?"

"I was near her all the time."

"What is this? No, she eluded you *both!*" So said the senior mother.

Time passed.

Now this woman had a very small dog. It was an old dog, it was small and old. It was very small. It loved her, and she loved it in her own manner.

Time passed for them there.

At dawn, Mityi departed, going out to herd the livestock.

The senior mother said to her little dog, "Please go now. Go and dis-cover what Mityi is eating out there among the livestock. When you have found out, bring the information back here."

The little dog went then, its tail behind. It trotted off, heading for the cattle. When it came to the cattle, it sat far away; it did not go to the girls.

The dog just sat there, watching. It saw them crushing each other's lice, and sleeping. It saw them crushing each other's lice there. It saw Mityi getting up, it saw her gathering firewood. It trotted along, so that when she went to this side, it saw her—and she was still gathering fire-wood. It saw her as she piled the firewood, as she bound it.

Then she went and put the firewood down.

It watched her: there she is, looking surreptitiously about, looking about, watching the other girl, making certain that she is still sleeping. The dog saw her; it was on the other side, far away; it was nowhere near her. It saw her, it saw her as she hurried away and disappeared. It saw the ox, hurrying, also disappearing.

And when the ox had hurried away and disappeared, the little dog ran. It ran and appeared on the other side, on the other side.

It saw Mityi eating from dishes that were spread in front of her, as the ox stood over her. It saw the dishes, it saw them disappear, and it saw her when she gargled with the water. It saw her stand up, and go over to the firewood.

She arrived and took the wood, then started to walk with it. She walked along, singing.

The dog saw the ox get up and then mingle with the other cattle. It saw Nomehlomathathu awaken, and say, "Oh! Where have you come from?"

The dog went back to the homestead, and it said, "Where does Mityi eat? This ox!"

The senior wife said, "Where does she eat? What about the ox?"

"She eats by means of the ox! She is fed by the ox! I saw her being fed by the ox. She eats a lot, and it's not like the food that she gets at home." So the little dog said.

This girl was left behind, not knowing what was being spoken by the little dog.

The dog had arrived at home, and said, "Mityi eats by means of the ox."

"Where is that ox?"

"She is fed by that ox, the great ox. She eats with it. They took it with them this morning, among the other livestock. When she finished gathering firewood, she was fed by it. It stopped in front of her, and she ate and ate and ate—much food! Then everything disappeared, it was swallowed up by that ox!"

"So you say! The others will see now why Mityi is full!"

The girls returned then.

The wife said to the husband, "Now, this is what has been happening. Do you know what your daughter has been eating? I asked a long time ago about that ox! I saw it chewing something once, it chewed this food—continually bringing it out, giving it to this Mityi of yours! This ox! Oh!"

"There is no ox like that! No, really, Wife, you're saying some incredible things! I don't know about any ox bringing out food! All I know is that the ox eats grass here."

"All right!"

They arrived, the people appeared from herding. Mityi put the firewood down, she closed up the livestock.

Then her sister entered the house. She said, "Mother—"

"You have a dog! It saw Mityi! The things that she ate! She eats by means of the ox!"

"I didn't see her!"

"The dog says so! It says that it saw her! It said so, it says, 'I saw her! I saw her! I saw her!'"

Time passed.

The next morning, the wife said, "Father of So-and-so, I'm not well."

"What's the trouble?"

"Something rises here in my stomach. This thing rises, and it closes off my breath!"

The woman had planned all of this carefully.

In the morning, Mityi went off with the cattle in the usual way, not knowing what had been spoken by this little dog. Nor did her sister whose lice she had crushed, and who had fallen asleep.

She went, Mityi went with the cattle and herded them. She herded and herded, she herded, then at the proper time she gathered firewood. She bound the wood, then put it down, and walked away and disappeared. The ox went after her, and when it came to her it stood in front of her. They looked at each other.

The ox said, "Mityi."

She said, "Mm?"

"You were seen by a little dog yesterday. That dog went up into these mountains, and it saw us quite clearly. Now *I* am to be slaughtered, because your mother does not want me. She has learned that I am the one who has been bringing you up, and that that is why you haven't been eating at home. Your father will agree to her plan, and I shall be slaughtered. They'll discuss it, and your father will agree."

"Oh!" Mityi cried. She cried, she cried and cried.

The ox said, "Stop crying! When you cry, you make me weak. Stop crying, you're making me weak! But I *shall* be slaughtered. They will first meet in council, various people will be called, and I shall be slaughtered. I shall be slaughtered."

Mityi said to the left horn, "Please do it."

The dishes came out as they customarily did, and she ate from the four of them. Then three of them disappeared. Water remained, and then the other dish disappeared as well.

The ox said, "Look, they're meeting in council now."

And indeed, they were meeting in council—the father and mother were discussing the matter now at home.

Mityi gargled, she drank. The water then disappeared into the horn, and she cried.

The ox said, "Don't cry, don't cry! You'll make me weak by this crying! Just be quiet. Don't do anything. I'm going to be killed and eaten. Don't cry!"

They travelled then that day. Mityi took the firewood, and they travelled. She arrived, and put the firewood on the woodpile. When she had done that, she closed the livestock in the two kraals. Then she stayed outside, and time passed for her, time passed. It was difficult for her to go into the house because of what she knew.

She thought about it, then went into the house. She washed her hands, she washed the dishes. Food was dished out, and it was eaten. Then, when the eating was at an end, she washed the dishes, she scraped the pots, and went out. When that was finished, it was said that she must beware of the little dog. She went out and poured the food for the dogs and the pigs. Then she slept at the side of the pig pen in her skin.

The next day, in the morning, she opened the kraal for the cattle, and she went with them to the pasture. They arrived in the pasture, and she herded the cattle, she took them to water when it was time, then she gathered the firewood, bound it, put it down, and went away. She went away, and disappeared.

The ox followed her, then said, "You see now, tomorrow I'm to be slaughtered. In the morning, when the kraal is opened for the cattle, I'm to be slaughtered. Now this is what you must do—you must not even *think* of crying! No matter what happens, you must not cry! When the announcement that this ox is to be slaughtered is made, don't be startled. When that has been said, they'll seize me—be happy, don't be upset! Be happy about this meat that you'll be eating too! But this is what you must do: you must climb up on the kraal gate post over there. Climb up on the post, and remain there on top of it. I'll be snared, and when the rope is taken, then you climb! You'll be told to beat the ox, and you must tear off a stick from that post. You'll be told to tear off a stick. They'll say to you that you should tear off a stick and beat the ox—that when you have torn off the stick you should beat the ox. You must watch, and when I've been seized, I'll come to you. I'll come to you when they say, 'Beat it! Beat, beat it!' Then you must get up, and leap! Climb on me! Climb on me here, climb on to my neck and cling to my horns! If you climb on to my tail, then hold on to me here!"

Then the child cried again.

"I said you're not to cry! When you cry, you make me weak! Now stop! Dry your tears."

Again, she said to the left horn, "Do it."

It produced the usual things, and she ate. There was plenty there. She ate it, and was finished.

Then she said, "Let it disappear," and it disappeared. She took water, and gargled, then she drank. The water disappeared into the horn.

She took her firewood, then gathered the cattle and went home. Time passed for her. When she had arrived, she stayed outside. She did not go into the house to wash the dishes.

It was said, "Now where is this fool? The dishes haven't been washed yet. Is she awake?"

She was called, "Mityi! Go and wash the dishes!"

She went into the house, and washed her hands. Then she washed the dishes, she finished.

She heard her father calling for his knife and the whetting stone, saying, "There'll be a slaughtering in the morning!" She knew that already, she knew that this ox was to be slaughtered.

Now she scraped these things, and went outside. When she got outside, she poured out the food for the dogs, she poured it out over there for the pigs. Then she went to sleep by the side of the pig pen, she slept there.

She slept there, and when it was morning, she saw some men arrive. She kept saying to herself, "Oh!" She knew that they were coming to slaughter the ox. She saw the men come out. They were told to open the cattle kraal. Then they were ordered to go in and seize the ox. Mityi was sent by her senior mother to take a large pot for cooking meat from the other homestead. Mityi hurriedly went to that homestead.

She arrived and said, "Mother says that I should come here and borrow a pot."

It was given to her, because it was known by the women that the men who were now there would be slaughtering.

Mityi hurried back with the pot. She put it down, then went to the kraal.

When the men had entered the cattle kraal, Mityi's father said, "Here is the ox that is to be slaughtered! My wife here is not well, she has a thing that comes up in her. When I went to the doctor, I was told that this ox must be slaughtered for her, and that she must be fed milk. This is the ox that is to be seized."

"Oh!"

The men then did the things necessary, they surrounded the beast, attempting to seize it. Mityi climbed the kraal gate post, holding her stick — it was the stick with which she herded the livestock.

The men said, "You're in a good position, Mityi! Beat the ox! Beat it there in the gateway!"

Then she tore out the stick, and mounted the ox. It went round the kraal, the ox went round, it went around the kraal, and the men kept coming closer to it. Finally the ox, holding high the tuft of hair at the end of its tail, came to the gateway, and then it went out.

"Beat it! Beat it! Mityi, beat it!"

She feigned an attack on the ox, pretending to beat it on the horn, but she was actually holding on. She climbed onto the ox, and it fled with her.

"Seize it! Seize it, Mityi!"

"Seize it!"

"Don't let it go! Don't let it go!"

The ox fled with her.

"Don't let it go!"

The ox crossed rivers, it was pursued all that day.

"Don't let it go, my daughter!"

"She's departing with the ox!"

"Seize it!"

"The ox is departing with her! Don't let it go!"

"Don't let it go! Don't let it go!"

"The ox is leaving with her!"

"She's holding its tail! She's holding its tail!"

MITYI, THE CREATOR

"PROVIDE FOR ME, HORN OF THE OX OF MY MOTHER."

The ox crossed numerous rivers, it ascended many ridges. When the sun had set, the men pursued it. All night, they tracked the ox, asking people if it had passed by their homes. And they were told, "No, no, no!"

In the clear light of dawn, they continued their quest, but they did not see the ox at all. There was not even a trail to indicate where it had been.

One of the men said, "No, there's nothing. It's not here."

"We'll die if we continue this search."

For three days, they pursued the ox, but it was not seen.

"No, no, there's no ox here."

They feared that if they went on they might be hurt.

"Let's go back."

The land was so vast that they slept on the roads as they made their way back to their homes. Sometimes, they had to ask for places to spend the night—they were that far from their own communities.

In the meantime, this ox travelled on with this child. When the sun had set on the third day, it put her on the ground, and asked, "Are you hungry?"

Mityi said, "Yes, I am hungry."

The ox first ate some grass at a distant place. Then it moved to where she was standing, and, stopping in front of her, it stared at her.

She said to the left horn of the ox, "Please do it," and her four dishes came out. Mityi ate until she was satisfied. Then she said, "Let them disappear," and the dishes disappeared. Water appeared, she rinsed her mouth, and drank. Then the water disappeared into the ox's horn.

The creature said, "Mityi, you've left your home now. You must never return to those people. This is what you must do: you must be firm in your heart, you must be steadfast. Our journey has been a difficult one. We're in a country that is not like that of your home, it is a land that I do not know. But I know this: My enemies will converge in this region. And this is how it will happen: we shall continue to journey just as we have been for three more days—that'll be six days altogether. Then we shall meet with a red ox, a bull, and that's when it will begin. That bull will charge at me, it will gore me with its horns, attempting to kill me. I may be able to overcome it, but it may conquer me. If it fails to overwhelm me, I shall let you know. But if it does defeat me, you must not despair. Just take these two horns of mine with you, and travel on."

The child wept when she heard the ox's words.

The ox said, "Mityi, your crying will make me weak."

So she was silent again. She mounted the ox, and it started moving at once, walking, walking through forests. It emerged from the forests, then travelled across plateaus. When it had completed its journeying across the plateaus, it ascended cliffs, and escarpments. It finished those climbs, then it crossed rivers—advancing, reaching the top. And then, far off, it would descend. So it went, through country after country, travelling night and day. Then, when it was night, the ox lay down and slept. And immediately, it travelled again.

It said, "Mityi, eat now. Look, that bull is coming!"

Mityi ate from the left horn of the ox of her home. She was almost in tears, but she ate from her four dishes, she gargled, she drank, and the dishes disappeared.

Then the bull appeared, saying, "Bo bo bo bo bo bo bo! Bo bo bo bo bo bo bo! Bo bo bo bo bo!" It struck the ground, moving about. Then it stopped.

Time passed, and finally the bull came to this ox. They confronted each other.

"Mityi, get away!"

The child moved away from them.

Then the ox of Mityi's home fought the red bull. They fought and fought, they fought and fought and fought. They disappeared from Mityi's sight, on the hard, stony ground. She watched for them to reappear. They caused one another to disappear for a time. The ox of her home was on the bottom, and she was convinced that "It's dead! It's dead! It's dead!" But then it overturned the other beast, and it was on the top. Then the other one submitted, the bull lay on the ground.

The ox returned then, and stood in front of Mityi.

"Get on! Let's go! I've finished that one."

The child got on, and they travelled all night. The next day, when it was clear, they were in another country that she did not know.

When this child looked, "Hey!"

The ox stopped. It again said, "Mityi, get down and eat."

She descended, and then said to this left horn, "Do it." Her four dishes came out, and she ate from them all as was her habit. When she had finished, water appeared, and she gargled, then drank. All the things disappeared.

Then the ox said, "You see, Mityi, today a yellow bull will come along. That bull is very dangerous. If it conquers me, I shall die today. If I'm able to overwhelm it, then *it* will die. But I am tired."

The child cried, because she realized that the ox was fatigued by all the travelling and the fighting.

The ox said, "Don't cry. You'll make me weak."

She stopped crying. They travelled, they travelled and travelled and travelled. Far in the distance, the bull could be seen descending.

Wiiiiiii! Wiiiii! Wiiiii! Wiiii!

The child stepped aside, remaining by the ox of her home. And this bull arrived.

The ox and the bull met, and they fought, they fought and fought, they fought. All day, they fought. They caused each other to disappear, one of them fell and then got up. All day, Mityi watched, fearing that the ox of her home would die. But then the yellow bull fell, and it died.

This ox returned, it came to her and stopped. It said, "Get on, let's go."

The child got on, and the ox travelled, it travelled and travelled and travelled—night and day, they travelled.

The next day, the ox said, "Aren't you hungry?"

She said, "I'm hungry."

It said, "Please eat."

The child: "Why is it, Ox of my mother, that *you* haven't eaten yet?"

It said, "No, I'm not ready to eat now."

The child ate her four foods that came out of the horn then. She finished, she gargled, she drank. Then the things disappeared.

A bull came roaring fiercely down the hills, goring the earth, shaking the earth.

When this bull came near, the ox said, "Mityi, go over there. We're going to fight."

The child went over there, and remained.

They met—they fought and fought, they fought all day, they fought and fought and fought. It was obvious that it was a difficult struggle. But in the end the bull yielded—it fell, vomiting, and it died.

The ox said, "Get on, let's go."

The child got on. They journeyed then, they travelled through forests all the night, not conversing. They did not talk, they travelled silently. They said nothing during that time, they travelled and travelled and travelled.

Then, in the morning, the ox said, "Get down and eat. You see, there is one that is coming: it will finish me. This one that is coming will finish me today. It is just a short distance away now. You must take both of my horns—and don't cry. You must not even *begin* to cry! Take both of the horns. One of them will provide food for you—this horn of food will provide food for you, all kinds of food, no matter what, no matter what, no matter what, even foods that you have never seen. And this other horn is the horn of clothing, it will provide everything for you—it will even make a house for you, and what not, and what not. It will make cattle for you, and pigs and dogs, sheep, houses. And your clothing. You must guard these horns, carry them with you no matter where you go, no matter where you turn. But you must not go back. You must travel here on the road. When you wish, speak to one of the horns. And when you wish, speak to the other."

The child was quiet. Time passed for her.

Then a dark bull appeared.

It appeared, goring and striking.

The child remained there, and the bull stopped, it stopped when it came to the ox.

Then, when the bull was approaching, the ox of her home said, "Go over there. We're going to fight. Now, when I have struggled, I shall die."

The child went over there and remained.

The beasts met. They skirmished and grappled, a fearsome struggle. They fought, both were bloody, both were bloody.

As she watched, Mityi said, "Oh! They're both bleeding!"

No, the one of her home would die.

The ox of her home fell to the ground.

The child remained where she was.

The ox of her home died.

And the other creature departed. It disappeared at the place from which it had come.

Mityi got up and struggled with the two horns; she pulled them out. She walked away with them, continuing along the way she had been travelling all those days.

She travelled then, she journeyed on. The sun set. She wondered what she would do now that the sun had set. She did not know the country, it was a forbidding place. She was in a forest, she saw no homestead.

Then she took that right horn, and said, "The ox of my mother said that it was able to provide for me. Now provide for me, Ox of my mother, so that I may sleep."

A house appeared!

It had a door, and she saw that the house was lighted. She stared into the horn, the horn that was here by her side.

She said, "Provide for me, Ox of my mother. You said that you would provide for me."

A sleeping mat appeared, along with blankets. Then four dishes appeared, with water at their side. She took the first dish—it contained two ears of roasted corn, and she ate them both. They were hot, as if they had just been taken from the hearth. She finished them, then dipped into another dish four times, and she dipped into yet another four times. She dipped into the other four times, and then she was sated. She took some water, and gargled. Then she drank.

She said, "There they are then." And the dishes ceased to exist, they disappeared—she no longer saw them.

She took her blankets and covered her body completely, on all sides now, unlike in the past, when she had a dried skin that covered only a part of her body. She went to sleep, and she slept well, fearing nothing. There was nothing that bothered her now.

The next morning, when it was light, when she saw that it was dawn, she sat and thought. She thought, then said to the right horn, "Do it, Ox of my mother." The door was open, the house disappeared! When the house had ceased to exist, there was no mat, there were no blankets. And when she looked at her body, she found that she was wearing the dried hard skin that she had worn from the beginning, from the time she was at her home—the dirty skin that covered only one side of her body.

Warm water appeared now, and she washed her body. She finished that, then white clay appeared, and she anointed her body and face with it. Everything that a person put on her body then appeared. She fastened her clothes nicely—being a girl who was cultivated, she wore fitting things. When she had finished doing that, she said, "Do it!" And all those things and the water that were in front of her ceased to exist.

She took the horns, and carried them in her hands. She walked, she went again in the direction that she had been travelling with the ox. She had not turned around at any time since she had come out of the cattle kraal. She moved out now and ran, going in the accustomed direction. She now looked, she looked over there, and now she travelled in that way. She did not stray from the path, she travelled at once and she walked all day. When she felt the turn of the sun, "Oh! I'm hungry now. I'm hungry."

So she sat, and said, "Provide for me, Ox of my mother. It was said that you would provide for me."

When she had said that, she saw a house. And when she was in this beautiful house, she said, "Provide now." And all of her dishes appeared. She now ate from each of the four dishes, dipping in her customary way four times. She finished, she gargled, she drank, and she finished. It was the time of the turning of the sun.

She said, "Do it then, Ox of my mother."

The house ceased to exist, and she was left alone. She again got up and travelled along the way that she had been going. She travelled, she travelled. The sun set. As she travelled, she crossed rivers; she descended, she ascended, she walked across land after land, one land not resembling the other. She passed by villages, homesteads, but she went to none of these homesteads. She walked on the path only, the path that was in front of her; she did not deviate at all from that path, even when other paths forked off from it. She walked only on the one that went straight ahead. When she walked among the homesteads, she would pass them by, she went to none of these homes. Then, when the sun set and she was unable to travel any more, she did not go to any of these homesteads. Nothing was ever spoken to her, and she herself did not speak.

Then she stopped, and spoke to the right horn: "Ox of my mother, provide for me. It was said that you would provide for me."

She saw that she was in a beautiful house, it resembled the first house. It would always be that house. She came out, and said, "Provide now," and her food appeared, four dishes. She ate from each of the four in the usual way, dipping four times; and she finished. Then she took water and gargled, and she drank. She finished, then said, "All right, do it now." A mat materialized, along with her blankets—everything, including pillows. She took her blankets and spread them, then she undressed and went to sleep.

Sleep descended on her, and she slept well, fearing nothing at all. There was nothing that bothered her. She was relaxed and happy, and she slept.

Finally, it was dawn, and when she saw that it was morning—she felt even in her body that it must be morning—she said again, "Do it now, Ox of my mother." The house ceased to exist, she was left behind dressed in the usual way.

She got up again and walked. She walked, taking that journey along the same path; she did not turn off at all, walking in the customary direction.

Not one person asked her who she was. Even when she saw people, they did not come to her. The people travelled over there. No one on the path that she walked even came close to her. She would always look at them over there.

So she walked, she walked and walked. Suddenly, she came to a mountain, the top of which she could not see. But from where she was standing, she could not even tell that it was a mountain—"because I see trees, I see grass, I see land, I even see rocks, but *it* is so huge!" It went beyond her sight, she could not see where it ended. She stopped, and stared at this mountain. She could see that the path went up the mountain, but she could not see where the mountain ended. She could not see its summit. She stood there, then walked on; she walked along this path, and ascended. She ascended the mountain, all day she ascended. She walked up the side of the mountain. She did not travel in the same place, her foot would rise as she walked, and she understood that "I am walking,

I am not treading in the same place." But she did not reach the top, she did not arrive there. The top of the mountain was far off. She went up the mountain. When she looked at the sides, she saw the place below from which she had come—because there were the hills that had been near her. She continued to walk in this way, and she was unafraid. She felt no anxiety, nothing, no uneasiness because she faced such a mountain, the top of which she did not see.

At dusk, she stopped and looked at the mountain: Oh, this mountain! The top of it could not yet be seen!

She walked on, she journeyed all night, ascending this mountain. She heard sounds at night—fowl seemed to be crying out, but she saw no homestead, she did not even see a fire. She just heard the sounds, the crying out of the fowl. She walked on, she was not tired. She walked, she walked and walked—and then she felt that, well, she was hungry now.

She stopped, and said, "Provide for me, Horn of the ox of my mother. It was said that you would provide for me."

She was suddenly in that house, in that usual way. Then she said, "Provide it now," and her four dishes appeared. When they appeared, she ate from the four of them, and when she finished eating, she took some water, gargled, and drank.

Then she said, "There they are," and the dishes ceased to exist. When they had disappeared, she said, "Provide it now," and her mat appeared, along with the sleeping blankets. The door of her house was closed, but there was light inside. She took her blankets and slept, and nothing bothered her at all. She thought about nothing, not even about the mountain that she was climbing, the mountain that had no end.

Time passed for her, she was happy; sleep descended easily on her. Then she felt in her body that morning had come. She continued to hear the sounds of the fowl.

She said, "Do it now, Horn of the ox of my father." She said that, and the door opened, and suddenly there was no house. She was left alone there, dressed in her usual way.

When she looked, oh! the place where the mountain ended could still not be seen, it was still far above her.

She walked again, moving along the path that she had been travelling for such a long time, and she walked all day. In the afternoon, she found herself on a plateau, a massive plateau. She saw that there were many villages in the far distance, but she did not try to go over to them.

The sun strained to turn, and she stopped and thought. She thought, then said, "Horn of the ox of my mother, provide for me. It was said that you would provide for me. I see this fine plateau. I don't know what it is. *You* know it, you knew it. Provide for me."

Suddenly, she saw cattle appear. These cattle were put there, and so time passed for her. She looked at them, and they went round her. They got up, and stood there; they stood apart from her. Then their calves came to her, passing by her, going to their mothers. Their mothers were lowing, and the calves arrived and went around Mityi. She continued to watch them as they went around her. The calves walked then, and went to their mothers, to those cattle. They arrived there. As Mityi continued to watch, the finest of the cattle appeared. There were oxen and heifers, all sorts of cattle. There were also bulls, and they surrounded her, then they departed, going to the others. Time passed, she watched, and while she was watching, many sheep suddenly materialized, all coming to her. They surrounded her, then again departed; they went to stand by the cattle. She continued to watch all this, and as she was watching, many horses suddenly appeared, all coming to her. They went around her, then they too departed; they went to stand over there with the sheep.

While she continued to watch all this, the sun set.

Suddenly, goats appeared, all coming to her. They went around her, then went to stand over there.

These things continued to come, then to move on to the others that were standing over there.

When all that had happened, something occurred that was strange to her. What it was precisely, she did not know. Dust rose like smoke, and an immense multitude, with which she was not familiar, approached her. The throng arrived, and everything was there, every creature that is raised. All different sorts were there, diverse sorts, various kinds, and they all passed her by. When they had done so, they stopped and stood over there with the others.

Time passed for Mityi.

When things were like that, there suddenly appeared four men, moving to her. When they got to her, they stopped at her side, asking her nothing. These men sat down, and time passed, time passed.

When that had happened, four women suddenly took shape, and they too approached Mityi. Then they turned and went to sit at the side of the four men. They sat there, saying nothing.

These people did not speak to Mityi, but they did talk to one another. They spoke only among themselves, they did not direct a word to her.

Time passed for her, time passed, then she stood up. She stood, and said, "Horn of the ox of my mother, provide for me. It was said that you would provide for me."

When she had said that, kraals suddenly came into being. There was a kraal for cows, a kraal for various kinds of oxen; there was a kraal for sheep, there was a kraal for goats, a kraal for horses. There were little hen houses, there were pig pens, there were sleeping houses for dogs.

And there was silence.

A Xhosa woman

The silence continued. The cattle were in their kraal, and so on: all these creatures were in their appropriate kraals.

And time passed for the child.

After a long time, Mityi again got up. She grasped the right horn of the ox of her home, and she said, "Ox of my mother and father, please provide for me. It was said that you would provide for me."

When she had said that, many houses suddenly arose; they were scattered all about. These were Xhosa-type houses, built in the manner of rondavels, and they were separate from each other. They were beautiful houses. Among them were four that were large.

Time passed for Mityi in that way, as she looked at these houses. After a short time, she said to the horn of the ox of her mother, "Horn of the ox of my mother and father, please provide for me. It was said that you would provide for me."

Then she saw a path leading away from her to one of the houses. She got up and left those people behind there. She entered that house.

In the house that she entered were mats. She saw in her house the mat that she usually slept on—her blankets were there, the ones that she slept under during the days that she slept out along the path.

She sat on her mat, and again she said, "Provide it now." When she had said, "Provide it now," her four dishes appeared. She ate from the four of them in her customary way, dipping four times in three of them, taking the corn first. She finished eating, she had enough. Then she took water and gargled, and she drank. The dishes ceased to exist then, and she was left behind. Time passed for her, time passed.

She stood and said to the horn of her mother, "Horn of the ox of my mother and father, provide for me. It was said that you would provide for me."

When she had said that, the four men got up and came to her. She was inside the house. They came to the house, and knocked.

She said, "Come in."

They said, "Greetings, Young woman."

She said, "Yes."

The men sat.

She asked, "What do you men want?"

The men said, "We have come here to you."

"Please say why you have come."

The men said, "We are looking for work."

She said, "What kind of work do you want?"

The men said, "We seek whatever work you have here."

She asked, "Do you know how to herd? Do you know how to milk?"

The men said, "Yes, we know how to do that."

She said, "Can you count?"

The men said, "We know how."

Then she said, "Please begin, then, by counting the sheep. How many sheep are there? And how many horses? How many goats?"

The men went out, they went to count the sheep. They counted, they counted and counted the sheep, and when they had finished, it was seen that they were mistaken. Many of the sheep had not been counted.

She said, "Have you finished counting the sheep?"

The men said, "No, Young woman, we're unable to count them. We seem to be in error. When we've finished counting, others come along and spoil our count."

She said, "But I instructed you to count them."

They said, "Yes."

She took the horn of the ox of her mother, and said, "Do it for them."

Then the horn: the sheep got up and followed, one after the other, they lined up one behind the other.

When they had done that, she said, "Count them now." And the men counted the sheep, they counted and counted and counted. Finally, they reached a figure that was enormous, hundreds upon hundreds of the creatures.

They returned, and said, "It seems, Young woman, that there are many thousands of them."

She said, "That's better. Now then, which man among you reached that number?"

One man said, "I'm the one who reached it."

She said then, "You must herd the sheep." And again, she said, "Go and count the goats."

The four men went off to count the goats. Everything was thrown into disorder when they counted them: the goats refused to be counted. They kicked, struggling for freedom, and so the goats got mixed up all that day.

Again, Mityi said, "Have you finished yet?"

They answered, "No, Young woman, these goats run all over the place, and we don't know how many they are. We haven't finished counting them. When we finish, we have to go back to the beginning and start all over."

She again turned to the horn of her mother, and said, "Do it, Horn of my mother."

And the goats got up and followed each other. They stood in a line, they went in a procession, all in a row. And the men counted them quite easily now, one over there, one over there, and finally they finished counting them.

They went to her and said, "Well, we've tried."

She said, "Tell me then, how many are they?"

They said, "They're the same number as the sheep!"

She said, "Who is the one who realized that?"

One man told her.

She said, "Come over here, and herd the goats."

And again, she said, "Please count the cattle now, the ones with calves."

The four men went, they counted and counted and counted these cattle. And the counting of the cattle was the same as the counting of the other creatures. They counted and counted the cattle, counting them again and again.

And once more, Mityi arrived at the usual time, and asked, "Aren't you finished counting yet?"

They said, "No, they're all mixed up. These cattle look exactly like each other, and that makes it difficult for us to count them. They're all mixed up here."

She again spoke to the horn of the ox of her mother, and said, "Horn of the ox of my mother and father, please do it for me. It was said that you would provide for me."

When she had said this, the cattle followed, and opened up. They gave each other space, they went in a procession. Then the men got up and counted, and when they had finished counting, they went to her and said, "Really, it seems—"

She asked, "What number did you reach?"

The men said, "Well, the number is the same as the other."

Mityi said, "Who among you counted and reached that number?"

They mentioned one of the men, and that one was told that he must herd the cattle.

Then they were told to go and count the various kinds of cattle, the oxen and the heifers and the bulls, all of the various sorts. The four fellows went there, and they counted.

But these cattle would not be counted at all, the men were unable to determine how many there were.

Again, the time when they would be questioned approached, and Mityi said, "Haven't you finished counting yet?"

The men answered, "No, Young woman, the cattle will not be counted. We try to count, but again we've been confounded."

She spoke, then, to the horn of the ox of her mother, saying, "Horn of the ox of my mother, please do it. It was said that you would provide for me."

Then all the cattle stood in a line, they lined up so that they could be counted. The men counted them, they finished; and when they had finished they went to her.

They arrived, and said, "Well, really, we're finished."

Mityi asked, "What number did you reach?"

They said, "We reached the same number that we reached in counting the others."

She said, "Oh. And the one who will herd the cattle, where is *he?*"

It was said, "Here he is."

She said, "There's your work."

The next day, one man would come out with his cattle, another would come out with his cattle, another would come out with his sheep, the other would come out with his goats.

"That's the four of you. Now, there's still a job for which there is no person—the work of herding the horses. Let the horses be divided among you."

The men agreed to do this.

She said, "Now you should not all stay in one place while you're living here." She pointed to some houses. She said to one of them, "You stay in that house over there, the one near the cattle kraal." She said that another must stay in the house over there. And another must stay in yet another house, over there—in a large house near the goat fold. And the other, she said, must stay in that house away over there.

The men did it in the way she had directed. The man of the various kinds of cattle went to stay in his house, the one of the cows went to stay in his house; the one of the sheep and the one of the goats went to their respective houses.

The four women were left behind, remaining in the place they had come to, at the side of the men.

Mityi went then, she entered the house. When she had gone into the house, she said that the men must come to her. The men came out of their houses, and went to her. When they had gone into her house, she said, "Do the four of you have no wives?"

They said, "We do have wives."

She asked, "Have you any children?"

They said, "We do have children, but they are still young. They are children who do not know how to herd."

She asked, "Are you satisfied, living with your wives?"

They said, "We are satisfied."

She said, "Each man, then, who was hired, go and bring your family. Each person should live with his family in his house."

The men departed hurriedly, going to their wives.

When the men had departed, the four women got up and went to Mityi's house. They arrived, and knocked.

The young woman said, "Come in."

They greeted her, and she responded.

She asked, "What do you wish to say?"

The women said, "We do wish to say something."

"Yes, speak."

"We are speaking: we want work."

She asked, "What kind of work?"

The women said, "We want whatever work is available, the work of people who have fastened the belt.[6] We want it all."

She said, "All right, then, if you want work of fastening the belt. You can begin to work now. Do it, Horn of the ox of my mother. You said that you would provide for me." When she had said that, four dishes of water appeared in the usual way. She said to the women, "Take the dishes and put them in those houses. Put them in those houses."

The four women went out, they went to put the dishes of water into those houses that had been indicated, the houses in which the men, the new employees, lived. They arrived at those houses, and put the dishes there, then they returned.

She said, "Do it. You said that I would be provided for."

When she had said that, cooking pots appeared. The women took them and put them into those four houses. Then the dishes: they carried the dishes to those four houses. And the blankets: a blanket for each man.

Then Mityi told those women that they must sleep in one house, in a large house. The next day, they would be told their work.

They had not yet gone to sleep when the men who had been hired returned, with their wives—some of the wives carrying a child on their backs, some children travelling on foot. Each person climbed to his house with his family, and they went in and settled down.

There was a lot of noise in this homestead, the place was filled with all sorts of livestock.

Time passed well, the men herding and the women doing the washing here at this place. The men inspanned the oxen and broke up new ground; they made gardens, everything. The women hoed, preparing all things properly.

Mityi asked the women, "Why do you want to be hired?"

The women said that they wanted to be hired for the sheep.

She asked the men, "Why do you want to be hired?"

The men said that they wanted to be hired for the cattle.

Time passed then, and there were many people now at this home; they did not know where their food appeared from. They only carried the food into the houses.

In the morning, the women helped bring the food into all the houses. They did not know the origin of the food. But this person—Mityi—remained in her homestead and was not cooked for, there was no person who cooked for her. She was not prepared anything by anyone at all. She would only speak to the horn of her mother when there was anything that she thought about in her heart. When she thought of something, no matter what it was, she would speak to the horn, so that things would work out the way she wanted them.

MITYI, THE QUEEN

"THIS IS GOD'S PLACE."

Time passed, time passed here—and in a certain village there were tumult and confusion. It was that distant village that she had seen when she had reached the top of the mountain. As she had ascended the mountain, sleeping along the way, she had seen villages far off, on the plateau. And there was confusion in one of those villages because the king of that place had died. He was dead.

The people of that village had seen this homestead of Mityi's, but they did not know what kind of homestead it was. They were afraid of it, some people had concluded that it was the place of God. The homestead was a big one, and it was filled with livestock. They did not know whose homestead it was, they did not even know what kind of person its owner was.

Finally, it was said, "The king is dead. Who will rule?"

The king had died having no son.

A meeting was convened in the main village, and the people discussed the matter.

One person said, "Why not send someone to that homestead over there?"

That homestead was huge, unsurpassed in vastness. But no person was seen there. They wanted to know what kind of homestead that was that had arisen over there so suddenly. It was clear that the entire gathering could not go over there to that homestead, so some men were selected to go there, to go and have a look, to discover precisely what it was that was over there.

Those people, six men, went over there.

They arrived at the homestead. They arrived there, and stayed in the place where the people were staying, the four men and four women. When they got there, they found many people in the great homestead— a turbulence of people and children.

They remained there, but no person came to them.

The people were in the house, discussing the matter. One of them said, "Let the six men be asked their business."

The others said, "No, when we came here, we were not asked our business."

"And these women, too, they were not asked their business."

"We must not do what is not done."

The matter was left at that.

Mityi looked at them from her house, then took the horn of the ox of her mother; she took it, and said, "Horn of the ox of my mother and father, provide for me. It was said that you would provide for me."

When she had said this, the men over there got up and came to the house to see her. They arrived, and knocked.

She said, "Come in."

They greeted her, and she asked, "Do you men wish to speak?"

They said, "Yes, Young woman, we wish to speak. We have a bit of confusion over there where we live. There has been a lack of restraint because of it. It is all because of the death of the king."

"People came together over there, to advise one another. It was then determined that we should come to this homestead—we wanted to see it with our own eyes, because there was no one who could explain to us whose homestead it is."

"We don't know how it got here, because we did not see the homestead being constructed. It seems to us that it is the place of God, because we never saw it being built."

"And it is a great homestead, unequalled in greatness. We have never seen anything like it. We have decided that it is the place of God."

"If that is the case, if this is the place of God, then we thought that we could come over here to be given advice as to what we might do in our situation over there."

The young woman answered, "I have heard your statements. When God arrives, I shall tell him that people have come here to see him. Yes, this *is* God's place, but God is not here right now. He shall arrive in his own time, I don't know when because he tells no one that. He may arrive today, or tomorrow. When he does get here, I shall tell him about your visit, and he shall advise you. I watch over the homestead when God is not here."

The strangers thanked her: "We thank you, Young woman. We look to you for help, and believe you when you tell us that you do not know when God shall return."

So they said, and then they requested permission to go. They went home after she had given them permission to leave. So those people went home. They went home, travelling and talking.

One of them said, "You heard that? We were right, that place *is* the house of God!"

Another said, "Yes, there is no doubt about that. You saw the homestead that is not a house, you have seen the livestock of that homestead. And the many people, the livestock, a beautiful homestead—such a very beautiful homestead! It is indeed the place of God. We haven't actually seen God, but he has purposely established that homestead for us!"

They all agreed with this. "God is here in this land, in the very place where we live! We've been living there, and God has been living here!"

"Well, she is expecting God to return. The young woman will tell him, you heard her—the nice way she talked. She said that she would explain our situation to him. She said so, my friend!"

"That's right. She said, 'Well, *he* shall advise you, I shall tell him.'"

"Yes, yes, yes, I heard her say that!"

The men travelled on then, and they came to arrive at the gathering of men at their home. When they got there, they were very happy men who had seen the homestead of God.

They said, "Oh, Fellows! It is the truth, the saying that you don't see God if you don't love him."

The men said, "So, so."

These men said, "We went and arrived at the place of God."

"Mm mm, at the place of God. There was nothing happening there."

"We arrived at the place of God, and sat outside. We saw people there, but they did not speak with us. They passed us by, as we watched them."

"They were gentle, they were happy, they were not cruel. But they said nothing at all to us."

"We sat there and waited. Then, after a short time, we went to the large house, and when we got there we knocked. We were told to come in, so we entered. There was a person there—a young woman."

"She was lovely! That young woman was lovely!"

"She asked us what we wanted to speak about, so we pressed on. We told her that we had come there because of the confusion in this village of ours. We told her that our king had died, and that he had not left a son behind. We told her how baffled we were, that we were at a loss, because there was no one to advise us."

"Then we told her that we had looked over there, to that homestead, and wondered if it was God's place. We had seen a great homestead, a homestead we had never seen before, that we had not even seen being constructed!"

"It is such a big homestead, and it is unbelievably beautiful!"

"We told her that we wanted to tell God what was perplexing us. The lovely young woman who was there said, 'You are right. This *is* God's place. It is God's place, but he is not here right now.' God had gone away. And when he had left, he had not mentioned when he would return. He'll arrive some time, he'll arrive one day."

"He might even arrive today, we were told, or tomorrow. 'But when he arrives,' she said, 'I shall tell him about you.' This beautiful young woman spoke eloquently, and we thanked her, as she said that she would tell God when he arrives."

"We come with these fine words. It seems indeed that we have seen

God, as we have seen the young woman who stays with him. She will tell him."

"That young woman is respectful, she seems to be accustomed to speaking with older people."

When all that had been said, the men said, "So that is the way it is. It was to be expected. You found the place of God! We'll keep a watch, since we were not told the day he'll return. We'll be able to tell when he has come back. Perhaps God himself will come to us, because we visited him."

The men stopped speaking of this matter, it was necessary that they disperse now and return to their homes. They travelled then.

It was night. That night, when everyone went to sleep, that young woman took the horn of the ox of her mother, and said, "Horn of the ox of my mother and father, it was said that you would provide for me. Provide for me then."

When she had said that, the young woman found herself at a great homestead. It was dusk, and she arrived and knocked at the homestead that was beside the homestead where the king had died. It was the place from which those men had come, those who had come to the place of God.

The young woman arrived there at this great homestead, and she knocked at the door. It was opened, even dogs did not bark.

When she went in, she said, "Greetings. I hope that it is well for all of you in this house."

The people responded, they awakened—they had been reclining. Many men were here in the house, it was filled with men.

Those men said, "Oh! Where does this person come from?"

The young woman said, "I have come from the place of God. Some men came to the place of God yesterday. These men told of the death of their king; they told of the confusion that resulted, of not knowing who should rule in the dead king's stead. The men told of the fact that the king had not left a son behind. They said that they wanted a person who would be able to advise them, because their land was troubled. They said that they had seen a certain homestead, and they wondered if it was the homestead of God, because they had not even seen it being constructed. They saw the appearance of a great and beautiful homestead, a homestead that could contain the whole of this village together. The men told of their problem, that life here was anything but tranquil because there was no king here. No one was on the throne of kingship. They wanted God to advise them.

"I now come to you with advice. I have been sent with this advice by God. After the men had departed, God arrived. He arrived at dusk. He was told what the men had said, and God has resolved the problem. He says that he wants his daughter to rule this land, because his daughter knows all the laws, all the judgements, the mediations and customs of the person who is bereft of his customs." So she said, and the child who was a young woman now stopped.

A man said, "Oh! What is this, Fellows? What should we do? because we're alone now. Those men who went to God's place are not here, and they will not even be here tomorrow—even if they were to be sent for now. Is it necessary that God be answered now? Would it be possible for us to respond to him tomorrow? Or will he say that he won't hear us if we wait until tomorrow to answer him? How would it be, Young woman, if we just went to those men who are sleeping over there at the royal residence? Because over there at the royal residence are men of good character. They are staying in the village now because things are going so badly."

The young woman said, "All right, but you must hurry this night, because the time God has given me will also run out."

The men travelled then, and the young woman went out. She stayed outside, she did not remain in the house. They travelled, they went a little distance to the royal residence. They arrived there, and knocked. Those inside were reclining, talking, not yet asleep. The door was opened for the visitors, and they greeted them.

They said, "No, the chiefs are not to question this. Here at home, a messenger sent by God has arrived. Those men went to see God recently. Now it is said that God arrived, and he wants an answer from us. A person has been sent to us, and is to bring our answer back to God. We must meet. We didn't want to bring her here, we must go to her."

The men stood then, they were happy. They went to her, they arrived—many of them, because the royal residence was filled with men from the village.

When they arrived, the young woman was outside.

The man who was in front said, "Aren't you the one who was sent? We have come to you."

The young woman said, "I am she. Now I have something to say to you, then I must go. I have been here too long already. We must push on with this business, Fellows."

All right, they would push on.

The young woman said, "I was sent here by God. He came home after the departure of the men who had come over there to the place of God, the men who told the bad news about your king. The men told of the confusion that resulted because no one rules here. They told of the king not leaving behind a son. No advice has been forthcoming, and life here has not been calm. The men were determined to see God, and they thought they had reached the homestead of God because it is such a huge homestead, they could see that it is a huge homestead. They had lived in this land, but had never seen any homestead in that place. Now, they suddenly saw a homestead that would house their entire village with room to spare. The men said that the beauty of that homestead was astonishing. But it seems that God was not there that day, he is there only when he chooses to be there. God has sent me here with the advice that those men were seeking.

"God says that he wants his daughter to rule."

She paused.

The men then said, "Oh, his daughter."

"Mm!"

"Oh! It is right that we should be ruled by the daughter of God. She'll know things that we should all be provided by God. Let us speak as one on this, Fellows!"

It was said, "Call the young man from that homestead up there."

The young man arrived immediately, and he was told about the young woman who had been sent by God. "A group of people had been sent out, and now they returned saying that when they had gone to that place God had not been there. There was a beautiful young woman there, and she said that she would tell him."

The young man said, "All right, *I* am satisfied."

The young woman then said, "God says that the men must be ruled by his daughter, he says that his daughter will rule the men well, his daughter knows the customs and will expand them, his daughter knows how to mediate, his daughter knows how to make judgements."

She stopped there, and it was said, "It is all right. Let us be ruled by that daughter. God himself does not come, but he sends his daughter here, and we are to be ruled by her. He gives us his daughter."

The young woman responded, "God does not travel all the time. He has agreed to watch over this affair from afar—but even if he is not seen, that does not mean that he will not govern. What he rules is not neglected. *He* won't come here, he has sent me."

Then some other men said, "Where is that daughter?"

The young woman said, "This must be done. If you agree to be ruled by her, then you should raise your hands at God's place."

It was said, "That is it, Men. We must now go over there one day, we must go over there to the place of God. We shall raise our hands, and this daughter of God will rule us."

"Well then, you must tell God that we have heard, and we greet him."

The young woman then requested permission to leave, and she was given that permission. She went away then, and arrived at her home. Then she waited for the men. She waited for the men now, she waited for them, for they would arrive that day. And when they arrived, the young woman would go outside so that she could receive the salutes of the men as they raised their hands—she was God's daughter. Now the men would be ruled by God's daughter.

Time passed for the young woman, time passed, and she awakened in the morning, eating her fine food, sitting alone here in the house. And time passed for her in this house, time passed for her, time passed.

Then she saw that "Oh! They're coming!"

Suddenly the men were here . . . and here . . . and here . . . and here. They arrived, and sat outside. The place was filled, it was filled, the place of God was filled. It was filled completely.

She saw them, she looked at them. She prepared her things. She saw that "*Hayi bo!* They're all here now! Not another person can fit out there!"

The people stood there—but the residents of this homestead did not speak to them. They spoke only among themselves, they conversed among themselves, ignoring these others. They ignored them without rancor, with love, having looked them over carefully. But they did not speak to them.

Time passed for this young woman. Then, in her own time, she went into the house, and took the horn of her mother and father. When she had done that, she said, "Horn of my mother and father, please provide for me, it was said that you would provide for me."

When she had said that, hot water appeared, and she washed herself. She finished, having washed in that way, and then something appeared— it seemed to be a throne. This throne went out to remain among the people, in the midst of that throng of people.

They stared at the throne, and said, "Oh oh oh oh!"

"This is truly the place of God!"

"Yes!"

"Indeed!"

That throne remained there, it was draped elegantly with a cloth, covered with a cloth. Then suddenly the young woman appeared. She came out, carrying a staff—a black knobkerrie. When she arrived, she sat on that throne. She sat there, and after a long time she stood.

When she stood, the entire mass of people also stood. Not one among them sat. All stood on their feet.

She said, "Today some men arrived, coming to the place of God because of their suffering. Now this is the daughter of God! God has told me to come and stand among you. I must deliver you from the thing that has befallen you, that weighs on your hearts. I shall rule you, so that you live well. When I am your ruler, you should tell things to me, you should ask me things. Today, you are my guests, until tomorrow. Now if there is someone who is not here, you must tell him so that he is present the next time we gather." So said this woman, and she sat down.

When she sat, all the men stood up—all of them, all all. She sat.

They said, "Child of God, we shall be ruled by you! Our wounds will be healed, we shall be healthy again."

"We salute you!"

"When God arrives, convey our greetings to him!"

"Your councillors!"

"Choose your councillors yourself—those who are present here have been here a long time. We want you to choose your councillors yourself."

"You choose them, let them be selected by you so that you're satisfied with them, Child of the Great Person."

When they had said that, the young woman said, "I am happy to hear you say that." So she said, and then she covered herself, she was covered and what she did was not seen.

She grasped the horn of the ox of her father inside her cape, and said, "Horn of the ox of my mother and father, provide for me. It was said that you would provide for me." She said that, emerged from the cape, and sat down. She sat down now.

Then two men from the other side came and stood in front of her. Two men came from below and stood in front of her. And two of them got up from another side, they came and stood in front of her. And again, two of them from above came and stood in front of her.

These men came to her in twos—they were eight altogether. The eight men stood there, and she saw them.

She said, "Here are my councillors."

But these were men who had never before, at any time, been councillors.

She said, "These are mine. I have been given them by God—my councillors." They thanked her then, and she said, "My councillors, it is necessary that they be left here. They can travel tomorrow. First, I want to tell them of my desires."

The men agreed, and the others asked permission to leave. They broke up, and went over there to the royal residence. They had previously departed from the royal residence and come to Mityi's homeland. Now they returned.

They left the eight men behind.

Then the eighth one said that they should go into the one big house among the others. They went in. When they had gone in, when the time for sleeping came, they said that they should enter her house. They entered her house, they arrived there, and the men remained there.

She said to one of them, "You are a councillor of your village: you must never agree to a thing that is improper. In your village, never agree to anything that is improper.

"Never sell something to any person. Never, when a person wants something from you, whether it is a deserted homestead or whatever, say that person must first pay you for it. Leave him the deserted homestead if it is seen that the homestead is nice.

"When the sun sets, you must not remain at a beer party. You are a councillor, and the sun might set, and the things to be done at the time of the setting sun may be many. And who will go to do them? If you remain there, the people will flee to a person who rules properly.

"I want you to be under my instruction, under my command. I want you to accept my kingship, so that I can take care of your court cases. You must be attentive, you are councillors and you must bring the people to me. You may say that you have seized this person: but you have not seized this person at all, you have seized us!

"Now, I wanted to say these things to you, and I also wanted to give you these garments of councillors. Wear them, so that you will not be cold in the morning."

Then the men saluted her, they saluted the daughter of God at her home, they saluted the daughter of God, saying, "We salute you, Queen! We salute the child of God. The words that she speaks are significant. There are many things that people are involved in. She will deal with them well, things will go well with her, and so we salute her!"

Then she said, "Go, and sleep."

When the men had entered their house, Mityi called her young women, the four young women, and said that they must bring eight garments to these men, similar garments. She said that the men should be told to wear these garments when they removed their older ones.

The young women took the clothing, and went and entered the house of those men. They knocked on the door, and the men responded.

The young women went in, and said to them, "We have been sent here by the queen. She says that these garments are those of her councillors. She says that you should wear the garments when you have removed your own and when you speak in the courts. These are the robes of authority. There are eight garments, one for each of you."

The men took the garments, they took them—each one now had his own garment. Then they slept there.

At dawn the next day, they requested permission to leave; they were going to travel. But before they left, they would like something to eat. One of the eight had come to say this.

The young woman, Mityi, said, "Horn of my mother and father, provide for me. It was said that you would provide for me."

Then eight dishes for the councillors appeared. The young women brought the dishes to each of them. They ate, and finished. Then they drank some water. They prepared themselves, then travelled and went home.

They arrived at their homes, and followed her instructions. They did the things the queen had told them to do.

A long time passed, then two people accused one another about a matter of inheritance.

One of them insisted that the inheritance of cattle of his home belonged to him. And the other said, "No, they are mine, because *I'm* the one who was employed by my father to look after them!"

The two accused each other, their father no longer being there.

All this took place in the area of the first councillor.

So one of them went to the law, the one who did not agree with the other in the matter of the cattle.

It was said, "Explain."

The younger one explained then. He said, "I demand the cattle from my elder brother. I worked very hard with those cattle, I was hired and was paid, and the cattle of my father increased in the kraal. They grew to a large number. Then my father took my cattle so that he could take a wife for my elder brother. My father took my ox to do what he wanted to do at his home."

He was asked, "What brand do these cattle have?"

He said, "The brand of my father. I never attended to it, I never thought that I should use *my* brand, because my father was still there. But then he took many cattle to get a wife for my elder brother. And I had not attended to the branding of the cattle, my father had done that. The reason that I want these cattle now is because my elder brother again wants a wife, he wants to marry a second wife. But *I* do not yet have a wife, I do not yet have a wife, *I* do not yet have a wife! *He* has a wife. For a long time I have been a man, but my elder brother just passes me by, saying nothing. That is what he does. I did not know that my father would not be here, that he had not yet prepared this matter. I have therefore called you myself, because I too want a wife, but he does not agree to let me have the cattle."

Then the elder brother was asked by the councillor to speak: "Please speak, Elder brother. How do you respond to your younger brother's accusation?"

The elder brother said, "My younger brother has no cattle at home. He has never had them branded with his brand, so there is no proof that they are his cattle. He is lying! He is a child. It makes no difference how much he worked with the cattle, his work is his payment for being brought up by my father. It is his payment to my father for being brought up. In no way are the cattle his."

Then it was said to the elder brother, "And you, his elder brother—how many cattle have *you* herded?"

He said, "I have never herded an ox."

"He is the son who herded then?"

"He was a child. I was older, and *I* did no work. I was never made to work, to herd the stock of my father." He had not herded the cattle, he had not been made to do that work.

Then it was said, "The younger brother had said that when he returned, he would herd the cattle. But how could that be, seeing that he had no cattle? And how could his work be doubled?"

He worked at home, and then he would go and work at other homesteads. Then he would return, and add more cattle to the stock, again and again. He would watch over the stock, making certain that it did not get lost or stray. "And that's the way you've been living? And there is a person—you—who just sits. How then can it come about that he has nothing? Whose homestead did he come from?"

The elder brother said, "An inheritance is never eaten by a child. The inheritance is that of the elder one in the homestead. What I speak is the truth."

Then it was said in this court, "Where are the grown-up people? Here is a person who does not know how to do anything, who cannot work!"

Then the elder brother said, with dignity, "No! Not so! I do not have to find work, because I am my father's first born!"

But the elder brother was judged by the councillor, who said, "Those are not your cattle over there. They belong to your younger brother. He herded the cattle as his payment to his father for his rearing. He was left with the stock by his father, he herded the cattle even though he did not have a wife."

So the elder brother was judged.

Then, when he had finished the case, the councillor walked away and went to the royal residence of the place of God. He went to that woman, to Mityi, and when he arrived there he went in to her. He explained to her the case that had just been adjudicated, about the two fellows who had accused each other. And he told her how the case went, how the younger brother and the elder brother had accused one another regarding the cattle. He told her that he had found against the elder brother.

The woman thanked him, and told him that he had judged well. He had examined the elder brother's way of life, the kind of work that he did, how he was in the wrong.

When the case had been judged, the younger brother had not spoken, he had gone home joyful because he had heard the decision of the court. When the councillor had been given the garment, the queen had said, "You should not speak anything that is untrue"—and so that one was now seen to be rejoicing as he went home.

One day, the queen called the men to her, saying that she wanted their number to be complete. She wanted to find the man who would live with her here at home.

On the appointed day, the men came along, and when they got there, they sat in the courtyard as usual—with no one to say that they were present. Time passed, time passed, and then, when it was afternoon and the courtyard was filled with men, the queen said, "Let an ox be slaughtered for them, let the slaughtering be done by the four hired men."

They took an ox, they seized it and slaughtered it for the men who had been called there by the queen. Then the four men cut it up and cooked all of it, so that all the people who were there would have enough.

When it was taken off the fire, the queen said, "Just put it there." They did that, putting it over there so that it would cool.

When things were like that, the queen went to her house, and she took the horn of the ox of her mother, and said, "Horn of the ox of my mother, provide for me. It was said that you would provide for me."

When she had said that, all the dishes came out, the dishes for the meat. Everything appeared, everything, everything. The dishes were distributed to the various men of the company—this group had a dish, this group had a dish, this group had a dish. There was enough for all the men, dishes with meat.

Then she said to the men who had been hired, "All right then!" and the men ate and finished. When the men had arrived, she had said, "Eat, all of you."

So the men ate, all of them; they ate that meat. When they had finished eating, the men did not see the dishes disappear. They did not see them depart or anything, they only saw that the dishes were no longer there. What they saw in front of them, at once, were other dishes, these containing soup. That is what now stood in place of the meat dishes. The men sipped the soup then, and they finished.

When the men had finished sipping the soup, the queen took her horn. She blew it, saying, "Ox of my mother, provide for me; it was said that you would do so."

When she had said that, a young man got up. He had been over there with the men. Now he made straight for the house. When he got to that house, he greeted the queen, and she responded.

The queen said, "Do you have something to say?"

The young man said, "I am not speaking, I want work."

She said, "What kind of work are you seeking?"

And this man, still quite young, said, "No, Queen, I seek work with *you*. I want to be your person, and I want you to be mine."

The queen said, "And will you stay here at home?"

The young man said, "Yes, I shall stay here at home, because *you* are not able to go and stay with any person."

The queen said, "Go then, go to the men. Go and declare yourself, tell them that you are mine. And return when you have declared yourself. Do you have parents?"

The young man said, "Yes, I am the last born in our family. We are a large family. My father is here, among the men, along with my older brothers. Some of them are here also among the men."

Then the queen said, "Go and declare yourself then."

The young man got up and went to the men. When he got to them, he just stood there, not knowing what to say. He stood there, at a loss as to what to say, fearing now to discuss this matter before his father and his elder brother and all the people of his homeland.

The queen looked, and she saw him, she saw that "He's embarrassed, he doesn't know what to say."

She again took that horn, and said, "Ox of my mother, provide for me. It was said that you would provide for me."

When Mityi had said that, the young man over there said, "Stop, please stop what you are doing, all of you. All of you—Father and the rest. My older brothers, younger brothers. I have something to tell you today. I want you to know that I am in harmony with this queen who rules us. And because of that harmony, I shall live with her—not just to visit her. I want her to be mine, and I shall be hers."

It was said, "Huleeeeee! We have heard!"

"Oh, Fellows! What is this?"

"This young man!"

"Hey!"

They stared at him.

It was said, "*Hayi bo!* We have heard this thing!"

They were in agreement with this. Time passed for the young man, and the others applauded him. They raised their hands, saluting him, because he was the husband of the queen.

The young man walked away from them. He went to stay in the house with the queen. They were happy with one another: he was her husband, and all was well. They lived together, walking one behind the other, accustomed to each other, loving each other.

In time, the husband began to try court cases. He did not come right out and try them. He would finish a case, being taught all necessary things by his wife.

She said, "When men come, no matter what the problem, go ahead. If you're puzzled, I'll be here."

When the young man was baffled by a court case, his wife would take the horn of her mother, and speak to it. Then the young man would finish trying the case.

Part Two

AMBIGUOUS PROMISE

"IT KEEPS ON HAPPENING, IT KEEPS ON HAPPENING"

Everything ordinary had something supernatural about it.
                                    —*Gabriel García Márquez*[1]

INTRODUCTION

The tale-teller is the person who most regularly and persuasively touches every member of the community. This creator moves behind the facts of history, and clarifies, defines, and elucidates the experiences of the people. She thereby sustains the society's traditions, those institutions that give context and meaning to daily life.

Noplani Gxavu's story "Malikophu's Daughter" and Emily Ntsobane's tale "The Deadly Pumpkin" are developed in similar ways: each has to do with a transition and a resulting transformation in the life of a young person. But there is an important distinction here as well: Gxavu's story of a boy's puberty ritual is decidedly positive, while Ntsobane's depiction of a girl's rite of passage is fraught with uncertainty. If storytelling contains promise, it is at best an ambiguous promise.

ONE

"The art of composing oral imaginative narratives," said Nongenile Masithathu Zenani,[2] "is something that was undertaken by the first people—long ago, during the time of the ancestors. When those of us in my generation awakened to earliest consciousness, we were born into a tradition that was already flourishing. Narratives were being performed by adults in a tradition that had been established long before we were born. And when we were born, those narratives were constructed for us by old people, who argued that the narratives had initially been created in olden times, long ago. That time was ancient even to our fathers, it was ancient to our grandmothers. And our grandmothers said that *iintsomi* [oral tales] had been created years before by *their* grandmothers. We learned the narratives in that way, and every generation that has come into being has been born into the tradition. Members of every generation have grown up under the influence of these narratives.

"But those ancient stories were quite different from those of the contemporary age. The current stories, those that we hear now, tend to be written down. As if from nowhere, we suddenly find that they are being written.

"But the genuine *iintsomi* were never, at any time, written down. They were composed orally by the old people. And when we too asked how this tradition came into existence, we were told that it was a craft that had been practiced at the very beginning, in the old times. Such stories go back as far as ancestral time, to the age of the first people. But these works did not resemble what we have in contemporary times."[3]

149

Southern African folktales are not always of the happily-ever-after variety. Storytellers confront life realistically, and, while it is true that they deal in fantasy images, those images are meant to give dimension to reality, not to embellish it. True, the images shape our experience of the real, and if stories are hopeful they are not unrealistic in their yearnings and their goals.

There is a dualism in storytelling in southern Africa, with some stories emphasizing the positive, suggesting hopeful realities; other stories, while containing such hope, give pause to the unbridled imagination, allowing the narrower confines of reality to limit and discipline the desires of the imagination.

The two stories in this section reveal this uncertainty, even nervousness, between the reach of the imagination and its reining-in by reality. Both were performed in the Transkei in September of 1967, one by Noplani Gxavu, a Gcaleka woman of thirty-five, living in Nkanga, in Gatyana District; the other by Emily Ntsobane, a forty-year-old Hlubi woman living among the Mpondo in Mgugwani, in Lusikisiki District.

TWO

Underlying the historical facts of Ndumiso Bhotomane and the epic grandeur of Masithathu Zenani is the tale, the basic production of the oral tradition. It is in the tale that myth is given contemporary form, that epic is localized, that history is legitimized. Tales typically treat momentous changes in the lives of individuals as they navigate the arc of life: the rites of passage, the movements from one state to another, and all the attendant uncertainties and dreads and hopes. To understand the history of a people, to comprehend a society's epic tradition, one must first grapple with the tale tradition, on which all else in the culture depends.

The crucial generating unit of oral narrative performance is the image.[4] Images, when organized into eductive patterns, evoke an emotional response from members of an audience. Message in such imaginative performances is the emotional experience of forms and relationships between forms. Surface homilies, etiological comment, and cultural data are among the materials of composition of the oral narrative; they are the means to message, not the end. Since the message of oral narrative is emotional, it is not easily paraphrased in words. "[T]o dance is to discover,"[5] argues Léopold Sédar Senghor; Susan Sontag suggests, "To interpret is to impoverish, to deplete the world. . . ."[6]

If a key emotion-evoking device in narrative is the image, the major shaping tool is repetition, the patterning of various kinds that includes anticipation and predictability as essential aesthetic adjuncts. Patterning

The eternal storyteller. Nohatyula Miyeki, a Xhosa storyteller, and her grandchildren.

of image, moreover, continues to elicit emotions even as it shapes and clarifies that response. The artist manipulates images, the emotionally experienced activities of diverse characters projected by means of words and the body, to establish the contours of form. The audience is, in a sense, both spectator and participant; it is a part of the raw material of the performance. In oral narrative, the artist initiates movement, guiding the members of an audience to an experience of relationships between characters based on that movement, thereby creating form. The artist patterns these movements of characters, assuring the uniformity of such movement through repetition.

Various devices and activities arouse the emotions, then sustain and mold them. The performer works with an audience that has the same repertory of images that he has, and this provides a necessary common experience. There is, moreover, aesthetic satisfaction in the predictability of the narrative. But it does not mean that the emotional responses are identical. Though all members of these audiences are closely related, though all come from the same culture, indeed frequently from the same neighborhood, individuals in the audience nevertheless have unique histories and experiences of such images. The close relationship between audience and image means that divergences in sensory reactions are of a peripheral rather than substantive nature. But the differences are significant, for performances require both emotional diversity and similarity for their effect, not only for the tensions that they produce but also for the activating of various elements of the narrative. The artist traps emotions in images and patterns, and thus begins to shape them, so that what begins as a somewhat diffuse set of responses is slowly worked into a response that is communal and harmonious.

The images are known, the patterns are familiar. The precise organization of the images and the arrangement of the patterns are not necessarily known for the specific performance, and this unidentified factor introduces a tension which contributes to yet another reservoir of emotions. Alteration of the predictable image-sequence which has been patterned into form is vital to performance. The options open to the performer are many, so that the exact nature of the shattering of the pattern and the timing of such shattering are not known. No matter what the knowledge and experience of the members of the audience, the patterning always contains an element of unpredictability, and anxiety and nervousness are elevated to a kind of aesthetic tension. That is, the anticipation of the breaking of patterns frets predictability with uncertainty. The audience knows that the pattern is to be broken, but it does not know when, and frequently it does not know how. The resulting anticipation provides an emotional accompaniment to audience expectation established by the regularity of patterning.

There is the common experience of narratives, then, and this results in emotional homogeneity; there is also individual experience of images, and this elicits emotional diversity. In the performance itself, the artist works against tensions and idiosyncratic experiences, striving to weld these into harmonious forms. The tensions involved in this artistic process contribute to the establishment of such forms. The artist's body may have a part to play in this—his hands, his shoulders, his face. The music of the language, the rhythm of the patterns—muted song and contained dance—help to develop uniform experiences of uniquely sensed images and image sequences. Even if the body of the artist is not active during a performance, the message remains primarily nonverbal, for the ultimate reaction of an audience is not to words but to forms established partially by words. The language of oral narrative is tonal, and the artist exploits this verbal music, the inherent poetry of the language. The audience's response to these aspects of performance is of a nature different from that aroused by individual images. It is not so particular, it is abstracted, and does not depend on a history of specific evocations with regard to a single image. It is not so charged; it is controlled, a regular rhythm, and it therefore plays a role not much different from the patterning of the image sets. In fact, the two kinds of activity frequently reinforce each other.

The regular grid of repeated response elicited by the patterned verbal and nonverbal elements of the performance provides a rhythmical framework for the more varied emotions evoked by images. Patterning is constructed of emotions, and such patterning gives shape to the sundry responses to specific images. The regular, rhythmical aspects of the performance elicit emotions that have a controlling effect on the other emotions. This is because there are few differences in the way the audience responds to the grid, because it is an act of the unique performance, wholly under the control of the artist, not dependent on the audience's separate histories. Emotions shape emotions, as the varied reactions are ordered by the similar.

The kinds of emotions called forth, then, are not the same: some result from the audience's intimate knowledge of the narrative being performed; others flow from the specificity of the unique performance; emotions are involved with expectation and predictability, the shattering of patterns; and emotions are cradled in the rhythmic movement of pattern, sound, and motion. The audience, thoroughly caught up in performance, as the preceding sense of incompleteness evokes emotion, is involved totally in the move of the narrative toward final unity, the climaxing equilibrium. The performer molds the various kinds of reaction into forms, and the forms are developed against and with the assistance of the regular grid. The one reveals the other, even indicating similarities among images of a very different nature.

The artist always works his way back to unity. Formal unity is purposely broken, but the images are reassembled, and the pattern reestablished, or a new pattern is initiated—wholly new, or born of the remnants of the preceding sequences. The audience reacts to the activities of the characters, which may be heightened, exaggerated, and highly selective. The performer frequently introduces violent actions and anti-social images into his narrative as units that evoke emotion. The audience does not experience these images in a literal way, but rather as a part of a total performance. Emotional involvement is such that the audience makes no judgments about specific images, but allows the performer to initiate such images for his own purposes. Conclusions about specific images cannot be made until the performance is complete; until then, the imagery, the patterning and the experience of the members of the audience are in the process of becoming. Shocking images do indeed evoke responses from the members of the audience, that is their function; but these do not constitute the message of the performance. They are a part of the total experience within a closed world of art, and they do not by themselves carry cultural values. The audience knows what kind of world it is entering with the pronouncement of the opening formula of the narrative; its members understand that this is not the real world, and they do not respond to it in the way they respond to real world events. The more outrageous, the more exaggerated, hilarious, bawdy and frightening the

Organizing the audience's emotions. A Xhosa storyteller.

images the better, for emotions are thereby elicited which can then be shaped into new forms. It is the full experience that is the concern, not the experience of specific details and images. The art of the performer involves a constant elicitation of responses from members of an audience who are thoroughly caught up in the work of art. The performer greedily gathers all these emotions, the tensions that exist between him and his audience, the music of the performance, the movement of the body, the clapping, the singing, the tones and stresses, the movements, images, patterns.

The performer is in no way seeking to imitate reality. Certain aspects of the real are a part of his raw material, and these are blended with materials from the art tradition. But he is not attempting to project a three-dimensional view of the real world. Even when—as it often does—the performance begins in that familiar world, warm and secure, with realistic characters and activities, a physical movement typically takes place away from this known environment, and out to the veld, to the forest, to another village, to a house of marriage. That place "out there" is not known; it is unfamiliar territory, threatening, cold. Danger is there, the fantastic is there. The spatial poles are matched by a polarity of emotional response.

But what happens out there is not all that fantastic. One of the significant aesthetic sensations of oral narrative is the experience of the identical nature of image sequences which, on their surfaces, have no similarities whatsoever—and may involve opposing emotions. This is accomplished by means of emotionally perceived relations between characters, a perception which is sometimes achieved through deception, disguise, illusion. The characters "out there" in the threatening space who seem so different from humans are not so different after all. Some of them were once human.

Out there, characters are never what they seem. In that strange world, situations are established which are identical (once deceptions and disguises are understood) to those which are occurring in the familiar world. Disguised creatures act out human roles, and humans react to the creatures as if they were in fact human. Only the audience realizes that deception is being perpetrated. Contrast becomes possible, contrast between identical forms: one situation is contrasted with its reflection. But that reflection, because of its composition (fantastic creatures, fabulous activities), is more than a mirror of the initial set of relationships. It becomes a kind of play-within-a-play, formally related to the other set of images, and the aesthetic experience of the performance is the emotional recognition of these formal relationships. If the narrative has a cognitive function as well, that is revealed only in the experience of the formal linkages between contrasting events. The artist thus ties a small number of characters in many different ways. The patterning of the actions of such characters reveals to the audience, through its emotional involvement in the performance, the identical nature of the relationships.

The essence of patterning in oral narrative is simplicity. Narratives do not become complex except as new forms are introduced to work with existing forms. In some narratives, the relationship between major forms is serial, almost picaresque, one set of images attached to the next, along a chronological axis. But this is not the only possible relationship that can be established between forms. It is also possible to develop patterning simultaneously. A dominant pattern may be ruptured by the performer to introduce other patterns which supplant, co-exist or entwine with, and otherwise relate to the dominant form. Complication of form allows for a complication of message, when message is viewed as emotional rather than cognitive. In narratives that are composed of two or three distinct narrative movements, the relationship between them is established and revealed by identical patterns. In such works, disguise and illusion may become important narrative tools. As narratives become more complex, as formal elements multiply, a finite number of characters will have more than one role to play. There is a growing necessity for ambiguous characters and events, mediatory agencies, and disguise, to aid in the revelation of relationships among the forms. The basic pattern still dominates in such narratives: All other patterns either reinforce the basic pattern, complicate it, or comment on it.

The shattering of an image-sequence gives birth to a new set of images identical to the preceding set but in which shattering has now become a part of the repeated pattern. In fact, the breaking of the model becomes the dominant feature of the new pattern; other repeated images can be worked in, so long as they contain the crucial element of shattering. This makes possible the subtle alteration of the dominant pattern into something quite different. This principle of the alteration of pattern seems central to the aesthetic experience of oral narrative. In effect, the dominant pattern is opened so that other patterns can substitute, and such substitution often occurs at a point of shattering, though it does not have to. The move to a new pattern is sometimes slow, other times abrupt. But the principle remains: a set of images molded into one kind of pattern is altered by a shifting of imagery so that the model is changed. In other cases, that dominant pattern is simply interrupted by a new set of patterns, which then operates serially or simultaneously with the initial pattern. The audience, caught up in the separate patterns, now begins to experience them in combination, and this has an effect on their experience of the first pattern; the combination of the two itself becomes a new pattern and therefore a new experience. In this way, a performance builds on patterns that are segmented or full, interrupted or developed at length.

The American painter Stuart Davis made use of words in his art, not for their meanings but because of their forms. He observed, "A painting is a collection or complex of colored tones of definite shape and size, that's all. Every thing that is expressed through the medium of painting must live through these properties of size, shape and color."[7] Words, sounds, and the body have similar effects in oral narrative performance. They provide patterns and forms, and everything that is expressed in such performances is expressed through these properties. Paul Klee speaks of a synthesis "where what is static, well-balanced and, often, quite symmetrical, is given a touch of the dramatic,"[8] and this describes precisely the aesthetic experience of forms in which audiences of oral narrative are involved. As in painting, the message of oral narrative is expressed through forms; in narrative, these forms are composed not simply of words, but of music and dance, the movement of the body, the sounds and silences of words. Balanced forms are the result. The dynamic element is introduced when balance is momentarily upset, then restored once again. This pulsating symmetrical/ asymmetrical exchange is central to the oral performer's art. He establishes form, only to shatter form, and in the shattering he produces yet another form. He establishes form, then breaks into that form to introduce yet another formal set of relationships. All is based on repetition.

Leonard Bernstein speaks of "nonmusical meanings" that interfere with our experience of such musical works as Beethoven's Sixth Symphony; such preoccupation diminishes our experience of "such things as inversions and subdominants, to say nothing of deletions and permutations. . . ." He argues that nonmusical meanings "form a kind of visual curtain of nonmusical ideas, a semi-transparent curtain, so to speak, that interposes itself between the listener and the music per se."[9] Oral narrative analysis suffers from the same kind of curtain, an emphasis, for example, on homiletic content and cultural data shielding us from the essential experience of such performances.

In one of her short stories, Doris Lessing creates a character, Michele,[10] who is assigned to build a small village for a military demonstration. "At the end of a week, the space at the end of the parade-ground had crazy gawky constructions of lath and board over it, that looked in the sunlight like nothing on this earth . . . , just bits of board stuck in the sand." But at night, when the lights were trained on this assemblage of squares and blocks, "Instantly, a white church sprang up from the shapes and shadows of the bits of board"; the lights were "briefly switched on, and the village sprang into existence. . . ." It was not a real village, it was a work of art that could not be fully realized except under the correct conditions, when the proper relationships between the shapes and light could be established and perceived.

The process of rupturing formal constructions is one of the most significant of the aesthetic characteristics of oral narrative performance. It allows for the complicating, unifying, and sophisticating of narrative, through the technique of interlocking. And it provides for acceptable interference with the chronological movement of the narrative. Interference incorporates complexity through the interlocking of basic forms. That is, complexity is achieved not in the forms themselves, but through the process of fracturing forms, then incorporating and interlocking other formal patterns. Serial composition is thus displaced by simultaneous composition of form, as artists bring into their productions the patterns and images they have experienced from childhood, linking them through this process. The audience, by means of several kinds of emotions involved in performance, experiences these forms and their new relationships. Those emotions include the somewhat diffuse reactions to separate images and image clusters, the more controlled reactions to the patterns and grids, the tensions between performer and audience, the nervousness and anxiety elicited by suspense, those aspects of performance that are not predictable, and the more pleasant sensations involved in expectation and predictability. The forms are composed of the varying kinds of emotions evoked by the artist's voice and body, and it is in the interplay of the emotions (the particularized emotions, for example, played against the regular rhythmic emotions) that the forms are perceived by the audience, which leads the members of the audience to an awareness of their relationship. The emotions are molded by the artist into forms, and it is by means of the emotions that the forms are perceived: the correct conditions are carefully established by the artist, so that the shapes and shadows of the narrative suddenly "spring into existence."

THREE

In Noplani Gxavu's story,[11] "Malikophu's Daughter," the storyteller details Gxam's growth to maturity, but it is Malikophu's daughter who is the focus here. She is the other side of Gxam, his positive side, his creative possibilities, while her father represents his ugly side, his potential for destructiveness.

In a story containing a typical transformation, Gxam moves away from home, the reason being poverty. He and his two fellow travellers are destitute, and they are journeying, seeking work among the whites. His friends turn against him to get his food; they blind him, and leave him to die. Now he is in the world of fantasy, away from home, in a physical and psychological state of betwixt and between. This is where the transformation will occur, and it occurs, as is characteristic of stories dealing with such matters, as he is tested and helped. His testing is his blindness, his sense of helplessness. His helpers are creatures of nature, crows in this case. The crows have compassion when they hear his story, and, in a pattern, they bring him life-sustaining food. They "take the eyes of a sheep belonging to the white man who has domesticated us," and they transplant those eyes onto Gxam, restoring his sight. And they sustain him with the food of that sheep. They refer to Gxam as "father." Then, in an elaborate plan, they instruct him as to how he can restore his sight. "He could see nothing at all," but the crows have made him "hopeful." But "dawn seemed a long time in coming." He follows their instructions, and can see albeit in a blurred way: "[O]ne eye could make out some blurred silhouettes." Slowly he moves into a new state. Then, after "he could see clearly with one eye," the crows instruct him to perform the same operation on the other eye: "It too will be capable of sight!" And so his sight is recovered, and he sees life anew: "What land is this? Where have I been?" He and the crows are in harmony: "What can I say, wonderful birds of life?" And they tell him, "You're free today!" They send him into his new life, warning him that "it's important that you conduct your affairs carefully in that land that you're going to, the land in which we live." They tell him, "It is a difficult land." They caution him, "Terrible things happen there."

So it is that Gxam moves into the final stages of his regeneration, to the fantasy land of the villainous Malikophu. A woman in Malikophu's house tells him that "this is the homestead from which no one ever departs," and indeed it is, for Gxam will emerge from the experience a new man. He is guided through his phase of his transformation by another creature of nature, a bee.

The second half of the story has a pattern of danger, with Malikophu attempting to destroy Gxam, and Malikophu's daughter saving him with the six eggs, symbols of rebirth. The relationship between father and daughter is complex: "Do you value that young man more than your own life?" Malikophu asks his daughter during the chase. "And mine?" She can only respond, "The decision has been made." And she thereby tests Gxam: "Do you see my father? Because of my love for you, I'm going to put the fifth obstacle in his way. I wonder, Gxam, if you'll treat me well." Gxam insists, "I shall even die for you." And, later, she makes the exchange even clearer: "Do you see this egg? It is *the* egg, the mother and father of all the other eggs. This egg is the life of Malikophu." But it is also the life of Gxam: "If I use this egg, my father will die, and we shall be able to go to the place to which you want us to go." When Malikophu challenges her one last time, "My daughter, are you actually accepting this man at the expense of my life? And your life too? And his?" she responds, "You have mentioned three lives. But you've grown quite old now, you've savored a long life, and now you must give way to this young man."

Malikophu is dead, the daughter's work as a guide is complete. Now Gxam is on his own: "I have been telling you what to do all along the way. Now, however, I won't be instructing you anymore. I'll only give you one piece of guidance. After that, I shall be submissive to you. I shall be under your protection, I shall acquiesce to you." That final piece of guidance: He must not reestablish relations with his past, which he has now left behind. If he does so, then he will forget her, that is, forget all that he has undergone, all that has made his rebirth possible. It is his last test, and he initially fails it. She has cut herself off from her parents, while Gxam restores his relationships with his: "Gxam, don't you realize that while you expressed affection for *your people,* that *I* had killed my own *father,* that I had left my *mother* behind, alone?" This final revelation brings Gxam and Malikophu's daughter into unity, and the story comes to an end.

Emily Ntsobane's story "The Deadly Pumpkin" is similarly constructed, containing the promise implicit in rebirth and regeneration, but this performer is less certain than Noplani Gxavu about the outcome.

The roles of Malikophu and Malikophu's daughter are in this tale taken by a pumpkin which has both life-giving and death-dealing capabilities. The storyteller signals the meaning of the events that are about to occur in the story: "Mabani," says the father of a daughter to his wife, "I want to initiate this child of mine into womanhood." The remainder of the tale will be a storyteller's dramatization of that move to maturity and responsibility, a move fraught with danger and suffused with hope and promise. The pumpkin comes to represent these two aspects of change and rebirth.

Now the members of the girl's household leave her behind, going "a far distance" to tend to the harvest, leaving "the child alone in the house here at home." This is a necessary condition for the transformation: the child is alone, separated from the sustaining influences of her family. She is in the betwixt stage now. It is at this point that fantasy enters the story, in this case in the form of the pumpkin that now becomes at once her assailant and her guide to womanhood. In a pattern that progressively robs the girl of her identity and securely places her in the betwixt stage, the pumpkin claims her for this middle ground: she must speak its language, not the language of her family. Each time the pattern occurs, the pumpkin alters her dramatically and violently: "[T]he pumpkin made her fall, then tore her flesh, it cut her body, rending her flesh again and again." Then it prepares food for her, the combination of violence and generosity representing the destructiveness and creativeness of the dualistic pumpkin. And always, it leaves her with the admonition, "And don't dare tell your mother and father that I have arrived." This is between her and the pumpkin: there can be no assistance from her own people until the process is complete. Each day, the pumpkin returns, testing her linguistically, tearing her flesh, feeding her, always departing with the interdiction. And always, when her parents return, they are astonished when they discover that she accepts no food from them: "Really, I am not hungry." Her parents' suspicions deepen: "Perhaps the child is not well." They detect an alien smell in the house, "they smelled something that was rotten." And when the mother uncovers her daughter, she finds "that her daughter's body was really green. It had become putrid." Something is happening, the daughter is changing in a dramatic way: "What's the matter with you? Why are you like this, Nobani?" And then the daughter tells her mother all, revealing the encounters with the pumpkin "that cuts me and does these things to me, bringing me close to death. . . ." The parents take the child and hide her behind a screen, precisely what occurs in reality when a girl goes through the puberty ritual. But the pumpkin finds her: "Come out, I'm your sister!" And this time, because she informed her parents, "It tore her flesh, it tore her flesh, and her bones also were bared today." And the pattern again is repeated. The parents are bewildered: "[I]t's a witch of a pumpkin. It is a menace. I carried it home, thinking that I was just carrying a pumpkin. But it was not a pumpkin."

Now they involve the king himself in the matter. The initiation ceremony must go on: "We cannot cut it short: it is necessary, according to the customs of African people, that the ritual move to its conclusion, in order that the initiate have good fortune." The child is then brought to the royal residence of the king. The girl's body is now changing rapidly, "her body overflowing with the maggots that she carried on her back." She is putrefying, her old body is dying. When the pumpkin returns, the king's men stab it, spear it. But they are not able wholly to subdue it: "[P]umpkin pips sprang up, they sprang up, sprang up, sprang up over there in the courtyard," the storyteller's repetition suggesting the eternal presence of the pumpkin. So it is that the girl is healed, she is now in health.

The story could end here, and might if it were constructed like "Malikophu's Daughter." But this storyteller is less certain. As the story comes to an end, the pumpkin, unlike Malikophu, continues to live: "In that place over there where the pips had sprung up, a pumpkin came out. This pumpkin came out, it emerged, and it grew and grew, spreading out." The young woman returns to her home, marries, and bears children. But "When she had had three children, these pumpkins arrived and ate the children of this young woman. No sooner had the young woman borne the children than she buried them in the ground, because of the pumpkins." And the story ends on this ominous note: "There is nothing that can be done about it now, because it is now present. It keeps on happening, it keeps on happening." Stories contain promise, but images of reality are never far from the surface. Implicit in the grand fantasy of the stories, the hope and promise of the past, is the danger of the present, always threatening to undermine that hope and promise. This, Emily Ntsobane argued, is what apartheid did to the promise of the stories.

Uncertainties and beliefs: that is what these stories show us. On the one hand, they contain the conservative, certain reassurances of an artistic system that has always celebrated tradition. On the other hand, the stories contain images that raise questions about traditions, inject an uncomfortable stratum of uncertainty which, if it does not undermine and belie the beliefs implicit in the traditions, enables audiences to see limitations, dangers, and ultimately the reality of the oral tradition: that it masks the vagaries of reality, providing certainty where there is no certainty.

Noplani Gxavu

MALIKOPHU'S DAUGHTER

(XHOSA)

Noplani Gxavu, a Gcaleka woman about thirty-five years old, performed this story on September 17, 1967, along a hillside in Nkanga, Gatyana District, in the Transkei. In the audience were seven women, three men, and five children. (673; tape 13, side 2)

In another time, three destitute men journeyed to seek work. There were no vehicles for transporting people in those days, so the men set out on foot, sleeping along the way.

On the morning that began the second week of their journey, they were resting beneath a big tree. Two of the men, having inventoried their provisions, discovered that not much food remained. They ate what little food was there.

The other man, whose name was Gxam, had exercised self-control, with the result that, even though the men had all left home at the same time, many of his provisions remained untouched.

Seeing this to be the case, the other two men conspired against Gxam: They knew that their journey was far from over; what they did not know was how it would end. Because the lands through which they had been passing contained no white people, there was no place where they might seek employment. And this other fellow still had so many provisions.

"We've got to do something about this," said one of them. "We've got to survive. He can't be the only one who gets a job, who earns money and then returns home. He'll relieve his family of its problems, and we'll die of starvation. Let's grab him, let's kill him. We'll take his food, we'll be the ones who live on. He's alone, there are two of us. It's not right that one man should survive, while two of us die."

All this time, the second man had remained silent. Now he said, "I'm of the same opinion. This man is alone, and the two of us are in agreement. Let's strangle him, then take his food, and move on to seek employment from the whites. He's clearly been shrewd. Otherwise, why is his food so plentiful, while ours is almost gone? We'll die of starvation, he'll survive."

Well, Friends, they fell on that third man, Gxam, they seized him.

"What are you doing?" he asked. "How can you kill me? They trust you at my home, I left in your company! Give me a reason why you must kill me, tell me why! You can have my food. Take it, eat it. Let me starve to death, you don't have to strangle me. After all, we left home as companions!"

163

"They pricked his eyes so that he could not see." Noplani Gxavu, a Gcaleka storyteller.

One of the men, suddenly filled with compassion, said, "He's right. Let's not strangle him. Instead, we'll put out his eyes. No white man would employ a blind person. We can take his food and eat it, but without actually dispatching his soul."

"You're right. He did leave his home with us, we could become culpable. If we just blind him, we can argue that he got hurt. Then, even if he should accuse us later, we won't be executed because we shall not have murdered him."

The big tree under which they were resting was a thorn tree. The two men took some of the thorns, and pierced Gxam's eyes with them. They pricked his eyes so that he could not see.

Gxam could not proceed on his journey.

When the other two men had taken his food and had eaten some of it, they went off again to seek work, which had been their original intention.

Gxam remained behind, groaning in pain, his eyes throbbing because they had been pierced by the thorns.

He was left there without food.

He remained in that place, and in the second month he still had no food. He was finally able to obtain something to eat when two black birds, crows, called "princesses" arrived.

The crows arrived, and they perched in the thorn tree.

"What is the trouble, Father?" said one of the crows. "Why are you sitting here?"

"We've been watching you for some time," said the other. "We've seen you each time we've passed this place."

Gxam was able to understand the voices of these crows, and he responded to them. They would start off by cooing like birds, then they would speak in the manner they had been taught in this land of the Xhosa.

"This, Crow, is why I'm here. There were three of us men. My suffering has to do with the food that I brought from my home, the provisions that we took with us when we left home to find work.

"It turns out that I, unlike my two companions, am not a man who eats a lot. So, as we travelled along, the food of the other two decreased. When their food reserves got low, they conspired against me because my supply of food remained plentiful. My stomach, you see, is small, I don't eat much. I become hungry quickly enough, but I fill up quite rapidly.

"So they conspired against me. In my very presence, they schemed against me. They didn't even move away from me, Crow, as they planned their actions. They intrigued against me in my very presence. They were so confident that they did not feel the need to go to one side to plot against me. They knew that if I resisted, they would easily overwhelm me and do to me whatever they wanted to do. So they determined that I must be seized, and killed: my food could then be eaten. It was then that

I spoke up. As they seized me, I asked them why I had to die, considering that they had set out with me from my home, the three of us going off together to seek work from the whites. 'Now that you have found that you do not have sufficient provisions, why not just take my food and eat it? Let me die of hunger, instead of killing me with your own hands.' After all, I said to them, they had set out with me from my home.

"Then one of the men took compassion on me. He said, 'Well, Friend, let's not kill him. This tree we're standing under can provide us with an alternative.' The tree he was referring to was quite a big one, a thorn tree. And it had huge thorns. 'Let's take these thorns and blind him, put out both of his eyes! If we do that, he won't be employed by the whites. He'll not even have a way of getting to the white men, because he'll be blind.'

"Well, that is just what they decided to do, and that, Crow, is what they did."

The crows considered his words, and they had compassion. One of them said to this man, "We'll tell you what you must do. We won't ask for any remuneration for what we're about to do, because we don't know yet if you'll have the wherewithal to repay us. In your condition, there's nothing in the world that you can do."

"Now just remain here," said the other crow, "where you are. We'll do whatever we can to help you, though we're powerless to take hold of anything. After all, we only have wings. But procuring food is no problem for us."

The crows flew off, and the man remained there, suffering from the pain caused by the deliberate piercing of his eyes.

Time passed.

Then, before sunset, the crows returned.

"Father?"

He responded.

"Are you still here?"

"Yes."

"We've had a difficult time in the land we've just been visiting. We thought about you, sitting here without food. And we realized that you prefer food that is unlike the food that we eat, small insects that dig up the soil."

"We also eat maize, but we don't cook it."

"We eat it raw."

"We clearly had to find something for you to eat, even if it were about to die."

"Just as long as it was slaughtered before it actually died."

"So we made thieves of ourselves. We decided that we should take the eyes of a sheep belonging to the white man who has domesticated us, then transplant those eyes onto you."

"We also decided that we should dig into the raw flesh of the sheep with our beaks, so that we could bring some meat to you."

"Here it is. We tried our best."

"But we know that you don't eat this meat raw."

"Bring us a can, a big one."

"Even if it's dirty."

The crows put the meat into the can, then dipped some water at a dam near this great forest. They poured water into this can.

Because they were in a forest, there was plenty of wood. Well, dear friends, they asked for fire from some boys who were tending the village herds. They got the fire from them, and a fire was kindled there. The meat was cooked.

Then the crows said, "We might well be killed by our owner, because we're really supposed to be the guardians of the sheep. If they get lost, we're supposed to tell the boys where they are."

"But today, we won't be entirely reliable. We'll have to pretend ignorance as to where this sheep has gone."

"You'll have to be satisfied with the meat, Father, even though it's unsalted."

"We really couldn't go directly to our owner and ask for salt for the sheep we had stolen from him."

The man, blind as he was, was grateful. He ate and ate, and as he did so the land about him began to seem different to him; this was, after all, the second month of starvation for him. And he had no one to talk to all this time. He ate now, he ate and ate.

Then, because this man's jaws had locked, one of the crows said, "You really must try to drink the broth, even though it's unsalted, so that your blood begins to flow again."

He drank the broth, as the crows had suggested. They thereby helped him to unlock his jaws; he was not even speaking properly. He drank the broth from this big, dirty can in which the meat had been cooked. When he had finished drinking the broth, he was fed the meat by the crows. Again and again, they fed him, using their beaks. The crows' beaks were ugly, but the man considered them beautiful, because they had brought him back from death. He was grateful for that, Friends.

Then the crows departed. As they did so, they said, "We'll do all we can to help you to see—at least, to see a little."

The man thanked them, and the crows flew off.

Time passed for that man. This was his condition: the pain remained as intense as ever, but his stomach was full now. So time passed for that man, and dawn came.

The crows returned.

"Father."

He responded.

They asked him how he was.

He said that he was much better, at least as far as his hunger was concerned. But the pain in his eyes still troubled him. Even though he had a full stomach now, "I'm still unable to leave this place and set out for my home. I haven't found any work, and the problem that originally drove me from my home will remain unsolved if I should turn back now. The problem is unsolved, it still waits on me."

The crows spoke to him:

"What you say is sensible."

"Follow this little plan. When it dawns and you get up, take the dew from the grass. The grass will be wet at dawn, take the dew from the grass. Then urinate. Urinate on that hand, mix your urine with the dew. Then splash yourself on these eyes. See if there isn't at least a little change."

Gxam thanked them. The birds left him a few things to eat, things that they had taken from their master. They gave these things to this man, to assuage his hunger.

Then the crows departed. When they had left, the man, Gxam, remained behind here. He was hopeful now, because his hunger pangs had been alleviated somewhat by these crows. Maybe his eyes, too, would get better. As of that moment, this man could not see even a blurred image. He could see nothing at all.

The crows departed, and the man remained behind, hopeful. To tell the truth, even the food brought by the birds did not taste very good anymore. And dawn seemed a long time in coming. He slept.

Morning came.

By the time the first cocks crowed, this man was already on his knees. It was hard for him to sleep that night, as he waited for the next day to come so that he might touch the dew.

Well then, Friends, dawn came. And the first cock crowed.

Gxam immediately got up. He stood, blind as he was, and fumbled around. Soon enough, he discovered that there was dew. It was as if it had been raining, yet there had been no rain at all. He gathered that dew and urinated on it, as he had been instructed. He urinated on the water that he had gathered from the grass, he urinated on it. Then he splashed this liquid into his eyes, and waited for what would happen.

He poured the last bit of the liquid into his eyes, repeating the process again and again. He poured it into his eyes.

Time passed.

Tears came from his eyes.

Tears came from his eyes, tears came from his eyes, tears ran from the eyes of this man. He persevered. His eyes continued to tear for a time, and he repeatedly wiped them. He wiped his eyes again and again.

Now, everything was blurred. There was some blurring now in his eyes. Then, one eye could make out some blurred silhouettes, the dim outlines of a human being, of a tree. A tree made an impression on him. He could see, he could see clearly with one eye.

He could not see with the other eye yet, but he could see with one. He was grateful for the sight of one of his eyes, it was better than blindness.

Time passed. Time passed, and at sunset on the day that he had splashed himself with dew, the princesses arrived, the crows.

"Father."

He responded: "Yes."

"How is it?"

He said, "You wonderful birds of God! You have freed me, truly you have! No matter that it's only one eye. Today, I can see you as you perch on this tree. Before, I was unable to see you at all. I could only hear you talking, I couldn't see you. You yourselves had to tell me that you were crows. But now I can see you with this eye. The other eye still cannot see well, it only sees a blur."

The crows were delighted. They laughed, and made sounds characteristic of crows. They were filled with happiness, having discovered that they were magnificent healers. And now they became eager to bring all of their skills to bear on this fellow, to make him whole. In this way, they would acquire a reputation among the other crows.

So, my friends, they said, "This is what you must do, Father."

"You can see that the sun is about to set. Now, when you awaken tomorrow, perform the same action with the dew."

"Concentrate even more on this eye."

"But don't neglect the other one. It too will be capable of sight!"

So the man again slept on his knees.

And the dawn came.

When it was morning, Gxam threw himself on the dew, gathering the dew, gathering it. He gathered the dew, then urinated on it. Then he poured the liquid into this eye. The eye would fill up, and the liquid would spill over into his ears.

Well, the man kept doing this with vigor. He poured it into his eyes again and again, then wiped himself off. This continued for a long time.

He was able to see with this other eye, too!

The man began to look around.

"Oh! What land is this? Where have I been?"

He had become slightly deranged during these past weeks; it had been some time since this person had parted from his brains; it had happened when he had been blinded. He had not been able to see nor to eat to fill his stomach.

Well, there he was, looking around in that way. And he waited there. The crows had not yet returned.

He could see now!

He could see, with the second eye as well. Both eyes could see clearly now. Thoughts of the journey that he had undertaken were on his mind now. But he was certain that he would not depart until he met with these crows who had freed him from his plight. So he waited.

The sun set, and the crows had not yet arrived.

In the morning, before the sun rose, the crows returned. While they were still far off, the man was already saying, "I am here, dear friends! I am here, my dear friends! I am here, wonderful birds of life!"

They approached him. They too were filled with happiness.

"Why is he looking around like that?"

"As if he can see with both eyes!"

The crows were talking to each other. They eventually arrived, and perched there.

"Father."

He responded.

"How are you?"

"What can I say, wonderful birds of life? I am well! I am so well that I am thinking about resuming the journey that I had undertaken. But I did not want to leave until you returned, you who have liberated me from my predicament. Though I possess nothing, I want to make a promise to you."

"Oh!" The crows were pleased. They appreciated the honor being given to them.

They pushed back Gxam's eyelids and examined him, looking into his eyes. They threw some little things a distance away, then suggested that he go and fetch them—very small things, he was sent to pick them up. They satisfied themselves that he could see well now.

They said, "You're free today!"

"You can proceed on the journey that you had undertaken until you were blinded under this tree by your friends from your own homeland."

The man thanked them.

They asked him, "What is the purpose of this journey of yours?"

"I wanted to go and find work. And I also wanted to get married, I haven't married yet."

"Oh."

"Yes."

"Well, that's all right. We release you."

"But it's important that you conduct your affairs carefully in that land that you're going to, the land in which we live."

"It is a difficult land."

"Terrible things happen there."

"There are people who forget to return to their homes once they get there."

So Gxam went on his way, he walked on, and finally came to a homestead, where he ended his journey. He was determined that, once he had obtained a job and had earned some money, he would take a wife in that same land, if he could find a suitable woman.

Well, Friends, he proceeded and finally came to that homestead. When he got there, he discovered that the man who owned the house was not there. Only his wife was at home.

When he had entered the homestead, the woman asked him where he had come from. She asked this even before he had entered the house.

The man responded, "I come from home, I've come to seek work."

She said, "Oh!"

"And I'm also anxious because I'm still a bachelor and have no wife. Once I have a worthwhile job, I hope to find a wife for myself. When I return to my home, I should have a wife."

This woman said, "Haven't you heard about this place? Didn't you ask as you travelled? Didn't you ask if this is the homestead from which no one ever departs?"

"No, I didn't inquire about that."

She said, "Look here, no one ever leaves this homestead! Many unusual things must have happened to you along the way, you couldn't have missed them! Those things should have suggested to you what happens here!" She went on, "One thing is certain: it is rare for anyone to return to his home once he has come to this place. The man of this homestead is very cruel."

Now Gxam became concerned; he could not understand what was happening. To the casual observer, this was a beautiful, respectable homestead. He could in good conscience have become a servant here, he could have taken work that would have enabled him to obtain the things that he wanted.

She said, "This is what you must do. There is no way I can help you, because you're already here. Surely, when you were sitting under that tree, something occurred before the crows arrived."

It was the wife of the man of this homestead who said that.

Gxam could not imagine what the man himself looked like.

He said, "I was in great pain at the time. I remember now that the first thing that came by was a bee. But because I was in such intense pain—my eyes were aching horribly—I didn't pay much attention. However, on the third day, I did manage to pay some attention to the words spoken by this bee. It kept calling me 'Gxam,' and I responded, because Gxam is my name.

"I was very hungry, I had been sitting under this tree not eating. And I could hear that there were many bees under the tree. There was also a crevice. I wanted to crawl towards the crevice to get some honey to eat.

"Then this bee came out and said, 'Gxam, don't eat any of this honey! If you don't eat the honey, one day, when things are difficult for you, I'll help you!'

"That's what I heard from this bee. But I was in such pain that I didn't heed its words.

"On the fourth day, the bee came again, just as I was crawling to help myself to the honey.

"And once again the bee remonstrated with me: 'Don't eat our honey. One day, when you're in difficulty, I'll help you.'

"So I left the honey alone. The thing that kept me from raiding the honey was the arrival of the two crows. That's what really kept me from going to the hive for honey.

"It was on that fourth day that the bee said, 'Look here, your condition will be alleviated by two crows, they've taken pity on you. Now, you're going to meet a person irrigating plants in the forest. That person will say to you, "Please convey my greetings over there at Malikophu's home. Say that I, the one who must irrigate endlessly, ask what I can do. What can I do to terminate all this?" You should walk on then. Next, you'll encounter a person who is walking upside down. He'll say, "Hello, Gxam! Convey my greetings when you get to Malikophu's home. Tell of me, the one whose fate it is to walk upside down, who has long since become tired but has no way to end it: What can he do to walk properly?" You should listen to his words, but don't reply. Just keep on going. When you reach that place, you'll find the woman of the house, and she'll question you. But even as she questions you, you'll know all about it already. Approach the house in the normal way, she knows that it's the way people come to her home. But her husband kills such people. The woman will take pity on you.

"Now, this is what you must do. When her husband arrives, he'll get a scent of you before he even enters the house. You'll have arrived before he gets there, and the woman will take you and hide you in a cupboard. Remain quiet in that cupboard, don't move. Do not make any commotion, don't turn over, do nothing. Move only during her husband's absence. You will hear him speak once he has entered the house. You must keep still then!"

That is what the bee had said, the bee that would not allow Gxam to eat its honey under that thorn tree. And Gxam was grateful for the bee's advice.

He recalled the matter of the bee because of the woman of this homestead he had now come to. When he had regained his sight, he had rushed off to this homestead, and everything that the bee had said had been forgotten. He had remembered only what the crows had said, the ones who had restored his sight and enabled him to continue his quest for work.

Well, Friends, he just sat there. Time passed in that homestead, in the home of the man he could not at all envision. And when the woman had questioned him regarding the bee, he pondered all these things.

The woman said, "This is what you must do. Sit here, in this cupboard. I'll lock you in. I'll give you riches. You'll be wealthy in your own land, if you can reach your home with the fine things that I give you. But many people die before they obtain my husband's riches.

"My husband's riches—his feathers!

"If a person should get even one of those feathers, he shall become so wealthy that even his offspring will become notables! I'm going to reward you for your perseverance in coming here, and because of all your needless suffering under that tree. I shall steal four feathers for you from my husband—his name, by the way, is Malikophu. I'll try all sorts of tricks to keep him from noticing you, to keep him from getting up once he is resting in the house."

So, Friends, he remained there in the cupboard, anxious, trembling. Because it was her house, the woman had nothing to worry about: she was well looked after. She had some vessels that were on top of the cupboard. Even though the man inside the cupboard was not saying a word, the vessels on top of the cupboard were rattling because he was trembling inside.

She said, "Let me just take these dishes and put them inside. The noise the dishes are making! As soon as my husband enters, he'll want to know why the cupboard is shaking like this!"

So the woman of the house hurried about; she took all the vessels down, then packed them and put them into the cupboard. She told Gxam to sit on top of them. They would not shake so noticeably there as they had when they were on top of the cupboard. So he had to put up with that.

Time passed. But the quaking did not stop, because Gxam could not be sure of anything: he was worried because of the things that had been said about this man with the feathers, a man who kills people and devours them.

Time passed, Gxam waited.

The approach of Malikophu, the monster, was unmistakable. He came with a storm. The house, situated among trees, trembled; the trees shook. Gxam remained in the cupboard, exercising self-control.

This thing came in. When it had entered, while still standing at the door, it inquired of its wife, "What's this unusual smell?"

The woman said, "What smell?"

"There's an unusual smell here at home! When I sense such odors, I usually do something about them!"

"No! No, there's nothing here. What could it be? I have nothing that smells!"

He said, "No, it's not you who smells. There's the unusual scent of sweat here at home."

By "sweat" he meant the odor of a strange person. "Or perhaps it's the smell of an animal clinging to you."

The woman denied that there was anything like a strange odor in the house. She bustled about her husband, insisting that he have something to eat. He ate what she offered. He was calm, not in a hurry, and then he said that he was tired. But she did not suggest that he go to bed. She thought, "Going to bed might be awkward." Then: "Why should I make you walk to the inside room? Why don't you just sleep here, with your head on my lap, while I delouse you a bit?"

So Malikophu put his head on his wife's lap, and she deloused the man. Gradually, he fell into a deep sleep.

After a while, as the man slept, she took one feather—quickly, vigorously, she plucked it, then put it beside her.

Time passed, then this man said, "I had a dream. It was as if there were a human being, someone who seems to have come looking for a job at Malikophu's place. It seems that you told him that you would give this person great wealth, that you would give him four of Malikophu's feathers and thereby enrich him, because he deserved such wealth, considering the hardships he experienced in his travels, in his efforts to find a job."

The woman said, "No, there's nothing like that! Dreams are only dreams, they don't mean anything. Sometimes they merely portend what is still to come. After all, you would have seen such a person. And you can see that there's no one here at home."

So he went back to sleep. When he had again been overcome by sleep, as she stroked him gently, massaging him, caressing him as he slept, she again swiftly plucked a feather, the second, and she put it beside her.

Again, the monster stirred. "I had a dream. It seems that this person was in a cupboard. His eyes had been put out by other men. He had met with someone who was irrigating plants in the forest, who said to him, 'Convey my greetings to those at Malikophu's place. Ask Malikophu what can be done to help one who must irrigate endlessly?' Now, Human-who-is-in-the-cupboard, this is what you must tell that being who irrigates endlessly: Malikophu says that he should rise early and take the dew and splash himself with it the way you did when you followed the advice of the crows. He'll immediately terminate all that."

When he had said that, the monster almost got up. But his wife soothed him, and said, "No, it's only a dream, merely a dream. You know what a dream is like. One may dream, one may dream of something, yet it hasn't happened yet. It's still to come, it's something that hasn't happened. Because the fact is, I haven't seen anyone here at home like the one you mention. And you would have seen him too. There's the cupboard over there. You can see for yourself that it's empty. There's nothing in it. Now take a nap, while I delouse you."

So she stroked him, she caressed this man. And sleep came to Malikophu. Then she plucked another feather, the third one. Now, only one remained: four were needed.

The monster woke again, and said, "I dreamt about that man in the cupboard again. As he was coming to my homestead, he met someone, a person who was walking upside down. This person who was walking upside down asked him to convey a message at Malikophu's place: when someone walks on his hands, with his legs in the air, what must he do to walk properly?" Malikophu said, "This is what you should say. Say that Malikophu says that this person should take an egg that was laid by a hen, then hit himself with it on the forehead. He'll be able to stand on his feet then, he'll be able to walk upright on both feet. Then he can stop walking on his hands, with his feet dangling in the air."

During all this, Gxam, that person over there in the cupboard, was listening to everything that Malikophu was saying. He knew that Malikophu was answering all the requests made of him during his journey.

So, my friends, this monster now said, "Someone did ask that question! And what I have said should be reported to that person."

When the monster wanted to get up again, his wife gently restrained him: "Sleep on, my dear. You're tired. Sleep, you are tired. Don't allow dreams to awaken you. Dreams are signs of health. One might dream of something that hasn't happened yet. And sometimes one dreams of something that happened at some other place, but not here. Now go to sleep, let me delouse you."

She kept massaging her husband, stroking him, talking softly to him. Malikophu, overcome by drowsiness, again fell asleep. Then his wife plucked another feather, the fourth.

When she had plucked that feather—well, Malikophu woke up. When he had awakened, he said, "I dreamt that the person in the cupboard now wants to leave. Not only that, he has an understanding with my daughter, that my daughter should become his wife."

The woman said, "Well, we haven't heard anything about that yet. Sleep, go to sleep. If that were true, we would know of it. After all, she is your daughter! You would hear of it directly from the fellow who is seeking your daughter in marriage, not in dreams. I haven't even seen the fellow you're talking about."

So the monster went back to sleep. And when he was sleeping soundly, the woman slowly moved him onto the pillow and put him to sleep; she covered him gently with his blankets. But she plucked no more feathers from him. There were enough feathers now, four of them.

Then she took that fellow, Gxam, from the cupboard, and told him to leave.

She said, "Look here, you must go! And be prepared. If he wakes up while you're still near this homestead, you're as good as dead! Now, as for the daughter of this homestead, the one you wish to marry—reach an understanding with her—she is his favorite daughter. She knows more about her father's magic than even I do."

Magic is an evil business. It is witchcraft, a secret means of support.

She said, "Now, I have two daughters. The younger one has her father's skill to an extraordinary degree. She's the one you should want. And both of you should leave, now!"

The fellow was delighted. He talked to the young woman, and they reached an understanding. The woman admonished her daughter, telling her, "Look here, if you accept this suitor, take some of your father's feathers with you. You know all about your father's magic, you've shared his secrets. You'll be able to save this child who comes from another homestead, as well as yourself. If I should even appear to be associated with this plan of yours, your father will kill me."

The daughter expressed her thanks. Then, while her father was still sleeping, she hurried to a tall tree that was in this homestead, and she took down some bird's eggs. A certain bird that belonged to her father had laid some eggs up there. She took the eggs down, six of them. Then she took her father's horse. She mounted the horse, carrying those six eggs. Both she and the young man, Gxam, got on the horse, and they set off, as the dust swirled around them.

Off they went on the horse, on the back of that horse. They departed, riding on the back of the horse, on the back of that horse. This horse was called Horse-of-the-wind.

When Gxam and Malikophu's daughter had gone a great distance, the monster woke from his sleep. And when he had awakened, he said, "I dreamt that I had sustained great losses. It seems my daughter had run off with my Horse-of-the-wind, and she also took my magic eggs! She left with the eggs in the company of that fellow who was in the cupboard, the very man I mentioned earlier."

His wife said, "Well, I can't respond to that, because I know of no one who was in the cupboard. You're the one who slept and dreamed all this. All the while, I was wide awake, I was not dreaming. My eyes have been wide open, and I saw no one in the cupboard. I should think that if you had seen him, you would have seized him."

He said, "My daughter has run off!"

And Malikophu ran outside, in a rage. He caught his other horse, and gave chase. Off he went at a fierce speed, raising dust as he pursued them.

They were a long way off when the young woman looked back.

She said, "Gxam!"

He responded.

"We're as good as dead!"

"Why do you say that?"

The young woman said, "There's my father, over there! Do you see him? Over there! That's my father! You can see the cloud of dust that's coming this way! I'm dead today, and so are you! Can you do anything for me?"

He said, "I'll do what I can, because I'm the one who took you out of your father's gates. You saved me, too. You and your mother saved me."

She said, "All right, let's push on."

They pressed forward. The horse that this young woman had taken had more of Malikophu's magic than the one that Malikophu was riding. And the young woman thoroughly understood her father's mind.

The horse that Malikophu was riding was second to her horse. The young woman had the horse and six eggs, and therefore had the greater advantage in this chase.

She had taken the bundle of eggs and had buried it at the place where her father would have taken some grass from the bundle. Now her father would not find the bundle: all he had was the horse.

Then, dear ones, they came to that person who was walking on his hands. He had been the last one the young man, Gxam, had met on his travels, and now he was the first one they met on their way home.

He said, "You told me to ask for advice as to how you might be able to walk properly. Well, you must hit yourself on the forehead with an egg that has been laid by a hen. Then you'll be able to walk normally."

That fellow expressed his thanks.

Then they came to the person who had been irrigating endlessly in the forest.

"The reply to you, you and your endless irrigating, is that you should splash yourself with dew."

He expressed his thanks, and Gxam and Malikophu's daughter passed on.

But the monster was gradually closing in on them.

Once again, the young woman said, "Gxam."

He responded.

She said, "My father has all but caught up with us. Because of my love for you, I shall put him through some painful business, even though he raised me. How will you treat me then?"

Gxam said, "I'll treat you as well as I am able."

She said, "Just watch. I'll put my father through some changes before your eyes. Right now!"

She took out an egg, a green one, from among those six magic eggs from her home, and she took aim at her father's forehead. She hit the target. A great forest immediately appeared, it rose thick and dark before her father. The daughter and her husband were on the other side of the forest.

This young woman said, "You see now, Gxam."

Gxam said, "I see."

"When he began to chase us, he forgot to take an axe with him. He must return to my home now. And that's a great distance from here. We've crossed three rivers. My father must go home to fetch an axe, so that he can cut down all these trees. Now, how will you treat me?"

Gxam said, "I'll treat you well, no matter what happens."

Malikophu, confronted by the forest, stopped his horse, and said, "My daughter got me this time!"

He turned back to get an axe from his home, so that he could fell the trees of the forest, to cut a way through. There was no way he could penetrate the forest on horse-back. He had to return to his home to get an axe.

Meanwhile, the other two were pushing ahead.

Malikophu reached his home, and took an axe. Then he mounted his horse again. But the horse was by now quite tired: it did not have the same strength as Horse-of-the-wind, the horse that the young woman was riding.

Malikophu cut down five trees, then he rested. He reclined in the shade, resting. He was tired.

The others continued to travel on. They did not rest.

At length, Malikophu demolished the forest. He did so by means of his magic. You see, the axe was not an ordinary axe. He had cut down five trees. Then, when he had cut the sixth, the entire forest collapsed. The axe was enchanted. And Malikophu himself was potent with magic. The entire forest came down. He left the axe there, he did not have time to take it back home.

He resumed the chase, he pursued them.

Gxam and his wife, very much in love, were far distant now, so they sat down for a while under a big tree to stretch their limbs. The young woman knew what her father was going through back there; she knew that he would have a hard time overcoming the obstacles that she had placed so quickly in his way. So they sat down for a while, and reclined here in the shade. She rested there with her husband.

Then the young woman said, "Let's go on! He's fairly close now, he's just back there. He'll come into view any minute now."

And, indeed, as she and her husband began to mount the horse, Malikophu suddenly appeared on his steed.

The young woman said, "Gxam."

Gxam responded.

She said, "There's my father! He keeps chasing me, I have to create a second difficulty for him. I've already made him cut down a huge forest, now I must put another obstacle in his way. Even though he is my father, even though he is the one who reared me, I shall do this because of my love for you."

The six eggs were not of the same color, each was different. The young woman took one of them, a white one this time, and, when Malikophu was fairly near, she took careful aim. She was mounted on her Horse-of-the-wind, the horse that belonged to her father, and she aimed at the forehead of her father's horse. She threw the egg, and suddenly everything turned into an expansive lake; there was no way for Malikophu to cross it.

He tried to pursue them, but there was no way now for him to proceed. So he dismounted, and sought a plan whereby he might deal with this problem.

What could he do about this?

"I'll go back home and get a bucket. I'll empty the pool, I'll bail the water out, and pour it onto the rock. Then, when the level of water in the lake has been lowered, I'll be able to cross."

So Malikophu turned back, to fetch a bucket from the house.

Meanwhile, the others travelled on, they hurried on.

Malikophu got a bucket, and he drained the lake. He dipped five times with the bucket, and when he dipped the sixth time, the lake dried up, and he crossed over.

He took up the chase again.

When Malikophu's daughter and Gxam were a long way off, the young woman said, "Gxam."

Gxam said, "Yes?"

She said, "That's my father over there! What shall I do to my father now? I'll pitch a third obstacle in front of him. I shall do this to him, even though he is the one who brought me up—I shall do it because of my love for you. Will you take care of me?"

Gxam said, "No matter what happens, I shall care for you. If necessary, I shall die for you."

Malikophu approached, covered with dust now, soiled and wrapped in dust. He advanced towards them, he came on relentlessly.

The young woman took another egg. She took another egg, and threw it, and hit his horse.

Great cliffs suddenly appeared. There was no way a horse could move in such a place. The young man and his wife were on the other side of the cliffs.

She said, "You see now, my father is on the other side of the cliffs. We're on the opposite side, travelling on a level road."

Gxam said, "Yes, let's pass on."

So they moved on, they travelled on.

Malikophu was puzzled. "What shall I do?" The cliffs presented a problem for him. "What'll I do? I must go back and get a pickaxe and dig this cliff up. I must make it fall, so that I can go on."

So he turned back, to fetch a pickaxe from the house. He came back with the pickaxe and with crossbars for leverage. He intended to roll the stones down, to clear an open road. With these implements, he dislodged six rocks, and, amazingly, a level stone surface appeared. He and his horse quickly moved onto this surface. He left the pickaxe behind.

When they were still a long way off, the young woman looked back and said, "Gxam."

He said, "Yes?"

She said, "Can you see my father? He must have dislodged those rocks by now." She added, "You see, all he has to do is remove six rocks, and the entire cliff will crumble, the way will again be clear for him. Look there! You can see him, there's my father! He's coming! What shall I do?"

Gxam said, "I don't know. I'm depending on you. I know nothing about your father's magic, you know that."

She said, "Well, this'll be the fourth obstacle that I shall create for my father. I've already put three difficulties in his way. Now, I'll put a fourth. But will you look after me?"

Gxam said, "Of course I'll look after you."

"All right then."

The young woman took another egg, the fourth one, a red one.

When her father came fairly near to her, he said, "My daughter!"

The young woman responded.

He said, "Do you value that young man more than your own life? And mine?"

The young woman said, "The decision has been made."

So saying, she threw the red egg.

Flames rose, and the entire forest and all the grass that was in front of them were instantly ablaze. In the midst of the flames as it was, Malikophu's horse was unable to go on.

The husband and wife moved on, they were on the other side of the blaze.

The young woman said, "Gxam!"

Gxam said, "Yes?"

"Do you see where my father is? He's over there, I'm scorching him in this firestorm. I am with you!"

Gxam said, "I hear you, I can see what's happening."

"Will you look after me?"

He said, "Yes."

They travelled on.

Malikophu and his horse turned back; he took the bucket that he had left behind, and he dipped water from that pool. He dipped water with this bucket, and poured it on the flames. Immediately, the fire was put out, and he moved on, in pursuit.

When they were a long way off, the young woman looked back, and said, "Gxam!"

Gxam responded.

She said, "Do you see my father? Because of my love for you, I'm going to put the fifth obstacle in his way. I wonder, Gxam, if you'll treat me well."

Gxam said, "I shall even die for you."

Malikophu was approaching on his horse. The young woman continued her flight on Horse-of-the-wind. How many eggs remained now? There were two eggs left. There were only the fifth, the one that she was about to use, and the last one, the sixth.

Her father drew nearer, he came straight towards them. As he gradually came nearer, the young woman said, "You see now, I'm going to put my father through a lot of trouble again. I really don't know what will come of all this, as far as you are concerned."

When her father was fairly near, the young woman took one of the eggs, the fifth, and she threw it at her father. When she had thrown the egg, great rifts appeared in the earth. It was not possible to walk on such riven ground, ruptured all over as it was. This occurred just in front of her father; there was no way for his horse to get across.

The animal that Malikophu was riding lacked the particular magic that the other horse had. Had he been astride the steed being ridden by the young woman, he would have been able to fly across: the horse on which the young woman and her husband were riding could do that. But the one that Malikophu was riding derived its power from keeping its feet on the ground.

He could only stand there and say, "My daughter! You're actually going off with this young man!"

His daughter said, "That is the way it is!"

Her father turned back then; he went to fetch spades and pickaxes from his home so that he might fill up these canyon-like crevasses and then move on with his horse.

Meanwhile, the young woman and her husband were continuing their flight. As Malikophu turned back, they went on.

Malikophu went back to get those pickaxes and spades, so that the fissures could be filled and a way made for him to continue his pursuit. While the two travelled on, Malikophu filled the gorges with a spade and a pickaxe. Then he again gave chase, following his daughter and the young man who was running off with her, that young man who had come to seek his daughter. They pressed on, but Malikophu kept stalking them, not knowing that this time might be, for him, disastrous. Still, rather than turn back, he wanted to destroy his daughter. By this time, he wanted only the life of his daughter and that of the person who was running off with her, that was all he wanted.

When Malikophu was fairly close to them, the young woman said, "Gxam!"

Gxam responded.

She said, "Do you see now? The eggs are finished. There's only one left, it's the last one!"

Gxam said, "Yes, I see that."

She said, "Do you see this egg? It is *the* egg, the mother and father of all the other eggs. This egg is the life of Malikophu. Watch now, I am about to kill my father. I must do that, because if I have compassion on him and allow him to approach close enough to lay hands on us, then *we* shall die. It won't help if I leave him alone. If I use this egg, my father will die, and we shall be able to go to the place to which you want us to go."

That was what she proceeded to do.

Malikophu was filthy, he was grimy with dust. His eyes were bloodshot, full of savagery and cruelty. And when he was quite close to them, he uttered his final words, although he had no idea that these would be his dying words. But the young woman knew.

He said, "My daughter, are you actually accepting this man at the expense of my life? And your life too? And his?"

The young woman said, "You have mentioned three lives. But you've grown quite old now, you've savored a long life, and now you must give way to this young man."

She said that, then threw the sixth egg, and she hit her father on the bridge of his nose.

Malikophu died. So did his horse.

The couple pressed ahead effortlessly now.

Malikophu died, and so did his horse.

The young woman, astride her spirited horse, rode on with the young man.

After the death of Malikophu, she said, "I have been telling you what to do all along the way. Now, however, I won't be instructing you anymore. I'll only give you one piece of guidance. After that, I shall be submissive to you. I shall be under your protection, I shall submit to you."

So it was that the young woman had killed her father with the last of the six eggs. Her father was dead, he did not get up again. And Malikophu's daughter journeyed on with that young man. As she did so, she instructed him one last time: "In time, you will arrive at your home with me. But before that happens, you must leave me for a time. I shall remain in a certain place, I shall go nowhere else. I shall wait for you, just as you waited for me as I struggled with the task of vanquishing my father."

The young man, Gxam, agreed. By now, he was able to see the land of his birth once again; he was in the country of his people—actually, quite near to his home.

When he reached the final river, preparatory to entering the vicinity of his home, he took the young woman to a certain place and told her to remain in a large tree. He hid her securely, so that he could go home and tidy up, so that he could make his home presentable because he was returning with a very beautiful person.

The young woman continued with her final instructions to him: "When you get home, do not greet your people with a handshake, just salute them verbally. If you should shake hands, then you shall forget about me. Remember that, you should not even touch them with your hand. Express affection only with your eyes. If you so much as brush them, they'll take away my magic. You'll feel as if you're touching me, and then you'll forget about me."

So the young man went home, leaving the woman in the tree that was overhanging the place where the people of his area dipped water.

He arrived at his home. As he was approaching his homestead, his dogs rushed out to welcome him and to express their affection. Feeling good about this, Gxam found himself lifting one of the dogs. Then he put it down, and went on to the house. Because he felt so good, he shook hands expansively; he had, after all, been blinded, and had thought that he would never again be able to see his people. So he did all that, greeting and petting his dogs, raising some of them to his chest.

And he forgot about the bride he had left in that tree that was overhanging the place where the people of his area dipped water.

Time passed there. Night came, and he slept.

The next morning, his youngest sister went early to dip water, so that breakfast could be prepared. When she reached the river, as she was dipping with a vessel, she looked into the water.

"I can't dip water and put it on my head! I'm too beautiful for such a task!"

She would not go on, she took the empty bucket and went home. And she reported what had happened.

She was asked, "Where's the water?"

"There were plans," someone said, "for an early breakfast."

She said, "Well, when I looked into the deep pool, I saw how beautiful I am. I could not bring myself to do menial tasks such as dipping and carrying water!"

"And how did you suddenly find out that you're so beautiful?" asked her older sister.

As she said this, she abruptly took a bucket herself, and went off to dip water.

She got to the place, took a dish, and began to dip. But when she looked into the deep pool, she realized that, "No! I cannot possibly dip water. I'm too beautiful! I've not seen this beauty of mine when I've looked into mirrors!"

You must understand that the comeliness of which those young women boasted was actually the splendor of that young woman who was up in the tree. When they saw the bride's reflection in the pool, they thought it was their own likeness, because they knew nothing of that bride. They imagined that somehow, mysteriously, they had become beautiful.

So that young woman returned home as the first woman had, and she too returned without having dipped water.

Now, how would this be resolved?

"There she is, Mother!"

"What?"

"There's my older sister, she's coming back! She's also returning with a noisy bucket. At this rate, there'll be no breakfast in this homestead!"

The mother said, "What you're saying is preposterous, my child, Gxam! Are you suggesting that the child is returning with an empty bucket?"

"Yes, she's coming back with a noisy bucket! Look at her, there she is."

The mother, upset by now, looked.

"What is it?"

"Well, Mother, when I looked in that pool and discovered how attractive I am, I realized that it wasn't really proper for me to do such things as carry a bucket on my head!"

"And how did you suddenly discover that you're so attractive?"

She said, "That surprised me, too! I decided that God had created me anew."

Her mother quickly, angrily, took the bucket herself.

Her son said, "No! No, Mother!" because his mother was quite old, and walked haltingly because she had difficulties with her legs. He said, "I should be the one who goes. I can go quickly, Mother. You just stay here. These two sisters of mine have gone too far. Breakfast is being delayed too long."

So Gxam took the bucket himself, and he hurried to the pool so that breakfast could be prepared, and he still felt very warm towards these people.

And he was hungry.

When he reached the pool, he looked in.

"Oh!"

He remembered.

He remembered, and he cried. He fell on his back. He remembered now the rendezvous that he had set up with Malikophu's daughter, the one who had been prepared to die for him, the one who had gone so far as to kill her own father out of love for this young man.

When he looked into the water, he did not make the error of saying, "The reflection is of me, Gxam."

It all came back to him.

"It's that young woman! I left her in this tree!"

He got up, still dazed.

The young woman gazed at him steadily from her perch in the tree.

"What did I say to you?"

He said, "No, please don't go into the details. I have disregarded your injunction because of some small thing. Please don't punish me for one small act against you. We have many years ahead of us yet before we die. I pledge myself to tolerate many things that you might do, just as you have tolerated me. I did forget about you. When my red dog leapt up at me, I spontaneously raised it to my chest. And I picked up the black one by its foreleg. Then I dropped the dogs, and greeted my mother and those with her, then the memory of the episode of my blinding became vivid to me, how those crows had come to my aid, how I wondered if I would ever see my friends and relatives again. So I forgot about you."

Malikophu's daughter responded, "Gxam, don't you realize that while you expressed affection for *your people*, that *I* had killed my own *father*, that I had left my *mother* behind, alone?"

Gxam pleaded for pardon: "Forgive me! What you say is true, I have committed an offense against you. Don't censure me! I have seen your capacity to inflict punishments even more severe than your father's! My own father does not have that ability. I pledge my life. Watch me, and see if I ever commit another misdeed like this one. Please, let's go home!"

The young woman said, "I feel compassion for you. Take me down."

Gxam swiftly climbed the tree, he slipped and broke his skin again and again. His legs bled, because he was attempting to climb in such a hurry, as if this young woman might take it all back, as if this young woman might do to Gxam what she had done to Malikophu, her father. So Gxam allowed himself to become bruised as he climbed, and fell.

The young woman said, "Don't rush! I just said that you should take me down. Be steady as you climb."

So he steadied himself, he ascended, going up the tree to get the young woman and to bring her down. He descended with her then, and took her to his home.

She became his wife.

His parents rejoiced when they saw the magnificent person who had appeared to those children when they had gone to dip water, and who had mistaken her image in the water to be their own. That image actually belonged to Gxam's wife.

"Gxam has taken a wife."

He was honored, sheep geldings were slaughtered. When someone has taken a wife among the Xhosa, there is a ritual slaughtering. A goat is slaughtered, so that the bride might taste the food of this homestead.

They slaughtered a gelded goat for Malikophu's daughter; it was a fully grown goat, one that had all eight teeth, so that she should taste the food of this homestead and know herself to be a wife.

Time passed. When this daughter of Malikophu had given birth to her second child, she suggested to her husband that they go and fetch her mother and bring her here. They were very happy together, and Gxam was always very obliging to his wife. He worked hard for her, and now possessed magic that enabled him to become wealthy in a short time. He had obtained this magic from Malikophu's daughter, largely because of those feathers that had been plucked from Malikophu, those four feathers.

So Malikophu's wife was brought; she came to live here at her daughter's homestead by marriage. They built a handsome homestead for the mother, so that she would be happy living here with her daughter.

So it was that Malikophu's daughter became Gxam's wife. They had now completed the process of marriage. And Gxam made his wife happy by bringing her parent to his homestead. He had accepted the woman with warmth, he looked after her and built a homestead for her.

Emily Ntsobane

THE DEADLY PUMPKIN

(XHOSA)

Emily Ntsobane, a Hlubi woman, performed this story on September 28, 1967, in the late afternoon. The performance took place at the back of a home in Mgugwani, Lusikisiki District, in the Transkei. Mrs. Ntsobane, originally from Matatiele District in the Transkei, was forty years old. The audience consisted of some fifteen children and teenagers. (786; tape 18, side 1)

A certain man married. His wife arrived at his home, and she conceived; she bore a child who was a girl. Time passed, and that child grew up.

During the time of harvesting, this wife regularly went to the fields with her husband, she went to harvest all day with her husband.

And this child grew up.

One day, this woman returned from the fields carrying a pumpkin on her head. When she got home, she planned to kindle a fire.

But when she was on the upper side of her homestead, the pumpkin fell down, it slipped and dropped from her head. It rolled down to a river, where it disappeared.

"This pumpkin! What is this thing that fell from my head?" she wondered. "It rolled all that distance to the river, then it sank!"

No one answered her.

The wife entered her house, and kindled a fire. Then she put her baby on her back, and told her story to her husband: "Father of Nobani, I was coming back, carrying that pumpkin—you saw it yourself, when I was picking it up. I carried it with me when we returned from the fields. Now, when I was just above the homestead, the pumpkin slipped and fell. And it disappeared in the water of the river. I'm puzzled by this matter. What caused it? What does it mean?"

The husband said, "Wife, how were you holding the pumpkin when it fell from your head? How were you holding it when it dropped from your head, when it came to fall?"

She said, "I was carrying it the way I have always carried things."

"Well then, this is an evil omen! You were carrying something on your head, it slipped and fell, and disappeared in the river. Why didn't you catch it? Were you unable to seize the pumpkin as it slipped and fell from your head?"

"I was rattled, it was a bewildering situation."

"Well, light the fire," he grumbled. "It was my food that you allowed to disappear in the river."

"This pumpkin emerged, it grew and grew." Emily Ntsobane, a Xhosa storyteller.

"You talk as if it's the first time that you've seen food," she said, as she continued to kindle the fire.

The husband was silent. He put tobacco into his pipe, and smoked. He was angry because of the loss of the pumpkin. He had hoped to eat some pumpkin porridge.

Time passed for them then, and they slept.

They got up in the morning, and returned to the fields. They harvested.

That child of hers was growing up: finally, breasts appeared and she was prepared to enter womanhood. The father said to his wife, "Mabani, I want to initiate this child of mine into womanhood. I want to initiate her, I want her to enter womanhood now."

She said, "Will you take it upon yourself to initiate her?"

"Yes, I shall do it. I shall slaughter three oxen and two hogs for the ritual."

"All right. When you initiate this child, you must prepare her to grow up in good health."

"Yes, I agree with you, my wife."

So it was that on a certain day the husband gathered his family to provide the initiation rite for his daughter.

The family arrived. They said, "Our brother, are you sure that you will initiate her with a properly elaborate celebration?"

He said, "My friends, and you my elder brothers, the celebration will be appropriately large, I swear to it. I shall slaughter three oxen here above the kraal and two gelded hogs—not just little hogs. I am well off, I'm not a starving wretch."

"Please, Brother," these men said, "please, our brother, we will watch what you do. Please brew some beer."

"I shall brew a great quantity of beer," this man said in connection with his feelings about his child. "I shall brew a great quantity of beer. I shall brew this beer, no one will complain about any vessel of beer and say that he is hungry. I shall apportion food to all of the assembly. I won't apportion little dishes to them. No, I shall bring out pots that will stand in front of various groups of the assembly. They'll all get something, I'll see to it."

"Well then, please go on, Son of my father, we shall hear from you, lest, perhaps, the matter prove too much for you, the matter which you are in such a hurry to conduct."

It happened then, on Friday, that he said, "The women should first stand in the yard and sing ritual songs."

So the women first stood in the yard, they sang the ritual songs.

Then, after dinner, he stabbed one of the hogs.

His daughter entered the house, the girls picking up grass to spread on the floor of the initiation house, singing fine songs.

In the morning, this fellow killed the three oxen and the hogs as a part of the ritual for his child. This fellow conducted this ritual for his daughter in grand style.

His brothers were heard saying, "We did not fully understand the matter that is being carried out by the son of our father, we did not believe that it would succeed."

They spoke as he took the beer out of the vats and pots, apportioning it to the people. Now he was directing the ritual, and it was clear that not one person would complain that he was hungry. He was taking out meat now in style, providing the ritual for this child here, providing the ritual celebration for his child's coming of age.

As for the child, she was to remain in the house. She would not soon emerge from the house.

In the morning, people ate what was left. On that day, the feet and head were cooked. It happened on that day that the man said, "It is necessary that we travel a far distance now. We must travel and go to harvest in the fields, because that corn over there will be spoiled, the livestock may tamper with it, and we'll begin to have irritating troubles. The people have caused my corn to be eaten by the livestock, we have been negligent here at home and have not gone to work on our corn. When we go, we shall leave the child alone in the house here at home. We must harvest, and we shall leave her behind, having cooked for her. We must again return and give her food, that she might eat."

Her mother said, "You are right, Father of Nobani, and I, too, I don't see anything amiss about this. We shall leave her behind, having cooked for her, and we shall return in the afternoon. She will remain by herself here in the house."

They got up in the morning, and travelled to the fields. They left this child behind, remaining alone here in the house while they were harvesting in the fields.

Then, at breakfast, the pumpkin that had disappeared over there in the water was heard ascending:
Rumble-rumble-rattle,
O ye ye ye eha.
Rumble-rumble-rattle,
O ye ye ye eha.
The pumpkin arrived, it stopped at the entrance. It rolled into the house, and fell on its side.
The pumpkin said, "Girl!"
She said, "Yes?"
It said, "Whom do you live with?"
She said, "I am alone."
It said, "Why do you say 'I am alone' instead of 'I am awone'?"
She said, "I am awone."

It said, "Come out, I'm your sister."

This girl came out, and the pumpkin made her fall, then tore her flesh, it cut her on the body, rending her flesh again and again. When it finished with her, it cooked maize in a great hurry. It ground the boiled corn, it mixed boiled maize for her.

The pumpkin said, "Eat, be full. And don't you dare tell your mother and father that I have arrived. Just do it, and you'll know all about me."

The girl was silent, she ate this porridge and finished it. She remained behind the screen, and the pumpkin rolled again:

Rumble-rumble-rattle,

O ye ye ye eha.

Rumble-rumble-rattle,

O ye ye ye eha.

It disappeared in the river.

Soon enough, in the afternoon, her mother and the other women arrived. They prepared the food here, her mother preparing food for her child. She prepared food for her child, and gave it to her.

The child said, "No, Mama, I'm full!"

"Oh! We've been away so long, how can you be full? Aren't you hungry? What's the matter with you?"

She said, "Well, Mama, I'm full. Really, I'm not hungry."

She did not discuss this thing that had arrived there, this pumpkin that had attacked her.

They slept then.

Again, in the morning, they got up. The girl's mother cooked. She got up, and she cooked. Then they left the girl behind.

The mother and father travelled, they went again to the fields. They arrived, and harvested in the fields.

Again, that pumpkin ascended. It arrived,

Rumble-rumble-rattle,

O ye ye ye eha.

It arrived there at the doorway, rolling.

It said, "Girl!"

This girl said, "Yes?"

It said, "Whom do you live with?"

She said, "I am alone."

It said, "Why do you say 'I am alone' instead of 'I am awone'?"

The girl said, "I am awone."

It said, "Come out, I'm your sister."

This girl came out.

Then the pumpkin tore her flesh, it tore her flesh, making incisions over all that body.

Again, it hurriedly cooked maize, it ground the boiled corn, it mixed boiled maize for her. It said, "Eat and be full. And don't tell your mother and father that I came here. If you do tell of me, you'll know all about me!"

The girl entered the house.

She ate hurriedly, then returned to the screen. She remained there.

When the pumpkin was sated, it disappeared in the river.

In the afternoon, her mother and father returned. Her mother returned, she came to the house where the girl was. She arrived there, and cooked hurriedly. She dished up food for her child.

The child said, "No, Mama, I'm full."

"Oh! Nobani, why are you full? This is the second day that you have not eaten! What do you eat?"

She said, "No, Mama, I am full. Really, I am not hungry."

Her mother said, "I'll have to see this thing of yours, this thing that has made it so that you are not hungry for as many as two whole days! You have been staying here behind the screen. While we were still here at home, not yet having gone to the fields, you were eating food and there was no problem."

She said, "No, Mama, don't be distressed because I am full."

They slept then, and early in the morning her mother got up. She cooked food, and told her husband, "No matter when I give Nobani food over there, she says that she is full. I'm puzzled about what she might be eating that causes her to say that she is full."

The husband said, "Well, maybe there is something that she eats, but why worry about it? There is no way you can know when she is hungry. If she were hungry, she would not be saying that she is full."

"Oh, no, Father of Nobani, it confuses me. Perhaps the child is not well."

"Don't have bad thoughts like that about the child while she is in the enclosure. Let's go and harvest."

They travelled, they went to the fields to harvest. They harvested, and as they harvested the pumpkin again ascended.

It arrived at the girl's place:

Rumble-rumble-rattle,

O ye ye ye eha.

It arrived, and stopped at the doorway. It said, "Girl!"

"Yes?"

It said, "With whom are you living?"

She said, "I am alone."

"Why do you say 'I am alone' instead of 'I am awone'?"

She said, "I am awone."

It said, "Come out, I'm your sister."

The girl came out, and the pumpkin beat her, it tore her flesh, it beat all her body, cutting her. This girl already had a slight rotten smell about her in these places where she had been cut by this pumpkin.

Then the pumpkin cooked maize in a great hurry, it cooked it and finished it, it took it out, it ground the boiled corn, then it quickly mixed the boiled corn for her. It gave it to her, saying that she should eat it.

She ate. When she had finished eating, the pumpkin said, "Don't dare tell your mother and father that I have arrived."

Then it returned to the water.

Her mother and father returned from the fields. When they entered the house of this daughter of theirs, they smelled something that was rotten.

Her mother said, "Oh, Nobani!"

She said, "Mama."

"What is it that smells here in the house?"

"I don't know, Mama."

"Could it be a dead mouse?"

"No, Mama, I don't know. It's not likely."

"Something smells here in the house."

The girl said, "No, Mama, I don't know what it is that smells here in the house."

Her mother said then, "Please stand up a little, that I may look here under you. This smell appears to be coming from here, from you."

When the girl stood up, the smell was very strong.

Her mother said, "This thing is here, on you! Let me look at you."

The mother uncovered the girl's body, and found that her daughter's body was really green. It had become putrid.

"What's the matter with you? Why are you like this, Nobani?"

"Mama, there is something that comes here continually. It says that I should never tell, that if I do tell it will take me away. That is the thing that created the fear in me. I was afraid to speak of this thing here at home."

"What is it that continually arrives here at home, cutting you up like this, so that your body is green like this? Yet you conceal it all from us, you do not tell us."

"It is a pumpkin, the pumpkin that you were carrying some time ago when I was still small, when I was a child. It rolled down from your head and disappeared in the river. Now, it continues to come out from the river, it comes here to me, arriving and saying, 'Girl.' I say, 'Yes.' It says, 'With whom are you living?' I say, 'I live alone.' It says, 'Aa! Why do you say "I am alone" instead of "I am awone"?' I say, 'I am awone.' It says, 'Come out, I'm your sister.' And so I come out. Then it tears into my flesh, all over my body, until I am green like this. There is no other cause, that is it. There's one thing more: you neglected me, Mother, leaving me to the mercies of this pumpkin that cuts me and does these things to me, bringing me close to death, making me die because I was rotting. Look at these maggots falling here from me. These wounds are the result of my having been cut by this pumpkin."

"Please stop, my child," her mother said, speaking with this daughter of hers. "Wait, my child. I shall just go here to your father, I will tell him about this matter." She said that, crying out, making a loud lamentation about her child who, unknown to them, was rotting, about her child who was rotting.

She went, she entered that house where her husband was. She entered the house, crying.

Her husband said, "What is the matter with you?"

She entered in tears, as if she were being tormented by smoke.

She said, "Father of Nobani, don't ask me in that manner! My child over there has been injured, she is in danger."

"Which one?"

"We have only one child. How do you dare to ask me that? You know the child, over there behind the screen, in that house."

"How has she been injured? Is she sick?"

"She is not sick, Father of Nobani. You know that pumpkin that I had carried when she was younger."

"Which pumpkin?"

"The one that I carried when we were coming from the fields. I was kindling the fire coals, and told you about this wonder, how the pumpkin had rolled down and went and disappeared in the river. You thought that I had wasted your food."

"Yes, I remember the pumpkin. What of it?"

"It's that pumpkin that has continued to emerge from the river. It comes up and cuts the flesh of this child here in the house. The child says that the pumpkin rises,

Rumble-rumble-rattle,

O ye ye ye eha.

It arrives and stops here at the door. It arrives, and says, 'Girl.' She says, 'Yes.' It says, 'With whom are you living?' She says, 'I live alone.' Then it says, 'You should say, "I am awone." ' She says, 'I am awone.' It says, 'Come out, I'm your sister.' Then she comes out, and it cuts her, it cuts her. Oh! Just wait and see the child. She is green! Maggots overflow from her body! You will see how rotten her body is. And I don't think she'll get well."

"My wife, there's only one thing we can do. We must move the child out of that house. We must hide her in another house, so that she goes through her initiation there."

"We must do that this very morning, Father of Nobani! Not another day must pass!"

"The child should be brought into this house and hidden here."

They went to sleep then, and awakened in the morning when it was about to dawn. It was not yet dawn, it had not yet fully dawned.

They took the child, and brought her to this house. They arrived and put her in that place, behind a screen; the child stayed behind this screen.

They left the child there, and departed. They went to the fields. She was left behind, staying alone there.

The pumpkin could be heard rising from the river. And it went directly to this house in which the child was hidden.

Rumble-rumble-rattle,

O ye ye ye eha.

Rumble-rumble-rattle,

O ye ye ye eha.

It came to the door, it forced its way in. It rolled in, and fell on its side in this house in which she had been hidden.

"Girl!"

"Yes?"

"With whom do you live?"

"I live alone."

"What's that? Why don't you say 'I am awone'?"

"I am awone."

"Come out, I'm your sister!"

The girl came out. The pumpkin cut her, it tore her flesh, it tore her flesh, it tore and tore her.

Then it said, "I'm going to do it as if for real today, because although I warned you and said that you must not tell of me, you did tell of me, you told your mother and father!"

It tore her flesh, it tore her flesh, and her bones also were bared today. The pumpkin tore her flesh, it tore all this body of hers. Then it turned around and it cooked maize in a great hurry; it ground the corn, it poured thick milk over the boiled corn.

Then it said, "Eat! And if you even try to tell about this again, you'll know all about me!" So it said, and it again disappeared into the river.

The girl stayed there, crying in pain.

At dusk, the others arrived; they arrived, and her mother came to the house containing the girl. She got there, and went in.

She said, "How is it? How are your pains today?"

She said, "Oh, Mama, I'm in great pain!"

"The pumpkin didn't come today, did it?"

"No, it didn't come." The child was withholding the truth, because she feared that the pumpkin would again do something to her.

Her mother went out then, she went and told the father, "Well, Nobani says that the pumpkin did not come today."

Her husband said, "I would really be surprised if it ventured this far, to this place where we caused her to flee from the pumpkin."

But no matter how often the mother offered food to the girl, she did not eat. The mother concluded that her daughter did not want food because of her pain.

They went to sleep then.

They awoke in the morning, and returned to the fields to harvest.

And this pumpkin returned to the homestead:

Rumble-rumble-rattle,

O ye ye ye eha.

It arrived, and stopped at the door. It forced its way in, then rolled in, and fell on its side.

"Girl!"

"Yes?"

"With whom do you live?"

"I am alone."

"You must say 'I am awone.' "

"I am awone."

"Come out, I'm your sister."

The girl came out. It cut her, it tore her flesh, it tore, it tore her flesh, this pumpkin tore her flesh again. Then, in a great hurry, it cooked the maize, it ground the boiled corn, it caused her to pour milk over the boiled corn. It gave her the food, and she ate it. She ate and ate.

Then it said, "Now, if you tell your mother and father about me, you'll know all about me!"

Well then, it rolled again, rattling, and it disappeared into the river.

At dusk, the girl's mother and father returned. They arrived, and her mother cooked, she cooked for her child. But when she gave the child the food, the girl did not want it.

"Father of Nobani! Father of Nobani!" she said, turning to her husband. "You go to this child! Don't say that you won't enter the house of an initiate! Please go in today. Speak a little with this child yourself! She might tell you what she's hiding. She'll tell you that this pumpkin comes in, and that it is because of this pumpkin that she's intimidated. She's afraid of what this pumpkin might do to her if she tells."

The man said, "Oh!" So saying, he stood up, and went off. He arrived at the house, and went in. He called his child by name.

She replied, "Father?"

"Why are you not eating?"

"No, Father, it's nothing."

"No, my child, please tell me. I beg you, tell me! This pumpkin that you say has been arriving here: Does it still come, even now?"

The child said, "Yes, Father, it comes even now. The thing is, I'm afraid to tell you about this pumpkin because, after it finishes cutting me up, it makes threats, warning me that it will kill me if I tell. It's for this reason that I'm inclined not to tell."

"Oh!" the father was heard saying. "What can be done about this matter? This pumpkin—what is it really about? Is it an annoying thing that has come to vex this homestead of mine? Can it be the means of my child's demise? She has been harassed by this pumpkin. Why does the pumpkin not come when I'm here? I would chop it up!" So he said, and the child said nothing. So the man said, and he called his wife.

"Mabani!"

"Father of Nobani?"

"Come here."

The woman went to him.

"This child says that the pumpkin is still coming here."

"She says that it is still coming here, Father of Nobani?"

"Yes."

"But what can we do about this pumpkin, Father of Nobani? Originally, it seemed that I had simply spoiled your meal because of that pumpkin. Then it seemed to be merely annoying. But it's a witch of a pumpkin. It never was a real pumpkin, even when it was over there in the fields. It is a menace. I carried it home, thinking that I was just carrying a pumpkin. But it was not a pumpkin. What shall we do about this matter, Father of Nobani?"

"Well, we'll have to take her and hide her over there in the homestead of the king, in case the king won't agree to send out some people to watch this pumpkin and finally kill it."

"All right," her mother said, "she should not sleep here any more, because it is clear that whatever we do with her, the pumpkin senses her trail, and it proceeds by means of that trail, then it comes to the place where she is hiding."

"I must attempt to meet with the king over there," he said, "and speak with him, because now he is not likely to agree, my wife, when he sees us arriving with a burden like this, one that is as difficult as this matter of the pumpkin."

The woman agreed.

The sun was setting when the man travelled then, he went to the king.

"Hail, Majesty!" he said to the king.

The king acknowledged the salute with his head, and raised his hand.

"King, I have come to you."

"What is it?"

"Well, King, over there at my home, this wonder befell me. My child has been cut up by a pumpkin! I was in the process of initiating that child into womanhood. She is being harassed by this pumpkin, it is cutting my child. I tell you, King, her body is crawling with maggots, they're all over her body. I am perplexed about what I should do about it."

"Well, Man, why don't you take the child to some other place?"

"King, I've already despaired of that. I helped my child to flee, but the pumpkin followed her. It follows her even when she has been taken from one house and put into another."

"What do you suggest I should do about this?" asked the king.

"King, I have come to ask that you keep her here. Could I come and hide her at your place, just for the duration of her initiation?"

"Why don't you terminate the rite now?"

"King, it wouldn't do for me to bring her out of the initiation ritual now, before the usual time. We cannot cut it short: it is necessary, according to the customs of African people, that the ritual move to its conclusion, in order that the initiate have good fortune."

"Please stop," the king said. "Please stop! Allow me first to call my wife over there in the house, so that she should come and listen to the strange thing that you are speaking of. Is there such a thing as a pumpkin that does this to a person?"

"King, you will see the same omen in this thing that I see. But it is my misfortune, because I did not beget any other children, she's the only one." So he said, and the king went then, going to his wife in the house, calling her by name, saying, "Come here!"

His wife stood, and went to this husband of hers, to this king.

"What is it?"

"Please help me, listen to the strange thing spoken by this man about his child. Please tell it again, Man."

"What has happened?" asked the wife of the king.

"Well, Queen, I'm puzzled by my child over there. She has been harassed by this pumpkin. It has been cutting her, it cut her entire body. It perplexes me as to what I ought to do."

The wife of the king burst into laughter. "Was there ever such a thing as a pumpkin that cuts a person?"

"Queen, this thing puzzled me, because this pumpkin began to work on my child over there at home! It cut her. I helped her to flee. I brought her to another house, and it followed her to that place!"

"What do you want the king to do?" the wife of the king asked.

"I've requested a place, Queen, to hide this child here with you, with the hope that the king might send out men to guard her from this pumpkin, and the hope that a way be found that the pumpkin might be killed."

"Well, all right, you may come with her," the king said. "Bring her here to this home. And yes, I'll send out men to guard her from this pumpkin. It cannot possibly succeed inside the court, here at my place!"

The man said, "You have helped me, King. I shall try to bring this child here this very night, because I am troubled here within me."

He went home then, and when he got to his house he knocked.

His wife admitted him.

Before the man spoke, she said, "What did the king say, Father of Nobani?"

"Well, he says that we should bring her over there to him. Nothing will happen to her over there. I went and explained what the pumpkin had done. They did not believe that a pumpkin can cut a person. But that is because they have not yet seen it. This situation is bad."

The wife said to her husband, "It's because they haven't seen this. We too, we have not seen it with our own eyes. It has been seen only by this child."

"Well, we must get her, and take her over there to the king. Get up, don't just talk. Get up and prepare the child's things."

"Sit down."

"No, I'll stand up! Stand up now, don't just be that heap down there! Stand up, let's go!"

The woman got up, she went to bring the child to the king's place. They got her up.

"Get up!"

The girl got up, her body overflowing with the maggots that she carried on her back.

"Is it all right if I carry you on my back, my child?"

The child said, "Yes, Mama. Carry me, because I'm unable to walk. You can smell this odor already, the odor of my rotting. Death is now close to me."

The mother carried her child. They journeyed with her, going to the king. They arrived at the king's place, and sat with the girl at the side of the house.

The king came out. "Take her to that house over there, the one that is on the side. That one over there, on the side."

The woman and her husband took the girl and placed her in this house.

The king said, "Will you go home? Or will you sleep here?"

The father of the child said, "Well, we'll just sleep here tonight, and then at dawn we'll get up and go home. We don't want our trail to be seen, so that it'll be known where we have come from."

"All right," said the king. "Now, Man, you must come here, away from the place of the initiate."

"Well, I wasn't going to sleep there in any case. It's my wife who'll sleep there. Even though people do not normally sleep there, my wife will sleep in the house of the initiate."

"All right," said the king, speaking to this man. The man was returning from the house indicated by the king. It contained people of the king's place, and the girl's father made room for his child there.

In the morning, they got up, and the man went home with his wife, leaving the child behind.

The king gathered the men of his village together.

He said to them, "I will not choose any one of you. I want all of you to take up your weapons and come with them. Bring your weapons, whatever is sharp, with you. I want you to lie in wait for this pumpkin. I have been told that the pumpkin has been cutting up a child at her home. If it comes here, you must kill it, slaughter it!"

The men heard the king: "A pumpkin? What is it like?"

He said, "They say it is a pumpkin. From the fields—a typical pumpkin, the kind that you eat. That is what is cutting this child up!"

"Oh, King! We could not possibly be outmatched by a pumpkin!"

The king said, "I shall see what you do today, because this pumpkin is not a real pumpkin, exactly. It is a weird one!"

The men stayed there then, lying in wait for this pumpkin.

After breakfast, the pumpkin was heard.

It was said, "Everyone should go!" The pumpkin should be seen only by those men who were hiding, waiting for it, and even they should not be in plain view. They must not be seen by the people nor by this pumpkin.

The pumpkin came up then, coming here now to this king:

Rumble-rumble-rattle,

O ye ye ye eha.

Rumble-rumble-rattle,

O ye ye ye eha.

The pumpkin was inside the court. It was coming, it was coming. It arrived at the door.

It said, "Girl!"

She said, "Yes?"

It said, "With whom do you live?"

She said, "I am alone."

It said, "With whom do you live?"

The girl said, "With whom did you expect me to be?"

It said, "With whom do you live?"

This girl said, "With whom did you expect me to be?"

It said, "Why are you so bold? What are you relying on?"

She said, "I rely on this thing that you wanted me to rely on."

The pumpkin got up angrily, it was jumping energetically into the house.

These men suddenly emerged. They speared the pumpkin, they stabbed it.

The pumpkin fled, and they pursued it. When it was in the courtyard, the king's men speared it, and pumpkin pips sprang up, they sprang up, sprang up, sprang up over there in the courtyard.

Well then, this girl remained now in health. Finally, she was healed here in her body.

In that place over there where the pips had sprung up, a pumpkin came out. This pumpkin came out, it emerged, and it grew and grew, spreading out.

Then this young woman came out of the initiation house, and she went home. She lived at her home, no longer suffering, and finally she was seen by a young man who began to court her. She married then, and after her marriage, at her husband's homestead, she became pregnant. She was pregnant, and she bore children.

When she had had three children, these pumpkins arrived and ate the children of this young woman. No sooner had the young woman borne the children than she buried them in the ground, because of the pumpkins.

There is nothing that can be done about it now, because it is now present. It keeps on happening, it keeps on happening.

Part Three

THE THREATENED DREAM

"THE LAND WAS SEIZED"

At his best the ancient hero had something of the divine in him. God, demigod, godlike, or intimate with the gods, he provided a transcendental link between the contingencies of the finite and the imagined realm of the supernatural. Time and the timeless, man's mortal state and the realm of eternal laws, were brought through him into conflict with each other. Through him also these orders overlapped.
—*Victor Brombert*[1]

He is a man, and that for him and many is sufficient tragedy. . . . It is the theme in its deadly seriousness that begets the dignity of tone: . . . "life is transitory: light and life together all hasten away."
—*J. R. R. Tolkien*[2]

INTRODUCTION

Like the storyteller, the poet and the historian take the names and events of the past, and cast these into metaphors and stories that give them cultural meaning. The poet takes history and, by placing shards of history into the resonant embrace of metaphor, links people and their acts to the mythical essence of the culture.

If the poet adds metaphor to history, the historian adds story to names, facts, time-lines. Each has the effect of theatricalizing history, giving it an artistic dimension that seems inattentive to fact but is moving to a conception of truth. One comes to such performances not for a realistic view of experience but an analytical study of human events. So it is that Ndumiso Bhotomane, in his historical comment, "The Land Was Seized," gives dimension to the genealogies that he earlier created.

Poems by the Xhosa poet and historian Mdukiswa Tyabashe about the Mpondomise people, by the Swati poet Mtshophane Mamba regarding the experience of Africans during the second world war, and by the Xhosa poet and historian Ashton Ngcama regarding Xesibe leaders provide the metaphors that give meaning to the acts of leaders of the present and the past.

In his poem, "So Tall He Touched the Heavens," Tyabashe tenderly savors the images of the past and, juxtaposing them to images of the present, makes a scathing comment on leaders who owe their place and their power to the apartheid regime in Pretoria. He created this poem in the presence of the king, Diliza Iintaba Mditshwa, and his wife and two of the king's closest advisors. In attendance also were about two hundred Mpondomise people. To the left of the king were about fifty plaintiffs and witnesses who had come to the royal residence to conduct their various legal cases. In the back were scores of horses belonging to people who had ridden to the residence of the king. Women were grinding and cooking food, children roamed about. Cows, sheep, goats, chickens, geese, and dogs were in abundance. A tractor stood nearby, and from time to time people came to the residence leading teams of oxen which pulled sledges filled with thatch. When the king arrived at his chair, outside in the courtyard of his residence, the poet dramatically gave voice to his images.[3]

Mtshophane Mamba's poem, "Snapping at the Water's Foam," contains images having to do with the developing relationship between Africans and Europeans during the second world war. While he warns the Europeans ("Whites of Durban, / Remove your shoes: / See him [i.e., King Sobhuza] walking / Rumblingly / In the red shoes / Of his enemy Mjingane"), he also understands that a major change is occurring in Swati life: "Montgomery[4] and his people / Were summoning you, / They were sending you a message. . . ."

Xhosa homes

Ashton Ngcama, in "The Land Has Grown Old" and "Tears in Your Stomach," indignantly uses poetic images to provide vitriolic assessments of the seizure of the Africans' land by the whites and the complicity of contemporary black rulers.

Tyabashe's lengthy oral history of the Mpondomise people begins in the great lakes area of eastern Africa and moves along the southeastern coast to what is today the Transkei. Tyabashe's abilities as a historian bring to mind Nelson Mandela's description of Zwelibhangile Joyi, the "most ancient of chiefs," who influenced and educated the young Mandela: "It was from Chief Joyi that I began to discover that the history of the Bantu-speaking peoples began far to the north, in a country of lakes and green plains and valleys, and that slowly over the millennia we made our way down to the very tip of this great continent."[5] In his history of the Mpondomise, Tyabashe describes in narrative form the eroding impact of the whites and other Africans on the traditions which the Mpondomise people have historically claimed as their own.

ONE

A South African poet recalls how in the early nineteenth century the Xhosa king Hintsa (c. 1790–1835) regularly appeared before his people to conduct the affairs of the nation.

Here at the place of the Gcaleka people, in the land of the Xhosa, at the royal residence, at Mgwebi's place, at Mhlontlo's, there was a king whose name was Zwelinzima. Whenever he was about to try cases in the morning, when he conducted the affairs of the entire land and determined the way things should be ordered in the land of his people, he would come out of the house carrying his skin mat which would be spread outside. The king would come out of the house wrapped in a kaross made of the skin of game animals. The cape was made of a variety of animals' skins that were joined together to form a blanket. His headgear was also constructed of game, sometimes made of the feathers of exceptional birds.

And there is the poet.

The poet approached the court one day, and, with a familiar image from the oral tradition, moved at once to transform the moiling crowd into a responding audience.

This is how the poet operates, profiting at the royal residence by excelling in his poetic skills, speaking and singing praises. He approaches the homestead from above, then speaks to that king, the scion of Mgwebi. This bard was a Cira fellow; he would come down from above the homestead (it was located below a hill). He would appear, and say:

> *Hoyiiiiiiiiiiini na! Hoyiiiiiiiiiiini na!*
> The late-riser has foolishly seen nothing
> because he will never see the python uncoil. . . .

The lines were ambiguous, but it was quickly apparent that they told of a lack of military preparation for a war that seemed imminent. As he revealed his foreboding, the poet strode through the throng to the motionless figure of the king. His theme was urgent, the realities of contemporary history were plain; to relate theme and reality, he constructed a set of imaginary events having to do with forbidden sexual dalliance. He boldly addressed the king with such epithets as

> You-who-expose-your-loins-to-the-door

and

> Thrower-forward-of-the-penis
> Not-to-anyone-in-particular,

imposing upon him the role of fictional miscreant. He combined fanciful image with his perception of historical event to create a metaphorical admonition: the king was dawdling while disaster menaced, his traditional accountability to the people emphasized by his supposed self-indulgence.

> The girls do not wipe their bottoms,
> They fear being pricked in the ass!

the poet cried.

> What do the puberty ritual girls do
> When the battle of the penises approaches?

In the end, the images of reality and fantasy clearly bonded, the poet turned on the king:

> Eee, what is the matter with this man
> That his testicles are swollen?
> Is it because he ceaselessly picks the young fruit?

Why, he wondered, are "gleaming weapons" not to be seen at the royal residence?[6] Shameless antisocial activity had become identified with a disregard for the symptoms of war, and, as rebukes evoked by one set of images were transferred to a second, a specific time in history was generalized into a cultural statement.

The poet, singing his poem, reached the royal residence.

When the poet arrived, he put his hand on the ground, his body not being covered. (A bard does not wear a cape over his body, he puts it over one shoulder.) When the poet arrived at the royal residence, two men got up and went out to meet him.

They said, "You praised the child of the king well! How did you come to know the child of royal blood? Where do you come from, you with such a rare respect?"

And how did the king himself respond? He began to murmur, "E! E! E! Ee! Ee! Bring him here, please, so that I may see him!"

Then it was said, "Go on out in front! The king wants you, young man. In front!"

He obtained a beast then, a brightly colored cow, as a reward for his poetry, for his praising of that fellow of Hintsa's domain, because the king had been praised by the Cira clansman.

TWO

In the poem, history is fragmented and linked to the metaphors that are generated by the tale tradition. If the tales contain the wisdom of the society, they lend that wisdom and the sanctions involved to history, but only on their own terms, when history is shattered and reshaped into poetry.

While such poetry is not a historical document, it nevertheless has no existence outside history. Images, selected at least partially for their power to elicit strong feelings from an audience, are first removed from their mainly historical contexts. Certain emotions associated with such subjects as heroism and kingship are intensified and reordered. Because contemporary events are thus routinely measured against cultural values, history is constantly being revived and revised. The poems depend on this enhanced narrative, reproduced, atomized, and redefined. It is a subjective accounting, but the poet, using all his magic to convince his listeners otherwise, contains these as yet unchanneled bursts of energy and gives history a new gloss. Not surprisingly, the oral poet is frequently a competent historian. He is a composer and public reciter, a person of wit honored by the community, as A. C. Jordan, the Xhosa novelist, has observed, and he also has a background in the history and culture of his people.[7] The poet, assuming an intimate knowledge of those subjects on the part of his audience, freely selects details necessary to the composition of his poetic patterns. If such references are sometimes elliptical and often seem obscure, he is confident that those witnessing his performance will suffer no confusion. It is not that they will as a matter of course supply what is missing: the poet does not allow them to force the poetry back into its causal origins. However, the historical connection remains, a linear echo arousing a requisite tension with the developing lyric. The poem establishes no new relationship with history; rather, it reshapes an already present linkage through the patterning of discontinuous images. These are placed in novel alignments, as the poet shifts from the perspective of historical sequence to that of didactic argument—and, simultaneously, to the nonlinearity of lyric intensity. The poem has its origin in a temporally defined realm, and converts that sense of time into a set of images, sounds, and emotions by means of which the historical moment provides insight into cultural infinitude. When the images thus disjointed recover their form, they represent a new dimension of history, an experience in which images of real time and place are reformed by the poetic line because of its capacity for rhythmical duplication.

The minimal unit of the poem is the reconstituted historical image. A combination of sound and movement, it is controlled by the poet and designed in part to induce sensations in the audience's imaginations that have to do with physical experience as well as memories of shared artistic and historical events. Images containing limited inventories of the community and its cultural activities unite the central character with nature, history, and fantasy.

Images are worked into a network of sounds to become part of a predictable pattern. In its simplest form, a pattern is created by verbal repetition with little or no deviation. As the variations of this pattern become more complex, sufficient similarity among the lines that compose it will be preserved to assure a sense of repetition, but enough diversity will be introduced to provide interest, aesthetic quality, and development of argument. On this level of patterning, verbal and sound qualities complement one another. To accommodate genealogical data, names of people and places, and historical and cultural images, the poet makes use of simple formulas, altering each repetition to supply, for example, a different name.

Oral poetry is a complex interplay of images. It is more than mere accumulation, but that is where it begins, as the solitary image wrenched from its wonted environment is pulled into new contexts. The Swati poet, Mtshophane Mamba, an official bard at the Entfonjeni royal residence in Swaziland, created a lyric in praise of the reigning sovereign, King Sobhuza II. The images, developed in tightly organized groups, seem self-contained:

> Thundering shield!
> He is a flowing spring—
> We drink only tepid water,
> For too long
> We have been drinking tepid water.
> Herdsmen,
> Having gathered their stock,
> Come to you.
> You are a grower of trees:
> Grow them, nurture them,
> Because the red bull of Mahlokohla
> Is maturing,
> And he will pull them up,
> Roots and all.[8]

As the series of separate images is evoked—thundering shield, flowing spring, destructive bull—they begin by their simple accumulation to reveal a certain attitude toward the king: he is a warrior, he protects and provides for his people. In a poem about Shaka by Nombhonjo Zungu, a Zulu bard, repetition is not readily discernible either:

Hero who surpasses other heroes!
Swallow that disappears into the clouds,
Others disappearing into the heavens!
Son of Menzi!
Viper of Ndaba!
Erect, ready to strike,
It strikes the shields of men!
Father of the cock![9]

In place of verbal repetition, the poet supplies apparently different images, but swallow, viper, cock, each with its stated or implied extension, in some way affirm or reinforce the sense of the opening line. Subsequent images repeat the theme, intensifying the mood or feeling. The Swati and Zulu poems are dependent on sound rhythms and thematic parallels for their form.

S. K. Lekgothoane concludes that oral poetry "is a stirring up of the emotions."[10] Feelings, tied as they are to discontinuous images, enable the poem to become oriented in the history and traditions of the people; they become progressively denser as more emotions are caught up in the images and are systematically organized by the rhythmical patterning that the poet imposes on the work. The grid, which is the combination of patterned lines, is also charged with feeling, furnishing poet and audience with a predictable emotional field, molding memories, echoes of past experience, and emotion into patterns. As new images, with their trapped sensations, flow across the grid, they are evaluated according to their new context. Feeling becomes a means of commentary, as the poet controls the developing experience of the poem through patterning.

The selection and arrangement of images frequently seems random, but the combination of line, sound, and emotion binds images as disparate as these:

He is a cherished child, Ndaba's brown one,
Mark of the daughter of Tsonyana of the Kwayi,
And placed at the court of Nothembu.
He is a bird of prey of the Hala
That tore the face of Xhelo's wife,
He is the pierced buffalo, deeply wounded in the back,
Shot with a rifle, a fine European gun.
He has nails blackened by mimosa gum,
A large kraal managed by Mityo and Mntalana—
Despisers do not dispute the airing of trifles;
He has a great forest, Mkamkam,
Held by Nkombi and Madongci.[11]

"Hero who surpasses other heroes!" Nombhonjo Zungu, a Zulu poet.

The line ties subsequent images to a model pattern that becomes more relentless in its control with each repetition. Successive historical fragments are swept into this unique metrical organization that connects events emotionally, in ways they may not be linked in time and reality, so that they are experienced in novel combinations. A fresh view of history is generated, as the discrete images are moved by contiguity and new rhythmical affinities into new relationships. The process seems random only if the observer is seeking the chronological sequence of history. But there is in such poetry a new alignment of materials, as the line blends emotion and image, as rhythm gives these an illusion of continuity, allowing the argument of the poem to move into the foreground. This argues for new relationships which taken together form an attitude toward history that transcends cause-and-effect linkages and enables history to move to a new level of cultural insight.

Emotions are aroused not only by the images but also by the unique use of language involved in their evocation. The poetry is "highly figurative,"[12] composed of "speech which concentrates all of the eloquence of the . . . language"[13] in a context that is theatrical, as realistic images are transformed by means of intonational configurations which, if they correlate at all to normal speech, represent an exaggeration and refinement of such usage, often moving nonpoetic treatment to its limits. Delivery is always rhythmical, the images forcibly declaimed, sometimes sung or chanted, frequently uttered at a rapid pace. "The poet," Edison M. Bokako observed, "freely indulges in ornament, entertaining contrasts between major and minor personalities. No man is presented under ordinary light, no man is allowed to appear only with what strictly belongs to him, no circumstance in which he appears is presented except as a swelling spectacle."[14]

Feeling and its containment and ordering have primacy in oral poetry: the poem reveals the sentient progress of the artist's thought. Images are aligned in logical patterns; complex associations are uncovered among images as the poet brings past and present time into sometimes uncomfortable union, generating unaccustomed emotional responses from the audience. Nonverbal rhythms and, frequently, verbal repetition fashion the image-evoked emotions into a form that gives symmetry to those experiences. By channeling feelings into the new environments that he has created, the poet expresses his own feeling. But he cannot make public his private feelings without the emotions of the audience. The Zulu writer Benedict Wallet Vilakazi notes that in certain poems "is seen the height of lyric quality," which "reveals ecstasy of feeling and a perfect imagery." Such poetry, he contends, "passes from being an objective presentation of great deeds to become poetry of feeling and intuition."[15]

Magema Fuze describes how, when the Zulu king Shaka proclaimed his father's greatness in poetry, his entire army was swept with emotion.

Such was the force of the poetry that it was as if the enemy were actually there; Shaka's men were prepared to fight at that moment and to die in battle. And when the king sang his grandfather's song, "Ndaba is king!" his followers were overcome with fury and in their excited state ready for death.[16] Everitt Lechesa Segoete found the same affective power in the performance of the Sotho poem "Mokorotlo," the "Song of the Enemies," called by some the Sotho national poem. Segoete notes that the words of the song have such power that "There is no Sotho person who listens to them without feeling his heart rise." It is, he adds, "an ageless song, unchanging. It treats of death and war, of vultures eating the bodies of men."[17] And Azariele M. Sekese tells how Sotho warriors during times of war composed songs in praise of themselves. Some leaders, among them Lejaha Makhabane, also created poems for themselves. In a dramatic performance, a warrior would recount the details of his heroic conduct on the day of battle. Having done so, he would stab the ground a number of times equal to the number of enemy soldiers he had killed. As he did that, the group that surrounded him would join in, crying out each time he touched his spear to the ground. Then he would jab his weapon toward the enemy, continuing to shout out the lines of his poem:

> Whirlwind of the enemies of Lejaha,
> The whirlwind destroyed the people,
> They were swept off in a shower of spears.[18]

The warrior, writes C. L. S. Nyembezi, a Zulu poet and novelist, "did not fail to get himself praises or add to those he already possessed."[19] Indeed, the poem was, according to Bokako, describing the Tswana panegyric, "a story of endeavor, of resistance overcome, of something accomplished. In it an individual was glorified, a momentous occasion recalled, or the achievement of victory celebrated."[20] It was no trivial matter. "It was the highest distinction conferred for valor and for safeguarding [communal] permanence and security. To the soldier it was a highly coveted prize, the highest reward for courage and manliness."[21]

On ceremonial occasions the Zulu poet "would recite the praises one after the other until he ultimately ended with those of the reigning sovereign."[22] Magolwana was the poet of King Mpande and was considered one of the great Zulu bards. When he composed poems, he would utter impassioned apostrophes to the king: "Lion, he silences speech!" Then he would stamp his heels on the ground, his ornate costume quivering violently—*gqi! gqi! gqi!*

> He silences speech, Beast!
> He silences speech, Great Elephant!

Then, abruptly, the poet would stand utterly still, looking suddenly in the direction of the king. The gathering of people was silent. Magolwana would again begin to praise the sovereign, more calmly, now standing still, now walking about. And the king, with his advisors, watched, saying nothing, but he would whistle when he heard something that pleased him—no one else dared to whistle. And Magolwana would chant and proclaim, sing and shout the praises, moving restlessly as his royal leader watched, whistled, and pointed at the poet with his finger, leaving the king very excited.[23]

Such praises were not idle fictions. R. R. R. Dhlomo, a Zulu writer of historical novels, argues that kings must not be praised for things they never did or applauded for improper attitudes. Images in the poetry "should be appropriate impressions of deeds in regard to that king, perhaps giving an impression of the deeds of prowess which are said to have been accomplished by the king during his reign."[24] Archie Mafeje adds that praise is not the only attitude taken in the poetry; the bard also "criticizes the chiefs for perverting the laws and customs of the nation and laments their abuse of power and neglect of their responsibilities and obligations to the people."[25] That more is involved in such poetry than simply praising a leader is also suggested by Ernest Sedumeli Moloto. He tells of how Montshiwa, a Tswana chief, with his fellow warriors assassinated the emissaries of Mzilikazi, a rival Nguni king, in about 1832. The bards commemorated the event in what appeared to be a negative way: "Those men were the emissaries of Mzilikazi," chided one.

> He had sent Boya and Bhengele to visit us,
> But you crafty son of Tswana ate them up!
> Yours will similarly be craftily eaten up—
> Remember, you are not a mad dog, but a man.

Moloto comments, "The point at issue . . . is that there was . . . suspicion simmering between the [Tswana] and the Nguni." And he asks, "Who says Mzilikazi's intentions were honest? And who says the denigration of Montshiwa by the bard is not intended to forewarn and therefore forearm him? That is the role of the bard. The bard is a constructive institution. He is a loving critic."[26]

Oral poetry aroused cultural consciousness, Bokako argues, "and the atmosphere it created of ancestral might and liberty kindled the desire for the greatest effort" on behalf of the community.[27] Lekgothoane goes further. The poems refer, he contends, "to past history, to past events and to the future. There is great prophecy in them, they are a prayer." In them heroes are extolled, cowards ridiculed. "If a man has been afraid he will not fear again. Furthermore, [poetry] is deep learning. We are enabled to establish harmony between ourselves and God and the departed spirits by means of praises. [Poetry] is rejoicing and weeping with which we cry to God." A person "whilst praising or being praised can walk over thorns, which cannot pierce the flesh which has become impenetrable." If any of the great doctors "were to praise God and the ancestral spirits, the rain would fall and the sick be healed."[28]

Like the poet,[29] the oral historian fashions a number of unique images in the process of recounting events in the social and historical life of his people. These result from a combination of significant cultural feelings linked to important historical events. The convergence of the two creates historical motifs that are as useful to the historian as they are to the artist. In history as in poetry, they are valued for their own sake and are frequently removed from their linear contexts, transcending the moment of history.

THREE

In Mdukiswa Tyabashe's poetry, heroes are tied to the past. "The moderns," including the living chief before whom he is performing, refuse to consider the wisdom of the past. The very presence of the incumbent leader is painful to the poet: "An old sore has been hit again, and I am hurt!" Tyabashe reflects on the distinction between the office of chieftaincy, symbol of tradition and continuity, and the current holder of the office. Today, "the country is ruled by lay preachers," he sighs.

> This country
> Is ruled by evangelists,
> This country
> Is ruled by women's church leaders.

It was not so in another time:

> It was splendid to see Gqirana
> Stalking astride the Malephe and Mjika Rivers.

The hero of the past

> . . . was so tall
> He touched the heavens.
> And he was beautiful.

As for the present chief,

> . . . the real successor
> Surpasses this little fellow
> Even in the sound that he makes![30]

Magagamela Koko, old, frail, and cynical, had his corresponding complaint: everything he had as a youth is gone. Who would care for him? he wondered. Who would nourish the old? In his poetry, Koko turned himself into a symbol of tradition and equated the ill treatment and indifference that he as an elder received from the young to ignorance of the past. He was as skeptical as Tyabashe:

> A man will exploit another;
> He himself feels the burden,
> And merely clutches his own knees.[31]

What was it like in the golden time? A Zulu poet, Umhle Biyela, recalls, speaking of an ancestral figure: "Ndaba stepped hard, and a lake appeared." It was a period of astonishing events.

> Bird weighed down by its tail,
> Lake that was pulled down by elephants.

Fantasy touches Biyela's descriptions of the great heroes: "Milk that curdles without foam," is the way he depicts the character of one prince. Another is

> Awesome cliffs of the wilderness,
> Whenever I called them they responded.

It was an era when man and nature were in harmony.

> Little hare, run away,
> And the land too will run away;
> Cliffs, come back,
> And the land too will come back.[32]

The Tswana chief Kgamanyane ruled the Kgatla people between 1848 and 1874. He composed a poem that referred to an 1858 war between the Afrikaners, who were then in control of the Transvaal, and the Sotho people. With other Africans, the Kgatla were conscripted by the Afrikaners as servants in this clash. For Kgamanyane, special conflicts of loyalty emerged because he was the son-in-law of the Sotho leader Moshweshwe. He spoke of this dilemma in his poem:

> I'm a two-pointed awl of the Masonya,
>   that pricks both cloak and sewer,[33]

another of those equivocal images common in oral poetry but carrying special relevance in this case. Ernest Sedumeli Moloto wondered what had gone on in the hearts of Africans used in wars against other Africans. "Who else could capture their honest attitude but the bard? Who else could sense their moral fibre?"[34]

Biyela and Nombhonjo Zungu describe heroes of the Zulu past, and so glory in tradition. It is when such figures are placed into the context of present time, as in the poetry of Tyabashe and Ashton Ngcama, that tensions between the two periods surface and a political statement results. The poet, as chronicler of the past, concludes that contemporary problems can be solved only by reference to former times. As he moves from objective recorder and historian to advocate, he mythicizes antiquity. And because he uses the past to set standards for the present, he does not have to criticize today's leaders in any personal way. He speaks not for a king but for a tradition, and, to the extent that he represents it, the leader is given praise or blame.

In present time, argue Tyabashe and Ngcama, there are no heroes. Leaders are forced by realities to relinquish traditional power, to deal with Pretoria, to give up authority first to the whites and then to puppet black rulers, and so contemporary chiefs are inevitably assailed by the poets. In the poem addressed to King Jojo, Ngcama voices a theme with a pair of comments about the gap between the two periods:

> We eat meat but have no cattle.
> We have sheep but have no knife.

As the poet constructs his poem around these lines, he reviews Jojo's triumphs, when his rivals were attacked and defeated. Then he turns to the current leader who is sitting before him:

> I'm not referring to *you,* Child of the King—
>   *You* were doing a lot of moving about,
>   Questing after the kingship.

But we do not know your legitimacy, the poet adds, "We did not even know your origins." For those who have thus been cut off from their past, Ngcama has a message: "Lean on Jojo's land." He insists upon a return to cultural values. "People of Jojo's land, why aren't you acting?" he asks.

> Why do you not go and fetch the king from the forests?
> This is why things have gone bad here on earth,

> This is why the land has grown old.
> It is because you have put these moderns in the land
> And left the truth behind.

Jojo had connections with the ancestors, and because of that he had access to truth. But missionaries came into the land, the poet remembers, and the past was neglected as people accepted the homilies of Western teachers. How can this unhappy imbalance be corrected? The answer is to be found in the poem's refrain:

> Please fetch the kings, bring them back!
> Let them return from the forests!

Ngcama evokes images meant to shock his audience and to buttress his argument:

> Today, the land of Jojo confuses me
> Because the women are exposing their asses
> Contemptuously to this land.
> The women go naked in the middle of the realm.

They reveal their bodies with imported fashions; they no longer follow Xhosa custom.

> Respect the land of the king!
> It is because of you that it is declining,
> It is because of you
> That the king is embarrassed over there
> In the river where he stays.

In a dream, the poet learns the truth:

> Leave the white men alone,
> They are seducing you from your traditions.[35]

For Mdukisa Tyabashe, oral poetry was not a relic of the past preserved in the memory; it was an active social force, performed always in the presence of subject and audience. If the chief had not been present, he explained, "there would be no purpose for the poem." If it happened that the poem's hero were absent—if, for example, he were dead—the evocation of images relating to him would require a contemporary reason for performance. Otherwise, Tyabashe insisted, the poem lost immediacy and purpose. Ngcama required an audience, too, although he insisted that he was oblivious to its members once the performance was in progress. And he too had to have the physical form of a subject; without that, there was for him no inspiration.

Tyabashe, born in 1897 (he died in 1970), spoke of his craft. "You saw me coming into the chief's court this morning," he said after completing a poetic performance at the royal residence. "What I must do first at the great place, before doing anything else, is face the chief. Then, having praised him, I go to his retinue and sit there." The art of composing oral poetry in southern Africa, he explained, is not the responsibility of a guild, nor is the art necessarily transmitted from father to son. "My father was not a poet. I'm the first one in my family," he said. "If my sons wish, they may become poets, but only if they are interested." There is no formal apprenticeship, "no place to learn oral poetry, except when you witness others creating it." Then, he said, "you begin to wish to do as they do."[36] As for actual composition, "You take a phrase from one poem, and when you hear someone else construct one at a certain place, then you take a phrase from that one." The poems, he argued, "are in the mind. . . . You learn the techniques, you learn and learn, and then you finally manage to put the poetry together." The fledgling poet thinks deeply about the craft: "[Y]ou think and think about it, and then the first time you attempt to do it, you say so much. The next day, when you try again, you'll say more. And on the next day, you'll say more, and so on and on. My first poems were quite brief, they kept getting longer and longer as I became more experienced."

Poets vary in their approaches to the art, Tyabashe said. "The way a poem is expressed depends on the poet himself. Some people are slow and gentle, others are more forceful. That's because their spirits push them." It made no difference if everyone else at the royal residence was feeling festive. "If my feelings are indifferent to what's going on, then my poem will reflect this. The poetry must come spontaneously. If I'm not in a good mood, then I won't be so eager in my poetry, and this will be obvious." Nor did Tyabashe create poetry for antiquarian purposes: "I know the history of the royalty . . . and in my poems I include events that are praiseworthy. If there are events that occurred before the time that the chief being praised was reigning, or after his reign, or long before it, one thinks about such events, and includes them in the poem if they are relevant."[37]

Ashton Ngcama agreed with Tyabashe that a poem must be a spontaneous event, but was rather more mystical about its creation. Ngcama, born in 1923, did not become a serious poet until he was about thirty years old. Because he is a poet, he reasons, he is a patriotic person, loyal to his people, their history and traditions. The one implies the other — though, as his poetry shows, this does not mean a toadying allegiance to his society's rulers. And he is a keenly sensitive artist: "Whenever I see a person, I'm simply touched. A person doing something good touches me. Or if what he is doing is bad, I feel it, I feel it." He adds, "If a person speaks on behalf of the people—good things, trying to teach the people good things—I feel it. And I feel like praising what he has done." Ngcama views the composition of a poem as essentially an inspired activity. The images come to him during the actual process of performance, he says, as in a dream and without his conscious knowledge. He had to see a certain mountain to call forth images about it; he had to see Jojo, or at least a Jojo surrogate, a descendant of that ancient king in regal garb. He argues that he stores these images in his mind; then, when he composes, he subconsciously brings them to the surface. "They simply come." When he created the poem about Jojo, he was not conscious of what he had said. It was, he says, as if he had been in a trance. "When I am praising, I cannot repeat the poem once I have completed it, because it is not I who says it. It comes on its own. When I visualize something . . . the brain wave gets to me. When it has come, then I have to say something about [the subject]. And when I have said it, I won't know it again. I won't be able to repeat it. Now I don't know where this thing comes from. It's as if I were dreaming, because when I'm praising I don't think. My mind stops functioning, I cannot think." One does not undergo training to learn to master this art, he insists. "It's a feeling! It's a feeling!" Ngcama has been asked by many chiefs to compose poems for them, "but I can't, because I don't remember. . . . It belongs to the world of dreams."[38] And "if the world of dreams has picked someone in a family to have the same spirit[39] as we have, then I think the tradition will continue." He concludes, "I don't know why the spirit comes to me. But it is the spirit that causes me to do it."[40]

Such poetry cannot be produced artificially. It necessitates the intricate lacing of time and space; it requires event and spontaneity, and loses its identity when frozen in memory or writing. Performance reveals among the images links that are not always obvious beyond the poem's framework. Reaching outside the poem for guidance through its dense imagery and historical-cultural allusions can be enlightening, but it distorts the poem and its purpose if external devices interfere with its patterning and that critical network of relationships between poem, creator, and audience.

Tyabashe, like Bhotomane, was interested in genealogical lists. But he was also, if somewhat nervously at times, concerned to provide story, to give meaning to the names. Tyabashe lies in the fascinating middle ground between historians like Bhotomane and storytellers like Masithathu Zenani. Tyabashe's history, "All the Land of the Mpondomise," is at once a story eulogizing the Mpondomise nation and its past, and a threnody, a song of lamentation regarding its fall.

Tyabashe is not at all averse to introducing into his history not only factual stories regarding the characters and events with which he is dealing but also tales clearly identified as *iintsomi*, the fantasy tales of the Xhosa oral tradition. Hence it is that, in the first part of the history, he recounts the tale "about the emergence of the twins," and, in the second part, a tale about Malangana, the "master of magic." He recounts the narratives of King Ngcwina and the rhinoceros, of Ngcwina and the Thwa people, to explain in storytelling terms the relationship between the San and Xhosa peoples. He tells the story of the antagonism between Ndosina and Cira as they struggled for the Mpondomise throne, and he remembers the narrative about the legendary Majola, the snake sacred to the Mpondomise. One of the most fascinating episodes in Tyabashe's history is that of Mamani, Phahlo's eldest daughter, the woman who would be king, a thread that runs throughout the history of the peoples of southern Africa,[41] and a subject that is also important in the epic of Nongenile Masithathu Zenani. Tyabashe also details the attacks on the Mpondomise by the Zulu king, Shaka, and by the Thembu people, and the internal dissensions that finally tore the nation apart, resulting in "the disappearance of the Mpondomise way of life." Its power broken, its fiefdom in twain, the Mpondomise were easy prey to the whites: "I have no land," laments Mditshwa. "What I have is people. I come therefore like a woman carrying children on her back." So it is that the quality of Mpondomise came to an end, and the whites were in charge: "They came in then, they came in, they came in." The refrain throughout this story, "All the land between the Mthatha and the Mzimkhulu [rivers], between the Drakensbergs [mountains] and Mpondoland," is patterned to powerful effect, during the good times, during the bad. Tyabashe is at some moments playing the role of John of Gaunt, praising "This blessed plot, this earth, this realm," and sadly observing that his "earth of majesty" has "made a shameful conquest of itself."[42]

Ndumiso Bhotomane is more succinct but no less melancholy in his description of the defeat of the Africans during the war of Ngcayechibi: "The land was seized; it was then ruled by the [white] government, and it continues to be so ruled to this day. . . ." The momentous event is given human dimensions by anchoring it in the story of "the princes who crossed [the river] at the time of Ngcayechibi's feast," and the party that ensued. This seemingly negligible event became tied to the larger issues and themes of the time, the white government became involved, with the result that "[T]he land was seized. . . ."

Mdukiswa Tyabashe

SO TALL HE TOUCHED THE HEAVENS

(XHOSA)

The Mpondomise poet, Mdukiswa Tyabashe, was seventy-four years old when he performed this poem on August 12, 1967. Mr. Tyabashe was formerly the official poet, the imbongi, *of Chief Lutshoto of the Mpondomise. This poem was performed at the royal residence of Chief Diliz' Iintaba Mditshwa at Mdibanisweni, Tsolo District, in the Transkei. In the audience were about two hundred Mpondomise men and women. (122; tape 3, side 2)*

Shu! Shu! Shu
The pain goes deep!
An old wound has been laid bare.
It has been laid bare,
And the pain goes deep:
This old wound,
A new torment
Has been inflicted by Diliz' Intaba,
Perpetrated by Diliz' Intaba.

Diliz' Intaba!
The one
Who topples mountains,
Cold, lofty mountains,
The Drakensberg Mountains,
The Nomkholokhotha Mountains:
He splinters them!

He is the grain of the people,
We are all given life's grain,
We are all given life's grain
He gives it to the favored ones!
It was given to Matiwane,
It was given to Bushula's people,
It was given to those of Bhungane.
We saw it,
We watched from a distance,
From across a river.

"He touched the heavens, and he was beautiful." Mdukiswa Tyabashe, a Mpondomise poet and historian.

Matiwane arrived,
And struck a man with a millet head,
Catapulting him to the Free State.
He alit there and left a wonder,
He arrived there and left a sign
Which I shall not divulge.
I swear,
I shall not reveal to you
The omen left by him
Because this country
Is ruled by preachers,

This country
Is ruled by evangelists,
This country
Is ruled by women's church leaders,
People whose sensibilities
Are as delicate as a hen's chicks.

I have said it again!
I have said it again!

I have said that
The heroes of Ntibana revealed it,
Blinded as they were
By the sun of Makhandezinyoni!
Those heroes,
The children of Mqangqeni's daughter,
Are beautiful:
It was splendid to see Gqirana
Stalking astride the Malephe and Mjika Rivers
Because of Makhandezinyoni!

Makhandezinyoni!
He was so tall
He touched the heavens.
And he was beautiful,
This forebear of Diliz' Intaba:
He was beautiful
Because he lived up to
The standards set by Ngubenani!

I have said it again!
I have said it again!
I have said that
The heroes of Jengca have class.
The children at Xhwangu's place
Are distinguished
Even though . . .
Even though . . .
even though they are old now,
So old they have worn-down teeth.

These contemporaries—
Rambatotshile's people,
Falase's people:
They do not compare
To this child of Matshiliba.
He fought against growing old,
He contested age.
He clung with his legs
To the milk-skin,
He drank ravenously
From the calabash.

Zebangweni was startled:
He considered himself
The great one at his home.
But we know the heir
Of the great ones of the past,
We know that the real successor
Surpasses this little fellow
Even in the sound that he makes!
He is the child of Makhamba
Who was exposed at Mabilokazi's place:
It was said that he was a puny thing;
A feeble thing!
He did not go to Madubedube's place;
Even though we begged him to do so,
Our voices were ignored.

I say to all of you,
To the old woman who was fined
In the court;
I say to all of you:
I spoke to Matheguda,
The rough one,
But no matter how I approached him
He remained elusive.
Even though I gave my hand to him,
He turned his back to me.
He turned his back,
And left me.
I am a gentle person by nature,
And I was humiliated.

Diliz' Intaba!

Mdukiswa Tyabashe

ALL THE LAND OF THE MPONDOMISE

(XHOSA)

Mdukiswa Tyabashe, seventy-four years old, was a respected Mpondomise historian. This history was related on the evening of August 10, 1967, before an audience of six Mpondomise elders. It took place in a home in Ngcolosi, Tsolo District, in the Transkei. (119; tape A-1, side 2)

FROM THE BLUE REGION

THE EMERGENCE OF THE MPONDOMISE NATION

On the origin of the Mpondomise. . . .

A nation emerged from above, from the lakes in the blue region. It was known as the Mbo nation, it came out of the blue region. It is not clear exactly what lakes these were, whether Lake Nyasa or Lake Tanganyika; it is only said that the nation appeared from the lake area.[1]

That Mbo nation came down and eventually arrived at the Zambezi River. It remained a long time at the Zambezi, then it crossed that river. We are not told by the histories who the king of the Mbo people was at that time, that leader who had come as far as the Zambezi. Nor are we told the name of the king who crossed the river. It is simply said that, when the Mbo people had crossed the Zambezi, they travelled on, building as they went; they journeyed, constructing, and eventually came to the country now known as Zululand, in what is now called Zululand and Swaziland. It is said that the Mbo people reached that area, that when they had arrived there they conquered the people of that country. It is not clear to me which nation they vanquished, which people it was. But those Mbo arrived and subjugated that nation, overcoming those who inhabited the lands now known as Swaziland and Zululand.

We are told that, during the period that they were in this region, there was a great king whose name was Sibiside, the ruler of the Mbo people. This king had many wives and many children, children who are now Mbo nations.

It is said that in the royal house of that king was a son, Nyombose. The progeny of this son are still living in the country of the Zulu, to this day, and are known as the Thethwa. Yes, it is those Thethwa who settled in that country of the Zulu where Shaka would one day appear.

227

Shaka was one of those who served at the court in this nation of the Thethwa, during the time when Dingiswayo was king. Shaka subdued the Thethwa nation, and so it was that the practice of calling the land of the Mbo people in the north "Mboland" came to an end. In the distant past, it was Mboland, but it came then to be known as Zululand. It had properly been called Mboland, because the Mbo people had come there and conquered. Then, because Shaka was of Zululand, all of that land became known as Zululand.

There is a question about this Shaka's lineage, a question as to whether he himself had his genealogical roots in Mbo history and tradition. But in fact he was never a member of that nation, he had nothing to do with the nation of Mbo.

That king was Sibiside, and, as I said, he had many sons. Among them was this son whose kingship was overthrown by Shaka. That son was a ruler in Sibiside's line, but he was not necessary a *direct* son of his, this one who was overwhelmed by Shaka. And among these "sons" of this king were twins, Mpondomise and Mpondo. They emerged as leaders in the country of the Swati. The site of the homestead was on the Mhlathuze River, that is where Sibiside's homestead was.

An *intsomi*[2] of the Mpondomise people says this about the emergence of the twins: When they moved out of the royal residence, one of the twins, Mpondo, travelled at first with the Mbo people. His followers were not yet called "Mpondo"; they were still referred to as "Mbo," and Mpondo was a king of the Mbo people. He moved out then, and Mpondomise also emerged. When Mpondomise went out, he kept close to the Drakensberg Mountains, and when Mpondo went out, *he* hugged the coast. So it happened, then, that those Mbo who travelled with Mpondo were ruled by him; and those Mbo who travelled with Mpondomise were ruled by him. Now, when those who were ruled by Mpondo had gone out, they had their own kingdom; those Mbo who were ruled by Mpondo had their own kingdom. And in the generations that followed the rule of Mpondo, the people stopped being called Mbo and became known as Mpondo. To this day, they are known as Mpondo.

Just let me go on with Mpondo's genealogy—this twin brother was the younger of the two. I'll soon be finished with him; just let me go on with Mpondo's side, until I have completed it:

Mpondo fathered a son, Sihula,
Sihula fathered Mkhondwane,
Mkhondwane fathered Sukude,
Sukude fathered Hlambangobubende,
Hlambangobubende fathered Hlamandana,
Hlamandana fathered Tobe,

Tobe fathered Msiza,
Msiza fathered Ncindise,
Ncindise, then, fathered Cabe,
Cabe fathered Gangata,
Gangata fathered Bala,
Bala fathered Chithwayo,
Chithwayo fathered Ndayeni,
Ndayeni fathered Tahle,
Tahle fathered Nyawuza,
Nyawuza fathered Ngqungqushe,
Ngqungqushe fathered Faku,
Faku, then, fathered Mqikela,
Mqikela, then, fathered Sigcawu,
Sigcawu fathered Poto,

this one who is now the king, the paramount chief of the Mpondo, the one who rules that nation that went out with Mpondo, the nation that came to be known as the Mpondo; it was no longer called Mbo.

I shall leave the Mpondo at that point. They have their own land and their own histories—they must be told by them. They can tell of the various things that happened to them in that land.

THE HUNTER AND MASTER OF MAGIC

MALANGANA AND THE PERSONS OF THE FOREST

Mpondomise, that other son of Sibiside, was the elder twin. I have already noted that Sibiside was the king of the Mbo, and that his homestead was on the Mhlathuze River in the land now populated by the Swati. The history says that Mpondomise went out from his home, and established a homestead at a place called Dedisa, somewhere among the rivers in Natal. It cannot be said with precision just which river was called Dedisa in the old days, there is no longer a river having that name. But the history says that Mpondomise built on the Dedisa River where he had arrived. The traditions say that Mpondomise constructed his homestead there. These Mbo, it was said, had their own king now, and they were called the Mpondomise; they are still called that to this day: those Mbo who followed Mpondomise are the Mpondomise people.

Mpondomise's grave is there at the Dedisa.
Mpondomise fathered Ndunu,
Ndunu's grave is also in the country of Natal.

Ndunu fathered Sikhomo,
Sikhomo's grave is also in that country.

Now, about this Sikhomo. People today have a tendency to become confused about the matter of Sikhomo. The Sikhomo of the Mpondomise has no connection with that Sikhomo of the Xhosa. The Sikhomo of the Xhosa is the son of Ngcwangu; the Sikhomo of the Mpondomise is the son of Ndunu, and is older by far than the Sikhomo of the Xhosa.

Sikhomo's grave is also in that place, in Natal; I do not know the exact site of his grave. We are not told in what place he had stopped.

Sikhomo fathered Njanye,
Njanye's grave is also located in Natal.
Njanye, then, fathered a son
Whose name was Malangana.

It is Malangana who led this nation of the Mpondomise and with them crossed the Mzimkhulu River. So they left the country of Natal. Malangana led the Mpondomise people, and he came to stop in this place in which they are now located. As for Malangana's crossing, the history says that he crossed the Bhisa, a river located in what is now the district of Mbizana. The sources of this river are in a mountain called Ngele. He built there, Malangana built there. History says that he arrived here at the Mzimkhulu, in a marvellous forest having the name Zana. Zana is a forest on the Mzimkhulu River.

An *intsomi* of the Mpondomise says that persons of the forest, swarming in great numbers, arrived there. A person of the forest was a leopard. When someone says "a person of the forest," he means a leopard. The Mpondomise arrived here in this forest, and, because the skin of the leopard was valuable in those days, the Mpondomise remained there at the Bhisa River and hunted the leopards.

Leopards tear people to pieces, leopards kill; they mangle dogs, they maul people. And the leopards were being killed in their turn.

The *intsomi* says that Malangana was a master of magic—yes, a king having exceptional magical ability. Now, in those days dogs were huge creatures, and Malangana's dogs did not flee from the leopard. It is the law of a dog that when a dog appears a leopard will run. Even though Malangana's dogs did not know what a leopard was, they fought it. A person would come along and stab the creature, and the dogs would continue to fight on. A great commotion would then take place over there in that forest.

Rudulu was the paternal uncle of Malangana; he originated the clan that is today known as the Rudulu clan. Rudulu was a son of Sikhomo,

Njanye's brother (Njanye was Malangana's father). It is said that Rudulu and his retinue distinguished themselves greatly because of their bravery in that forest of Zana. The Mpondomise kings in those days of the crossing of the Mzimkhulu were Malangana and Rudulu—Malangana was the king, Rudulu the maternal uncle. They are the ones who ruled the Mpondomise during the period of the crossing of the Mzimkhulu River.

Malangana was a great hunter, so when it appeared that the Mpondomise had almost finished off the leopards over there, they migrated to the country between the Mthatha and Mzimkhulu rivers and hunted animals there. The people who lived in this area were the Thwa (San) people, the Thwa who had never fought with the Mpondomise because they lived by themselves in little groups over there in the mountains. They were organized in little groups, and there was no fighting. They had not yet met the Mpondomise, but there was no fighting.

Malangana went on, and finally came to a river at Chizela, a river over there in Thembuland. He travelled on then, he moved on, and when he arrived there he turned around and went back to the Bhisa River where he died.

The poets used to say,

> Malangana is the sun that went into an elephant's ear,
> He is Dyamfu of Chizela, he is Nongawuza,
> He is the root that ate the calf.

He is not at all connected with the Xhosa; only the names are connected.

THE DREAMER

THE MPONDOMISE AND THE THWA (SAN)

When Malangana died, a son survived—his name was Ntose. That Ntose became known as a king who married many women. Yes, Ntose married many women. And this is the way the Mpondomise became the Mpondomise: sub-clans issued from Ntose, including the Cwera, the Mpinga, the Debeza, the Nqanda, and others not so easily remembered. But these four are the significant clans: they are sub-houses of the Mpondomise that developed from these people, and members of those sub-houses became many. Let me say that these four have become great clan names, because they are so full.

Well, this Ntose ruled all that country. It was his, from the Mzimkhulu to the Mthatha, from the Drakensbergs to the country of the Mpondo. It became his country, all of it.

Ntose's grave is in the district of Mbizana, there at the Bhisa. A son, Ngcwina, survived him. It was Ngcwina who migrated from the Bhisa; he moved the royal residence, and went to build it at Matatiele—in the area where the Mvenyane school is now located. He arrived there, and constructed his royal residence; he built his royal residence when he arrived.

He loved to hunt, as Malangana, his grandfather, did. He loved very much to hunt, and was always taking his regiments out so that they could go hunting. One day, his regiments went off to hunt in the Drakensbergs in that district of Matatiele, and a very dangerous animal sprang up—a rhinoceros. Yes, a rhinoceros sprang up—history tells us that the rhinoceros was dangerous to people because it was so difficult to kill. When one approached it, the creature would do ugly, fearful things. So it happened that when this rhinoceros made a disturbance, someone who was a marksman hit it on the horn (as you can see, it has only one horn). He hit it with a weapon, he hurled his weapon at the animal and its horn broke, and the rhinoceros was killed. That event, among the Mpondomise, has not been forgotten even to this day: as people dance before going to war, the Mpondomise say: "Who are they who broke the horn of the terrifying monster in the Drakensbergs?" What they are actually saying is, "Who are those who killed that rhinoceros over there in the Drakensbergs?" They ask that question because of that heroic incident. You see, when a rhinoceros is hunted, a trap is laid for it. It is never attacked by hand. People do not use their hands when they wish to kill such an animal. But it happened that the Mpondomise did kill this rhinoceros by hand! This valiant event of the rhinoceros occurred at the time of Ngcwina.

Ngcwina was the king. He was a dreamer, he was always dreaming of many things. Once, he dreamed that the Mpondomise had gone out to hunt. They returned from the hunt, having killed their quarry; they returned with a wild creature without hair. They had gone out to hunt, and when they returned, they did so carrying a wild creature without hair. This dream troubled Ngcwina greatly. He called the nation of the Mpondomise together, and told the people of this dream. Then he ordered that a hunt be organized, so that it could be discovered if the dream portended something.

History says that the people of the nation of the Mpondomise went out then, they went out to hunt. For three days, they surprised no animal. Nothing even resembling an animal was seen. Nothing was surprised, nothing happened in the hunt. Then, on the third day, over there on that mountain—Mount Ayliff now, at Ngele—the dogs were making a noise in a cave. The hunters went there, they arrived and looked above a rock. They went up on the rock, and found a person there, a Thwa woman. They came to this Thwa woman, and all of the regiments were called.

It was said, "This is what the king's dream was about!"

"It has been fulfilled!"

"Let us go back!"

They departed from Ngele, returning to Mvenyane, and they were dancing because the king's dream had been fulfilled. They came to the royal residence with this Thwa woman. When they arrived over there at the royal residence—well, then, this Thwa woman was retained. She was a girl, and it was observed that, as far as cooking was concerned, she did well. She cooked very well indeed, the Thwa woman cooked foods that were especially savory. It was said, therefore, that she must be kept here in the palace; she was to cook the food that was to be eaten by the king— a testimony that, among women, there was no one who knew how to cook as she did.

At the time this Thwa woman was cooking there, Ngcwina's wife who was in the palace was Mangutyana. The name of the Thwa woman was Manxangashe. Now then, Manxangashe cooked in the palace at Mangutyana's place, cooking for the king. She remained there as a cook.

It was found that this Thwa woman was chaste. Among the women of the Mpondomise in those days, it was very important that a woman remain pure while she was unmarried: she would know a man only after she married. This Thwa woman was found to be one of the women among the Mpondomise who were pure.

Well, time passed, then one day it was observed that "Oh! The Thwa woman is pregnant!"

Those at the royal residence were startled, and they asked her, "What is this?"

She pointed into the air.

When she did this, it was known that she meant that she had been made pregnant by the king. No one repeated the charge, not a person spoke; no one asked her again why she was pregnant. All the people were silent now.

This Thwa woman was seen at the royal residence, preparing now for womanhood. She stopped dressing and acting as little girls did.

One day, Ngcwina, the king of the Mpondomise, called some trusted men at the royal residence, and he said to them, "Please go with this woman, Manxangashe. She must return now to her home, to her home on the mountain. Go with her."

They went with her then, journeying from Matatiele to Mount Ayliff, to that mountain at Ngele. When they arrived over there at the mountain, this mountain at Ngele, Manxangashe kindled a fire. She kindled a fire, she looked around and behind. She looked around, then she scattered the fire.

They walked on, and again she kindled a fire. She again looked around and behind; she looked around, and again she scattered the fire.

They walked on, and again she kindled a fire. And when this fire was smoking there, it was seen that there was also smoke far off, in the distance, over there on the mountain.

She said to the trusted ones, "Stay here until I return."

She left them, she went over there—above, to the place where the smoke was. She remained there for three days, and the councillors stayed in that place, waiting for her.

On the third day, they saw her coming.

Manxangashe arrived, and said, "It is said that, as I am pregnant, I must be given a dowry, because all women are given dowries. I have been told to say, 'Let two oxen be brought.'"

They left then, and went to report this at Mvenyane. The trusted ones arrived at the royal residence, and reported the matter to the king of the Mpondomise, that the Thwa people were requesting a dowry.

"They said, 'Let two oxen be brought.'"

The oxen were produced.

The Thwa woman had told them, "When you come back, you must come along kindling a fire just as you saw me do it—kindling a fire, extinguishing it; kindling, extinguishing; kindling, extinguishing. Now when you have kindled a fire and it is smoking, and you also see smoke on the mountain, then you must stay at that hearth. Do not leave it."

So it happened then. When they got there to the mountain, they kindled a fire, then they scattered it. They went on, they walked on. Then they again kindled a fire, and again they scattered the fire. They walked on, they travelled on. And they kindled a third fire. This time, there was smoke over there on the mountain. They remained there, and eventually Manxangashe arrived. She arrived, and drove the two oxen away. She went up to the mountain with them. She went off for a time, and then returned.

She said, "It is said, 'Come with two more black oxen like these.' And when you return, do the same things again. Kindle a fire just as you have kindled this one. And when you see smoke, do not move from where you are."

The trusted ones travelled then, they returned to the royal residence. When they arrived at the royal residence, they reported what had occurred. The king answered easily, and produced those two cattle—they were four now.

The trusted ones took the cattle, and when they arrived over there on the mountain, they did exactly what they had been doing—continually making a fire. Again, at the third hearth, there was smoke, and they stayed there. Manxangashe arrived; she took the oxen, and went up with them. They were four now, the cattle that had been produced. She hurried off, then returned.

She said, "It is said, 'Come with two black oxen.'"

As before, they returned to Mvenyane, and the king again produced the oxen.

They travelled then, and did the same thing they had been doing. And again, at the third hearth, there was smoke on the mountain, and they stayed.

She came, and said, "It is said, 'Come with two black oxen, so that there are eight of them.'"

When they had returned and reported this to the king, he again brought out two black oxen. They took them, and went back to the mountain. When they had arrived on the mountain, they did just what they had done before. And again, at the third hearth, there was smoke. When the smoke appeared, Manxangashe arrived. She took the two oxen, and departed. They waited.

"Why isn't she coming back?"

"Why isn't she coming back?"

"Why isn't she coming back?"

"Not a sound!"

A week went by then, a week passed, and still she had not returned. Then, as they watched, they saw some people coming over there on the mountain. They were carrying something. Those people approached, and when they were some distance away, they unloaded these goods. They unloaded them, continually ascending and descending, putting the goods down at that distant place. Then they returned to the mountain, and Manxangashe came down to the trusted ones.

"They are Thwa people, and today it is said that I have been married to the Mpondomise. The Mpondomise have been accepted by the Thwa on the basis of the dowry of these eight black cattle. It is said that we should now go and take those goods, those things over there. It is said that we must go over there in a hurry, because this is the nature of an agreement in the Thwa manner: when a suitor is accepted by the Thwa, it usually rains. So a big rain is coming. Let us hurry!"

The rain affirms the agreement, affirms that the Mpondomise have been accepted by the Thwa; it is an indication that the Mpondomise have been approved by the Thwa.

They took the goods then, and returned to the royal residence at Mvenyane. Then the rain came. The rain came, and thus was originated a practice among the Mpondomise: when there is a drought, they go to the Thwa to plead for rain. That custom was born on that day: if there is no rain, the Mpondomise go to ask for rain from the Thwa. And the Thwa make efforts to produce rain when the Mpondomise experience a drought. That is how the practice began here among the Mpondomise.

STRUGGLE FOR THE THRONE

SIBLING RIVALRY

The Thwa woman remained at the royal residence as a wife. Now that she was a wife, a house was built for her by the king below the cattle kraal, and she lived there; it became the place where she lived. This Thwa woman was pregnant, and when the time came she quickly gave birth to a child who was a boy.

The other wife of the king, the one from the Ngutyana clan, was utterly barren—yet she too was suddenly seen to be pregnant. She was evidently jealous of the Thwa woman's pregnancy and deliverance, and now she too produced a baby—yes, even the queen from the Ngutyana clan hurriedly gave birth to a child, and this child of the Ngutyana woman turned out to be a boy. So it was that these two children were more or less of the same age, and when one of them began to play in the courtyard, the other joined him quickly. That is the way they grew up. They were children of almost equal age and size, and they grew up together. Now this child of Manxangashe, the Thwa woman—it was said that his name was Cira.

What is meant by this word "Cira"? No one knows what the name means. The Thwa woman constantly played with the child, and when she did she would say, *"Cir'! Ngci! Cir'! Ngci! Cir'! Ngci!"* And the Mpondomise could not understand these sounds, the people just could not fathom what she meant. So it was that this child of the Thwa woman was given the name "Cira."

As for the queen from the Ngutyana clan, her child was called Dosini. It is really an alteration of his proper name. His mother originally called him Ndosina, meaning that people rejoiced and danced because they had children, and now she too would dance.

"Yes, I too will dance like the other women! I had no child all this time, and these women of the royal residence were gloating about it. Now I'll dance like the other women!"

Time passed, and the practice of calling this child "Ndosina" was stopped, and he became known as "Dosini." The son of the Ngutyana woman was Dosini; the practice of calling him Ndosina stopped.

These children grew up then, these growing children. Actually, the children of the king here at this home were many. I am limiting myself to these two children. There were many, the children of the king. These children grew up then, but something happened while they were growing up, and this confused the people. They wondered why the king did this: Whenever there was feasting, he would say that the two boys should go and race each other. They should go off, and when they were at a distance, they should turn and run, returning with speed. As they came

Xhosa children

running, this father of theirs would take meat in this hand and that. He would take meat in that fashion, and the meat in the right hand he would give to Cira; the meat in the left hand, he gave to Dosini. If Dosini happened to be on the right hand side, and Cira on the other, the king would cross his arms and give to Cira with his right hand; if Dosini was on this side, he would cross his arms and give to Cira with the right hand. Never on any of those occasions when the boys raced did he give meat to Dosini with his right hand.

Well, they grew up; and when they had grown up, they were men, they were circumcised. When they had been circumcised, and as they continued to grow up, this Dosini loved very much to herd. As for Cira, when they had become young men, he liked to sit in the court. When Dosini had become a young man, he had a tendency to do something which was very bad. He would take the cattle out, and, when he got to the pasture, he would take mud and smear it on his face. Then he would go to other boys who were herding cattle. When they saw someone with mud on his face, the boys would leap up and beat him.

"What is this thing?"

"What is this?"

"What is this thing?"

The boys would beat him, then he would wash off the mud.

When they got back to the royal residence, Dosini's escort would charge that boys from a certain clan had beaten the chief.

Everytime they looked, "He's been beaten again!"

That clan whose boys had attacked the chief would be fined cattle.

And Dosini would again go out to herd, accompanied by the escort with whom he customarily went—the escort's name was Sisusempaka,[3] a son of the Thithiya clan. When they arrived over there in the pasture, Dosini would put his garments down and smear himself with mud. Then he would go to the other boys who were a distance away. When he came to those boys, he would provoke them, and then be beaten. That would then become a court case, it would be said that the boys of such-and-such a place had beaten the chief, and that clan would be fined.

One day, he was repeating this thing that he was in the habit of doing, and he went to some boys. He again smeared himself with mud, and they beat him. Sisusempaka then came up, and made the charge at the royal residence. That clan was to be fined—it was the Nyandube clan:

> Khwetshube, son of Xhwangu,
> Valley in which birds sleep!

The Nyandube clan was fined. It was a heavy fine, resulting from Dosini's ruse that had caused him to be beaten by the children.

A young Xhosa man

But then the Nyandube clan departed, the entire group went off to Mpondoland. They stopped being Mpondomise, they stopped being Mpondomise because here in Mpondomiseland was a chief who appropriated the people's cattle in an underhanded way. And they went to Mpondoland.

Then the people realized that "No! People are refusing to remain in Mpondomiseland! They're scattering because this business goes on unendingly, and the guiltless suddenly become guilty!"

Ngcwina called the household together, and said, "This Dosini is disrupting the Mpondomise community! Seize him!"

He was seized.

"Bring him here to the entrance!"

He was brought there.

The king said, "Bhukwana!" referring to his first son. "Jump on him!"

Bhukwana refused.

He said, "Nxotwe!" calling another of his sons. "Jump on him!"

He refused.

Then he said, "Zumbe!" All of these were names of his sons. "Jump on him!"

He refused.

He said, "Cira!" Cira was the son of the Thwa woman. "Jump on him!"

And he jumped on him.

Then he said, "Jump on him three times!"

He jumped on him three times.

Then he said, "Tell him to say, 'Older brother'! Make Dosini call you 'Older brother,' Cira!"

It was clear that Dosini did not want to say this.

Then the king said, "Here! Here is a spear! Stab him in the stomach three times, and make him say, 'Older brother'!"

Cira took the spear and stabbed him, and said, "Say 'Older brother'!"

And Dosini said, "Older brother!"

The father said, "Now make him say, 'I have abdicated'! Stab him three times, and force him to say that he has given up the kingship to which he is heir!"

Cira stabbed him like this! and this! and then he said, "Say that you relinquish the rights of the firstborn!"

"I relinquish the rights of the firstborn!"

Then the father said that Dosini should be released, and he was released.

It was said, "Today, your rights to become king in your father's place have ended! Those rights have ended because you were exploiting the nation!"

After a few days, Dosini left the royal residence. He departed from

Matatiele, and after a time reached his mother's place in Mhlabathi in Tsolo District. He remained there, and built a homestead: that was to become Mpondomiseland.

Soon after Dosini had departed, Ngcwina the king died. When Ngcwina had died, Cira became king, that same Cira who had been instructed to jump on Dosini, who had made Dosini say to him, "Older brother," who made him say to him, to Cira, "I relinquish primacy, I hand it over to you." And when Ngcwina had died, Cira became king of the Mpondomise.

Just before Ngcwina died, he said, "I'm sure that Dosini will give you trouble. To diminish the chances of that happening, you must move the royal residence. You must go and settle in the very place that he has settled, because all the land between the Mthatha and the Mzimkhulu rivers belongs to the Mpondomise. The place where Dosini has settled is still within Mpondomise jurisdiction. He'll make claims, he'll insist that he is the king of those Mpondomise he lives with over there. Now when you begin your rule, you must go and settle in the very place that he's living in, so that he'll have no way to stir up the nation, to make the nation rise up against you!"

So it was that a few days after Ngcwina had died, Cira moved his royal residence from Mvenyane in Matatiele, and came to establish it here at the Lothana, a little river that is very close to Mhlabathi where Dosini had settled. The two places were in the same area. By that act, the royal residence of the Mpondomise was moved from Matatiele to this place where Dosini was living.

Ngcwina's grave is at Mvenyane, at the place where the seminary school is now located—the place called Mvenyane, in Matatiele.

Now the rule of the Mpondomise was in the hands of Cira, the son of the Thwa woman. He was king of the Mpondomise now; he ruled all the land between the Mthatha and Mzimkhulu rivers, between the Drakensberg Mountains and the Mpondo nation, until the end of his life. His grave is here at Lothana. The Lothana is in what is now Qumbu District.

And that is the story of Ngcwina's son, Cira.

Cira left behind one son; his name was Sabe. Cira was one of those Mpondomise kings who had one wife, and he left behind a son, Sabe.

Sabe ruled then; he became the king of the Mpondomise. An *intsomi* of the Mpondomise says that it is doubtful that there will ever be a person as handsome as Sabe. He was exceptionally handsome, a good king who loved social gatherings and joyful occasions.

One notable event that occurred during Sabe's reign was the arrival of messengers who had come from Tshawe, the king of the Gcaleka, the Xhosa. These messengers had come to ask Sabe for help. Tshawe was at variance with his brother, whose name was Cira—not this Cira of the Mpondomise, but the Cira of the Xhosa. To Sabe, son of Cira, came people who had been sent by Tshawe, and they said, "Tshawe! Tshawe says that we should summon you. He is having problems with Cira. He needs your help."

Sabe granted the request; he sent out the members of the Rudulu clan. These Rudulu are the progeny of Sikhomo, by that time quite a large group. He sent the Rudulu to go and help Tshawe. And so that force of Rudulu went, and when they arrived they assisted Tshawe in the battle that was taking place. Cira was defeated by Tshawe, and Tshawe then assumed the kingship and became the king of the Xhosa.

Tshawe said, "These Rudulu must not return to their homes!" He would give them much land. Because the Rudulu had assisted him, whenever there was a charge and the army was fighting, it became a custom for the Rudulu to invoke "Sikhomo's cattle." They would say, "We are Sikhomo's cattle!" So it was that Tshawe said that his grandson, a child fathered by Ngcwangu, should be named "Sikhomo." And so it was that the Xhosa came to have a man whose name was Sikhomo, taking it from the Rudulu when they had acclaimed themselves in that war, saying, "We are the cattle of Sikhomo!" So Tshawe said that his grandson was to be Sikhomo. That is why there is this confusion about the Rudulu, why the Rudulu seem to be Xhosa. But they are not Xhosa, they are Mpondomise. They had only gone there to help. The Rudulu are Mpondomise who live in great numbers in the land of the Xhosa; they are Mpondomise, close to royalty and respected in that country. They are more numerous in the land of the Xhosa than in Mpondomiseland because of the great honors that they gathered there.

Sabe, then, ruled over the land of the Mpondomise—a handsome king who, during his reign, had among his sons one who was very handsome also, who resembled him. When there was dancing and the king came out, it would be said that the son who resembled his father should come out first. The women would ululate when the son and the king came out. They would say, "*Ki ki ki ki kiiiii!*" Then, following each other, came the "twins," Mhaga and Sabe. But Mhaga is the *son*, not really Sabe's twin. Because of the ululating of the women, considerable confusion was generated among the Mpondomise, so that among those Mpondomise who are the Haga, it was believed that Mhaga was Sabe's twin. But Sabe was Mhaga's father.

Sabe ruled until at length he died, dying there at the Lothana at the site of the death of his father, Cira. Sabe was survived by his son, Mhle.

THE SACRED SNAKE

MAJOLA AND THE SNAKE

Mhle became a very vengeful person: he nursed grudges and caused much commotion in this land. He had a son whom he loved, a son whose name was Ngxabane. This son was not born to be king, but Mhle nevertheless desired that the land be ruled by Ngxabane. That led to bloodshed. The Mpondomise refused to accede to that wish; they insisted that the son of the great house should be the one who would ultimately rule, the one whose name was Qengebe. And as for the question of Ngxabane being pushed forward by his father because Mhle loved Ngxabane's mother, no! that matter must end! Still, because of it, blood was spilled, the cause being the tumult created by the king because he loved Ngxabane's mother.

I, who am speaking, have the Ngxabane clan name because I am of Ngxabane stock, the same Ngxabane who was denied the kingship. It was right that he was not the king: the matter was rejected, and the upheaval ended. What prevailed was that the rightful son should rule, the one whose mother had been so "created"—that is, Qengebe.

When it became evident that, to the Mpondomise, Qengebe was in the proper line of succession, they put an end to this question. But Qengebe was removed by Mhle, who said, "Go back, further back, go to where we lived in the past. Go and establish a homestead in the Mzimvubu valley. Go back over there, to that side! As for this land that is Nyanda, the land that is called "At Nyanda," I shall give this to my favored son to rule." He was referring to the land now ruled by Chief Poto [of the Mpondo]: this became the land that he gave to Ngxabane, and he said that the heir should rule this very land between the Mthatha and the Mzimkhulu, all of it.

So it was that Qengebe ruled. Mhle died; his grave is at the Lothana, in Qumbu District. Now Qengebe moved the royal residence; he established his headquarters at the Mzimvubu, more or less in the area where Kokstad District is now. His royal residence was there, in one of those areas; Qengebe's royal residence was located there. And Qengebe became the king of the Mpondomise, because the Mpondomise said that they wanted him to be their king. Qengebe ruled then, and when he had assumed the leadership of this land, he married the queen mother. We are not told the name of this great wife. He married the queen mother (the queen mother is the one who will bear the heir). After the marriage, the queen mother became pregnant. And after she had become pregnant, dear friends, when it became evident that she was having labor pains, the women went as was customary to be the midwives to the queen.

Then the women were suddenly seen running, rushing out of the house!

The men hurried to that place, and next to the queen they found a huge snake!

"Oh! What has happened?"

The snake had obviously come out of the stomach of the queen! They decided not to kill it.

"No, it must not be killed."

They coaxed it, they coaxed it, then took it away. But they did not kill it. They just nudged it along, then released it some distance away.

After that, the queen gave birth to a man child. When the queen had borne this child who was a boy, it was said, "His name is Majola!"

It would happen that, when Majola was asleep, the snake would suddenly be seen right there beside him. But it would be left alone, and it would depart in its own time. If Majola happened to fall sick, the snake would suddenly appear, and the next morning Majola would get up, recovered—after the snake had paid a visit. This is quite a common snake, well known. But it had this peculiarity that it repeatedly visited this child; this child would be seen with that creature that had been beside him before he was born.

The child grew up, constantly being visited by this snake, constantly being visited then by this snake. Because the king's child was named Majola, as time passed the snake too was named Majola, after him.

Now this snake presents certain problems for the royalty here in Mpondomiseland. When a Mpondomise woman, a daughter of chiefs, is married, if the snake make its appearance it will be known that she is about to become pregnant. If, among Mpondomise royalty, a chief is facing a lawsuit or something like that, should that snake make its appearance it will be known in advance that the chief will escape whatever trouble he is confronted with. The snake's close relations with the Mpondomise date from that day that Majola was born.

So Majola ruled Mpondomiseland, and then he died. Regarding Majola's death: we are not told why it was that his grave should be made in a pool. But he was not buried like former kings of the Mpondomise. His grave was made in a pool, in the deepest pool in the Mzimvubu River. Majola was buried there. That occasion of Majola's burial—let me say, the manner of Majola's burial was the work of the Mbulu clan. "Mbulu" is a clan name that exists among the Mpondomise. The Mpondomise known as Mbulu, their clan name, went to bury Majola in the pool in great secrecy; no one knows what it was precisely that they were being secretive about. It turned out to be a significant event concerning Majola—that his grave should be in the water. But we do not know what led to that.

The reason is not revealed in history. He was buried in the Mzimvubu, in a pool in what is now Kokstad District, if I am correct.

When Majola died and was buried, he was survived by a son, a son whose name was Ngwanya. Ngwanya became a very great king, and he became very wealthy. He had a successful reign in this land of the Mpondomise. Ngwanya moved the royal residence from the Mzimvubu, locating it below the bridge that crosses the Thina River. And it was there at the Thina that he died. Like his father, Ngwanya was buried in a pool. I think that this pool is about a mile from that bridge that crosses the Thina; he was buried there in a pool, as was his father before him.

THE WOMAN WHO WOULD BE KING

THE STORY OF MAMANI

Ngwanya was survived by his son, Phahlo. Like his father, Phahlo became a prosperous king, a dignified king, a king who ruled the land of the Mpondomise well. We are told that Phahlo's great wife was a daughter of the Xesibe clan, she was a woman of the Xesibe clan. This queen who came from the Xesibe gave birth: she did not give birth to a boy, she bore three girls. We do not know into what clan or nation one of them married. One of them married into the Xhosa nation, she was the mother of Gcaleka. You know the Gcaleka people. Well, Gcaleka's mother was a Ngwanya woman; she was a Phahlo woman, a daughter from here in Mpondomiseland. Those people who are called the Gcaleka: Gcaleka's mother was a woman from here; she bore Gcaleka over there among the Xhosa. The name of that woman was Thandela, the one who bore Gcaleka. Phahlo's eldest daughter, whose name was Mamani, refused to get married; she said that she did not want to. And when her father died, she took over the powers, she claimed her father's throne. She did this in spite of the fact that there were many sons of Phahlo from the other wives of the other houses, but the great house was that of this Xesibe woman, and it was without a son.

Mamani came in and assumed authority. Against those who raised their voices, she sent the army and put dissenters to death. People kept their silence then, they did nothing; no one spoke up again. They ceased talking, and she ruled all the land of the Mpondomise, the land between the Mthatha and the Mzimkhulu, from the Drakensberg Mountains to Mpondoland. The land was ruled by this woman, Mamani; she was the queen of the Mpondomise. And this woman ruled harshly, everyone felt the effects of her reign.

Suddenly one day, a bridal party arrived, a party coming with a young woman. The party arrived, and was asked where it had come from.

Members of the party responded: "We come from Mpondoland."

"We have come to ask for marriage."

The bridal party brought with it a daughter of Nyawuza. This daughter of Nyawuza was brought to be married to this woman named Mamani.

When the Nyawuza woman had arrived—that daughter of Nyawuza, whose name was Ntsibatha—the nation was shocked, for Mamani had taken a man's place; she had set herself up as the ruler of the nation. And now, here was a princess, brought to her to be married! Mamani was not troubled by this; she simply produced the dowry—one hundred cattle.

The day of the wedding came, and Mamani married this woman; they got married, in a marriage ceremony. Then the stage was reached when the woman must go and kindle a fire in the bride's room.

One spectator commented to another, "Well, we'll see what happens now."

"Did two *women* ever copulate?"

"I tell you!"

Mamani went on, she said that the bride should go and make a fire. Well, she took her, and went into the room.

"I tell you!"

Mamani spent some time there; they conversed. And when Mamani went courting there in the bride's room, she took her brother with her.

Years before, when Mamani was a baby, her mother had asked her sister to come and be a nurse to Mamani, to look after the child. Mamani's nurse-girl became pregnant when she grew to be a young woman; she was made pregnant by Mamani's father, the king. Now the Xesibe woman had given birth to Mamani; and the nurse who had come to look after Mamani, also a Xesibe clanswoman, got pregnant and bore a child who was Sontlo.

So it was then, when Mamani went there to court, she took this boy; she went with him to spend some time together with him there. And when she departed, she said, "There's a woman for you!" She was addressing Sontlo, the child of her aunt, and she said, "Here's a woman for you!" So Sontlo chatted with the young woman as a young man chats to a woman.

In the morning, it was clear that the queen should come out as usual, that she should go to the courtyard to discuss business. And, Friends, over there in the courtyard, the official skin was placed in position—the seat of the queen. Then the queen took Sontlo and put *him* there, that same Sontlo she had said should cover that woman there—that girl of Nyawuza. She put *him* on her throne.

For her part, she sat down and said that the discussion of lawsuits should now proceed. As they discussed the lawsuits, she would say to Sontlo, "Give the verdict." And Sontlo would stand and pronounce the verdict.

"What's happened?"

Now someone else had been placed in the highest position, above the rest of the royalty.

"How can it be that a nurse's child should be so elevated?"

But because Mamani, if she heard anyone say anything about this, would have cut him up, Sontlo continued to rule. Mamani began to relinquish all of the duties of the queen, and Sontlo took up the reins and sat on the throne. Sontlo now became the king of the Mpondomise. Mamani limited herself to the activities of women. That daughter of Nyawuza, Ntsibatha, became the wife of Sontlo; she became Sontlo's wife. Sontlo was the king now, in place of the queen.

Then Mamani died. Sontlo continued to rule, and soon afterwards he died.

Sontlo said, "I know why I'm ill! I'm being bewitched by my older brothers because I took a throne I'm not suited for! That's why I am dying! Mgabisa!" he addressed one of Phahlo's children. "Mgabisa, look after this woman. If she bears a girl child, the child is yours. If she bears a boy child, then *he* is mine—mine, Sontlo's!"

So he died. After his death, in accordance with Mpondomise custom, beer was brewed, and that daughter of Nyawuza came and chose the person who would look after her interests—yes, and also become the regent for this thing here in her womb. Oh! the princes came back now, and the queen came out of the house, to choose. They sat there, the brother of Mngcambe, the sons of Phahlo. The queen came out, then pointed at Mgabisa; she chose him, that same Mgabisa who had been instructed to watch out for the child who would be born to her. She chose him, he being young, not one of Phahlo's older sons—a junior son. The gathering became rowdy now.

So this land of the Mpondomise was ruled by a regent, that one—Mgabisa—chosen by the queen. Mgabisa ruled this land. But when he had come to power, it soon became evident that his older brothers were not going to be obedient to him: they did not obey him—at all!

Everything was upside down now. There was no peace. Everyone did what he wanted to do.

Then Mgabisa set out, accompanied by the queen, Ntsibatha. They went over to Gcalekaland, to the land of the Xhosa, to Phalo's domain. Phalo was the king of the Xhosa at that time. They went there. When he arrived, Mgabisa put the matter to Thandela, Phalo's wife—Gcaleka's mother—saying, "My brothers over there do not obey me, even though I am the regent!"

She took two weapons and put them down, she put them in front of him and formed an "X" with them. She went into the house and took some magical medicines, and she poured them.

"Go, return home now. And rule! You are the one who should be the regent, who should hold the reins for the queen."

But there was something that Thandela wanted to know when they arrived at her place. The queen had already given birth to Sontlo's child—the child was already growing up. But there had not been another child after that one. Thandela wanted to know, "Why is it that the queen is naked like this? without another child? Go, go, go! You two go and— Go! Go, and kindle a fire!" So saying, she slapped him.

Mgabisa had been afraid to sleep with the queen, to treat her like a wife, because he was not accustomed to that: he had known her as someone of greater status.

"No," it was said, "you must marry this person. It is not right that you do not touch her as a woman."

So he touched her now as if she were his wife, and they returned. When they had returned, Mgabisa went after all his enemies, using the magic that Thandela had given him. He was now the agent of much bloodshed. Those who disobeyed him were thrown into confusion. He triumphed.

He triumphed, and they all submitted. Mgabisa ruled, reigning for Sontlo's child who had been left in his mother's womb by his father. Mgabisa ruled, and when he had known this queen as a woman, she became pregnant. And she bore a child whose name was Velelo. This Velelo came after Sontlo's child, whose name was Mngcambe. Velelo was Mgabisa's son, but his mother and the mother of Mngcambe were the same person—that queen, the Nyawuza clanswoman.

Velelo came after Mngcambe in birth. And after Velelo came Nkulu, a girl. Nkulu and Velelo were both Mgabisa's children; they were borne by the queen, and came after Mngcambe. Nkulu ultimately married into the Mpondo nation. She was Faku's mother—Faku, the king of the Mpondo, was borne by Nkulu. And Nkulu was the daughter of Sontlo: Mngcambe, then Velelo, then Nkulu, all were Sontlo's children. Yes, they were borne by the Nyawuza clanswoman, Ntsibatha, the daughter of Nyawuza.

Mngcambe grew to maturity. When he had grown up, Mngcambe wanted to assume his rightful place as the king of the Mpondomise; Mgabisa had only been regent for him. But Mgabisa refused to allow Mngcambe to take over the kingship; he wanted to continue to rule, even though he was only the regent. That caused bloodshed here in Mpondomiseland. Mgabisa was a wise man, and it was clear that, if an attempt were made to settle the matter in the field, it would not work. "Settling a matter in the field" means to fight. It was plain that it would not do to try to settle this matter in the field, because in the field Mgabisa could not be moved.

Then, from among the minor chiefs, there appeared from Ngxabane's lineage a man whose name was Phalo—not the Phalo of the royal house of Gcalekaland, but the Phalo of the Ngxabane household. (The Ngxabane are a clan of the Mpondomise here in Mpondomiseland.)

When Phalo appeared, he said, "No, we can do nothing to Mgabisa. But I'll try something. Mngcambe must just relax and stop thinking about fighting Mgabisa. He just can't do that! He just can't fight with Mgabisa."

So time passed. Time passed, time passed, and then one morning news came that Mgabisa was dead. Unknown people had broken into his house and murdered him, and that was that.

The royal residence of Phahlo, the father of Sontlo, had been at the Mzintlavu River; when he was buried, therefore, he was buried in a pool in the Mzintlavu. And when Sontlo died, he died at Mzintlavu; when he was buried, he was buried in a pool in the Mzintlavu. Now when Mgabisa died. . . .

Mgabisa had established the royal residence in Tsolo District, at the place where the homestead of Chief Mavu Mabandla is now located—that is where Mgabisa's homestead was, where his royal residence was. He had taken his wife from the Mzintlavu and had come to live with her here in Tsolo. Then Mgabisa died; he was murdered, killed by three men who went in and murdered him, and then ran out. It was not known where they had come from, but they had been sent there by the chief of the Ngxabane clan; they were sent to do this thing, to kill Mgabisa in this way, because no one was able to do anything to him.

When Mgabisa died, then, Mngcambe came to take his brothers and the queen, and they all returned to Mzintlavu. The royal residence in Tsolo came to an end, that royal residence that had been here in this district. The royal residence went back to the Mzintlavu, where it was then established. The queen, Ntsibatha, remained there with her son, Mngcambe. And time passed. Mgabisa had died and been buried in a pool here at the Tsitsa, in a deep pool at the confluence where the stream Mpukane joins the Tsitsa. Mgabisa had several children and several houses that should not be confused with those of the queen. He had wives other than the queen.

The queen herself remained the wife of Mngcambe, she being the wife of Sontlo. Yes.

So the land of the Mpondomise came to be ruled by its king, Mngcambe. And he ruled. All the land between the Mthatha and the Mzimkhulu, between the Drakensbergs and Mpondoland, was under Mngcambe's rule; he was the king of the Mpondomise.

SHAKA INVADES THE MPONDOMISE

THE IMFECANE[4]

Time passed for Mngcambe, and then occurred the episode of a quarrel between minor chiefs of the Ngxabane clan, a quarrel among themselves involving Bhodi and Nxokazi. Mngcambe went over to the district of Nyandeni to resolve that problem, to stop the quarrel, to stop these minor chiefs from spilling blood. And Mngcambe was killed. He died trying to arbitrate the war among the Ngxabane. He died at Gungululu in Tsolo District.

Mngcambe was not buried in the river as the five kings who had preceded him had been—they had been buried in a pool in a river. He is the first king who was not buried in a pool. Mngcambe died, Friends. His royal residence was at the Mzintlavu River in what is now Mount Frere District—yes, in the district of Mount Frere, at the Mzintlavu.

Mngcambe died, leaving behind a son who was Myeki. And because Myeki was still a child, it was clear that his uncle, Velelo, should become the regent—this Velelo who comes after Mngcambe in birth.

The land of the Mpondomise was now ruled by a regent, Velelo. So Velelo ruled.

Important things happened in Velelo's time, because he ruled during the era of Shaka. A major fight occurred over there at Mzimkhulu between Velelo and Macingwane, the latter being pushed from behind by Shaka. And there was a significant struggle between Velelo and Madikane, because Madikane wanted to cross the Mzimkhulu and come to this side. Velelo drove him back. There was another big fight, this one involving Ngozi, a Thembu clansman who was being overwhelmed by Shaka. Ngozi was also defeated by Velelo, and he too did not cross the Mzimkhulu.

Then a very big episode took place. Ngozi and Macingwane were chiefs who accompanied Shaka into battle; they were Shaka's equals, both of them great heroes in the land of the Zulu. The two joined forces on the other side of the Mzimkhulu River, then they crossed and entered Mpondomise country. A crucial battle was fought in Kokstad District, on a mountain called Nolangeni. If one travels through that area and asks, "Where is Nolangeni?" it will immediately be pointed out. A great clash took place there, a battle in which Macingwane combined his regiments with those of Ngozi; the Mpondomise forces were commanded by Velelo. And Velelo overcame both of those Zulu chiefs. He killed Macingwane, and Ngozi fled into Mpondoland.

Then it became clear that Velelo's time as regent was expiring, that

Mngcambe's son, Myeki, should now take over the kingship. So Velelo handed the authority over to him, and Myeki ruled.

One day during Myeki's rule, some people were seen driving a large number of cattle over there by the Mzimkhulu River—in those days, the Mpondomise occupied all the land right up to the Mzimkhulu. People were seen driving a great herd of cattle. Then they suddenly abandoned the herd, and ran off. They were pursued, and seized.

"What's this about?"

"Well, we're Mpondo."

"And these cattle?"

"Shaka is coming!"

"His armies!"

"The Dukuza Regiment!"

"Shaka's regiment is approaching Mpondoland!"

"Faku has instructed us to leave these cattle at a ford, where they can cross the river. They'll spend the night there."

"Then, when we see Shaka's armies approaching, we're to drive the cattle so that the Zulu follow them into *your* territory, into Mpondomise territory."

"We want the Zulu to stop coming into our land, into Mpondo country!"

"But we're wasting our time here!"

"The Zulu are coming!"

"The Zulu forces!"

The Mpondomise were then called together. A force was sent out to meet the enemy. Battle was joined with Shaka's forces, with the regiment known as the Dukuza. Myeki's armies wholly decimated that regiment. And someone hurried off to report to Shaka that the Dukuza Regiment had been annihilated by the Mpondomise.

The Lion of the land of the Zulu said, "Who dares touch Shaka Zulu? Who dares touch Zulu? Dingane! Go! Go, go and find the person who has dared to touch Zulu!"

A huge Zulu army set out then, moving toward the Mpondomise. That was in 1828. A mighty Zulu army went out, coming here. But in the interval, after the Zulu forces had been destroyed, the Mpondomise began to quarrel among themselves.

Zozi, a great man among the Mpondomise, said, "The land is now at war. But the ruler of the Mpondomise is weak! This Myeki is weak! Let the kingship return to Velelo, so that we can fight effectively against these other nations!"

That is what the Mpondomise were quarrelling about among themselves.

Zozi said, "We'll be crushed and defeated by the other nations now! The time has come when we must fight Shaka himself! But our leader is weak!"

The Mpondomise split over this. How could a king be demoted? The Mpondomise quarrelled, and fighting broke out among them. While the fighting was going on, they learned that Shaka was coming. Just when the Mpondomise were struggling over the question of deposing Myeki, Shaka was coming! The Mpondomise fled from the Mzimkhulu River, they moved off. And when they got to the ridges of Mbutho near the Xhokonxa, word came that "The Zulu have turned back!" When the Zulu had arrived there, they found no forces to fight against, so they turned back.

Then, because Velelo had made a claim against the king, those who favored Velelo insisted, "The king of the Mpondomise must abdicate!"

"The fighting must go on! We can never desert the king and be ruled by Velelo!"

The Mpondomise attacked one another. While the fighting was going on here at Mbutho, someone standing on a hill at Cingco said, "Just look across the Tsitsa! What's all that dust?"

And they looked: "The Zulu have returned!"

That was the day the Mpondomise were destroyed, slaughtered almost to the finish by the Zulu.

All the way from Mbutho, right up to the Mbashe River, there was a mat of slaughtered people, the Mpondomise liquidated by the Zulu without even fighting back.

When they finally reached the Mbashe, they were left alone. By the time the Thembu, the Xhosa, and the Gcaleka had taken up arms, the armies of Shaka had already gone, taking with them all the cattle of the Mpondomise, as well as people. All were driven ahead of the armies, taken all the way to the land of the Zulu.

Then the Mpondomise returned, sheepishly coming back to rebuild, having been emphatically defeated by the armies of Shaka.

During this era of Shaka, Sotshangane was ruling at a certain place in the land of the Zulu. Sotshangane, Shaka's younger brother, was a hero who had accompanied Dingane in this battle. Bards, praising Sotshangane, declared,

> "Sotshangane, the lion that drank
> The waters of the Mbashe,
> the Mbashe of the Xhosa!"

That was the day the Mpondomise were destroyed by the Zulu, when all of the Mpondomise cattle were taken. If you are ever over there at Tshali's place in Jengca, you can see the pass where all this livestock was located. It was taken from over there at Jengca, and driven all the way to the land of the Zulu—the Mpondomise cattle, the Mpondomise having been destroyed by the Zulu. That was the day the Mpondomise lost their status as the biggest nation here. They were crippled by Zulu.

A LAND DIVIDED

THE DISAPPEARANCE OF THE MPONDOMISE WAY OF LIFE

Then they returned, and settled here. And when the Mpondomise had returned to live here, it was clear that they should not have two kings— because Velelo, the one whom many had proposed should rule, had not been defeated. But Myeki, the one many had said should abdicate because he was weak, had not been defeated either. Because neither had been vanquished during the fighting, during the period when they had been interrupted by Zulu, both of them came to rule here. That is the reason that today Diliza[5] rules here[6] and the other one[7] rules across the river.[8] That is how it happened, how it came to be. So some of the Mpondomise were ruled by Myeki, the son of Mngcambe; and others were ruled by Velelo—and that is the way it is, even today.

Myeki and Velelo ruled then. During the time that they were ruling, the Mpondomise kings now being two, it happened that Madikane arrived. Refugees were on the move, coming down from the land of the Zulu. Yes, then came the refugees.

Let me put it this way: when the Mpondomise cattle had been taken away to the land of the Zulu in 1828, Shaka died. Dingane took over the kingship.

During the period of Dingane's rule, the chiefs of the north who fled from Dingane moved down here. Refugee battles without end were fought by the Mpondomise; chiefs who arrived here—Makinana and his followers, Golizulu and his followers, and others—were driven back. Then Madikane arrived. When he had arrived, Madikane pushed the Mpondomise, he drove them right back to the Thembu. In Thembuland, the Mpondomise were aided by the Thembu. Along with other nations, the Thembu assisted the Mpondomise, and Madikane was killed with his mother, Vatshile, together with many chiefs of Madikane's domain. That was before they had become known as the Bhaca; they were still called the Njoli at that time. The Njoli of Madikane were slaughtered by the allies, the Thembu and the Mpondomise, in Ngcobo District. After the defeat, Madikane's son, Ncaphayi, established himself in Qumbu District. The Mpondomise were far away, he had driven them off. He established himself, and remained in Qumbu District. The Mpondomise established themselves outside this territory. He had driven them from all this land; he became the ruler here in this country. And so it was. The refugees, the Bhaca, had come; they lived now at Qumbu in the land of the Mpondomise, and they killed Velelo. Myeki, the king, was at Rode in the district of Mount Frere, where he had fled.

Because matters had come to this, Velelo having died, it became clear to the Mpondomise that the Mpondomise way of life should disappear from this land, and that the land should become the domain of the Bhaca. The Mpondomise then established themselves in the area of Nyanda. Others built their homesteads far away. All this land was now ruled by the Bhaca. During the period that the Bhaca reigned in this land, they sent out force after force against the Mpondomise; one force and then another went out against the Mpondomise, and so on, and on.

Velelo was dead, killed by the Njoli; Myeki was far off at Rode. Velelo's son was Diko: on the day his father died, Diko was also seriously injured, and he went to die at Mngazi. The Mpondomise were now ruled by a regency that was set up to hold the kingship; Mandela was the regent. Then the Bhaca sent out another force to fight the Mpondomise and scatter them. A battle was fought in Ngqeleni District, a battle between the Mpondomise and the Bhaca. In that battle, the Mpondomise sought the assistance of a Hlubi herbalist-diviner whose name was Vuthela. This doctor took a python, he took a frog, he took some milk, and he concocted a magical potion. Having prepared it, he studied the potion carefully, then concluded, "Mpondomise, today you will overcome the Bhaca!"

Meanwhile, the Bhaca were upon them, and the battle was waged at a place called Mxhoxho in Ngqeleni District. The Bhaca were defeated and driven away by the Mpondomise; they were slaughtered. Thus massacred and defeated in the struggle, the Bhaca gave up their claims to the land of the Mpondomise, and they migrated then to Mpondoland. When they got there, they gave up their independence, and were ruled by Faku. When they had been over here among the Mpondomise, they were sovereign because they had defeated the owners of the land; now, they were ruled by Faku over there, and the Mpondomise returned to reestablish themselves here in their land as before. The Mpondomise returned and built here, and the Bhaca departed and settled in Mpondoland.

Among the Mpondo, Ncaphayi, Madikane's son, quarrelled with Faku. A great fight followed, a really great fight, and the Bhaca were defeated in that battle. And Ncaphayi was killed, Ncaphayi was killed. Then Ncaphayi's wife set out and journeyed to Qumbu, to the headquarters of the Mpondomise which were in Qumbu, where King Mbali was ruling on Mhlontlo's[9] behalf. When Ncaphayi's wife, a Juxu clanswoman, got there, she said, "I am a refugee [ndiyabhaca],[10] Mpondomise, and my people of Njoli and I beg to be sheltered by you." Mbali then gave her the land in

Four Xhosa youth

which the Bhaca live today, all of the land in Mount Frere District. She was given that land by the Mpondomise; she said that they were now refugees [*ayabhaca*], and Njoli no more. They were refugees [*amaBhaca*] because they had enough of war. So the Bhaca arrived and settled in this land. They arrived there after the Mpondomise had returned from their flight, after they had been established here again and were ruled by Mbali, Mhlontlo's regent.

So Mbali ruled.

During the reign of Mbali, about five years after the Bhaca had arrived, it became clear that Mhlontlo should be circumcised and become a man, so that he could take his rightful place. When Mhlontlo was going through the circumcision ritual, the Bhaca arrived and besieged the initiates over there in the circumcision lodge, and killed some of them. War broke out then in the land of the Mpondomise, war between the Bhaca and the Mpondomise. When the fighting started, the king of the Bhaca became Makhawula, the son of Ncaphayi. At the time when the Bhaca had first arrived, they had come with the queen; her son's regent was Diko. He held the reins for this Makhawula. It was Diko together with the queen who had said that they were refugees [*ngamabhaca*], and that is how they came to be known as the Bhaca people. Now the king was Makhawula. War broke out, and Makhawula went to fetch Jojo, a Xesibe, to assist him in the fight. Then he went to get Sidoyi of the Ntlangwini area. And he also went to get Msingaphantsi, a Bhaca, the one on the other side of the Mzimkhulu. And he went to fetch Sonyangwe, a Bhaca who was also on the other side of the Mzimkhulu. These Bhaca were there, and there were also two Sotho chiefs, Sirunyana and Lipina. This considerable army set out, then, to march against the Mpondomise.

When that great army got there, the Mpondomise regent said, "We can't fight that army! We must surrender! We must release all of our cattle and leave them for the army to take!"

Then Mhlontlo, the one who was in the circumcision lodge, said, "Go against these people, Uncle!"

The other said, "Take a rope and tie him up! He's mad! This is not a force to be fought!"

So Mhlontlo was apprehended and tied up, and the cattle were released so that the Bhaca could take them. As the Bhaca were rounding up these herds of cattle, someone decided to release Mhlontlo over there where he had been tied up. When he was set free, Mhlontlo and all those boys who were his fellow initiates crossed the lower Thina River, and moved right in among the Bhaca who were in Qumbu District. Mhlontlo's army of initiates was maneuvering over there in the land of the Bhaca, setting fires, creating clouds of smoke, raising a lot of dust among the Bhaca, columns of smoke rising into the air. Mhlontlo was cutting up the Bhaca over there. Then the Mpondomise who had been hiding came out of the forests, and attacked the force that was driving the cattle. Because it saw the clouds of smoke rising in the land of the Bhaca, this force of Bhaca suddenly turned and fled. That huge force did not know what was happening, and now it was decimated. There was an army in front, another at the rear, and all of it was cut down.

Then Mhlontlo said, "Finish them off! Kill them! They must be killed! Killed! Not one should remain! Don't return until they've been annihilated!"

At length, when those forces of the seven chiefs had been thoroughly destroyed, a missionary who was at Tshungwane, at Osborne, appeared.

He said, "Mhlontlo, Makhawula is over there at the school. He accepts defeat. So stop your armies. Make them stop slaughtering Makhawula's forces! Tell your forces to stop destroying Makhawula's armies, Makhawula is conceding defeat!"

Because Mhlontlo was a person who had great respect for missionaries, he stopped his armies, and he went to Makhawula.

Makhawula said, "I submit myself to you. I am your person, Mhlontlo!"

So the war ended.

As he had fulfilled the custom of circumcision, Mhlontlo was already king when he returned because of this battle, because his uncle had feared it. Mhlontlo had been the one who had caused the force to charge, and, in the battle that followed, the armies of the allies had been defeated—those armies of the seven chiefs. By the time they had returned, Mhlontlo was being saluted: "Hail!" From that day, he was king of the Mpondomise.

So it was that Mhlontlo came into his own as the leader of the Mpondomise; Mhlontlo came into his kingship. As for the Mpondomise of Velelo: Velelo had died, and had been succeeded by Diko. Then Diko died from a wound, and he was succeeded by Mandela who held the reins for Diko's son. At the time Mhlontlo became king, Velelo's Mpondomise were being ruled by Mditshwa, the son of Diko. He settled in the area of Ngqeleni and Mthatha. All this land was now governed by Mhlontlo, he being the sovereign of the Mpondomise.

CONFLICT WITH THE THEMBU

MPONDOMISE FIGHTING AMONG THEMSELVES

Time passed, the land belonged to the Mpondomise, and they dwelled in their land, sovereign over all the people who were there.

It was during this period that Mditshwa, the son of Diko (Diko, the son of Velelo), had a war with the Thembu when he was in Thembuland. He had a war with the Thembu. The war that Mditshwa had with the Thembu was a very difficult one, and, because Diko had warred against the Thembu, the Mpondo also moved into the struggle and helped the Thembu. The ruler of the Mpondo at that time was Ndamase:

> Ndamase fathered Nqwiliso,
> Nqwiliso fathered Bhokleni,
> And Bhokleni is the one who fathered Poto.

Ndamase sent out a force against Mditshwa, against the Mpondomise of Mditshwa. But it became clear that, when the Thembu force came, Mditshwa would defeat it, and that, when the Mpondo force came, he would overcome it as well. Mditshwa would be able to conquer the two forces separately. But one day, the allies came together, the Thembu and the Mpondo, and suddenly Mditshwa's forces were surrounded.

Mditshwa, scion of Diko (Diko, son of Velelo), said, speaking to his forces, "Today, we must act! We must not move from where we are, if moving means only to confront the group that will throw a spear into our midst, if it means throwing ourselves to the death on that spear!" So he said.

The child of Diko has two teeth—
Had they been three, Mtika would die:
Small Mtika of Mpondoland,
Ndamase who heaps up at Noqingatha
Because he lies on his back;
Ngwanya of Majola's place,
Lying there in front;
Joyi who loves war,
Because he stabbed with a spear
In the courtyard at Mngcayi's homestead,
And when he tried to pull it back,
It stabbed him in the small of the tail.
You became like this
Because you had a contagious disease,
You, the one who does not cleanse himself
More than Leopard;
Stick of Ndamase that ate Mbola's back,
And two bad things of Mpondoland beat each other,
And Qakaza farted
And startled Ndlebe of the Tolo clan.
It is, of course, a custom of the Mfengu
To fart at each other.
Bhani with wings, Gasa of Niphazi.

So he said, then he made his forces sit down. He said that they should sit down, and they sat.

The allied armies charged, and as they approached—but before they got within stabbing distance or, if they had guns, shooting distance—some ominous looking dust was seen coming towards them. When the cloud of dust arrived, anyone who was standing fell on his face! If anyone wielded a spear, that spear was wafted into the air, and it fell no one knew where! Soldiers fell to the ground on their hands, they threw their weapons away and lay down. Then the wind, the whirlwind, passed. When it had passed, it was late in the day; it was dusk. He who slept, slept there. The other merely wandered in the night.

On the following day, the war ended. No one wanted to fight now. Everyone wanted to go to his home. So these forces departed without a fight. Mditshwa and his people, the Thembu, the Mpondo forces, all departed and there was no fight because of that whirlwind.

Then it became calm, and a little woman came along, saying that the allies were again approaching—the Thembu and the Mpondo. They had given up the idea of coming singly, they decided to come together—at the same time, on the same day. Now the Mpondomise of Mditshwa fled from Mthatha District and Ngqeleni, and from Libode, to the place where the Mthatha River enters the sea. They migrated from that area, and the Mpondomise army was force-marched away. If you are ever over there at Jengca, you can see the ridge they were forced to march to; it is called "At Mkhalana." They were driven to that ridge, they were pushed right to that point. And they were ejected from all the land below. So they arrived among other Mpondomise here.

When Mditshwa arrived, he found a Thembu chief here whose name was Jumba. Since the Mpondomise had been driven out of that land by the Thembu, it was clear that the Thembu who were here should be driven out but not killed.

Those of Mditshwa's royal residence, and Mditshwa and his family went to "pour" themselves into the homestead of the royal residence; and each man sought the homestead that was suitable for his family, and "poured" into it. The Thembu fled when they saw the force coming in—not attacking, only coming into the houses. They fled, and Jumba crossed to the Thembu who were on the other side of the river. So the Mpondomise returned to their own sites of former days, the ones from which they had been ousted. This land—the land between the Mthatha and the Mzimkhulu, the Drakensbergs and the Mpondo nation—was settled by the Mpondomise. That land was resettled, and the Mpondomise were ruled by Mhlontlo, the king, and Mditshwa, the second most important leader.

Time passed. And as time passed in this land, those groups that you see here now—chiefs like Lubenye, like Luhane, Magwayi, chiefs like Sidoyi, all the chiefs—this is the way they came in. The chiefs who are now in these eight districts, in these eight offices, the chiefs came in asking Mhlontlo and Mditshwa if they could settle and build here. So the chiefs came in. Now while these chiefs were settling in, the Mpondomise quarrelled among themselves in the war of Phakana.

Phakana was a citizen of Mditshwa's domain. One day, a group of people from Mhlontlo's royal residence passed by, and the dogs here at Phakana's place attacked them. The group of people beat the dogs off.

Phakana objected: "Why are you beating the dogs at the same time that I'm restraining them?"

They said, "But they're attacking us!"

He said, "Where are you from?"

They said, "From Mhlontlo's royal residence."

Then Phakana said, "Is there anyone left at Mhlontlo's place? since there are just six people, Mhlontlo being the seventh? You impertinent people! How dare you beat my dogs? What makes you so proud?"

Well, they passed on their way. Then, one day, while Phakana was relaxing, he saw six horses appear; Mhlontlo's turned out to be the seventh.

They were coming straight to Phakana's house. Well, Phakana and his group got up and ran. Then Mhlontlo and his men arrived, and the cattle of this homestead were impounded because Mhlontlo had been insulted by Phakana. When those cattle had been impounded, it was obvious that the result of this would be war, because his majesty, Mhlontlo, had not properly instituted legal proceedings: he had simply begun fighting. So fighting broke out among the Mpondomise, war broke out, a conflict that was to be costly in Mpondomise lives. The war of the Mpondomise, the Mpondomise fighting among themselves, now depleted their numbers.

LIKE A WOMAN CARRYING CHILDREN ON HER BACK

THEY CAME IN, THEY CAME IN

In that war, Bishop Key, the missionary, was present. One night, in a home that was on the mission station—the mission was then still over at St. Augustine's—one night, Mhlontlo was seen arriving. He was heard talking outside.

"Mze!"

"Isn't that Mhlontlo? the one who's involved in the fighting?"

"Mze!"

"Sir!"

"Come out here."

He wavered, hesitated, then eventually came out.

"Let's go to Key!"

So they went to Key.

"Well, Teacher, there is a war. People are dying. How can we end this fighting? Do you have any advice?"

"Yes."

"What is it?"

"Ask the government to come and arbitrate between you."

"Where is the government of the English?"

Then Key advised him on what Mhlontlo, the king of the Mpondomise, should do. Key was present; Mze, the man who had been called, was there; Mhlontlo was there—the three of them, at night. Well then, Key finished speaking, giving his advice, and then Mhlontlo went out. The land was still at war, people were dying.

Word eventually came from the English government, saying that it wanted to meet with the Mpondomise at the place where Somerville is now. The Mpondomise went to that place where Somerville is now, and an army of Sotho along with some European soldiers arrived there. Accompanying the army was the magistrate, Joseph Orpen.[11]

The magistrate rose—at that time it was not known that he was a "magistrate"; the people just referred to him as "government." Joseph Orpen got up, and said, "Mhlontlo, why have you called the government?"

Mhlontlo said, "I have called him so that he should become the protector of me and my people."

"Will you stop killing diviners?"

"Yes."

"Will you stop sending out armies to kill people?"

"Yes."

"Will you obey the government and pay taxes to it?"

"Yes."

"Where is this land of yours, which you are asking the government to give protection to?"

"It stretches from the Mthatha right up to the Mzimkhulu, it ranges from the Drakensbergs to the Mpondo nation."

His excellency, Joseph Orpen, then said, "From today, this land between the Mthatha and the Mzimkhulu, from the Drakensbergs to the Mpondo nation, is under the hand of the government. From today, there will never again be bloodshed—as from today!" And his excellency turned and said, "What do *you* say, Mditshwa?" because Mditshwa had been fighting with Mhlontlo.

Mditshwa said, "I also come under the government. *I* have no land. What I have is people. I come therefore like a woman carrying children on her back. This is what I want: the government should speak to me, then I'll speak to the people. And the people should talk with me, and I'll convey what they say to the government."

When Joseph Orpen interrogated Mditshwa on those same points— would he stop cutting down diviners? would he stop sending out armies? would he stop—would he obey the government? would he stop—would he obey the government?—he agreed to all the things that Mhlontlo had been asked.

Then his excellency, Joseph Orpen, said, "From today, the sixth day of October, 1873, this land is the government's land!"

That is how the Mpondomise came under the control of the government; they were ruled from that time, they became the government's people.

Now during the time that they were being ruled by the government, some people suddenly arrived at Mhlontlo's, and they said, "A Hlubi chief, Langalibalele, wants to come and settle in this land." Langalibalele was like many chiefs who were continually coming into this area; he was coming to join one of his brothers, Ludidi.

Mhlontlo said, "He's all right. Let him come."

But when it was agreed that the Hlubi chief could come, they learned that this same chief, Langalibalele, was fighting the whites. The reason he was at war with the whites was not known.

His excellency, Joseph Orpen, said, "Well, Mhlontlo, Langalibalele is fighting with the white man."

"What are they fighting about? This Langalibalele who is coming here is one of my subjects."

"Well, he is fighting the government. Now, I want some people to volunteer to go and settle this matter."

Mhlontlo said, "I shall not fight with my child! I do not even know what they are fighting about!"

His excellency said, "Well, it's all right. Lubenye! Luhane!"

These were Sotho chiefs, Lubenye and Luhane, the chiefs who had come here between 1867 and 1870, about that time. But those chiefs came from Lesotho, and his excellency was now asking them to be volunteers. Well, they departed, and they subdued this chief, Langalibalele; that war of his was brought to an end. Then they returned.

Mhlontlo said, "Where are my cattle? These chiefs who went to fight over there are my children! Where are the cattle they're supposed to bring to the royal residence?"

The magistrate said, "The spoils of war go to the government. They do not come to you!"

"Then what was the point of coming under the government, if the spoils will not come to me? It's *you, you're* the one who has made this decision! The government would never claim such a thing! So it's better that you leave, that another magistrate come here!"

They quarrelled over this, and time passed. After a while, other magistrates' offices were set up. The first magistrate, Joseph Orpen, came and set up an office over there at Tsolo, at Somerville. After he had done that, Joseph Orpen became the magistrate of all Mpondomiseland—between the Mthatha and the Mzimkhulu, from the Drakensbergs to the Mpondo nation. Then he prepared for the introduction of other magistrates for the various districts. So the magistrates came in: Mount Frere, Mount Ayliff, Kokstad, Matatiele, Mount Fletcher, Tsolo, Qumbu, McClear. These magistrates were now introduced, taking their offices under the authority of his excellency, Joseph Orpen. They came in then, they came in, they came in.

FREEDOM-FIGHTER

THE MPONDOMISE QUARREL WITH THE WHITES

Then, a chief of Matatiele, Magwayi, refused to pay his taxes, the tax that the Mpondomise were supposed to pay. The magistrate of Qumbu District, his excellency, Hamilton Hope, said, "Mhlontlo, there is a subject of yours who refuses to pay his taxes. He has been warned. Now a force must be sent out."

Mhlontlo said, "That won't do! I cannot send out a force. My wife, a daughter of Sarhili, has just died. According to Mpondomise custom, I cannot even begin to talk about an armed force. I must remain silent, and not speak about such things as armed forces."

His excellency, Hamilton Hope, then said, "You're a liar! You're a liar! You said that you would obey the government. And now, you're not being obedient to the government! You're a liar!"

Mhlontlo calmly departed, and when he got home a Mpondomise meeting was called. All arrived. He slaughtered a bull, and the meat was eaten. When the eating was at an end, he said, "Mpondomise, I have called you together because I have been insulted by the magistrate. Did you hear?"

They said, "We heard!"

He said, "What do you say?"

Gxumisa said, "That magistrate should be expelled for what he has done! The government must be told that the magistrate must go. You, a king, should never be insulted! The magistrate must be driven out!"

He said, "What do you say, Mpondomise? Considering that I have been so insulted?"

The Mpondomise said, "We all agree!"

"We say the magistrate should be expelled!"

When that had been concluded, a colorful citizen of Mpondomiseland, Mahlangeni, a great provocateur of Mpondomiseland, very great, got up. If he happened to come to any homestead in which a creature was being slaughtered, meat with the name *gebhe* was cut and placed before him while he was eating—some meat from the chest of the slaughtered animal was cut and placed before him, this most prominent firebrand, who surpassed all others living among the Mpondomise.

Mahlangeni, this agitator who rivalled all the fomenters of those days, said, "What is this you're saying? What cowardice are you speaking? Just name me!"

It was said, "*Ntsuke-ntsuke!*"

And he said, "Please name me!"

It was said, "*Ntsuke-ntsuke!*" and he took his gelding and drove it through the kraal fence, then fell over with it inside the kraal. He swung it back, and drove it so that it came to fall on the outside of the kraal.

He said, "Mpondomise, who is this who's insulted? The king of the Mpondomise! Insulted!"

The Mpondomise said, "This magistrate must be expelled!"

"It's not the government that insulted the king! It is this person!"

"He must be expelled!"

And the meeting came to an end.

When the meeting had ended, his excellency, Joseph [Hamilton Hope], called a meeting, and it was held out on the veld. When everyone arrived there on the open veld, he said, "I still insist that you go to Magwayi! He refuses to pay taxes!"

Mhlontlo then said, "Well, I have heard what you have to say. But I shall not be able to go. Gxumisa will take my place. He shall listen to all the directives that you make. Here, then, are your Mpondomise. You shall speak to them. Come here, Sunduza!"

Sunduza was the son of the missionary; they went off.

Then his excellency, Hope, got up and said, "Mpondomise, I have called you to insist that you go to Magwayi in force, because he's been disobedient! I've talked with him a long time, Mpondomise!"

As the magistrate spoke, Mahlangeni said, "Please say 'Ntsuke-ntsuke!'"—that flamboyant incendiary over there at the royal residence.

It was said, "Ntsuke-ntsuke!"

He said, "I say, 'Please say, "Ntsuke-ntsuke!"'"

It was said, "Ntsuke-ntsu—"

Oh! He leapt up and fell on the magistrate with a spear. He stabbed him. And he stabbed another person, and another—for there were three white men there, and he stabbed all three of these white men. As he was stabbing the third one, Thethani, a policeman who was nearby, shot at Mahlangeni, but he missed. When the shot missed, Mahlangeni jumped on the policeman, then he ran into the tent.

As Mahlangeni was entering the tent, Mhlontlo arrived. "What is going on?" And he restrained Mahlangeni.

But all three of the white men had died.

Mhlontlo restrained him.

"No!"

"These policemen?"

"No!"

Then there was a pause. They were wondering what to do. They did not know what to do, what would happen now.

Mhlontlo said, "Let all the white people come here."

It was necessary that the white people go to the mission station at Shawbury, for otherwise they would be hurt by the Mpondomise. There was confusion now, and some people broke into shops and looted them.

When the shops had been looted—in Tsolo here, there was a magistrate, [Alexander R.] Welsh. When he heard what had happened, he ran; he ran to the jail over there at Somerville together with the whites who were present. They went into the jail.

Then Mditshwa went there.

"I'm here, Welsh! Come out, I'll go with you to Mthatha."

"No, I'm afraid of you! You must come in!"

"No, come out! I'll go with you! But I won't come in there!"

Then Mditshwa called Silothile and Mngcothane. Silothile's offspring now lives in the place called Noziyongwane, and Mngcothane's progeny lives on Tsolo Mountain. He called those two men, "Go and report at Mthatha. Say that Welsh should be fetched." So they set out.

After a few days, an army of Mpondo arrived, led by these two men. There were also some white men with them, and Mngcothane and Silothile came along with this army. They came to this place which is now Somerville. These men had been told to take care that nothing was done by the Mpondomise to help this magistrate in any way, and so these two men departed and were rewarded by the government. Mngcothane was given a chieftaincy, and Silothile was given a chieftaincy, and then they departed.

Now came the armed might of the white man. Well, there was not even a fight. The Mpondomise were scattered, scattered in this land; the Mpondomise were scattered now. On the day of Khohlombeni, which is over there in Qumbu, the Mpondomise were gathered in great numbers, and the white army came. The army of the white men came there. The armies of the Mpondomise were routed, the Mpondomise were pushed over cliffs, they were surrounded in that marsh of Khohlombeni. Then, in the night, they got up and walked in the water, and broke through. At dawn, the government armies poured fire on that place where the Mpondomise armies had been. When they found that there was no response, they let up. In the morning, they saw that the Mpondomise forces had broken through. So the white man's armies departed.

When the armies of the white man had gone, one fellow said, "My lord, Mhlontlo, Gxumisa is dead."

Gxumisa was that orator who had spoken briefly during Mhlontlo's meeting. He is that man who had spoken at the meeting at the royal residence, he is the man Mhlontlo had said would command the force that would go to Magwayi's place. They told Mhlontlo how Gxumisa had remained behind—that is to say, he was dead.

Mhlontlo covered himself, and was quiet. Then he got up and said, "Mpondomise, today the government has defeated us. So—those of the mountain, to the mountain! Those of the water, to the water! Let us disperse!"

The Mpondomise said, "How can we do that?"

"Wherever we turn, we'll be stabbed if we dare separate from each other!"

"We'll die fighting!"

He said, "No, if you appear before a group of people and they ask, 'Who are you?' you shouldn't say, 'We're Mpondomise.' You should say, 'We're Tikita,' and when you've said that, the people will know that you're not combatants. And they'll leave you alone. They'll even pick you up."

There was agreement that, "Well, we've been defeated!"

Mahlangeni got up then—that man who had stabbed Hope, Hamilton Hope. And he said, "Please say, *'Ntsuke-ntsuke!'* "

It was said, *"Ntsuke-ntsuke!"*

He said, "Please say, *'Ntsuke-ntsuke!'* "

It was said, *"Ntsu—"*

He said, "*I'll* never go anywhere!"

As he said this, he took a gun and put it here, and said, "I'll not go anywhere myself! I'll stay here!"

The nation dispersed then, the people went in all directions.

And Mhlontlo said, "Let's go to Lesotho!"

Mditshwa said, "No, if we depart from here, the quality of Mpondomise, the Mpondomise ethos, will come to an end. We'll become refugees who'll never have any land! As for me, *I* choose to surrender myself. And when I've done that, I'll be arrested. They might even hang me, if they so desire, but they'll leave these people alone to rebuild the land."

After he had said this, insisting that he would not go to Lesotho, that he would hand himself over, he called the Mpondomise together and took a cloth. He tied it to a long stick, and said that this cloth should be carried to Mthatha to signify that he was surrendering himself.

When he had said this, he said, "Nokhaka!" Nokhaka was an important aide of his. "Take this stick!"

Nokhaka said, "I'll be shot by the white men! I won't go!"

Then Mditshwa said, "Edward!" Edward was a lay preacher who had come with Bishop Key. "You can speak the white man's language, you take this stick!"

Edward said, "Have I, a Thembu, been wrong to fight for you to the very end of the war that you should now order me to go and die over there?"

There was silence, and when it was quiet an important man whose name was Nomlala shot up. He said, "Mditshwa, be quiet a bit and let us of the Nomlala clan speak. Manqophu!" Manqophu was his son. "Thembani!" Thembani was also his son. "The chief here is speaking. What do you say?"

"We have nothing to say."

As they said this, another fellow, Sibhalala of Somhlahlo, whose offspring lives right here now, got up. He rose and took the cloth, and said, "Let's go!" and they left, going to Mthatha.

They were gone for some time, then they returned.

"Well, the army is going to come. If Mditshwa has indeed been pacified, they'll be able to tell when he comes forward to this army. They'll shoot overhead. If he doesn't retaliate, but comes ahead, then it'll be all right."

The army arrived. When it had arrived, when it had come into sight, the Mpondomise stood still. Shots were fired!

The Mpondomise said, "This self-deliverance idea is a sham! We're being shot at just as we think that we're calmly surrendering ourselves."

They fled to the forests.

Those other three men got up then and went forward, they went to the army.

"What's the matter now? Why do you run? We said we'd only shoot over your heads! Where is Mditshwa?"

"Never mind! Come, I'll take you to him!"

Thembani, Sibhalala, and Manqophu went now to where Mditshwa was.

Well, Mditshwa emerged, and he gave himself up. And so he was in the hands of the government. Peace was made.

Now then, concerning Mahlangeni over there—the man who had said he should have been given ammunition belts, guns, bullets, that man who had remained there. Before long, the armies heard him, and they went to the place where he was. An exchange of fire took place there. Mahlangeni was dug in among the rocks, and—well, he shot it out. They tried everything, but they could not discover where he was. Then the soldiers came back and waited for him; they took out their food, and ate. Day after day, they waited. Then one morning, there was a fog. And when the fog had lifted—here he is, plucking maize cobs right there in the army camp! He was picking maize cobs! By the time he was hurrying to his horse, they had seen him. They gave chase, pursuing him to his stronghold. As they approached his hideaway, he looked back and saw Larry riding hard on a gelding, on Gcazimbana, Mhlontlo's gelding that had already been taken as spoils from Mhlontlo.

He said, "Larry! Larry, hurry! You'll hold the seed with your mouth! You'll know that you met Mahlangeni today! You'll surely know all about it!"

He drove the gelding harder.

When Mahlangeni got to his stronghold, he jumped off, and, drawing his gun, said, "Now is the right moment!" As he drew, he was hit by a bullet from Larry's revolver.

He fell, and that was the end of Mahlangeni.

It was the end of Mahlangeni, the one who had stabbed those three white men. That was his finish.

FLIGHT

THE END OF THE MPONDOMISE

Mhlontlo, in the meantime, fled to Mpondoland; he arrived in the land of the Mpondo. Then the government army arrived in force in the land of the Mpondo, requesting permission to seek Mhlontlo, asking to be allowed to search for Mhlontlo themselves.

The Mpondo said, "He's not here!"

Then the forces of the government said, "Let us search for ourselves!"

While that disagreement between the Mpondo and the government was going on, Mhlontlo sent a group of men to request refuge in Lesotho—the government forces had obviously learned that he was here in Mpondoland. These men set out, they stealthily approached the Letsie people in Lesotho, in Lerotholi's domain—I think he was chief at that time.

"I'm seeking a place of refuge," and he agreed.

The men must now return to Mhlontlo with the news.

"No, we can't go back now! Where will we travel?"

Tshayeni, a member of the Ngxabane clan, said, "We were sent here by the king! We dare not fail to return with the news!"

Then he got up and left those ten men, and returned to this land. Eventually, he got to Ntabankulu. There is a forest at Ntabankulu, it is on a mountain that is in Ntabankulu District.

When he got there, he was told, "The king is here in the forest. It won't be easy to get to him. Take three stones," and he took them. "You must throw a stone three times. If stones are returned in the same way that you throw them, then you'll know that they're coming from the place where the king is. That'll be his way of saying that you should approach."

He went there, and arrived. At a big rock, he threw one of the stones. He threw another. And another. There was a corresponding response—stones thrown three times, coming from the place where the king was.

So he went down to that place, and when he came into view, Mhlontlo appeared with his gun drawn.

He said, "Tshayeni!"

"Lord!"

"Tshayeni!"

"Lord!"

"Tshayeni."

"Lord."

Well, then, he received him; he put his gun down. Tshayeni went to him and made the report, that Mhlontlo had been given permission to come to Lesotho.

At about the time that Tshayeni had returned, on the following day, there was to be a meeting involving the government, a meeting concerning the search for Mhlontlo.

Mhlontlo said, "I'm going over there to the meeting."

He took a hat, a knitted cap, and put it on.

"Where is he going?"

"No, I'm going!"

"Are you going to the white man?"

"Even though they're looking for you?"

"No, I'm going!"

He took an old blanket, and pulled it tight around him; he took his spear, and went out.

When he got there, he found the government people talking: "Mqhikela, Mhlontlo is here in Mpondoland! So open your frontiers! Let the government search for itself!"

Mqhikela said, "No, he's not here! I cannot open the frontiers, because your armies will frighten our children!"

The government said, "We say, 'Open up!' We want to search for ourselves, because you cannot arrest him!"

Mhlontlo then said, "Well, my friend, go on and open up your frontiers for them! Otherwise, they'll continue to trouble you. Open up for them! Tell them that you'll permit them to search for themselves. If you don't, these government people will just give you a lot of trouble."

Mqhikela: "All right then, my lords, I give you leave. You can look for yourselves."

They said, "Right! That's what we wanted."

So the meeting came to an end.

Mhlontlo got up and left the meeting.

He returned to his hideaway: "The government's armies will soon be here! Let's go!"

The men came together, then they moved on. Mhlontlo fled from Mpondoland. When they were in the forests of this land of the Mpondo, travelling by night and not during the day, when they were in those forests of Mpondoland, Mhlontlo said, "Oh! oh! oh! oh! I miss my horse!

Gcazimbana,
Land-of-equals,
I'm just a human,

> A thing that has to move;
> I'm just a person,
> A thing whose spirit is not of iron!
> Where will I sing my praises to you,
> Gcazimbana,
> Land-of-equals?"

And he wept.

Somyalo then said, "Oh no! What are you doing? Stop that!"

Well, Mhlontlo covered his head, and wept.

This Gcazimbana was Mhlontlo's horse, the one he would have ridden in this struggle. It was a fast horse. But now it was dead.

Actually, the horse had been impounded by the Bhaca. It had happened one night as Mhlontlo was travelling. He came across two men. In that war, the Mpondomise had used a password: if you wanted to find out if a group of men belonged to your side, you would say, "Sinika!" If the other was a Mpondomise, he would respond, "Sinika!"

When he met these men, Mhlontlo had said, "Sinika!" and these men had responded, "Sinika!" It was clear that they were Mpondomise. But the Bhaca fellow jumped on him, he caught Mhlontlo and rolled over on the ground with him, and said, "I've sworn that one day I would bring you in alive!"

While the Bhaca was holding him, Mhlontlo drew a knife and stabbed him in the stomach. He knocked him down, and killed him. He made for his horse, but it was being taken away: the other Bhaca was fleeing on Mhlontlo's horse! And Mhlontlo was only able to catch the horse of the Bhaca who had died, and he rode it away.

Gcazimbana was gone!

That is how this Gcazimbana, which he said was missing, came to be abducted by the government armies.

Now, as he was fleeing, escaping to Lesotho, he said that he missed Gcazimbana greatly.

The hero of Mpondomiseland then said, "Be calm, be calm."

Well then, Mhlontlo covered his head and wept, and they went on their way.

Then this hero, Somyalo, son of Mgqatsa, suddenly mounted his horse and departed, leaving the others there. They went on, now travelling, now taking cover.

As they awoke early one morning during their flight, Mhlontlo said, "Oh! oh! oh! oh! Why do I dream of my horse? Why do I dream of my horse?"

As he was saying this, two silhouettes came into view.

He said, "That's it! That's Gcazimbana!"

The silhouette came closer.

"That is the horse!"

Somyalo had gone to retrieve the horse from the English army at Kokstad. He found it in a stall; he had seized it there, and brought it along. He arrived now, and delivered the animal to Mhlontlo.

"Now I'll enter Lesotho! Yes, I'll get there now!"

They travelled on. While they were going over Qhashe's Nek, they found the government armies awaiting them. And another army was behind those.

Mhlontlo said, "There is only one way now. We must cut through, amongst the people who do not know us. We have had enough of these others, they have defeated us. But the Boer army is not familiar with us, we shall find a way to break through them."

Well, that was a crisis. It was a crisis, and then a bullet was shot from this army that was in front. Someone there was clearly an expert shot: every time he shot, someone fell.

Every time he shot, someone fell.

Whenever he shot, someone fell.

The bullets were coming from one man among the soldiers in the army that was in front.

The bullet never hit the ground, it always hit some person.

Then Mhlontlo said, "Nomantyane!"

Nomantyane, a Thembu who had fled with Mhlontlo, was an expert shot.

"Let us just seek out the location of that bullet. At this rate, our people will be finished off."

They lay low, they lay low, lay low, seeking the position of this bullet. Before long—well, they had the fellow who was shooting from among the government forces. And this white man was shot by Mhlontlo, and he fell.

And there was a great commotion!

"Hii-i-i-i!"

This army parted, and the Mpondomise went over; they came into Lesotho. And so the war ended on this side. Mhlontlo had fled and reached Lesotho.

Mditshwa, meanwhile, had handed himself over to the authorities; he was convicted and sentenced to three years imprisonment on Robben Island.

Mhlontlo, having fled, remained a fugitive over there in Lesotho for twenty-five years. He remained in Lesotho all that time. Then, one morning during the time that he was there, he was seen departing. Towards midday, he arrived at a place where a church service was being conducted by Roman Catholic missionaries. He got there, and stopped.

"Missionaries, I am here to become a convert. Earlier today, I went to a mountain to kill myself. When I got to the mountain, I took a head cloth and blindfolded myself, determined to hurl myself over the cliff. But while I was running, about to do that, I heard a voice that said, 'Stop! Do not do that!' I took the blindfold off, and looked around. But I saw no one. So I took the blindfold again, and tied it. I tied it tightly. And as soon as I began—it was as if I were being held by the arm! The voice said, 'Stop! Do not do that! Go, and offer yourself to God! You shall find a church service being held, go there and pray.' That is the reason that I tell you that I am offering myself." So said Mhlontlo to these Roman Catholic missionaries.

He was accepted then, and he entered the church; he was in a state of being received into the church.

Soon afterwards, soon after he had offered himself to the church, Mhlontlo went to a Hlubi fellow who was a detective. He went to this person: "Go, and tell the government that I shall be at Bhulekane, at the shop, on a certain day. Do not say that *I* said this. Just report what people heard."

That day came. Mhlontlo set out with his son, Charles, telling the other members of the group to remain behind. He went to this shop. When he got to the shop, as soon as he had entered—well, the police came out.

"We know you! You're Mhlontlo!"

Suddenly, Mhlontlo drew a revolver.

"Who is this that you arrest like a dog?"

They were so startled by the revolver that they fell back.

"I shall not be arrested like a dog! I am a king! Let a magistrate come and take me. Let me be arrested properly, not like a dog!"

When he had drawn the revolver, his son went to him and restrained him.

"Ho, Father! What are you doing now? You said that you were going to surrender yourself!"

"Why are they treating me like a dog then?"

"Well, well, leave him alone! Arrest him politely. Urge him to go with you. Do not touch him."

Well then, he was arrested by the government. When he had been arrested, his case was tried at Rhini, at the court for lawsuits in Rhini.

I obtained the report I am going to give now from Titus Fadane, an observer at the trial. This is the report:

Mhlontlo said, "I am Mhlontlo, king of the Mpondomise. Now then, one day a magistrate died. When this magistrate had died, I called Abeli Phatho and sent him to call a Mpondo, Mkreqo. I called this Mpondo, and told him that he should go and report at Mthatha that some white men had died there. And, because the white men were dead, the prisoners who had killed the government people should be fetched. That was the situation, but then we suddenly saw the force of the white man already among us. And so war broke out."

A witness was sought.

The story goes on: they suddenly saw the witness being produced from down here on the floor, when the floor was opened. He went to the witness box. This person entered the box.

"I am Mkreqo, a Mpondo. Abeli Phatho came to me, saying that Mhlontlo was calling me. I went to Mhlontlo. When I got to him, Mhlontlo said, 'Go to Mthatha and report that Hope is dead. Let the white people be fetched.' So I set out and went to Mthatha with a group of men. When we got to this side of the bridge at Mthatha, they asked which side we were on. We answered that we were Mpondomise. Suddenly their guns were about to fire, even the horses that we were riding were taken from us! That is why I could not deliver Mhlontlo's message."

This was the judgement: "Mhlontlo, you are released by the court. You are not guilty of killing Hope, Hamilton Hope, and his aides. The bad judgement turns out to be with the government. You are therefore released, so that you can rule your land as you have governed it in the past."

So he was released.

But when he had been set free, the government did not agree that he should rule again at all. I really do not understand how the things of government are carried out. The government utterly refused to allow Mhlontlo to become the king of the Mpondomise again. Yet the verdict had gone the way I have just described.

Mhlontlo returned in about 1910, perhaps 1911. He came back to this land and remained here until he died, dying in Qumbu District. He died in the place where his reigning son, Ntabankulu, is now. His grave is there, Mhlontlo died there.

Because of that episode, the kingdom of the Mpondomise was drastically reduced, and it no longer has a status like the others, like these other areas—here in the Transkei, the kingdom of the Gcaleka came under government jurisdiction when Sarhili, the Gcaleka king, delivered himself after the Ngcayechibi War. As for the Thembu kingdom, in 1876, Ngangelizwe, the Thembu king, delivered himself to the government. In 1864, Sigcawu, the leader of the Mpondo kingdom, delivered himself to the government. In 1873, Mhlontlo, the ruler of the Mpondomise kingdom, delivered himself after the war of Phakana.

The Transkei, then, is in the state I have described. And the manner of annexation is as I have detailed it. The land became the land of the government. It was in this context that Mhlontlo died. He died, and was survived by his son, Charles.

But it turned out that Charles had serious blemishes, and he was therefore not acceptable to the government. Charles then fathered Sigidi, and Sigidi was acceptable to the government. But then he was deposed some years ago because of a mistake that he made: he fought with the police. The government later restored him to the chieftaincy.

Herdboys at sunset

When Mditshwa returned from prison, he arrived and died. He died here where the royal residence is, and he was survived by his son, Mtshazi. Mtshazi was taken by missionaries to England, to go to school there; then he returned to reestablish himself here. He also died, he died in that place where the royal residence is [in Tsolo].

Mtshazi was survived by Lutshoto, his son—his son who, when the other chiefs were given batons by the Prince of Wales, was not given one. That agitated him very much. Then there came a fellow from America, Dr. Wellington. He joined Lutshoto's retinue, and when he had done so, the government saw fit to depose Lutshoto, and he was deposed. But soon afterwards, when he had begged for forgiveness, he was restored to the chieftaincy. Then Lutshoto died, and left behind the king we have today, King Diliza.

Yes, and this coming Saturday, Sigidi, son of Charles, will be over there at Diliza's royal residence, and Diliza, the son of Lutshoto, will be there.

These are the royalty of the Mpondomise, of this land that is between the Mthatha and the Mzimkhulu, ranging from the Drakensbergs to the Mpondo nation.

That is how the history of the Mpondomise ends, as far as I have knowledge of it.

Mtshophane Mamba

SNAPPING AT THE WATER'S FOAM

(SWATI)

Mtshophane Mamba, a Swati and an official court poet, was about sixty years old when he performed this poem on October 9, 1972. The performance took place at the royal residence of King Sobhuza II, in Entfonjeni, Swaziland. The audience consisted of ten men, five women, and one child. (NS-1426; tape 33, side 2)

The long-eared Bhuza:
When he gets the word,
He hurries to his shield,
Thundering shield!

He is a flowing spring—
We drink only tepid water,
For too long
We have been drinking tepid water.

Herdsmen,
Having gathered their stock,
Come to you.

You are a grower of trees:
Grow them, nurture them,
Because the red bull of Mahlokohla
Is maturing,
And he will pull them up,
Roots and all.

You are a buffalo with horns widely spread:
You gore your enemy, piercing him
With your horns.

You are a backward-kicker like a viper:
You devour your enemy
As if he were engorged
By a missile.

275

You are a ford with wildly falling rocks:
Crossed not by cattle,
But by men.
You are the lofty pool at Mhosheni:
Drunk not by cattle,
But by men,
Drunk by Jobe and Mlotshwa.

The king attacked at Mphanda's place,
And they lost their leader.

You are a beetle with mouth widely spread:
You daily devour herds of men.

You are Ndaba's surging one,
You never tire of heaving,
You are like the sea
Which exerts itself
Night and day,
Never tiring,
Ever surging.

You gathered the regiments,
The Soldiers and the Locusts,
You gathered them in Manzini.
The men of Manzini were jealous
Because their women were attracted
To the Soldiers and the Locusts.

You are renowned
Among those on buses and motorcars
That move through Bethany.
You are known at Langwane,
Known at Mgungundlovu:
Woman of Mgungundlovu,
Slaughter sheep
To feed the followers of the king
As they move through your land.
You shape the country,
You sculpted the Zulu mountains.

Whites of Durban,
Remove your shoes:
See him walking
Rumblingly
In the red shoes
Of his enemy Mjingane.

You are a labyrinthine sea:
You confuse us,
You don't swim, you surge,
Leaving the crocodiles of the sea
Snapping at the water's foam.

Turn your back:
Let India's mountains
Strike their blow.

You are a duck that beats its wings:
When you got to Abyssinia,
You were asked:
"What do you see, Child of Ngwane?"
You responded,
"The long-eared Bhuza,
When he gets the word,   ·
He hurries to his shield,
Thundering shield!"

You crossed the Red Sea
Like Moses of Israel.

Cold one!
You are the frost of the North
That was bitter for the youth
Of the Soldiers and the Locusts,
Of the Serious Ones.
You crossed the sea at dawn,
You crossed into Palestine.
Palestinian women said,
"Whence comes this handsome one?
Handsome one with white eyes
Like the women of Palestine?"

You are the shearer of our country,
You are like the mole of Methula,
Shearing the sheep of the Serious Ones.

Montgomery and his people
Were summoning you,
They were sending you a message:
You were called to Palestine,
You were called to Libya,
And when you were called to Italy,
Tears fell from Mussolini of Italy.
All nations heard the sobbing.
You move in thunder,
Like the thundering birds of the sea.
The cold of your arrow
Is like an open grave.
You are a lion that devours.
I salute you!

Ndumiso Bhotomane

THE LAND WAS SEIZED

THE NGCAYECHIBI WAR OF 1877

(XHOSA)

Chief Ndumiso Bhotomane, an eighty-four year old Gcaleka, related this history on September 10, 1967, at his home in Rwantsana, Centane District, the Transkei. Three Gcaleka elders were in attendance. (589; tape 10, side 2)

Something occurred over there at Bawa, in Nqenqa's jurisdiction, among the Nzotshwa clan over there. There they are: beer was being brewed on the occasion of the marriage of the daughter of the son of Ngcayechibi. Khewuthi was marrying a daughter of Msamo, the sister of Nazo in Bawa. That feast occurred in 1877. Then Maphasa's forces came down. Maphasa had been assigned by Sarhili the land of Khobonqaba. . . .[1] At Gobe, yes. At Gobe. His homestead was there at Gobe, in this very place where Freddie Soga is, just where the old school was on the Goba River. Maphasa was there. His forces went as far as the Xhobane River. You see, the manner of settling in those days was quite unlike the crowding of contemporary times. The homesteads were spread out then. So Maphasa's group stretched right up to our land, and a boundary—the Thulura—was established between us and them of the Xhobane, over there. This is where the Maphasa group crossed, going to the beer drink at Ngcayechibi's.

These are the princes who crossed at the time of Ngcayechibi's feast. The chief of Tsonyane was one of those who crossed. He is Mxoli:

> Mxoli is the son of Mbune,
> Mbune is the son of Khawuta,

in the supporting house; he was created into a younger brother of Bhuru. Their mothers are the same woman. It is he who crossed, together with these men I am about to name:

> He came with Nkuzana,
> He came with Stemela,
> He came with Thwana,
> He came with Ludwanga,
> He came with Ncitha,
> He came with Thwana, a scion of the Bamba clan,

279

as well as other gentlemen. I am only mentioning the important men with whom he came. It is they who provoked the war of Ngcayechibi.

Towards sunset, when they had drunk enough, instead of going home they insisted on being given more beer. They wanted more beer. And when it was denied them, they said that they did not see the beer pots that had been loaned, and they looked for them. They refused to go, and having consumed much beer they were drunk.

This is what happened next: a Mfengu man, also drunk, was leaving the house to go and urinate. And he put his hand on this Mxoli. He was beaten for laying hands on the chief, since he was only a Mfengu. Fighting broke out.

That is how the war of Ngcayechibi started. It was the Tsonyane of Bhuru who caused it.

When Bhotomane heard about this, he sent a message to Sarhili, telling him that the Tsonyane had fought with the Mfengu.

Sarhili said to Bhotomane, "Fetch the cattle of the Mfengu!" because a thousand had been impounded. Bhotomane fetched them from Khobonqaba, at Maphasa's. The thousand were sent—not the original ones, they were mixed up now with other cattle. A thousand cattle were sent. Now, the government wanted to discuss this matter with Sarhili, to discuss the thing that had been done by Maphasa. But when the government came to discuss the situation, it brought its armies, its generals. There was an army that was at Gwadane—three big government divisions. Another was at Bika. And while Sarhili was conducting a meeting at Holela regarding this matter, that group that was in Gatyana decided not to go to the royal residence when it saw the armies in Gwadane. They feared that their families would be exposed while they were going to the royal residence; they feared that their families would be attacked and killed. They would rather die with their families. And so they charged. Fighting took place, and the government forces, that had started the war, were put to flight.

Now, Sarhili did not yet know that this force of his had put the government forces to flight and had defeated them. When this force returned, its members said, "We've defeated the government! We fought it over there!"

Sarhili said, "Who ordered you to go to battle? Who gave the command? Because *I* was having a meeting here! And *I* had told you to come *here!* So you were harassed—that should have made no difference to you, because *I* had called you! I don't want any fighting! And fighting over food is not good! It was the same thing with Maphasa's group, the group I'm still remonstrating with!"

Well, it was not good. The government attacked. And that is the origin of the war of Ngcayechibi. That is how this land—

[Member of audience: Sarhili was not anxious to fight.]

Sarhili was not at all anxious to fight.

Then something else happened. Everything was spoiled by the Velelo, the Ndluntsha, and the Mbombo of Ngubo; they provoked the European government when they saw its forces, and they concluded, "Oh! Here it is!" approaching them. They decided not to go over there to Holela and leave these armies that were already coming. They feared that the armies would crush their families, and so they immediately charged. There was fighting. And the government forces were pushed back a little at first. But the government came back for more. And that is how the fighting went.

A second battle was fought at Bika. Sarhili began to be pushed back there at Bika. Fighting went on from dawn to dusk during the important days of the war, and the battles took place at these locations: there was the day of Ngunduza at Msintsana—oh! the graves are in the plantation that is now growing over there at Ngunduza, the graves of the government forces. Yes, the graves of government soldiers are in the plantation that was sown then, those who were fighting against Sarhili. Those days included

> The day of Gwadane,
> The day of Bika,
> The day of Holela,
> The day of Ngunduza,
> The day of kwaKhwabakazi,
> The day of Chebe,
> The day of Sebeni,
> The day of kwaCentane,
> The days of Mphame
> And Cwede
> And Guze,

where Sarhili was being sought.

Having been defeated now, he went to surrender himself. Bhotomane, Ngubo, and Joyi were the generals of the armies. Those armies were annihilated. Sarhili was overwhelmed, and defeated in the war of Ngcayechibi. The land was seized; it was then ruled by the government, and it continues to be so ruled to this day. . . .

Ashton Ngcama

THE LAND HAS GROWN OLD

(XHOSA)

The poet and performer was Ashton Ngcama, a Mpondo, born in 1923; he has lived among the Xesibe since he was a child. This performance took place on August 24, 1972, in Mount Ayliff District in the Transkei. In the audience were seven Xesibe men. (NS-486; tape 15, side 2)

Salute!
Rise up!

The way we travelled
Skirted the forests,
Hopped from river to river,
Mountain to mountain.

Who would tell our origins?
We, whose story is known by none,
A story preserved in blood:
Who would tell our origins?
Our story was not preserved
By anyone: it was preserved
By God.
We did not see this God.
From whom did we hear of him?
White nations arrived.

I say to you,
The one who coughs on his way home,
The chewer of the ring,
One with a mouth that is long,
I say to you:

Things are spoken just below the hill:
They summon the Mpondo people.
The one who calls on the shoulder,
The namer of the unnameable:
The one being called will not hear.

The one not being called will hear.
We eat meat but have no cattle,
We have sheep but have no knife.

I direct these words to Mjoli's child,
To the one who builds for himself,
To the one who bites like a dog:
The people of Nqabana's place remember him:

He bit them,
As he bit the Mpondo, then left them living,
As he bit the Xesibe, then left them there,
As he bit the Nguni, beating them back,
As he bit the Thembu, then left them there.

I am not referring to *you*, Child of the king:
You were doing a lot of moving about,
Questing after the kingship.
But we did not even know your origins.
Still, people of the earth will talk.
We have no interest in your claims,
But we have heard you.

We must have faith in Jojo's land,
The land of Jojo is the land of the king.
Jojo was a king!

I am not speaking of these *moderns* —
These moderns begotten by Fikeni.
Only *Jojo* begets *kings!*

I do not know where this one came from,
I do not even know his status,
But it is said you were moving together.
I am saying this to you,
To the one who does not bask in the sun
As it was basked in by the Mpondo and the Khoi.

Come, Nations, and arbitrate!
A matter at Mthatha puzzles us:
A directive came forth from that place
And it went to Mzimkhulu.

Go, Child of the king!
People of Jojo's land, why are you not acting?
Why do you not go and fetch the king from the forests?
This is why things have gone bad here on earth,
This is why the land has grown old.
It is because you put these moderns in the land
And left the truth behind.

Because he had been given the real truth by an ancestor,
Jojo went and called Ayliff.[1] Jojo did that,
And Ayliff, terrified of the king's spear,
Fearful of the assegai of Mjoli,
Took his collar and put it in his pocket.
That genuine leader saw Ayliff in a dream:
He did not know him, but he heard in dreams
That *this* man was to be the king,
And he did not like what Jojo was doing.
But Jojo invited the light, he sired a teacher.

A wound remains, things are not going well.
Friends, please fetch the kings, bring them back!
Let them return from the forests!

I shall not be talking about *you*, Child of the king,
Because I do not know your genealogy.
You disturb me.
I speak because I want us to go home,
To go back to where we came from.

In the name of the owners of this land,
By virtue of assemblies and compacts,
By giving our daughters in marriage:
We initiated girls and graduated boys,
And we put the boys in the mountains.
The boys did not complain—the only thing,
They heard this from someone last night:
"I warn you, do not pass by Nompita's place.
If you do, I shall be cursed."

I heard people speaking, murmuring:
They told of
A man who was lying on a drinking vessel and porridge,
It was said that he belonged to Bhobhu's household:

You people of Bhobhu,
You lost the kingship because of your venality!
They told of
Miya's people who fled to the mountains,
Afraid of being stabbed by Jojo here below —
Yet Jojo stabs no one: he was the king!
He was not even stalking a beast of the hunt,
So that he should come out and go to the reeds.

I speak only once and for all,
I did not hear this from anyone else,
The news leaked out through Mount Nolangeni:
Today the land of Jojo confuses me
Because the women are exposing their asses
Contemptuously to this land.
The women go naked in the middle of the realm.

Respect the land of the king!
It is because of you that it is declining,
It is because of you
That the king is embarrassed over there
In the river where he stays.
Please, Friends, go and bring the king back,
Bring him back home!
Today, the king is amazed.

I am directing this to *you*, Calf of the beast,
You of the flashing eyebrows:
It happened that I also denied you to someone.
You saw the two people sitting in a deserted place,
By the prickly pear.
You, black ear of corn that was spewed out
From Mount Xholoxholo!
You, black thing that stays in stony places,
Who has been called by no one!
I did not call on you when I was about to speak,
I did not call on you when I was going to listen.
And so it was that I too denied you.

This is what I hear in my dreams:
Here it is, I can hear it now!
Leave the white men alone,
They are seducing you from your traditions!

They are taking you from your traditional ways
Because those ways tend to confuse the whites
As they get closer to you.
Our traditions make them uncomfortable,
So they give us soap instead.

And where did you ever see a king with one wife?
The king takes a wife because it is a cultural thing.
Which household shall we repair to when Mabani is difficult?
Which household shall we go to when this wife,
Loved by the king, becomes inhospitable to us?
A wife is institutionalized by tradition to bear a king—
It is not the king who is created to bear someone.

I salute you,
Creator of the earth!

Ashton Ngcama

TEARS IN YOUR STOMACH

(XHOSA)

Ashton Ngcama performed this poem on August 25, 1972, at the foot of Nolangeni Mountain in Mount Ayliff District, the Transkei. The audience consisted of about twenty men, women, and children. (NS-520; tape 16, side 2)

To the mountain!

Consider the mountain:
When we study the mountain, its stories are many.
We people love this mountain,
We say that the ancestral spirit moves there.

Go, Nolangeni, along with your things,
And age, for we see that you are now growing old.
But it is sad:
A drought appeared, and you were left alone,
Fearing even human beings,
Afraid even of white people.
Once, when they sat on you,
They erected stones on you,
Seeking to bring you to life.
We knew that you already had life.

Beyond you are people we do not know—
We do not know their language,
We do not know what they think.
But we know they are wise people
Because they tell us there are tears in you,
These tears that are inside your stomach.
We only see those tears when you cry,
Then we open our mouths and receive your water,
We rejoice when you give us your water.
It is then that everything becomes green below you.

The drought,
There is this matter that has plagued us,
There is this matter about which you should pray for us

"Consider the mountain." Ashton Ngcama, a Xesibe poet.

There with the ancestral spirit:
What is it that happened, that you are sere?
That you are patched white, as if you have aged?
Indeed, it seems that you *have* aged,
Because on this side are erosions,
On that side are streams, streams with no forests,
Streams in which nothing lives.
We see no wild game on your banks
Because their food has gone with the drought.

No, Nolangeni!
You are too important to the Xesibe,
Because you are the divider of the land:
You divided the Xesibe
And divided the Khoi above (the Khoi sold their land
And today it is called "The Republic,"
But we know it to be "The Transkei,"
Although it is inside the Republic).

You, Bird,
That repeatedly sings when flash floods
Descend from Mthatha,
The floods move along this snake,
This black snake that tears the soil,
Then comes to stop there,
Then here in the Khoi area,
Then here in the Xesibe region.
We fear the road that goes to Mthatha
Because there is something that is going to break through.
Well, let it break through.

We salute you, Beautiful Mountain!
Come out, Sun, so that we see you as go over Nolangeni!
Then the dew of heaven will descend
And you, Nolangeni, will rise
And become young:
Your youth is resplendent,
As green as the land of the people.

Part Four

UNCERTAIN HOPE

LIGHTING "AN UNCONTROLLABLE FIRE"

This phantom of the trickster haunts the mythology of all ages. . . .
—*Carl G. Jung*[1]

INTRODUCTION

The struggle for freedom and land began almost as soon as the Dutch set foot on South African soil in the mid-seventeenth century. A century of sporadic wars occurred from 1750 to 1850, and there were many efforts to resist the development of white apartheid which was present from the beginning, in fact if not in name.

Many Africans struggled, some dying in the effort, against white encroachment and hegemony. Two of the most interesting heroic figures lived in the nineteenth century. Both are frequently dealt with by contemporary historians as peripheral characters, moving on the edges of the more familiar history of Dutch generals and English commissioners, of voortrekkers and mining magnates, of bold and determined European armies and Dutch throngs struggling against faceless Africans. But names like Smuts and Botha, van Riebeeck and Rhodes[2] are less significant to Africans than names like Nongqawuse and Chakijana, figures too often treated with sullen disdain and condescension by European historians.

Ndumiso Bhotomane and Masithathu Zenani tell Nongqawuse's story, and Sondoda Ngcobo relates two stories of Chakijana. Ngcobo first recounts one of the myriad tales of the trickster, Chakijana, of the Zulu oral tradition; then, within that context, he recounts the story of the historical Chakijana. The oral imaginative and historical traditions come to a juncture here. Two other views of the role of Chakijana in the Bambatha Rebellion are given, one by an Englishman, Frederick William Calverley, the other by an Afrikaner, P. W. van Niekerk.

Like the names of other contributors to this volume, Sondoda Ngcobo is a pseudonym; he was sensitive about the stories that he told, worried about possible repercussions, but nevertheless insistent that they reach a wider audience. He requested anonymity.

ONE

Africans sought to maintain their independence against an increasingly hostile set of white settlers who moved north from the Cape. In contemporary times, one thinks of three major events that precipitated a free South Africa: the Sharpeville Massacre of 1960, the Soweto uprising of 1976, and the virtual revolution of 1985. But these were not isolated incidents: they were one of a piece, an unbroken effort on the part of Africans to remain free people.

In the nineteenth century, two persons caught the imagination of Africans who quested for freedom. Both seem, at first glance, to be unlikely heroes—one a girl, the other "Just a person." But each came to embody significant streams of resistance among the Africans one least often hears from, the Africans of the rural countryside.

One of these heroes was a Xhosa girl, Nongqawuse, the other a Zulu youth, Chakijana. During my wanderings up and down the southeastern coast of the continent, I heard their names again and again. On September 9, 1967, I went to Nongqawuse country, along the Gxarha River, in kwaNkonki in Centane District in the Transkei. I was with Mr. Velaphi Mzini, an eighty-year-old Ngqika man. We sat at the edge of the Gxarha River at one of the precise spots where Nongqawuse saw her visions. We were near the Indian Ocean, in a remote area at the bottom of a steep valley. On one side of the Gxarha River is a sharp incline covered with dense foliage and euphorbia trees which, it is said, cast their weird shadows on the water and resembled human beings. These shadows, said Mr. Mzini, were pointed to by the Xhosa people as proof of Nongqawuse's visions. The other side is the floor of the river valley. Nongqawuse lived in a house at the top of the sheer incline, and the pathway she used to come down to the river for water is still remembered. Several spots in the river were indicated as important areas in the history of Nongqawuse.[3]

"Nongqawuse, Mhlakaza's daughter, gathered the people together," said Mr. Mzini, "and she told them to come to this estuary of the Gxarha. And the people saw shadows here in the water. Nongqawuse said, 'Here are people, about to rise from the dead. The cattle must be slaughtered, the reserve corn-pits should be emptied—all that food must be disposed of. People will rise from the dead!'

"She preached about that, and the people did what she told them to do. They did that thing. The people of that time were not as alert as those who are living now. They were foolish: Who would observe shadows here in the water, then conclude that they are people? Some did not slaughter their cattle, but many did. And some people died of starvation. Those who did not follow Nongqawuse's instructions survived. And some, starving, went among the trees and ate apples.

"Everyone came to this place, and heard the strange news. Even people on the other side of the Kei slaughtered their livestock because of what she said. They had come here to witness the words of Nongqawuse, and they paid heeds to those words: they returned to their homes, and butchered their stock. They observed that people were indeed present here, in the water.

"But what they saw was not people, they only saw the shadows of these aloes—and they concluded that the shadows were those of the people rising from the dead! 'Truly,' they said, 'they are coming! Here they are, the people are coming!'

"The land suffered on Nongqawuse's account," Mr. Mzini concluded.

"She was an ordinary person, not a doctor. But she was unique, she had certain powers. Things were told to her in dreams. And everybody, including her father, believed her. But as it turned out, these 'people' were merely aloes, the shadows of the aloes here in the water, reflections of the plants in the water. Look, you can see those aloes over there, their shadows stretched right up to here.

"That was the reason people believed her."[4]

During that same month in 1967, I spoke to a number of other Xhosa elders, including Nololo Sibini, a headman. They discussed the question of Nongqawuse's motives; some were convinced that the Europeans in the Cape Colony had engineered a theatrical event to force Africans to migrate into the Colony to seek labor. Others saw the girl as an authentic hero, espousing and embodying the fervent desires of the Xhosa for freedom and the need for the Xhosa to recover their unity and ethos.

TWO

History is always understood and experienced within the context of story. In real-life depictions from history, it is the narrative drive that dominates, because it is narrative that gives meaning to human experience. Images of history are woven into the familiar narrative structures and patterns of tale.

In April, 1856, a seer, Mhlakaza with his fifteen year old niece, Nongqawuse, "a prophesying medium," preached a resurrection from the dead. Nongqawuse declared that she had had a conversation with the spirits of old heroes of the Xhosa. They said that they had witnessed with sorrow the ruin of their people because of the oppression of the conquerors from overseas. They wanted to save their people from destruction, and said they would appear once more in the flesh among their people, but first the people had to destroy all their animals with the exception of horses and dogs. All grain was to be destroyed and the fields were to be left unplowed. When this was done, vast herds would emerge from the ground, grains would be plentiful, and there would be food for everyone. The advent of this resurrection would be preceded by a mighty wind which would sweep off all Xhosa who had refused to obey the order of the spirits.

So it was that, throughout the land of the Xhosa, and especially in the Gcaleka part, cattle were slaughtered. Dogs were gorged on beef, vultures were surfeited, carcasses were left to putrefy, the air was tainted with corruption. After ten months of this, Nongqawuse ordered that within eight days all cattle must be killed. On the eighth day, February 27, 1857, heaven and earth would come together amid darkness, thunder, lightning, rain, and a great wind. All unbelievers, along with all whites, would be driven into the sea. The sun would rise blood-red on that day, and at noon it would suddenly descend not to the west but to the east.

But when the sun set in the west, leaving the usual darkness over the earth, thousands of Xhosa were disappointed. Starvation was now imminent. Kraals and corn-pits were inspected, but remained empty. People wandered about seeking food. Many deaths resulted, and the people began to move to Cape Colony where they sought food and work from the Europeans. Some twenty thousand people were said to have died; through death and migration, the population of the area dropped by two-thirds. One hundred and fifty thousand cattle died. For a long time, the countryside was strewn with bones. Among the dead was Mhlakaza. Nongqawuse lived for many years.[5]

Various interpretations have been offered of this event. "The nation's willingness to perish haunts me," wrote the Zulu author, Herbert I. E. Dhlomo (1903–1956), in *The Girl Who Killed to Save: Nongqawuse the Liberator*. In this fictionalized version of the story, he had a missionary say, "Nongqawuse may reduce at a sweep what legislation and missionary endeavor have so far failed to fight against—the power and influence of the witchdoctor, the tyranny of custom and tradition, the authority of the chief, the isolation of the Xhosa nation. By isolation I mean that the AmaXhosa are a self-sufficient community, hostile to, and not eager to come into contact with Europeans. The Nongqawuse Drama will break down this self-sufficiency, this hostility, and force the AmaXhosa to throw themselves—literally and metaphorically—into the arms of their white neighbors. Nongqawuse will give the AmaXhosa that dependence, by robbing them of their food and national solidarity, which spells progress." As the play comes to an end, Daba, a Christian convert says, "This is the host of those who perished in the Great Famine. Do you see these people, surrounding, thanking and laughing with Nongqawuse. They tell her that hunger and destitution drove them into the paths of life, led them to the missionary and his divine message; put them in the hands of God. So there is triumph in death; there is finding in death; there is beauty in death. Nongqawuse laughs as she tells them that she was really in earnest but was ignorant. They laugh and sing. They call her their Liberator from Superstition and from the rule of Ignorance."[6]

A. C. Jordan, the Xhosa writer, calling the Nongqawuse incident "the 'National Suicide of the Xhosa people' in 1856–1857," asserted that "The Nongqawuse cattle-killing episode had broken the economic independence of the Xhosa, hunger and poverty driving them in large numbers into the colony to earn a livelihood as laborers. Though not yet subdued, the Xhosa chiefs had lost their political and military power." He added,

"By 1870, the stage was set for the last phase of the Wars of Dispossession."[7]

In "Ingqawule," one of the finest poems in Xhosa literature, the poet, James J. R. Jolobe, wrote of the tragedy; he argued that Nongqawuse's experience revealed the need for a joining of the two warring traditions. The poet described the spectral ridges that were white with the bones of the nation, and considered how a proud nation had been humiliated and taught a life of servitude. When Nongqawuse had grown old, he said, a wagon drawn by eight yoke of oxen stopped in front of her house late one night. The driver, his face obscured by a cape, had come to get Nongqawuse, to take her home. As she boarded the wagon, she was transfigured; her strength was renewed, her skin became smooth, her beauty was restored. Then she met many of the people who had died in the cattle-killing that she had provoked.

A messenger came to her, and suggested that she had been unerring in her dream; it was the interpretation that proved to be incorrect. And he proceeded to analyze that dream: Those who had been feared as strangers were actually the leaven for our mental life, he said, for the purpose of spreading the knowledge that produces the means for good living—agriculture, the work of the hands and intellect. That is the meaning of the cattle of the dream, he said, the significance of the great harvest. This abundance will become attainable in our land when the Xhosa accept the new ways; this, he proclaimed, is the rebirth of the people.

As for traditional Xhosa culture, there was much that was beautiful in the traditions of the nation, but the wrinkles obscured the beauty and the new light exposed these blemishes. In the process of realizing perfection, the beautiful would come into strong relief, and a great nation, proud among nations, would be reborn. Again, the messenger observed that the ones who were feared as strangers had come with the lord of the heavenly home who was seeking to establish his reign in Gcalekaland, among the Ngqika, and beyond. Already he had sent Faith, Hope, and Love, three handsome young women, to be wed to humankind on earth. When these three were accepted, the great spirit would come and the sprout of manhood would grow in the land below. The messenger embraced Nongqawuse, congratulating her for the enigmatic foresight that she had shown when she was on the earth, musing at the pool in her homeland, foresight concerning matters of importance for eternity. Then, wrote the poet Jolobe, the messenger led Nongqawuse to the heavenly palace, and the Xhosa past and the Christian present were united: the knowledge that Qamatha, the traditional Xhosa god, was no other than Thixo, the Christian god, the giver of new life.[8]

Two views of Nongqawuse's story are offered here. In the first, "She

Spoke about the Resurrection," the Xhosa historian, Ndumiso Bhotomane, attempts to provide a factual account of the event, with some
details about the role played by his father. The second commentator,
Nongenile Masithathu Zenani, the Xhosa storyteller, is more opinion-
ated. In her account, "No Person Arose," she sees a sinister role played
by mysterious whites who convinced Nongqawuse to do their bidding.

At the trial of Chakijana in 1908 ("The accused Sukabekuluma, alias
Chakijana, cautioned, elects to give evidence, and makes declaration. . ."),
he was questioned by Mr. A. H. Hime, Counsel for the Defense[9]:
    "When were you born?"
    "I think at the time of Isandlwana I was a child."
    "Could you walk?"
    "No, I was still being carried."
    "Have you lived in Zululand all your life?"
    "Yes, I grew up there."
    "Who was your father?"
    "Ngazindaka."
    "What was he?"
    "Just a person—a commoner. He is now dead: he died while I was in
prisoner."
    "Who is his heir?"
    "Melele."
    "Who are you?"
    "Just a person." [10]
Much more than "just a person," Chakijana, who was born in 1866[11]
and died in 1963,[12] dressed in his khaki tunic and breeches, with leather
gaiters and helmet,[13] was known as a trickster: one of his praises
was *uSigilamikuba, kuvel' izindaba,* The-one-whose-pranks-give-rise-to-
matters-for-consideration.[14] His name was Sukabekuluma (literally, He-
who-goes-off-whilst-they-are-still-talking), and he was also called Dakwaukwesuta (literally, He-who-becomes-drunk-on-getting-a-full-meal)
and Gwazakanjani (How-do-you-stab?).[15] Because of his behavior and activities, he took on the nickname, Chakijana, from the oral tradition.
    In the Zulu oral tradition, Chakijana is a mongoose. His praise name is
uChakijana bogcololo umphephethi wezinduku zabafo, "Chakijana, the clever
one, medicator of the fighting sticks of the men." Many narratives reveal
this character's wonderful and often outrageous activities, describing the
untamed force of this Chakijana, his amorality, his seemingly endless
energy, uncontrolled and unchannelled at times, magnificently focused
at other times. And this trickster is always akin to the hero, as indeed
was the case with the historical Chakijana, the trickster and hero who
effectively fought the white man, then survived to fight once more.

One Zulu storyteller told me that Chakijana is a meerkat. Another said it is simply a cat. Others suggested that Chakijana is an old woman. A Zulu woman suggested that Chakijana is "like a cat," though larger, a cat that kills other animals. Another said that it is a very small animal, smaller than a cat, and that it eats other animals. But, unlike the hare, which people do eat, Chakijana is not eaten by humans. These different guises reveal one of the signal attributes of the trickster: he is characterized by deceit, disguise and illusion being his characteristic weapons. Now he plays the role of a king, and now he is "just a person." He is a boundary character at the same time that he is at the center of his society.

Ellen Biyela,[16] a Zulu storyteller, said: "The *chakide*[17] is an animal that is small and low to the ground. It is similar in shape to the cat, yellowish-brown. It has a rather bushy tail which it is able to curl into a bundle when it sits upright, or when it is excited or looking for something—hence, perhaps, the suggestion that it is a wise creature. When it runs, its tail extends straight back behind it. It catches fowl. Its praises are *uChakijana ngamcololo umphephethi weenduku zabafu*[18]": Chakijana even outsmarts people on their own territory—i.e., even though he has never been to a certain place, and even though the owner of that place makes every attempt to keep the *chakide* out, he invariably outwits that owner.

Ellen Biyela also said that the *chakide*, like a mongoose, eats fowl, rats, and snakes. And there are many mongoose around Zululand now. It is a fact, she says, that the mongoose will study a snake, its habitat, and its habits. It watches the snake and waits for it. It sleeps near the snake's hole until the snake comes out. When the snake leaves the hole, the mongoose burrows the hole bigger. It goes into the hole. Then it comes out and goes to find this same snake. When the mongoose finds the snake, it antagonizes it, frightens it, and the snake goes to its hole for shelter from the mongoose. But the mongoose runs to the hole also and gets there first and waits for the snake. The mongoose is inside the hole. As the snake enters the hole, it grabs the snake and bites its head off.[19]

Sukabekuluma, or Chakijana, is one of the authentic heroes of Zulu history, one of many rebels who through the years engaged in guerrilla activities against the encroaching Europeans. Chakijana is unique in that he has an existence both in history and in oral imaginative tradition. Sondoda Ngcobo, the performer of both the historical account and the imaginative story that follow, insists that the name of the historical Chakijana was not coincidental. Zulu people, he argued, saw the cunning mongoose of Zulu ancient story in the activities of the clever historical character of the same name.

As befits someone who lives in both history and legend, the historical figure is the subject of many stories. It is said that he harassed both camps during the Anglo-Boer War, that he was a double-agent effectively working both sides. Some tell of how he lived at Nhlazatsha Mountain, near Ndlebe. The mountain was held by the Boers during one battle, while the British held another mountain not far away. As they fired on each other, this agent provocateur was staying at a mission at the foot of the Nhlazatsha Mountain.

"[T]his phantom of the trickster," said Carl Jung, "haunts the mythology of all ages, sometimes in quite unmistakable form, sometimes in strangely modulated guise."[20] The trickster is an indifferent, amoral, undifferentiated force, as if God the creator had never got around to ordering this part of the universe. He is always on the boundaries, the periphery: Trickster is a liminal being. In the heavens, he is called a divine trickster; on the earth, a profane trickster. Disguise, deception, illusion are his tools and weapons. He is an ambiguous character: usually a male, he is often androgynous. Trickster moves through the universe undertaking to satisfy his basic appetites. If the divine trickster also creates something permanent along the way, so much the better, but that is not always his aim. The trickster is outrageous, obscene, death-dealing, uncaring, ignoble. This does not mean that he is incapable of socially acceptable practices and activities—but these are usually by-products of his acts rather than conscious efforts on his part. He remains forever an undifferentiated force: he is never tamed, never domesticated, although he may appear to be so at times, usually as a part of a sly plan to gain something for himself.

Chakijana moved into history as an archetypal trickster during the Bambatha Rebellion of 1906. A problem for whites was how to force Africans off their own lands and into the labor market, to work on white-owned farms as tenant farmers and to provide cheap labor for the white-owned mines in the Transvaal. Early in the century, Africans were prevented from purchasing more land, and, to further squeeze Africans from the land, a poll tax was imposed on African males.

The white government of Natal province imposed the tax on Africans, £1 a head, in that province in 1905. Certain Zulu chiefs, desperate, refused to pay, defying magistrates who attempted to collect the tax. Some Zulu people—twenty-seven followers of a chief whose name was Mveli, and members of an Ethiopian religious movement—also resisted, and when they were attacked by two white policemen in February, 1906, they killed the policemen. Whites feared a mass uprising, and demanded action against the Africans. Two were killed at once, twelve Zulu were publicly executed after perfunctory trials, others received harsh prison sentences with hard labor and lashes, and Natal colonial troops then moved through the African areas, burning homes and destroying fields of those who refused to pay the taxes. But the white authorities' determination to prevent a mass uprising led instead to a broader rebellion.

At that time, Bambatha,[21] chief of the Zondi people, was quickly heralded as a symbol of Zulu resistance. For six weeks, he waged a war of liberation, refusing to pay taxes, and he began to fight a guerrilla war in the Nkandla mountains. Many Zulu joined him. Whites, still nervous, demanded the immediate suppression of Bambatha and his followers. He sought refuge with the Zulu king, Dinuzulu, and when, in his absence, he was replaced as chief by his uncle, Magwababa, he retaliated by kidnapping Magwababa and fleeing into the Nkandla Forest. He was joined by other Zulu, under the leadership of the ninety-six year old chief, Sigananda. He ambushed a party of police, then moved deeper into the forest, adding to his force by arguing that he was operating under Zulu King Dinuzulu's authority. White forces, commanded by Colonel Duncan McKenzie, hunted Bambatha, and, after a number of battles, on June 10, 1906, killed him, with five hundred others, in the Mome Gorge[22] in Zululand. In two months, the rebellion was quelled. Thirty whites were killed, three to four thousand Africans lost their lives, seven thousand were jailed, four thousand were lashed. But there was, in Bambatha's rebellion, a sense of nationalism that would later reemerge to lead to the demise of apartheid and to a new South Africa. Africans had, Bambatha reckoned, lost their freedom on the battlefield, and that is where they must regain it.[23] This was to be the last armed insurrection until the 1960s, but Bambatha's message was clear: White supremacy would not be easily accepted. But whites had won the battle. Three years later, 80 percent of adult males in Zululand were migrant workers. "The rebellion also alerted white opinion in South Africa generally, and more particularly in Natal, to the need for white political unity to maintain control over the African population."[24]

Dinuzulu, the Zulu king, did not give the rebellion his support, although he was suspected of doing so by many of the whites. He was arrested and tried on twenty-three counts of treason, and was sentenced to four years imprisonment. He too became a symbol of African resistance to white rule.[25]

THREE

When Sondoda Ngcobo detailed his story of Chakijana, he did so within the context of the Zulu notions of the trickster. An understanding of the historical Chakijana, he averred, was not possible without an understanding of the imaginative trickster Chakijana of the Zulu tradition. So it was that he created stories of both, the one informing and giving meaning to the other.

In the imaginative story of the trickster, Ngcobo established two artistic patterns,[26] one having to do with the relationship between the trickster and the mother, as the former takes over the latter's child-rearing functions, as the trickster becomes the mother. Associated with this pattern is the conflict at the center of the story: The trickster owes the cannibals a living being, and this attaches the trickster to the cannibals, giving him his chief death-dealing characteristics. In storytelling terms, he is like the cannibals. The presence of the duiker further demonstrates the trickster's negative traits, showing him to be opposed to nature (the killing of the duiker) in the same way that he is opposed to culture (the killing of the human child).

The second pattern has to do with the purging from the mother of what the trickster represents, cleansing her of evil, an evil that is represented graphically in her callous attitude towards her child. This purging is effected by her illegitimate son, a boundary figure who orchestrates this grisly pattern, as the trickster flees, transforms himself, begs for mercy, and is in the end subsumed by the cannibals he represents. He is now eternally a part of them, and the cannibals, who will live forever, are a symbol of everlasting evil—sometimes, as here, masquerading as decent beings, without any real decency. Evil and death remain. The trickster has not been destroyed. He is here forever, and we must deal with him.

In storytelling terms, Chakijana takes over the role of the mother, becomes the mother, but he is also death-dealing, being equated with the cannibals. The story is a working out of a drama: the humans, having allowed evil to take over their world, are now in the process of cleansing their world of evil. The trickster is death-dealing in his tricks, and the people are in the process of cleansing themselves of him—of what he represents. Trickster's characteristic ambiguity and androgyny are exposed as he becomes the mother. But he is a dualistic mother, both life-giving and death-dealing. He is a fantasy character, mirroring the conflict within the real-life mother.

Trickster exists between the worlds, between the human and cannibal worlds. He preys on both. In the end, he is destroyed, but he remains in the guise of the cannibals, who are not destroyed. He literally becomes a part of them. He cheats both humans and nature, and even attempts to deceive the essence of evil, the cannibals. Trickster represents an impulse that must be brought under control. An eternal force that is morally ambiguous, he is a betwixt-and-between force that cannot be destroyed.

It is this boundary quality of the trickster that the storyteller uses in his creation of the story of the historical Chakijana. This man, who characterized himself as "just a person," must surely have been practicing his craft of trickery as he made that comment. All of his activities, including his clever evasion of the authorities and the fact that there were varied interpretations of his activities, behavior, and statement, are testimony to his linkages with the fabled Chakijana of Zulu tradition. More than Dinuzulu, whose protection he said he had, more than Bambatha, whose loyal follower he seemed to be, he was triumphantly prancing on the periphery of the Zulu struggle for freedom from the whites. He was a master of disguise, as Sondoda Ngcobo's story reveals. And, in Frederick William Calverley's version, "I don't know his name," says the servant, "but this is a trouble-maker." When William James Calverley recognized that it was Chakijana he was dealing with, "Then he knew that there was trouble." The whites were convinced that "Chakijana had committed many murders, sent of course by Dinuzulu. And the Government wanted him, dead or alive."

There was an element of fantasy associated with both the Nongqa-wuse and the Chakijana stories, as reality and myth united and, in both cases, collided with tragic results. In the case of Chakijana, it was argued that magical guns and bullets would be utilized by the Zulu guerrillas as they fought the British in the Nkandla Forest and the Mome Gorge. Those who followed Nongqawuse fervently believed that the sun would stand still in the heavens and that the whites would be driven into the sea.

Myth is useful to storytellers, historians, and poets as an artistic device. During periods of stress, people turn to their oral traditions, to their myths, and seek to give them credence by making them real, something myths were never designed to become. It is a mark of the pressure and misery being experienced by Xhosa and Zulu people in the nineteenth century that they attempted to make their myths reality. Out of these junctures of myth and reality emerged heroes, Nongqawuse and Chakijana. People saw them as links between story and experience: In the wreckage of this tragic linkage could be discovered the hope of the people.

Ndumiso Bhotomane

SHE SPOKE ABOUT THE RESURRECTION

NONGQAWUSE AND THE CATTLE KILLING OF 1857

(XHOSA)

The story of Nongqawuse was related by Chief Ndumiso Bhotomane on September 10, 1967, at his home in Rwantsana, Centane District, in the Transkei. The audience consisted of about twenty Gcaleka men and women. (589; tape 10, side 2)

In 1857, the Nongqawuse episode occurred.[1]

Nongqawuse was the daughter of Mhlakaza of the Ngqosini clan. She spoke here at Gxarha. She spoke in the village of the Thembu, the one Griffiths was in:

> Griffiths is the son of Dimanda,
> Dimanda is the son of Sibhozo,
> Sibhozo is the son of Nzabela,
> Nzabela is the son of Raba,
> Raba is the son of Faku,
> Faku is the son of Gcaleka.

She spoke here at Qolora, speaking of the resurrection of kings, about the wealth that would follow if cattle were slaughtered and the reserves of maize thrown away.

Hintsa sent my father, Bhotomane. Bhotomane was at Ndwe, up on the boundary of Lady Frere, where he had jurisdiction. He came from here at Ntlambe, and had gone to settle at Thulura. Before he went there, he had gone to settle at Khwangane in this place where we are, going with Sarhili who was on his way to Hohita, going to settle there. Now, Nzabela was here at Qolora. The girl spoke in Qolora, she spoke about this resurrection. Hintsa sent my father to see about this matter. My father came, and he believed. Sarhili came too, and so did these chiefs. The last meeting was at Hohita, at the royal residence. All the chiefs of the Xhosa had gathered there.[2]

This girl spoke at Gxarha, here in Centane in Nzabela's jurisdiction, here at Griffiths' home. She spoke about the resurrection, about wealth; she said that Hintsa would rise, she said that Ndlambe would rise, she said that Ngqika would rise, and so on. And those comments were believed.

Now then, in 1857, Sarhili called a big meeting, at which he said that cattle would be slaughtered. He sent to Sandile in Ngqikaland. Where was Sandile? He had settled at Cumakala—at Stutterheim, yes. That is where the royal residence of Ngqikaland was. But Ngqika's grave— Ngqika himself died at Xesi, at Mkhubiso. Sandile was now there at Cumakala—at Stutterheim. Mlawu and Rharhabe had died. Having gone to impound Thembu cattle, they died at Xuka. Ngqika was then very young, and he went to be circumcised by Khawuta, coming from here. Khawuta, coming from Nxarini, went to circumcise him at Qonce.

Now, let me come to the story that I am telling.[3] Sarhili called a big meeting, and announced that cattle should be slaughtered. That pronouncement could not be contradicted, because it was made by the king, and he himself had already sent to other minor chiefs who were under his authority. They had concurred with his decision that the cattle should be slaughtered because of misfortune and the European government's determination that it should possess the land. God is responsible for that, yes.

Maphasa spoke at that big meeting. His father, Bhuru, a chief, was present among the old ones, the parents. When he heard it said that the cattle should be slaughtered, this young man, Maphasa, pleaded with them. He said that, before they concluded that the cattle should be slaughtered, they should go to the pasture to study the grass, "that we may observe whether the grass could sustain the cattle, having been slaughtered and resurrected." They should go to the pasture. "I plead with you!" But no, his request was not heeded. It was ignored, discarded. Maphasa had to admit defeat.

The message was sent to Sandile, and Sandile slaughtered his cattle. They even sent to Sigidi, here at Mpethu. And the cattle were slaughtered. But at Ngqikaland, Tyhali did not slaughter any cattle. Khama did not slaughter, nor did some other chiefs; the majority of them did not slaughter. The same thing occurred in Gcalekaland. Sarhili did slaughter cattle, and so did others. And Sandile—both of them slaughtered cattle in great numbers, each according to his stature. Sandile said that what Sarhili did Sandile had to do. "I shall slaughter the cattle!" And he slaughtered them.

It was said that eight days would pass. That was a ruse; it seems to have been deliberately designed, a deception, for they knew that after eight days no one would be alive. Eight days passed, and the sun rose— it had also been said that, when the sun came up to here, it would turn around and go to set in the east. It did not do that. It rose and set as usual. The signs were never fulfilled, after the cattle had all been slaughtered. No signs were fulfilled.

It became clear that the people should now scatter. Sarhili went to the home of his mother in the land of the Bomvana; he had decreed that the Bomvana should not slaughter cattle. So the Bomvana did not slaughter their cattle. When the other cattle had been destroyed, when he saw that he had been lied to, he went to the land of the Bomvana and remained there at Moni's place. Maphasa went to his daughter's home by marriage, at the Gqili River among the Vundle clan. Bhuru insisted that he would not move, and he sat down; he said that he had been obeying the king. Therefore, if this project did not succeed, then he wanted to die there. So Bhuru sat down. Dingana, also a clansman of Gcaleka stock, came back; he came and sat beside him in the royal residence. Tyindye, a councillor who had gone through circumcision rituals with Bhuru, returned; he went and sat beside him. Maphonya, a scion of the Pinga clan, came back; he went and sat beside him. Ngqelenga, a member of the Bamba clan, came back; he went and sat beside him. Those councillors died with him, they starved.

About a million people died in the Nongqawuse episode. The rest of the people were scattered.

And Bhotomane, where did he go? He went to Mhlontlo's domain, to his in-laws, to the home of my father's mother.[4] At Qumbu, exactly. Exactly, sir; he went to stay there. Then, when it saw that there was no one in the land, the European government came in. Sarhili had departed, as well as Bhotomane—everything. The European government impounded the land; it took the Mfengu, which it had taken across the Nciba River, and sent them here, settling them at Gcuwa, at Ngqamakhwe, at Tsomo. And that land where Sarhili was, and where Bhotomane was, at Ndwe in the Cofimvaba area, the European government gave that land to the Thembu. The Mathanzimas began to come up, coming from the Gqili River; they came here now, but at the time when Sarhili was alive here, they did not dare to come near this area! No, they could not come near! But now, the European government gave them that land. These Mfengu whom you can see here—after Nongqawuse, they were given that land. Sarhili then sent Bhotomane and his son, Dalasile, to go and meet with the European government, so that he might return to this side, to this land.

The European government said, "I have impounded the land at Gcuwa, I have impounded the land at Ngqamakhwe, I have impounded the land at Tsomo. I have given these lands to the Mfengu, those same Mfengu whom I had previously taken from here, the ones I had taken to the Ciskei. I have returned them, now, to those lands. As for the land that was Sarhili's, I have given that to the Thembu. Now, I say that Sarhili should return to Centane, he should come back to the land of Centane. I give that to Sarhili. I also give him Dutywa and Gatyana. Let him come![5] And at Xhora!"

Sarhili returned then. He came to be here at Holela. Bhotomane returned; he came here at Ntlambe, at Ntlambe, yes, at Thuthura, at Nkondwane, at Rwantsana. Those are his areas.

Time passed happily, time passed, time passed happily.

Nongenile Masithathu Zenani

NO PERSON AROSE

(XHOSA)

What follows is excerpted from a lengthy account of the Nongqawuse story related by Nongenile Masithathu Zenani, the Xhosa storyteller, doctor, and historian. The account was given on July 20, 1975, in Mrs. Zenani's home in Nkanga, Gatyana, the Transkei. (3S-328, tape 18, side 2)

This is the story of Nongqawuse, this is the way it happened.

In older times, there was happiness in all the land of the Xhosa. There was no anxiety among the Africans. People dined on the products of their labor. They ate corn that they had planted, cultivated, harvested. In the homesteads, young men shared beer as they threshed the corn.

That corn was preserved in pits that were dug in cattle kraals. A person would dig a hole, calculating the number of sacks of corn that would fill one pit. When that hollow was full, he would dig another below that one. He always took care to cover the corn-pit carefully, knowing that otherwise water would seep in when it rained heavily. It was therefore covered with a large stone. The pit was dug in a place that had brittle rocks, rocks that were clayey, to assure that it was firmly constructed. Manure of cattle was taken and the pit was plastered inside, so that it was tightly sealed, with no defects. Then the pit was crammed with corn.

Throughout the land, there was nothing for one person to sell to another. If a man had no ox, he would ask for assistance from another. And the exchange was gracefully done. That person simply gave him one from among his stock.

That is the way it was then, and there was great happiness.

That is the way things were among the Xhosa in those days, that was the way of life in the land of the Xhosa.

Girls gathered firewood in those times. One day, while some of them were collecting the wood in their customary way, there appeared among them people who were white. The girls, not knowing where these people had come from, fled. These strangers, they saw, did not wear clothing that was familiar to them; they wore garments that covered their entire bodies. The custom of the Xhosa at that time was to wear clothing that did not have that effect; they wore skins fashioned of the hides of wild animals, and skins of goats, of cattle, of sheep. They had no other garments. Those who had suddenly appeared were handsome people wearing clothes that the girls did not recognize, beautiful attire to keep them from getting cold.

One little girl, not able to run as fast, had been left behind.

The whites spoke to this little girl: "Where do you come from?"

For a long time, she did not respond.

They told her that they would give her some clothes so that she too would be attractively garbed, so that she too would not be cold. Then they offered her money. But when they produced the money, she did not know what it was.

The whites remained there with her, attempting to persuade her, telling her, "We want to hire you. Such work will provide you with fine things."

The girl said, "What must I do?" Then, after a long pause, she added, "I do not live here. My home is far away, I live at the place of my mothers."

They continued to wheedle, to coax her, moving around her, entreating her.

Finally, she agreed to do as they said.

They told her, "We want you to remain here in the forest, to live above the river in the thicket near which people travel. We want you to speak to those people. We shall daub your body, we shall disguise you so that they do not recognize you."

They added, "Leave the things that you are wearing behind." They gave her new garments, clothing with which she was unacquainted, and they daubed all her face and body, her feet and hands. At the beginning, this girl's color was black, entirely black. Now she was a young white woman, a yellowish-white woman. She glistened in her whiteness.

They stayed there with her, and the sun set.

Then they walked with the girl, going to the place to which they had referred, telling her, "People dip water in this place, here where the water ends. There is a thicket above the place where the water is dipped, a little to the north of this point."

That thicket was a tangle of vegetation: a tall coiling tree, a vine without thorns, a towering cylindrical plant that twisted around; it was luxuriantly overgrown—winding, spiraling, curled together, interwoven, entwined.

They came to this place, studied it carefully, deftly equipped it, then said that she should live here, in this place.

She did that.

They gave her everything that she needed to eat.

And she did what they told her to do, said precisely what she was instructed to say: There will arise all of the people who are dead, all of the dead people will be resurrected. All of those who had died will arise. They will stand here, fit and well. They will be in perfect health—the young and the old, every person who has died.

But it was first necessary that the food that people ate come to an end.

"A new spirit will enter you." Nongenile Masithathu Zenani, Xhosa storyteller, historian, poet.

The old pit-corn should be destroyed. All the corn should be thrown out, abandoned on the hard stony ground. Food had to be taken from the houses also, and discarded. The corn-pits should be broken open, the corn cast out.

One of the whites said to the girl, "You will tell the people clearly that they should act firmly on this matter. Tell them that all the country should be assembled and told of this matter. All cultivating of the land must cease, livestock is no longer to be reared."

So it was explained to her. The girl was persuaded that what they said was truth, that it would result in great things, that she must persevere and do as she was told. She did not forget even one thing that had been spoken to her.

Later, certain young women descended, moving towards the river to the water below. As they did so, the thicket near which they walked shook violently. Yet, there was no wind. The thicket was quivering violently, and these women stopped, pointing out to each other what was happening. And wondering, What was this? What was the thing that caused this thicket to whip about so much without a wind, what caused it to be so agitated?

Yet, the weather was tranquil.

Then it happened again, and the kraal vibrated.

And the thicket was calm again.

Then they saw the white person, the girl who seemed to be a white thing. It appeared to be white, but they did not recognize the clothing. They had never seen clothing on a person other than animal skins. And they wondered, "What kind of animal is this?"

Never had they seen such a thing.

They went home and described what they had seen in the countryside —the marvel, the quaking of the thicket. "And a white thing appeared, a thing that we have never before seen! It shook!"

Some men then went stealthily, going to investigate the thing that had been described by the women, the figure that had appeared at the river. They moved furtively, going to the river by the usual way, determined to destroy that animal. They arrived, but stood far off, troubled by the trembling of the thicket—it whipped about wildly, then, and the men became anxious, troubled. They were afraid. They did not approach, they did not get near the thicket. Instead, they turned back.

But two of the men remained behind, watching her. As they observed, one of them said, "What is this thing? It does not get up, it simply stays over there."

They continued to watch, but they did not advance, remaining at a distance.

Finally, she spoke: "I have called you here, having been sent by the

Creator, the ancient one. To all of our people here, I bring a word. I have called you, all of you, because I want you to hear that word. But I shall not come to your homes. It is said that I should summon you here, to the place where I live."

The young men departed then, going to their homes. When they got there, they asked, "Fathers, what is this about? She told us, 'Young men, return here with the others. I have been sent,' she said. 'I have been summoned to explain things. I shall not come into any homestead. I have been put here in this place, so that I can explain things to you.'"

The word went out, the people were called. They were told, even at the royal residence, what had been spoken. The ruler decreed that the matter should be looked into. The entire country was told that it was a situation involving all the people. Some of them must go to that thicket at the river where the water churned, where the thicket shook.

Four men went then and stood in fear before this thing, before the thing that was apparently responsible for all this, the thing that stayed there below. Anxiety and tension were clearly present.

She said to the four men, "You must listen." And she proceeded to speak to them. She said that she had been sent by the Creator, that she was to instruct them that they must take the corn out of the corn-pits, that the pits must be opened and abandoned. There were some corn-pits in which there was much corn, other pits had now been devastated by the hoofs of cattle and fallen in. The girl explained that the lids of these corn-pits could be located with spears. People should go to all the cattle kraals until the pits had all been demolished. Not a kernel of corn should remain. Anyone who had a corn-pit should be certain that it contained no grain. Moreover, no ox should survive: "Destroy all the cattle. Let them be finished. Not a single thing should remain."

She continued, "If you do that, a new spirit will enter you. When you have finished doing this, the resurrection of the ancestors will begin. The children who are dead will awaken, along with their mothers and grandmothers. Everyone will arise, it will be a wonder.

"No hard-working person will ever be exhausted, no one will shiver from the cold. There will always be a fire for warmth, along with abundant food to eat. Nothing will be wanting. The person who wants clothing will be clothed. There will be soft, beautiful garments, and people will abandon those clothes that are ragged and dirty.

"That is the way things will be.

"You will eat things that will come with the Creator, things that are not now eaten. There will seem to be no corn to eat—yet, if a person has faith, there will be plenty of corn. He will see it, the corn will be there— so much that he will have to eat it. No one will long for anything. There will be no person who will want to be pregnant and not be pregnant.

There is no person who will again be thirsty, a person will never want anything. Death itself will be brought to an end."

And she added these words, "Destroy even the cattle kraals, raze the houses, and when you have done that you will have beautiful beginnings."

As the men, along with their wives, listened, this is what they thought: "God has sent her to us, so that we can be told what must be done. Even now, as we stand here, we are preserved by her. We shall, it is clear, have splendid things at the appropriate time. Our children who have gone will at that time arise. We shall become, each of us, a person who is well, who has no troubles. Those who do become ill shall go to the doctors, shall look to the traditions."

All of that matter was finished then, and those who had gone there looked anxiously about. Those who had gone there were persuaded by the words that had been spoken, the words that thundered, reverberated. All the people believed, and they withdrew, satisfied. They departed, believing; they went home, convinced.

The corn was taken out of the corn-pits. It was removed, then left outside, carried off and abandoned. Cattle were inspanned, and they hauled the corn away. It was forsaken on the rocks, and the people never saw it again because God had so commanded—God, who would do momentous things for them: the dead would be awakened.

When the people finished carrying off the corn and leaving it on the veld, they began to destroy their fowl, abandoning their chickens, carrying off the cattle. The cattle were butchered, the pigs were slaughtered, everything was surrendered. Animals and grain that had been cast out began to rot, those things decomposed there.

And in all the country, there remained only silence. Nothing else.

They continued these activities, and the meat was finished. Entirely finished.

Now the people were cold.

They were cold because there was nothing—nothing at all outside of the cattle that were seen in the pastures and the forests. And when the cattle returned and went into the kraals, the people finished them off, silently.

That is the way it was.

They watched and waited then for something that they might eat.

They continued to watch, they continued to wait for something that might appear, waited for the resurrection of the dead. They stared off into the far distance, and waited.

And when it was morning and when it was evening, not one person had risen from the dead.

No person arose, no person even intended such a thing.

And the people longed for the milk to which they had become accustomed.

But nothing was seen, nothing at all. Nothing.

The people remained there, eating water.

The people were dead, lying in rows. The people lay dead in row upon row.

The people were starving, in all the land their strength ebbed.

That is the way things were.

In time, it was discovered that certain plants could be eaten. The men who had been vigorous in their homesteads now walked feebly, seeking these plants—plums, cat-thorn fruits, flannel berries. They began to eat plants that they had never before eaten.

The girl herself was not present.

The girl who had said that she lived at the place of her mothers: it was not known where she was.

She was the child of the wife of Mhlakaza, at the place of her mothers. At Mhlakaza's place, it was not known if she was far away, it was not known where she was.

Where did she go? Did she go home? They had no knowledge of her, they did not know if she went home, they did not know what had become of her.

That is what happened. That is what was done by the young woman whose name was Nongqawuse, the daughter of Mhlakaza. She had destroyed the land altogether.

The foods were rotted, the people were finished.

They were dead.

Sondoda Ngcobo

CHAKIJANA, THE TRICKSTER

(ZULU)

The performer of this Zulu story about the fictional trickster, Chakijana, was Sondoda Ngcobo, a Zulu man about forty-five years old. The performance took place on February 7, 1968, in a home in Mahlabatini District, Zululand. The audience consisted of fifteen women, one man, and ten children. (3597; tape 70, side 1)

It happened. . . .

There was a woman who had a child, a small child. She had had another child in her maidenhood, before she had married.

Now this boy grew up, the one she had given birth to when she was still unmarried. And he became a fine young fellow. When he was already a young man, the one she had borne in her maidenhood, she gave birth to a small child. Then her husband died, and the wife remained behind with the small child and the son whom she had given birth to in her maidenhood.

One day, when she had gone off to hoe, she was approached by Chakijana. He said to her, "Mother, let me watch the child for you! I can see that the sun is too much for him."

The woman refused. She said, "No, I don't want you to watch my child! I'm satisfied with the baby strapped to my back."

She hoed on, then she went home.

The next day, the sun was very hot. Again, Chakijana came along. He said, "Mother, Mother, let me watch your child for you. Can't you hear that the child is crying?"

The mother said, "Well, you began all this by asking me to allow you to watch my child. Just sit nearby, and carry the child."

The mother gave the child to Chakijana, and Chakijana played with him. The mother hoed on. She finished, then prepared to go home when the cattle were returning from the pasture.

Chakijana said, "Will you come back, Mother, when the cattle return to the pasture?"

The woman said, "Yes, I'll come back—but only when it's cooler."

So Chakijana remained there, waiting for the mother to return to this field. She did come back in time, she came as the cattle spread in the pasture. Then Chakijana said, "Mother! Mother, let me watch the child for you."

The mother gave the child to him, she had no suspicions anymore. No more did she wonder "what sort of person this is who offers to watch my child," anxious lest he be some kind of monster who might bewitch the child.

Chakijana watched the child, and the mother went on hoeing. At sunset, she thanked him. She thanked Chakijana, and said, "I thank you, my child, for watching my child for me." And she said, "Well, I'll bring you some boiled mealies from home next time, so that you can munch on something as you look after the child."

Chakijana expressed his thanks, and said, "Well, Mother, I'll return in the morning."

The woman did not think to ask, "Just tell me, my child, where have you come from? Where do you live? You're so generous, all this time looking after my child in this way!"

The woman departed.

On the third day, Chakijana came. He came in the company of an animal—a duiker. He drove it ahead. As this woman hoed, he suddenly appeared.

"Mother, I'm here already! Isn't the baby crying?"

She said, "Oh! Are you already here, my child?"

He said, "Yes, I'm already here. Isn't the baby crying, Mother? Give it to me, I'll look after it." Then he said, "I want to teach him some games. I even brought something for him to play with."

"What have you brought, my child?"

"I've brought him this beautiful thing—he can throw it in front of himself, he can throw it in front. While you're hoeing, the child will not be crying!"

So the mother gave him the child.

Then Chakijana said, "Well, Mother, we'll just sit down under that tree, over there in the middle of the field."

Then he pointed to his duiker, and said, "There! The child can ride on the duiker!" He said, "Say, Mother! Say, Mother! Look how I play with the child!"

So indeed this mother was happy.

Then the mother said that she thought it was time for her to return to her home, to go and prepare food for that boy who was at home. So she said to Chakijana, "Chakijana, where's my child? Bring him back! Why don't I hear you talking to the child?"

He said, "Here he is, Mother! He's still here! He merely followed the duiker, that's all! The duiker went into the thicket there."

She said, "When did the child learn to walk? Come now, Chakijana, I know that the child can't walk! My child can't walk yet!"

He said, "The duiker's teaching him to walk, Mother. That animal! It's a very beautiful animal. He's very resourceful and wise. He's teaching the child. He'll bring the child back any minute now. He's gone to the stream with the child, they went to get a drink."

The mother was silent, she stared at Chakijana.

"Oh, Chakijana! It's time for me to go! Just look! You can see that it's about time for the cattle to come home. I must go and prepare food for my son at home!"

Chakijana said, "Well, Mother, I'll bring the child when he cries. You're in a hurry. Go on! Or don't you trust me, Mother? I'm not distrustful of you! You're my real mother!"

The woman said, "Chakijana, I really cannot leave my child behind! What will my neighbors think when they see me return without my child? And I'm still nursing the infant!"

Chakijana said, "Well, mother, trust me. I'm sure the duiker won't harm the child. He's just gone down to the stream for a little while, to get some water to drink."

But the mother would not be persuaded. She persisted, "No! I can't trust you, I want my child!"

Then Chakijana said, "Well, Mother, I'll go and look for the duiker. He disappeared just as we started to talk, you and I. He was here just now. They went away for a short time, he and the infant. They were playing here together."

The mother said, "No, let's go together, Chakijana! Let's go together and find them!"

When they set out, Chakijana made certain that he walked in front. He said, "Follow me then, Mother! Follow me! I'm the one who knows where they've gone, where they've disappeared to."

So the mother followed, walking behind Chakijana. As he went along, Chakijana devised all sorts of schemes, thinking, "I've already transported the child, he's no longer here! He's gone! Hey! Now how can I shake this woman from my back, this woman here?"

He went down to the thicket at the edge of the field, then Chakijana caused himself to fall.

He said, "Oh! I stumbled, Mother! I'm hurt, I'm really hurt! I'm badly injured, Mother!"

She said, "Oh no, Chakijana! Get on your feet! Give me my child! You must realize that it's getting very late! The boy will soon be driving the cattle home, and he won't find anything to eat there."

Chakijana said, "Mother, I'm really hurt! I'm really hurt! I'm unable to walk further!"

The mother caught hold of him then, and said, "Get up, Chakijana!"

Chakijana refused to get up, he went limp.

The mother said, "No, no! Get up! Show me my child, Chakijana!"

Chakijana refused.

The woman loosened her cape now, and she began to hit him with it. Chakijana endured it all. She hit him harder, Chakijana endured the beating.

She said, "I beat you on the shins, I beat you on the waist, but it makes no impression on you! I'll beat you on the ears with the strings of his garment! See if *that* won't make you get up!"

And the woman did that—she beat him on the ears. But Chakijana persevered.

She said, "Well, he doesn't feel any pain. I'll push him!"

So the woman pushed him, she pushed him and shook him by the ears, she pinched him. Well then! Chakijana burst out crying.

Then the duiker arrived.

He said, "Duiker! Duiker, turn back! The day has not yet arrived for us to go off with the child!"

Well, the duiker realized that Chakijana was crying here under the tree.

Then he said, "Mother, I told you that the duiker had gone down to drink! And here's the child, he's come with the duiker!"

The woman looked back and saw the child riding on the duiker's back. The duiker had the child on its back.

"Oh!" the mother said, "Chakijana! What you almost did to me! What is this?"

He said, "Well, Mother I told you that the duiker had gone for a drink. But you acted as if I had killed the child!"

The mother took the child then, and said, "Well, Chakijana, today I don't see how I can come back. You've given me a fright! But I do appreciate your looking after my child, I appreciate your keeping my child occupied so that he doesn't cry as I hoe these weeds. But after today, I won't be able to come back. I've already delayed too long."

So saying, the woman departed. Chakijana also departed, he went to the cannibals. As it turned out, Chakijana had been acting out all this craftiness because he had previously deceived the cannibals. He had tricked the cannibals, he had taken their cattle. Now the cannibals were demanding that he bring them a small game animal, their favorite meat—something like a human being. Chakijana had agreed to do this, and had said, "All right, I will bring it to you! I'll bring you young game, tender soft meat, not meat that has become tough."

They said, "Well, you bring it to us, Chakijana! Bring tender meat."

He said, "Another person would fail! But not me!"

That is why Chakijana had attempted to trick the mother. He was about the business of getting the meat that he had promised the cannibals, in payment for those cattle that he had consumed, that he had taken away, that the cannibals had then sought and could not reclaim.

The next day, the mother came back. When she got there, Chakijana was waiting for her in the field.

No sooner had she arrived than he said, "Mother, I've been here a long time, waiting for you! Now then, Mother, I left my bucket right here. I brought the bucket with me this time so that I can dip water with it. I thought you would be in the field already, I thought you would come early. But you had not yet arrived when I got here. So I've been waiting and waiting. I thought that I would be insulting you if I just went away."

The mother said, "Well, you did well to bring the bucket along, to dip water. When your throat is dry, you'll be able to drink. I should have brought a scoop from home, but I forgot it. You do help me, Chakijana."

Well, Chakijana remained quiet.

Then he said, "Just give me the child, Mother."

The mother was happy to do so, she did not have the slightest suspicion because of Chakijana's actions the day before. Here he was once again, Chakijana had again appeared to watch her child.

So it happened that Chakijana and the mother both returned on the day after the duiker and the child had been missed. Today, Chakijana had left the duiker behind, at the stream. When he was speaking of the bucket, he actually meant the duiker itself. Now he was asking for the back strap from the child's mother.

He said, "Well, Mother, give me the back strap. Untie it from your body. Give it to me, I'll carry the child on my back. I'll take the child to the stream, all right? Then I'll come back with some water, so that I can drink as well as the child. And you too, you'll become thirsty. The sun will be hot soon, you'll also be dry. And you too can drink some of this water, it'll be right here!"

Well, this mother said, "That'll be very good indeed, my child. I can see that the sun's getting hot. And I know that I'll get dry too. Go, get the water."

Then he said, "Well, Mother, I'll go with the child. I'll carry him on my back."

And she said, "It's still early. Let me get to work, it's still early. I can't go back just now, it's not yet time for the cattle to return."

Chakijana was pleased in his heart. He said, "Today, I'll get that tender meat, and I'll deliver it to the cannibals! The cannibals are pushing me now because of the debt regarding their cattle!"

So Chakijana departed, cooing to the child: "Oya! Oya! Oya! Oya! Oya!"

Then Chakijana disappeared, going to the stream. When he got to the stream, Chakijana took the child and gave him to the duiker. Then he took a stone from the stream, and he tied that to his back. He took the scoop, which he had been carrying all the time, which he had left here with the duiker. He took the scoop, and as he took it in his hand and carried it in the proper manner, he returned to the fields, all the time pretending to coo to the child: "Oya! Oya! Iya! Oya! O—"

Then the mother asked, "Oh! Is the child crying, Chakijana?"

He said, "Not at all, Mother! He's not crying yet! He's still quiet. I'm cooing so that he sleeps well, Mother, so that you won't be bothered by the child."

But the duiker was then going off with the child, right up the stream, going up the stream! There were some bushes on the river bed. The duiker went on.

Chakijana remained here. But all this while, he was calming and cajoling a stone! There was no longer a child with Chakijana. The child had gone off with the duiker.

When it was about time for the mother to return to her home, when the cattle were returning, she asked for the child.

She said, "Well, Chakijana, would you give me the child so that I can nurse him? I do trust you very much, but it's time for me to hurry home. I'll only nurse the child, then I'll leave him here with you. I'll come back quickly. I'll get home, prepare some ground boiled maize over there at home, so that my son can eat and take the cattle to the pasture. Then I'll rush back."

Chakijana said, "Oh! You may go. I'm very happy that you trust me so much." Then he said, "Mother, do wait a minute. Have patience with me. Just let me go and relieve myself. I'll come back presently. But actually, you can go right now, Mother. The child hasn't cried yet. And there's plenty of water here. As you say, you won't be long. You're going to prepare some boiled maize at home, that won't take long, Mother. You'll hurry and return. And you'll find me here. Today, I'm determined to leave when you return in the late afternoon."

The mother said, "Well, Chakijana, I'll not let you down this time, I really do trust you, my child. You're a very good person, you watch my child well for me. And you get along very well with my child."

So the mother hurried; she took big strides, hurrying to prepare food for the boy who was herding cattle. She got there and made the preparations.

The boy asked, "Mother, where's the baby? Why have you come home alone? Where have you left the child?"

Then she said, "There's my boy, over there! I left the child with him over there in the field."

"What could he possibly be eating, the child is still—"

"Well, there's a little food that I took with me this morning. I left instructions that he should continue to feed it to the child."

"Oh!" The boy was startled. He said, "How could Mother leave the child behind and just say, 'There's a boy who's staying with him'? It's not even a girl who is a relative of some kind!"

The boy began to think about this, and he said, "Mh! Mh! My mother's child is no more! But she refuses to tell me where he is! I'm certain that the child is no more! Perhaps he's been hurt by wild animals, perhaps he's been eaten by the wild animals!"

The boy remained quiet. Soon, his mother departed. When she appeared in the fields again, Chakijana went out to meet her.

"Oh, Mother! The child hasn't cried yet, he's very still. Listen yourself! He hasn't cried since you left! Not a sound! Your child—"

["—will soon appear!" says a member of the audience].

But the son of this woman had an idea. He decided to leave the cattle over there in the pasture, and he turned back with the dogs. He went off like a person who was hunting wild game. He walked on and on, silently. Then he saw this person here in the field—with his mother. He approached stealthily, little by little, edging closer. The dogs were chafing to go after him. But the boy restrained them, saying, "I want to observe this person very carefully. There are certain people who are said to go about with an animal. And I want to catch this creature with my dogs."

Quietly, the boy came closer, little by little, restraining his dogs. They came closer and closer. Suddenly, his mother heard: "Say, Mother! Say, Mother! Oh! The child—Is this the one who looks after the child?"

"Yes, my child!"

Then Chakijana said, "Well, Mother, just let me go and get a drink of water over there at the stream!"

She said, "Go quickly, Chakijana! I should go back at once, my child, because here's the boy who herds the cattle—he's here already. I'll be going back soon too, I must get some water for home."

Chakijana departed immediately, carrying his scoop. As soon as Chakijana had left the field, the boy let the dogs loose, saying, "Mother, this is not the child!"

As Chakijana was leaving, the boy was examining whether or not this was actually the child, because he could not see the child's head—and he knew that when the child is strapped to the back by its mother, with the back strap, one can usually see the child's head clearly, and the feet and the arms as well. Now the boy was looking closely, but he could not see the feet, he could not see the head, he could not see the hands! All he could find was a hump on Chakijana's back!

So the boy loosed his dogs. And Chakijana then opened the hump on his back, and began to run.

[Audience laughs.]

Chakijana ran away from the dogs!

The boy said, "Mother, look! You said the child is being carried on Chakijana's back. Where is the child now? There's Chakijana, and he's dropping a stone!"

"Oh!"

[Audience laughs.]

The woman and her child!

[Audience laughs.]

"Oh, my child! Chakijana has deceived me! Chakijana has deceived me!"

The boy gave chase with his dogs. And the woman seized her hoe, and she ran too. The woman ran! She came to the stream, and when she got there, she realized that—well, she had no stone with which to hit him.

The dogs also lost the trail. As they ran, the dogs did not look carefully. But Chakijana knew this river well, he had purposely lured them there. And when he got there, he moved to one side of the river. As the dogs came straight ahead, they reached a dead-end at the river's bank.

And as the boy moved along, he remembered that he should be with the cattle—the sun was setting, and the cattle would stray into the fields of other people.

But the mother rushed on. She said, "Well now, I'll go right here, to the place where he went in. I'll get there and catch him, wherever he is, this Chakijana!"

So she ran, the mother ran. She said, "Chakijana! Give me my child! Chakijana! Give me my child!"

But Chakijana kept running. They approached a second stream, and this stream was overflowing its banks. It had been raining further up, and the rain caused these streams to be full. Then the mother arrived.

Chakijana then turned himself into a stone. When he realized that there was no way to cross this stream, he changed himself into a stone.

When the mother got there, "I thought he stopped here! I thought he stopped here."

Well, all she could see was stones. There were three beautiful stones there, with very pleasing shapes. She looked across the stream, she looked downstream to see if perhaps Chakijana had thrown himself into the water, and the water had then swept him downstream. But she could see nothing. Then she looked upstream. No, the mother saw nothing. She looked on the banks of the stream, perhaps he had submerged his body and was holding to a root on the river bank. But no, Chakijana was not to be seen.

So the mother just stood there, and she cried. She said, "You did deceive me regarding my child, Chakijana! Where will I get another child? because I no longer have a husband, I don't have anything!"

The mother went on thinking in this way. Now and then, she would look across the river, but she did not see Chakijana. Suddenly, she took one of the stones, and said, "If I had him here, I would strike him with this stone! I would do this to him!"

Saying this, she took the stone and threw it across the river.

Then Chakijana said, "Hoho! You helped me to cross!"

[Member of audience: "Oh! My God!"]

"Hoho! You helped me to cross! Hoho! You helped me to cross!"

The mother now broke down and cried. She could see that "Now I've helped him to cross the river! And here's all this water, blocking my way!"

The mother fainted, she passed out. But Chakijana went on his way, and soon he met that animal of his, the duiker.

The plan now was to take this child to the cannibals. Chakijana caught up with the duiker.

"Now then, Duiker, where's the child of— Oh, here he is! Let's go then. Now you, Duiker, you must stay over there. I'll go in with this little game animal of the cannibals!"

As it turned out, while Chakijana was saying that, he had already deceived the duiker as well. That very duiker had been betrayed to these cannibals.

So Chakijana went on, and when he got to the place of the cannibals, he went in. As soon as he had appeared, as soon as the cannibals saw him, they were glad. They danced and danced.

They said, "Oh! Here's Chakijana!"

[Audience responds.]

"He's arrived!"

"Surely he's bringing with him the game animal that has tender meat!"

Well, Chakijana came along, and said, "Don't you see? I told you I would bring some beautiful game animal for you! Don't cause me any more trouble now because I robbed you of your livestock! Besides, you stole that stock too! It didn't belong to you, you didn't work for it! You didn't fight for it like the rest of mankind! After all, livestock is obtained only by acts of daring and heroism!" Then he said, "Well, I'll give you another game animal to make up for the cattle that I took."

The cannibals said, "You'll have discharged your obligation to us then, Chakijana!"

"Because here you are, you've brought this game animal of ours!"

"The one we've craved so much!"

Chakijana went outside.

He said, "Give me a rope! The animal's here, I'll drive it by myself. I won't carry it."

So the cannibals gave him a rope, and he went away.

When he got to the duiker, he said, "Now Duiker, come here. I want to tie you up. Then I'll go back with you, I want to take you back all tied up."

[Audience laughs.]

Then he said, "You'll be jumping around and struggling in the courtyard all the time, struggling, struggling, and just keep on struggling

when I've tied you to the posts of the house. Keep on jumping around."
He did not tell the duiker that "I have betrayed you, Chali!" He only said,
"Duiker, just say that you've come there to play and dance!"

The duiker cooperated, it did everything that Chakijana told it to do.
The duiker did it, and Chakijana tied it to the posts of the house. And the
duiker jumped around, round and round. They speared it, that was the
end of the duiker.

Then Chakijana moved on. He walked along, carrying his scoop. He
came to some boys. (He had taken the scoop from the cannibals.) Chakijana found these boys just sitting around, herding livestock in the pasture.

He went to the boys, and said, "How could you just be sitting around
here without water? Where do you get water when you're dry?"

"Well, we just go down to the stream when we're thirsty."

He said, "I could give you a fine container! Look, here's my scoop!
Who wants to go and drink? Who wants to go and drink?"

One boy said, "I do."

Chakijana made a quick trip to the stream. He scooped up some water,
then returned with it. He put the water down, and said, "Don't you see
how clever I am? But you don't carry scoops for water for yourselves! Just
look now! I've brought you something useful. Now you can drink water."

The boys said, "Well, Chakijana, make some scoops for us too, because
there are no drinking vessels at our homes."

He said, "Well, I could make some scoops for you. But today, we'll just
sit around a little, and you can drink from my scoop."

As the boys sat there, they said, "Let's parry a bit!"

"Let's parry a little!"

"Here are the sticks, they're here!"

"We'll spar gently with them!"

"We won't hit one another hard!"

So Chakijana took a stick, and they parried.

Then he said, "Why don't you spar among yourselves? You see now,
I don't want to take unfair advantage of you. This scoop—It would be a
good idea to have a contest, to determine who among you is the champion, who is the hero!"

Oh! The boys, because boys are always ready to fight one another,
were easily deceived. They took their sticks and fought. They fought each
other just above Chakijana's scoop.

And the scoop was broken!

[Members of the audience snicker.]

Chakijana was enraged over the broken scoop. He said,

"I want my scoop, my scoop!
The scoop that I took from the cannibals!

> The cannibals took my game animal,
> The animal that I got from the woman!"

The boys wondered what had happened.

"Chakijana, may we suggest that you take our sticks? Because you walk with no stick."

Chakijana said, "No, I don't want these sticks of yours—such as they are! Hey! Rather, get me some beautiful sticks!" Then Chakijana said, "Look here! Tomorrow morning, I'll be here to collect these sticks!" So saying, Chakijana turned around and departed. He said, "I really want those sticks! I'll not take this scoop!"

The boys said, "All right, Chakijana, but take it! And try to get another. As for the sticks, we'll bring them for you in the morning."

So the boys left, they looked for the sticks. They returned with some really fine sticks. And Chakijana also returned.

They said, "Here are your sticks, Chakijana. We've brought them for you."

Chakijana took them and examined them closely, admiring them. He looked at them carefully. He satisfied himself that they were indeed fine sticks. Then he said, "Stay well!" and he left those boys there.

He went on. And when he had gone on, Chakijana came to a forest.

He found two men fighting and wrestling with their hands.

Chakijana said, "I've never seen such fools! Big fellows like you! When you have a misunderstanding, you hit each other with your bare hands! Here are sticks! Take them, you'll get what you want out of each other!"

He took two sticks, and gave them to one of the men. He took two more, and gave them to the other. So these young men went at each other with these sticks. When they had been hitting each other with the sticks, the sticks snapped—they broke!

Chakijana became very upset about the broken sticks. He said,

> "I want my sticks, my sticks!
> Given to me by the boys!
> The boys destroyed my scoop,
> My scoop! My scoop!
> The scoop I took from the cannibals!
> The cannibals took my game animal,
> The animal I got from the woman!"

"Before Chakijana came, we were fighting in our own way. You gave us the sticks to fight with!"

"Well, Fellow, there's not much we can do. We'll replace your sticks."

"You just say how you want your sticks paid back to you, what will satisfy you."

Chakijana said, "I want clothes that are nicely decorated with splendid buttons or beads."

The young men said, "We'll bring them for you, Chakijana, because you did help us."

"We had contemptuous attitudes for each other all this time. Now, all that has changed."

"Our animosity toward each other has cooled."

Chakijana said, "Well, I'll come tomorrow morning. I'm going back there for a while, then I'll pass by here again. You'll find me right here, and I should find you here too!"

The young men said, "It's all right. We concede to you, Chakijana."

So Chakijana departed. He came back the next morning, and, true enough, he found the young men waiting for him.

They said, "Well, Chakijana, here we are. We're very happy to see you."

Chakijana, for all his craftiness, did not realize that the youth who was the brother of the child he had given to the cannibals had gone ahead of him. And now, Chakijana went on with his booty.

But he was going straight to this boy. The boy was just ahead of him, on this very road. When Chakijana got to a certain place, he found that he was moving towards a festive gathering. He encountered some young men who had no weapons.

Chakijana said, "Just look here! Here are weapons—you're not armed! I could supply you with weapons—beautiful ones, weapons that surpass those!"

Then he saw this boy.

The boy thought, "Here's the person who abducted the child of my home!" But he said nothing. He thought, "I don't want to strike him, I want to catch him. Then I'll kill him in a very painful way, because he killed the child of my home in a painful way. I don't have a sibling anymore because of this Chakijana."

The boy then attempted to persuade the other boys of his homestead—the homestead where the festivities were taking place.

The boy said, "Well, please give me two fasteners. I want two fasteners. I'll return with them in the morning. There's a little creature of mine that I want to go out and drive this way. I want to go and make it crawl, because I'm here by myself. I don't think I can drive it by myself. I'll just have to bind it, then make it crawl! And when it's too tired to run, it'll raise its head."

Well, the young men waited for him.

They said, "Well, hurry, turn it around, Fellow."

"The others will kill us when they demand their fasteners and don't find them!"

"I'll hurry, and then return them!"

The boy took these fasteners, and he made a lasso. Then he moved about like the other people who were bumping into each other in the dance. That is how he behaved. As he approached Chakijana, the other did not recognize him; Chakijana did not know that this was the brother of the infant he had sold to the cannibals. The boy came with these fasteners and things. Before he knew what was happening, Chakijana was trapped.

The others wondered, "Oh! Where has this young man come from?"

Because this Chakijana was a very crafty person, he could perform all kinds of tricks.

The young men were quiet, then they said, "Where is this young man from?"

Others said, "Don't you see that it's Chakijana? It seems to be Chakijana!"

Someone said, "Ho! He seems to be dallying with the boys! What's he doing? Now he's been caught by the boys! They seem to be playing."

In the meantime, the boy pulled the lasso, and tightened his hold on Chakijana. Chakijana struggled, and said, "Let go of me! Let go of me! Pulling me like this—where are you taking me?"

The boy said, "Come here! There's something for us to talk about!"

The boy tied Chakijana's hands, and dragged him. Chakijana did not know what to do. Because there were so many people here and because there was such a commotion because of the dancing, no one at the party took any notice. There were many people here, and they were minding their own business. They thought only of participating in the dancing. They took no notice of this activity that was occurring to the side of them and behind. They were observing only what they had come here for.

So the boy dragged Chakijana, pulling the ropes tighter and tighter.

And these other boys were watching him, and following. When he was out of the sight of the mass of people, he was joined by the others.

He explained, "This Chakijana is the one who killed my mother's child! Now I'm left alone because of this person!"

"Oh! Is that so?"

"Yes!"

Then the boys said, "Well, we won't kill him by ourselves! Let's go and call our brothers."

"Our brothers will beat him and kill him."

"We can't find it in ourselves to kill him."

The boy said, "Well, I won't find it hard to kill him! I have the same nerve he has, the one who killed the child of my home, an only child!"

Chakijana now began to go soft, then he turned himself into various things. He changed himself into all sorts of things, whatever the boys desired.

He changed himself into a goat.

Three boys

Then he turned himself into a cow.

The boy said, "I won't let you go, no matter what you change yourself into! I'll never let you go, you! I'll take you with me, Chakijana!"

When the boy got to a tree, he thought of tying Chakijana to it. Then he thought,

"No, he'll just untie himself."

So the boy dragged him on. He went on, going now to his mother at his home. He dragged Chakijana, and when his prisoner resisted the boy would flog him. Then Chakijana would cooperate. And when he changed himself into all manner of things, the boy beat him up. So Chakijana stopped changing himself.

The boy said, "Don't change yourself anymore! I want to do to you what you did to my mother's child!"

So the boy went on, dragging him along. And when they were close to his home, when it had come into view, the boy called out loudly, and said, "Mother! Come outside! And see! Here's the one who killed the child of my home! I'm coming with him! Burn that house at the side!"

Oh! Chakijana now began to beg him. "But young man, you're determined to kill me, hey? But I can bring the child back!"

He said, "Oh no! I'm not interested in that anymore! My mother's child is not here anymore! He's not alive anymore, Chakijana! You killed him long ago! We've already heard that he's been devoured by the cannibals, that he was devoured long ago. But you're still alive! And you must die also!"

Well, the mother came outside. At first, she did not know who was calling out so loudly.

Again, the boy said, "Mother, ignite that house on the side. By the time I arrive, I want to be able to throw him into the fire!"

Oh! The mother was perplexed as to why she should burn that house.

Then she saw that the youth was getting close, and he was saying, "Here's Chakijana, the one who abducted your child!"

The boy dragged him along, and he said, "Mother, I've been telling you to ignite that house!"

The woman said, "No, my child, wait a little. Let's just wait before we kill him. Let us beat him, let's beat him to satisfy our hearts. We've lost everything because of Chakijana."

Then the woman took the handle of the hoe, and she tried to remove the hoe from the handle. It was not easy to do, because in the beginning hoes were attached in a certain way. The boy took one end, and said, "Hold it here!" He realized that he too would be pulled. He pulled on the hoe, and pulled his mother. He said, "Well, hit it against this—like this. Mother, hit it here!" So the mother hit it, and it came loose.

Then the boy caught hold of Chakijana, and said, "Hit him, hit him, Mother! I'm holding him down!"

So she hit him, she hit him, she hit him.

And Chakijana said, "I'm as good as dead!"

Then Chakijana turned himself into a snake—a snake long dead.

The boy said, "Under no circumstances will I release you—no matter what you do! I'll never let you loose, no matter what you turn into, Chakijana! I just won't let go of you!" Then he said, "Mother, bring flaming firewood! I'll burn him! He will come out—here he is, he's turned himself into this!"

The mother said, "Wait a little, my child. There's firewood here in the wood pile."

The mother took it. Her son piled the wood on top of Chakijana.

Then Chakijana said, "Forgive me! Don't burn me, I've changed again. I'm a human being again!" Chakijana said, "Please forgive me. I'll give you many cattle! Right now! Cattle, and many other things! Goats! Because I've sold your child!"

The young man said, "Yes, I understand all that, Chakijana. However, I am demanding your soul, I want your soul to become like that of my mother's child, the child who is gone now!"

Chakijana said, "Well, they ate the child long ago, they finished it."

The boy said, "You agree then, Chakijana, that they ate the child long ago."

He said, "Yes, hey! I handed it over, together with the duiker that carried the child on its back. I'm telling everything now, so that you may pardon me, so that I may give you everything! everything! oxen! goats! to pacify you regarding the child of your homestead. I am pleading with you."

The boy said, "No, my one demand is that you allow me to take your life, and do to it what you did to the child of our homestead." Then the boy said, "Mother, get up early in the morning. I won't sleep, I'll tie him here until the break of day. I'll rope him here, I'll watch him."

The boy took his shield and his spear, and he tied Chakijana. He said, "If you but move, I'll stab you! Mother, you go and fetch the cannibals! I want the cannibals to eat him up right here before my eyes!"

The mother got up and went out, and when she had done so, she met a duiker. It said, "Hello, Mother."

The woman responded.

It said, "Mother, you travel as if you're troubled by something. And you seem to be in a hurry. Where are you rushing to?"

The mother said, "Oh, my child, I'm rushing to the land of the cannibals."

"Hurry, Mother, the day is all but gone!"

So the woman travelled on and on. Along the way, she met an old woman.

The old woman said, "Hello, my child."

The woman said, "Hello, Mother."

She said, "Where are you hurrying to? Where are you rushing to? You walk as if you're troubled."

She said, "Well, I am hurrying, I'm going a great distance—to the land of the cannibals."

"What business do you have in the land of the cannibals?"

"Well, there is certain business that takes me to the land of the cannibals."

"Well, you'll never find the cannibals!"

"Oh!"

"Go down this way. Go down this way, down there. I met them going down this way!"

The mother said, "I see, Mother."

Then the mother went on her way. She went up a ridge, then she came to a snake.

The snake said, "Madam, why is it you walk as if you're troubled? Are you sad?"

The mother said, "Yes, I am indeed troubled, Snake, at this time! I don't know whether my disease can be cured. My destination is the land of the cannibals. But a short time ago, I met a very old woman over there, and she said that the cannibals are not to be found in this direction, that they went up over this ridge."

It said, "Yes, yes, indeed, I too met them in this direction. But this distress of yours, Mother—do you think I can help you?"

The mother said, "Oh, I don't know, Snake. Could you help me to find the land of the cannibals?"

The snake said, "I'll find out for myself. You keep going forward. But if you can't find the land of the cannibals, come back. You'll find me right here on the road."

But this was one of Chakijana's tricks.

The woman passed on. And soon enough, she saw the dust of the cannibals, as they moved along.

The woman called out, she clapped her hands, and said, "Hello there! Cannibals, come this way!"

The cannibals stopped.

They said, "What is this? What is this that has spoken?"

"What's this that has spoken on this side?"

"She seems to be saying, 'Say, you of the land of the cannibals, come this way!'"

Well, the cannibals remained silent. Then they looked this way.

The woman called out and said, "Say, Cannibals! Come this way!"

The cannibals mumbled and said, "It seems to be an animal that has become tough!"

They said, "Speak up!" They were drawing nearer to her, and they said, "Speak up, speak up, speak up, speak up!" Repeatedly, they said, "What is it? What is your trouble?"

"Well, I have been sent to you! I have been told to come to you. We caught Chakijana, and now I have been sent here by my son. He says, 'Come on and take him!'"

"Really? Have you actually caught Chakijana?"

"Well, Chakijana deceived us also, he ate up our cattle, then brought us an animal in return, an animal that was quite small."

She said, "That animal that he brought to you was my child!"

They said, "Mother, was that indeed your child?"

"Yes, yes!"

"Oh! There is nothing we can do about that. We place the blame on Chakijana!"

"But we do mourn with you."

So the cannibals went along with the mother all that day, the mother showing them the way.

When the cannibals arrived, Chakijana again turned himself into an old snake, a snake that had long since rotted.

The cannibals remained silent. They said, "Mother, but where is Chakijana?"

She said, "He is here." Then she said, "Point him out to them, my child."

The boy told them to approach. They should come close so that he could talk seriously to them.

The cannibals came, and he said, "Do you indeed want me to produce Chakijana for you? Do you want to see him?"

They said, "Yes, yes! We do want to see him!"

"Do you really know what Chakijana is like?"

They said, "Yes, we do know Chakijana."

"But Chakijana is capable of changing himself into all sorts of creatures here on earth." Then he said, "I'll show you that I have apprehended Chakijana."

Oh! He said, "Mother, let me have that burning wood."

Chakijana immediately changed himself into whatever he turned himself into, and the mother came with the burning wood. She put the wood on Chakijana.

He said, "Oh! Forgive me! Don't kill me with fire!"

He said, "You can see what they are saying."

"Yes, yes!"

Then he said, "You see, I don't want to drive him away. If you'll eat him here, while I watch you, I'll give you these two oxen—to thank you. And you can sing my praises as I praise you."

So the cannibals said, "Now what shall we do to him?"

He said, "Well, I'll ignite this house, and we'll burn him in it. But we don't know if you want to cook him."

The cannibals said, "Well, we do want to roast him."

The boy remained quiet, and then he said, "Now, when you roast him, will he come out of the pot?"

[Member of audience: "Yes! He'll come out!"]

They said, "No! Never!"

He said, "Wait! It turns out that you are in league with Chakijana! You mean to let him go!"

The cannibals said, "Not at all! We would never let him go!"

"Chakijana has given us a lot of trouble too!"

"He has been slipping out of our hands all this time because of his cunning!"

"Now that you've caught him, we want to finish Chakijana off—so that anything by the name of Chakijana should perish!"

"Because Chakijana is responsible for the bad reputation that we have among humans and animals!"

Then the boy said, "Well, I'll show you a plan whereby we can kill Chakijana. Make a fire here. Here's a large pot, take it."

Well, the cannibals took this large pot, and they put it on supports.

He said, "Kindle a fire!"

A fire was made, the fire was kindled. Then the boy got large stones. He placed the pot on them.

Then he caught Chakijana, and said, "Let's put him inside."

The cannibals said, "Has water been put into the pot?"

The boy said, "No, you dare not! If you should put water into the pot, Chakijana will escape! No water should be put in!"

The cannibals remained silent. Chakijana cried now, realizing that the sun was setting for him. His last day had come.

"Oh! Are you really killing me, young man? Do you actually refuse the cattle that I would give to you?"

The boy said, "I am only making you feel what you made the child of my homestead feel!"

Meanwhile, the cannibals were saying, "Chakijana, you're making us angry!"

[Laughter in the audience.]

"We're hungry!"

[Performer also laughs.]

"We're hungry! We're anxious, we can't wait to eat, Chakijana!"

[Members of audience: "Don't make us angry!"]

"Don't make us angry! Don't try us!"

There was silence for a time, and then he said, "Mother, make a fire."

Immediately, the cannibals kindled a fire just beneath the pot.

[Audience: "He feels it!"]

They made the fire. Some were holding Chakijana. The pot began to heat up. It got hotter and hotter. Chakijana began to burn.

He said, "I'm dying! I'm dying!"

The boy said, "When you see him cry aloud, bring all the vessels of water."

Water was brought. Then oh! the cannibals came close. They were in a hurry to eat.

[Member of audience: "A hurry to eat!"]

So the cannibals were made to come close to the pot. And they began to share the parts.

"Chakijana is gone! If you don't claim these parts, I'll kill you!"

The cannibals then regarded the various parts. They also heard the word about killing, that "We might be killed, and such nice food has been offered to us!"

The cannibals then became serious about eating. The boy poured on the water. After a time, after he had poured on the water and Chakijana was boiling, Chakijana tried to come out! The boy beat him back with a club, and Chakijana went back into the pot. When he became agitated, the boy beat him with the club, and Chakijana went back inside.

So Chakijana boiled, he was cooked, and there was a meal for the cannibals.

When the cannibals had eaten Chakijana, the boy offered them the two oxen that he had promised them. He gave the oxen to the cannibals as a thanksgiving.

The cannibals thanked him, and they departed, driving the cattle.

The story ends here.

Sondoda Ngcobo

CHAKIJANA, ZULU FREEDOM-FIGHTER

(ZULU)

Sondoda Ngcobo, the storyteller, now becomes Sondoda Ngcobo, the historian. During the evening of February 10, 1968, Mr. Ngcobo related an account of the historical Chakijana, a freedom-fighter who was active during the Bambatha Rebellion. The performance took place in a home in Mahlabatini District, Zululand, before an audience of six men, six women, and three children. (3750; tape 73; side 1)

He is Ndaba of Chakijana!

Chakijana was, here in the land of the Zulu, a clever, crafty rebel, a re-sister. His way of life was resistance, as was that of some army regiments. He was involved in the wars against the whites. When the Boers fought against the English, Chakijana was there too. And, because at that time the land of the Zulu was in a state of rebellion, when the Anglo-Boer War ended Chakijana became a rebel in his own land. The Zulu had not yet given up their resistance. Guerrilla warfare of the type that Chakijana engaged in is similar to war: it involves people eager for combat, people who are prepared to fight at any time.

It was his artfulness that distinguished this rebel. Like the Chaki-jana of old,[1] this Chakijana was remarkably resourceful, able to respond effortlessly to a variety of challenges: it was as if he used magic. But Chakijana's wizardry was his cunning. This gaudily provocative trick-ster taunted the whites, disquieting them. Though the whites tenaciously pursued him, they were unable to apprehend him. Even when they watched his movements scrupulously, their efforts failed: he would no longer be where they had thought him to be. This canny guerrilla always eluded them.

Men like Chakijana were closely watched and feared in the land of the Zulu. "The guerrillas are here!" When such a warning came, a woman might fling herself into a barrel, and hide. A man might throw his gar-ment to one side when the guerrillas appeared, certain that "The sun has set for me, Child of my father!" When he saw the renegades appearing with such suddenness, he knew that they might abduct him and take him off to their hideout. But frequently they would merely be passing by, going to whatever place their chief had sent them. Their leader had pos-sibly instructed them to go to investigate something, and so they would go off, making people anxious wherever they went.

During the entire period of hostilities following the Anglo-Boer War, after the Boers had been defeated, Chakijana distressed these people. He did all sorts of things to the Boers. He rustled their cattle, and generally outwitted their forces. He became very nettlesome. And the whites continued to seek him; they doggedly persisted in their efforts to capture Chakijana, but always they were unsuccessful. Because he was constantly agitating, unsettling things, they wanted to kill him. He ceaselessly created disruptions in this land at a time when the land was finally moving towards peace, when tempers were at last cooling, when bloodletting had finally been arrested. Chakijana, it is evident, was fostering further carnage in the land. But whenever the Boers thought that they had surrounded Chakijana in his homestead, they were unable to seize him. He simply used his wit, and escaped. He had only to hear the words, "They're here!" He seemed to be endowed with a supernatural sense; it was uncanny the way he obtained his intelligence that the enemy was approaching. It was more than simple vigilance, it was beyond genius and eloquence. It truly seemed that there was something enchanted about him, something that enabled him to sense that the Europeans were almost upon him, about to ambush him. He would invariably find a means of escape.

Chakijana's craftiness was varied. He even changed himself into a woman once when he realized that "The white men are here!" almost upon him! and he had no opportunity to escape. He merely took his wife's garments and put them on; he took a blanket that belonged to his wife, and tied it around his head. When the white men entered and said, "Where's Chakijana?" his wives and his people said, "He's not here! Since he left this homestead, we no longer know where he's operating." But during this discussion that was taking place between the white men and Chakijana's family, Chakijana was himself right there. He had disguised himself as a little, very old woman, dressed in a woman's clothes, with a small blanket coiled like a turban around his head so that it was evident to no one that he was a man.

In the old days, men were quite distinct: it was easy to tell that "This is a man," because men wore head-rings. They wore head-rings and had ornaments around their necks. When the Europeans arrived to surround and capture him, Chakijana would hide those things.

Nor would the whites go away. They would search here and there, but always in vain. They would search, and find nothing. The whites would also look in the homestead neighboring Chakijana's.

Sometimes, a neighbor would say, "Well, my lords, the last time we looked, he was here. But now, we can't say. We just don't know. He's a guerrilla, you know, and such people don't remain long in one place. While we sleep, these guerrillas are on the move. As you know, they're people who are spilling blood constantly."

Then the whites would deliver a speech to the people: "You really should help us when you catch sight of Chakijana. When he comes here, you should inform us. We want him very badly. It's because of Chakijana that this land remains drenched in blood."

The people would agree to do what the whites wanted, and so the Europeans would depart. After the whites had gone, Chakijana would come out of hiding, and again go out and engage in still other exploits that ran counter to the government's laws.

As soon as the white men heard that "Oh! Here's Chakijana! Over here!" they would rush to that area and stalk him. And Chakijana would again disappear into the air. When he found a secure place, well, it was just impossible to dislodge him.

But the Zulu people also feared Chakijana as he went about, because he was a killer, the practice of man-killing being an integral part of guerrilla warfare. Whenever anyone saw him, he would run off, and the people would be unable to tell where it was that Chakijana had disappeared.

One day, Chakijana journeyed near the place where the whites were. He moved in the direction of the Boers, following in the tracks of people who were leaving the land of the Zulu, Nokheshengu's domain—those who were fleeing the land of the Zulu in dissatisfaction, some running because of what other people had done, others moving away from chiefs, still others fleeing in order to settle over there near the white men. The government had divided the land in two, and had decreed that one side belonged to the government, the other to the Zulu.

The people had a saying: "If you flee across the Mngcele, the government will catch you!" A Zulu no longer had the right to do as he wished on this side of the boundary, because on this side the government of the white people ruled. On the other side, the Zulu chief was the ruler. Zulu laws were operative on that side, but not when crimes involved death, because the government had banned the shedding of blood in the land of the Zulu. It no longer permitted a person to be killed in any illegal way. The government decreed that a person should only be arrested, not killed.

Chakijana, then, set out and went over there to the land of the white man. After a time, he began to miss the Zulu people. He returned to the land of the Zulu, driving before him a portion of the white man's cattle: he had fled with this livestock. He spoke to the Zulu in a provocative way, urging them to rebel, insisting that the land of the Zulu king could not be thus alienated with no resistance from the Zulu people.

Once again, the Europeans learned that "Chakijana is there!" They heard of his presence from their agents; the Europeans had placed many spies throughout the land of the Zulu to watch out for Chakijana. The people did heed the instructions of the Europeans; it did seem desirable for the government to overwhelm the rebels in the land of the Zulu. The rebels, after all, were the ones responsible for the turmoil in the land, they were always claiming that the land of the Zulu should be returned to its rightful owners. We, of course, realize that there can be no return of the land of the Zulu, because the white man fought against the Zulu, and the Zulu were defeated. Peace followed. Moreover, the government had not oppressed the Zulu so intolerably that the Zulu were in a constant state of rebellion.

Still, there *was* the urge to rebel. It is painful for one bull to be driven out of his kraal by another. But they had fought each other, and it was really quite appropriate that the Zulu should reconcile themselves to their fate, put down their arms and weapons, and become subject to the law of that bull that had triumphed over them.

And Chakijana should do likewise.

The whites continued to monitor Chakijana's movements closely: "This fellow is behaving in a suspicious manner!" He did not lack guns; the rebels possessed arms that they had obtained during the war between the whites, the war between the English and the Boers. Some Zulu soldiers had been recruited by the English, others had been recruited by the Boers. These Zulu took part in the war. When that war had ended, many of them did not return the guns to their white owners. Instead, when the hostilities ceased and the Boers had been defeated, each went home with his gun; each one returned to his home with a gun. Some Zulu did return their guns to the whites, but the majority did not do so. It was because people knew that he too carried a gun that Chakijana was feared. People knew that one should not approach Chakijana recklessly, because he would stun such a person with the gun that he carried all the time. It also happened that, when revolvers had been obtainable, Chakijana had managed to get one for himself. The rebels got such weapons because they were cunning, because they had the quick wit of killers.

Even though the whites were pursuing him, driving him before them, Chakijana managed to escape to his homestead, which was here at Ntlazatshe, below the Ntlazatshe Mountains. The whites came thundering after him on horseback, swearing that they would capture him that day. But they did not touch Chakijana. He arrived at his homestead, and they knew that "Well, he got it!" They hurriedly looked everywhere, but their efforts were futile once again. Chakijana had broken away from them. He seemed to enter the homestead, but in fact he had not entered at all. He seemed merely to merge with the wall; he disappeared on the other side of the house, then came out at the back of the homestead. There was a thicket near the Ntlazatshe Mountains, and Chakijana just blended into it. Then he disappeared into a cave.

They thought that they were following him. "There he is!" They hurried after him, saying, "Shoot him!"

Others thought better of it: "No, don't shoot him! It's preferable that this man be apprehended!"

"And arrested!"

"It'll not help to kill him, to shoot him, because the government will hold that against us. The government has prohibited bloodshed, it has banned the spilling of blood in an unlawful manner."

"No matter what a person has done, the government has decreed that he be arrested and brought before the government, to be convicted for the deeds that he committed."

So the whites chased Chakijana, seeking him here. But Chakijana had entered a secure place. Then they heard Chakijana jeering at them from high on top of Ntlazatshe Mountain. This mountain is not only large, it is not easily climbed by foot—not at all points, because there are cliffs in some places. In some parts of the mountain, there is no place to climb, even on foot, not to mention riding on a beast.

The whites went up the mountain, determined to capture Chakijana up there—but they failed. They failed to capture him. Chakijana had his own special cave, known only to him. This posed a problem for both black and white men. Even the Zulu chief was baffled by him. While the chief wanted the white men to kill Chakijana, he nevertheless was unable to lay hands on him because Chakijana was so cunning—because of this cave of his, which no one could enter, no matter how bold, no matter how much he might boast that "I am a man! I'll go in and capture him!" One did not dare enter Chakijana's cave.

Chakijana did not go down to his cave on foot, he did not get into it on foot. There were stones, and when he had navigated these stones, there were branches of trees coming out of the rocks, growing out towards the ground. Chakijana would swing on those creepers when he went to his cave. When he had disappeared into the cave, someone might say, "There he is! I saw him going in there!" but in fact he would be stepping on those stones, reaching out for a creeper. He would be out of sight for just a brief time, then he would be there no longer; he would already be down at cave level.

What could one do? It was impossible to traverse a huge mountain like the Ntlazatshe. You would only see Chakijana, you could never capture him, because he was above everything else very crafty.

Food had been put into the cave, so that no matter how they might harass and pursue him, he knew that he could survive a long time without starving, he would not starve. There was water there too; there was much water on the mountain, and water oozed through the floor of the cave. So he could drink. He lacked nothing.

The whites remained there, waiting for him, expecting him to come out. They fired their guns down at the opening of the cave, but with no success. Chakijana would not come out. There were all kinds of labyrinthine recesses on the ground level. Chakijana realized that if he stood in the middle of these recesses, the white man or whoever was on top "would hit me with his gun, and I would die inside there." When he entered the cave, therefore, he would drop to the floor with a thud, then go immediately to the chambers of the cave. And Chakijana would remain there, in good health. He would remain there for some time, then come out slowly, with circumspection, to see if there were anything up there, above the entrance to his cave. If he detected signs of danger, he would return to the bottom and remain in his cave. Nothing bothered this famed person, because he was well fed there. His food did not run short, because food was produced for him. When the tempo of the search had abated, food would be smuggled in. It would be put at the top of the mouth of this cave by children; then he would take it and put it inside the cave. People might wonder when Chakijana would appear: "When, under the pressure of starvation, will Chakijana come out?" But such questioners were ignorant of the fact that Chakijana was eating very well.

So it went, on and on and on, Chakijana being sought by the whites, Chakijana rumored to be all over the land. But this was idle talk. Chakijana realized that, well, the sun was setting on him. There was nothing he could do. His cunning was becoming less and less effective because he had given the whites too much trouble. Moreover, he had thrown the land into too much turmoil. The whites were constantly on the lookout for him. In the end, he realized that, well, everything was burning up for him, the last sun was now setting for him.

He realized in the end that every time he came out, he was watched. He would sneak to his home, and learn that, even at his home, "The whites don't give us a chance to sleep!"

"From our point of view, the best thing you can do is go to some distant place like Swaziland."

"Go up to the land of the Swati, or even farther than that, right on up to the lake regions. Maybe your notoriety will diminish over time, Chakijana."

Well, Chakijana said nothing. He was an awesome person: when you looked at him, you could not doubt that he was a killer, and a ferocious one. He had the character for the evil deeds that he was reputed to have committed. Chakijana and people like him went about in those days carrying revolvers wrapped in scarves that hung from the hip. One would conclude that these were mere items of clothing, but they were actually concealed revolvers. When people were determined to kill, they would simply shoot their guns. The government had prohibited anyone from carrying a spear around in their hands. It had been determined that, if a person walked about carrying a spear in his hand, that person was belligerent, and the government therefore confronted him with a lawsuit for disturbing the peace. Such people took to carrying revolvers that they had obtained in the course of their careers as killers and rebels. They carried such weapons around, and killed people with them. When they were after someone, when they wanted to murder someone, they would watch his movements, then go and surround him in his homestead; they would go there and hit their victim with the firepower of the revolver.

When he had heard himself being admonished by his own household, by his children and his wife, Chakijana departed. This great fellow of the Mdlalose clan set out (Chakijana's clan praise-name was Mdlalose). He set out, and considered going to the king. But he feared the king now, because the king was resentful of him; he bore grudges against Chakijana. He had heard of the bad things that Chakijana had done, reports had come to him from the government.

The king was also in constant anxiety: "Chakijana might just light an uncontrollable fire. Why does he do this? The great regiments have been disbanded. Why does he needlessly provoke the white man? What is Chakijana's purpose in doing such things? Because of such people, war will break out in this land of my father, a war to the finish! Even this last war, which decimated the Zulu, was not provoked by me, the king! It was not caused by my father's household. It was fomented by outside agitators, and now that war has destroyed the whole land! Chakijana is delivering a second blow, he's precipitating similar disaster!"

Chakijana himself thought, "Well, if I go over there to the king, I'll be exposing myself unnecessarily to danger. I'll be warming myself at a very hot fire over there at the king's place. He's been receiving reports for a long time, reports saying, 'We should stop rebelling, we should move through the proper channels. We must stop simply proceeding as we wish, according to our own designs.'" The rebels were obliged to go out and resist only when directed to do so by the king, for reasons determined by the king. The king was the one to initiate things. Why is this? So that when his messengers would come to those to whom they had been sent, they would have official status, and would therefore not be attacked by those people. They realized that "If we touch these emissaries of the king, we'll invite a lot of trouble. We might all die because of our actions." Nor would the king promote rebellion within the borders of his own land.

So Chakijana thought about this. Then, one day, he gathered the members of his household together, and told them, "Well, my children, I can see that the sun is setting for me. It's preferable that I go and deliver myself in person to the white men."

Wailing swept through his household. His family knew that if he surrendered himself to the white men, as soon as he appeared they would spray him with gunshot because he had made things so difficult for them. The whites had petitioned the government for permission to shoot Chakijana. It would be in order for them to do that to a person who was responsible for so much turmoil in the land. The government, considering what Chakijana had been doing, realized that, "This person is truly determined to set the land ablaze once more, to steep it in blood again!" Still, the government did caution against shooting Chakijana: "Just apprehend him! Try to seize him, arrest him! Bring him here, bring him before the law. Let him face up to the law. And, if that is the right thing to do, let him be convicted and punished. If the government so determines, then he shall be executed. If, however, the government determines otherwise, and does not find the offense serious enough to warrant execution, then Chakijana cannot be executed. He'll be convicted and sentenced to hard labor in prison."

A profound lamentation erupted within Chakijana's household when his children and wife heard that he was going to deliver himself to the whites.

They said to Chakijana, "What shall we do then?"

"When you depart, Mdlalose clansman, how will we live?"

"We'll be left alone! Where will be find refuge?"

He merely said, "Nothing will happen to you. I'm the one who is being sought, I'm the one who has been judged guilty. Many of the rebels I have resisted with have already died. They are no more. Only a small group of us remains. I'm not counting the newer recruits to the ranks of the resisters, the ones who are only beginning to resist. They're not made of the same stuff as the heroes of the past, those braves whose courage could be relied on in war."

All was quiet in the homestead. Everyone concluded that Chakijana was indeed departing.

But, as it turned out, Chakijana had not decided to go that way after all. He had changed his mind.

He said goodbye to his family: "Farewell! I'm on my way, my children! I'll go and surrender myself to the white men, they can do whatever they wish. I can see that, truly, my days are numbered. I don't have a day of life left."

Chakijana left then, saying that he was going to the white men. But he did not do that; he went south instead, saying that he wanted to go to the land of the spirits for sanctuary.

He went, now crouching and hiding, now moving on. It was not a direct journey, because government forces filled the entire land, seeking signs of the rebels who might incite hostilities in the land, because the land was now returning to peace. The government was trying mightily to keep the land peaceful, to keep it from erupting in anger, so that people might live in one spirit.

Chakijana departed. After he had gone beyond Mandlakazi, Chakijana learned that "Well, here are the white men, on this side." There were rebels who had defected to the whites, who seemed to want to get vengeance. When Chakijana realized this, he said, "I'll endanger myself!" And he turned back.

As Chakijana was returning, government police suddenly appeared, as if from nowhere. Chakijana fled. These policemen kept moving, and they encountered some people. They caught up with some people, and said, "This Chakijana whom we want so badly—he seems to be in this area! Is that so?"

"The police!"

"Where is he?"

"Well, he was here!"

"Chakijana was right here!"

"Did you meet him along the way, as you were walking?"

"No, we didn't see anyone!"

"Oh!"

"Where's Chakijana?"

"Is he around here?"

"Yes, he's certainly around here."

"You should have met him as you walked along."

The police turned back then, and sought Chakijana. But Chakijana was nowhere, he had already disappeared. When he had realized that they had turned their backs to him, he disappeared, and went all the way to the Mfolozi River. He now kept close to the Mfolozi. The police unit included some Europeans, and they were determined to flush Chakijana out; they were resolved to reduce the impact of his reputation, a reputation that emanated from this area of Mandlakazi. Meanwhile, here was Chakijana, going up the Mfolozi, making his way to the district of Ntlazatshe, returning to his homestead.

The police departed, having concluded that he had again eluded them. They turned back.

"Well, we'll come back when we've heard that he's been seen around here."

"Anyway, he's completely surrounded throughout the land."

"There's no chance that he could possibly get away."

So the government went off quite a distance, going down towards Mandlakazi to end the trouble that seemed to be simmering there. The government ended that trouble, it put a stop to that unrest, then it returned. Now the government was seeking Chakijana with great care. The ranks of these raiders were swelled now by both white and black people, all working for the government, all seeking this man—this scion of Mdlalose, this Chakijana.

They continued to stalk him, seeking to bring him out into the open.

Soon enough, Chakijana realized that—well, he might go this way or that: "Well, maybe this way again!"

The Europeans had closed all paths of escape!

Chakijana considered his plight, then said, "Well, what kind of craft will I require to get out of this? What'll I do? I can't join up with those rebels who belong to the king! If I did that, I'd be compromising myself. I'd rather be devoured by the leopards, if they should surprise me."

Chakijana spent some time here. The Europeans went to the wooded areas and found Chakijana asleep. When they arrived, the whites began to look for Chakijana in his homestead. The people recognized them as policemen.

"Where's Chakijana's house?"

They pointed it out. There was no possibility of concealing it, because the white men were right there; they filled the homestead in the night. The police were all over the place.

They said, "There's Chakijana's house!"

As it turned out, Chakijana had long anticipated their moves, and had devised yet another ruse to escape such encirclement. He had taken bedding and a mat, he took the bedding and spread it out neatly. Then he placed his kaross on top of that. He slid beneath the pile of blankets and mats.

When the whites came in, falling over each other and breaking the doorway as they entered—they found a light, but all they discovered inside was a bundle and the bedding and the kaross. Chakijana was in fact lying right there, under these things! The whites looked about carefully, but found nothing. They poked again and again, everywhere; they searched the place thoroughly, but with no results. Nothing moved here.

They came out of the house, and sought to squeeze more details from Chakijana's wives. Where was Chakijana?

"You said he was here! Now where is he?"

"We don't know, Sirs! He *was* here!"

"He *did* sleep here!"

"When we went to bed, he was here at home!"

But at the very moment that the whites were coming out of the house, Chakijana came out just behind them! While the whites were talking with his wives, here was Chakijana, making his escape!

He hurried over to his cave. The white men were silent, listening carefully for any sound. And they heard rocks falling, thudding rockfalls.

They said, "What's that?"

"What's moving the rocks over there?"

The rocks continued to fall. Some whites were hiding, waiting near the cave, because some people had shown the Europeans that "Here's

Chakijana's fortress! Here's where he takes refuge! A fine secure place!"

Chakijana realized that "Well, they've caught up with me now! My cave is well guarded."

But the whites resigned themselves once again, thinking, "Well, he must have made it into his cave. He has already gone in."

"We must wait until it's light."

"But this place must be sealed up, and well guarded."

Chakijana knew what he would do, even though he was surrounded. He began to climb over the cliffs, making his way tortuously until he had cleared the obstacles. In the meantime, the whites kept watch on the top, waiting for him to appear there, "because he's bound to come running up there, on foot!" They did not realize that they were waiting for the wind. Here was Chakijana, already entering his fortress-cave once again.

They heard him say, "Goodbye, stay well! Why don't you wash your hands?" He was addressing those who were standing guard at the top of his cave. He said, "Stay well! You might as well wash your hands, Children of the white men! I'd rather kill myself here, I know that you want to strangle me!"

They said, "Oh!" and they turned around. By that time, Chakijana had entered the cave and disappeared. The whites remained determined. "This man has given us so much trouble, some other plan must be attempted. Close the cave entrance now."

But they were unable to close the mouth of this cave, they could not find a stone large enough to close the opening through which Chakijana had entered. Even if they stacked rocks on the ground, they could not be certain whether Chakijana was alive or dead. They could not be certain because *he* was down below. Moreover, the white people of those days were not as resourceful as they are now; for the white people, too, cleverness develops bit by bit, so that today they are exceedingly clever. At first, the whites were comparable to the black people in cleverness; the wit that the whites have now they did not have in those days. So they remained there, waiting for Chakijana.

Time passed, and things continued until almost a month had gone by, as they waited for him, waiting for nothing as it turned out, because Chakijana was eating well inside the cave. Nor did he lack water. There was plenty of food in that cave.

The white men just could not believe that anyone would remain a full month inside that cave with no food. They wondered how he managed to survive. Eventually, they departed, saying, "Well, he must have died by now."

Meanwhile, Chakijana was observing them. He ventured out again and again, stealthily, moving almost to the top, watching the whites who were there at the top of the cave.

He satisfied himself that, "Well, they're not here anymore. They've underestimated me!"

So he went out to see what the situation was. He said to himself, "Well, I just won't come out in the daylight. I'll wait till the sun sets."

Chakijana remained there, and when the sun had set, when it was deep dusk, he came out.

But he came out to find himself in a hopeless situation. The government had placed people around there, people not known by the local inhabitants of the land of the Zulu. Well, Chakijana had moved into a trap. And that is how he was finally captured. He was captured by the Europeans, because he had delayed too long outside here, thinking that they had departed, that the whites had given up. But he himself realized that the sun had set on him, that he would not live long. As he was going down, they had seen him. Whistles pierced the silence. The sudden whistling startled Chakijana, and he attempted to fall back. He entered the cave, and never again re-appeared.

When Chakijana meant to come up to spy on what was going on outside, his pursuers were already on top of the cave. So they shot him with gunpowder, and he fell inside there. He buried himself right there, in his cave-fortress.

So ended the story of Chakijana.

Frederick William Calverley

SO EVERYBODY WAS AFTER CHAKIJANA

(ENGLISH)

This account of the historical Chakijana was related by Frederick William Calverley, an eighty-year-old, blind, white South African. He told this story on September 17, 1972, at his home in Melmoth village, Zululand. The audience varied, usually including from five to seven members of his family. (NS-852; tape 22, side 2)

Now, my dad was not very well educated. My father's name was William James Calverley. My name is Frederick William Calverley. My age—I'm close on eighty.

My father was a great Zulu linguist; he was brought up amongst the Zulu, the olden day Zulu, the gentleman Zulu—not this riffraff today. And he was a man who had plenty of brains, he used to walk six miles a day to get a few lessons at night. His people were very very poor. And he used to walk six miles back home. Early in the morning, he had to cart water for his mother. They lived down at Amanzimtoti on top of a hill overlooking the station.

The first job he got was driving a bullock wagon at thirty shillings a month, and then he worked himself up. Being a brilliant man, he soon worked himself up. He's had a shot at lots of things. His first job, as I said, was driving a bullock wagon at thirty shillings a month, for Mr. Asher in Natal. Then he was in charge of a whole lot of wagons after that; he was a conductor. Then he bettered himself. He got in with a Durban syndicate. And he managed a little gold mine down below the Nkandla Forest, at Nkunzana. They worked, he and his partner worked this little gold mine for some years, then after that he was asked by the Newcastle coal mining manager—the big noise in Johannesburg—if he could get a hundred able-bodied natives, take them to Newcastle, and work with them down in the coal mines.

He said, Yes, he'd try.

He went to John Dunn—he knew John Dunn very well—and he asked John Dunn to give him a hundred boys, able-bodied young boys.

So John Dunn said, "Oh, you'll stop with me for a day or two while I send the word round, then you can pick what you want, and you can take them along to Newcastle."

So he got the hundred boys after a few days, and he proceeded to Newcastle coal mines. And there he went underground with the hundred boys, and they worked. And after a month or two, he had a difference with the manager, with the coal mining manager at Newcastle, and he put in his notice.

So down came the big noise from Johannesburg, and said, "Calverley, what's the trouble?"

So Calverley told him what the trouble was.

So he said, "Right!"

Well, within a few days after that, they had a new mine captain.

And all the boys said, "Well, Baas, if you're leaving, put all our notices in. Every one of us will go."

So he said, "All right."

And then the big noise persuaded Dad to stop on another three or four months, so he did.

But he said, "I don't like the work, I don't like underground work."

So he said, "Well, just put in three or four months, and give me a chance to get someone else."

So still the natives said, "Put in our notices. We're going!"

So Dad told the manager, and he came down, and all the natives stood up with Dad and said, "We're giving in our notices, we don't want to stop here without our own *baas* that brought us down."

Every native knew him by the name of Willie, "*uWilli.*"

So that finished.

Then he went in for native shopkeeping. And he's a man that has four medals, I think three or four medals. He was in the '06 [Bambatha] Rebellion, he was in the Boer War before that, and he was in the Basotho Rebellion.[1]

Actually, he was the cause—that was long before the Boer War—he was the cause of winding the chief who had rebelled, winding that rebellion up. It was in Basotholand.[2] A Basotho chief had rebelled. You know they were under British rule. And he personally rebelled against it, and he took all his followers. And they went into a cave.

Well, Dad heard about this rebellion, so he got on his pony, and he went and joined up. They had a British force there that was attending to the chief's rebellion, and all the Basotho had got into a cave. After he had joined up, two or three days afterwards, he was walking around the cave in the evening, and was trying to find out something about it, because, as I said before, he was an intelligent man, and he liked that sort of thing. It was right up his street. All of a sudden, a tame cat came up to him and started rubbing itself against his legs. So he stroked it, and—and a thought hit him straightaway.

"Oh, by Jove! I'll take that cat down, and I'll see the big man"—you know, the man in charge of the British troops, you see.

So he went down, and he got into the tent in the evening.

And he said, "Sir, I want to talk to you."

So he said, "Yes." He said, "What do you want to talk about?" He said, "Sit down," so he sat down.

So he said, "A thought has just struck me. While I was walking around this cave, a cat came up to me," and he related the story. And he said, "I'm used to explosives. Have you any gelignite?"

He said, "Yes. What are you going to do?"

He said, "I'm going to put it on the cat's tail, take it up there, and then give it a whack. And it'll run right amongst the Basotho, and that'll play havoc with them maybe!"

So the officer in charge said, "Very good idea!"

So he looked around for some gelignite, and he found it, gave it to Dad with some fuse. He took the cat with him up to the entrance of the cave, and he fixed it all up, tied it onto its tail, and gave it a whack. And away went the cat! It sounds like a fairy tale, doesn't it? But it's perfectly true, every word of it is the God's truth! And away went the cat—because of the fuse burning it got a fright—went amongst the Basotho. And all of a sudden, there was a terrific explosion! And oh! that charge did tremendous damage!

The next morning, at six o'clock, every Basotho was out of that cave, standing in front of the entrance.

So the officer in charge said, "Yes?"

They said, "We're surrendering! Some terrible thing has happened to us, and we're surrendering!"

So he said, "Right!" And he took the whole lot of prisoners, and that was the end of the Basotho Rebellion.

After that, of course, the [Bambatha] Rebellion started.[3]

Well, they offered him to be captain in the ZMR, Zululand Mounted Rifles, and he said, "No," that he had a friend, Jack Hedges, who was better educated and better able to carry that commission. So anyway they made Dad sergeant-major, and put him in the Intelligence, Government Intelligence.

And they said, "Now you can get a whole lot of native levies to run amongst the rebels. Find out everything you can."

To cut a long story short, he used to go—

He knew the chief very well, Sigananda Shezi, because he worked there in the mines and he was a great shot. And there were plenty of buck about the Nkandla Forest. And he used to shoot the old chief a buck every now and again. He knew the old chief, Sigananda Shezi, very well, and he knew all about when Bambatha went into the bush, called up all the natives who were willing to rebel against the British, and all that. And Dad found out. He had his levies amongst the rebels, and they gave him firsthand information every day.

And he had a friend, Jack Hedges, from England, and a friend, Elias

Titlestad, from Ntingwe. You know Nkandla, you know when you cross the Ntsuzi River, going on towards the Thukela. Now Elias Titlestad had a big store there. And they were friends, those three. Right.

So, he found out that on a certain day every rebel would be concentrated for a beer drink and a great eating of meat, a great feast, at a certain spot in the Mome Gorge. So Dad went to Sir Duncan and told— Sir Duncan was in charge of the whole outfit, Sir Duncan McKenzie.[4]

So he went to him, and he said, "Now we can fix all this rebellion up in a very short time."

So Sir Duncan said, "How so, Calverley?"

So he said, "Well, on a certain day, all the native rebels will be concentrated at a certain spot—the Mome Gorge."

So he said—Sir Duncan said, "Right!" Below the Nkandla Forest, there was another British contingent. So he said, "Right! Now, have you got a man that knows the bush well? can take a shortcut to that camp at the bottom, the other camp?"

So he said, "Yes, certainly." He said, "I've got the man that worked with me in the mine. He knows every inch of the Nkandla bush."

So he said, "Right!" He said, "I'll write a dispatch, and you hand it over to that man, and tell him to go and hand it over to the officer in charge. He must go right now, as soon as I've finished the dispatch, because these niggers are going to be concentrated tonight, and we'll get to them tomorrow morning, before dawn." So Sir Duncan said, "Calverley, go and find a man—your man to take the dispatch."

He said, "Right."

So he went along, he knew where he was lying. And he touched him, he said—whatever his name was, I've forgotten his name—so he said, "Now, come on, I've got a job for you."

Another young chap was lying close too, and he said, "Sergeant-major, can I go too?"

He said, "Yes."

So another one: "Sergeant—"

"No, that's— No, two are plenty!" because too many, you see, would make a noise, and they had to be very stealthy going through the Nkandla bush to get to the other end. So Dad said, "Saddle up quickly, and report here at my tent."

By that time, he had the dispatch from Sir Duncan, and they had to bring those troops straightaway and get down— There's a nasty ridge, called Bobe Ridge, you've got to go down that to get to where the natives were lying, and feasting, and drinking. And— So they went down, they successfully got this—these troops, and they led them down the Bobe Ridge.

And Dad led Sir Duncan and his men down that ridge too. They met down there at two o'clock in the morning. And they sat there quietly, waited for it to become light. When it was light, they could see all the native rebels—oh, they had a big camp there! Sir Duncan was the first one to shoot. They surrounded the rebels completely. And—well, as Dad knew the country so well—he had worked down there in this mine—he placed them right round, and—unbeknownst to the rebels, because they were drunk, they were full of meat. And—the first nigger that jumped up, Sir Duncan put a bullet slap through his chest. That was number one, and then the fighting started all round. They shot practically every native there. Some of them got up trees, climbed to the trees, and they shot them down. Some of them got fallen logs, they got under these logs, they pulled them out of that. And—well, by six o'clock, everything was finished! Dead! Bambatha was amongst them at this time, but he got away, got into another part of the bush. By six o'clock, everything was quiet, finished. And niggers started rolling in, putting their arms down, because Dad sent word and told them that those that didn't get shot had to now surrender quickly. So they started coming in. And Dad knew all the natives around there. And the levies were sent and they notified everybody, and of course you know what the natives—silent telegraphy—it's very good! They stand on a hill, and they shout. And the next one stands on another hill. That can be taken from here to Dundee long before the day is done, before the sun is down today.

So they started bringing their arms in, and those who went there to see, the minute they heard of it they started bringing their arms too. Thousands came in, and lay down their arms. And thousands were killed. I believe the bones are still there, to this very day. Sir Duncan showed no mercy at all. He put them to death left and right! And those that were wounded, he finished them off, because—you've got to be severe with a native, you see. Because a native is not a human being, he's an animal. Do you know that? Well, I'm telling you. I've been amongst them for eighty years, and they are worse today than what they were eighty years ago! Mind you, that's not saying much. The Europeans are worse today than what they were before, aren't they?

Well, Sir Duncan's ZMR must have been five or six hundred. And his horse: he rode a grey. A dapple grey Irish hunter. And the horse wasn't frightened of any donga,[5] he used to put it—and he was a fearless chap!—and he used to put it at a donga, and it'd go flying clean over the top. And he'd expect all his followers to put their horses over. Well, they couldn't. They hadn't got horses—blood horses—like that.

Anyhow, a month or two after that, when everything was quiet, Sir Duncan was looking at my dad. My dad was a man of six foot in his socks, big, a powerful man, and well built.

And he said, "You know, Calverley, you're a man."

So Dad said, "Thank you."

He said, "This paltry few shillings that you get. You've risked your life over and over again with this rebellion." He says, "It's not worth it!" He said, "I'm going to see the government, and see if they can't give you something worthwhile—make it worthwhile for you."

So Dad stood up, and he said, "Thank you, Sir Duncan. It's very nice of you to think like that. But remember, I have two friends."

And old Sir Duncan—he was a short, thickset man—stood up, and said, "Ohh," he said. "Who are they?"

So he said, "Jack Hedges and Elias Titlestad."

He kept quiet for a little bit, and he looked Dad up and down, and he said, "You know, Calverley, I admire you. You're a man. Yes."

He never said any more.

And then, sometime after the Rebellion, the government, through Sir Duncan, gave Dad a sixteen-hundred-acre farm, freehold, for a present, for his services during the Zulu Rebellion. They gave Jack Hedges one, they gave Elias Titlestad one. They each got a farm. My dad gave his farm over to Puff [Louis], my brother, who has since died. And that farm was sold, with the rest of the other farms that were in Nkandla District, to the Native Trust. Yes, it belongs today to the Native Trust.

My dad had said, "If you do anything for me, do for them as well."

That's when Sir Duncan said, "Calverley, I admire you. You're a man!"

Well, that's the finish of the Rebellion.

Oh yes! Then Bambatha—a few days after they were in camp, in the evening, Dad's levies brought a young native of about twenty-two to his tent.

And they said, "Now there's the *umnumzana* [gentleman], the *inkosi* [chief]. Talk to him."

So Dad said, "Yes, *Mfana* [boy]."

He says, "*Qha!* [Well!] I just come to tell the chief that I am Bambatha's mat carrier. And he was shot at the Mome Gorge through the arm, they broke his arm. Then he got away, got into a— He had a rifle and ammunition. And he got onto a little ledge, a shelf, and he was there. Then some of the soldiers found him there, and they finished him off."

This was Bambatha himself. And this was his mat carrier, the man who was with him all the time, carrying his blankets and his mats. It was three days after the shooting took place.

And so Dad said to the boy, "Can you take us there and show us Bambatha's body?"

"Yes," he said, "I can."

So they gave him a feed, and they said, "Right! Come on!"

He took them right into the bush, right to where Bambatha was lying dead. So Dad, he— One of his levies—Bob was his name—he took a sharp knife out. It was in the summertime, they couldn't take Bambatha's body because— Dad had a couple of uncles in jail at Nkandla to identify Bambatha. And they couldn't carry the body up from the Nkandla Forest up to [the village of] Nkandla, because it meant men had to carry it, you see. And it's a rough country. So Dad had his head amputated, put the head into a nose-bag, and took it up—in a horse nose-bag.

Bob severed the head, put it into the nose-bag, and it was taken up to Nkandla. And Dad— It had several marks, you know. He apparently had been a bit of a fighter and all that. And they had described those marks, and when the head was taken out, they said, "Oh yes, that's Bambatha!"

"There's no doubt about it!"

"Just look, behind his ear, there's another scar."

And they found it, and Dad was very satisfied that it *was* Bambatha. Especially when they had his own mat carrier.

And Sir Duncan heard of this, and he ordered Dad to take the head back, put it on the body, sew it on the body, and bury him properly.

So Dad went down with the head, and did exactly as he was ordered, and they buried Bambatha properly.

That's all.

The king of the Zulu, Dinuzulu,[6] was— He knew all about this move. And he instigated the— Actually, when he heard about it,[7] he agreed, and said that it was a very good idea, and that he would help in it as well, help Bambatha. He wanted to see the white people put down. And Bambatha's wife, his young wife and child, were there at Mahatyini, under Dinuzulu's care. And Dad found out that he knew all about it.

Bambatha did not live in the Nkandla area, I think he lived in Msinga. I don't know quite where he lived, but he wasn't a Nkandla native at all.

He had a brush up with the police, he shot one or two of the police, then he got the guns, you see, and then his followers went with him, and they went and had a confab with Dinuzulu, and he said that the best place was the Nkandla Forest, and so they went to the Nkandla Forest.

Chakijana was a killer to Dinuzulu. When Dinuzulu wanted a man killed, he sent Chakijana with his rifle to go and kill him. He killed Sitshitshili, the Sibisi chief on top of the Tala Hill, he reigns there. He used to reign there. But of course this is many years ago. He went there.

He was sent to kill my dad, but they were too wide awake. He came to my dad's store in the evening, about seven o'clock. This was before or during the Bambatha Rebellion, because all the chiefs— Dinuzulu sent to the chiefs to tell them to join Bambatha, and some of the loyal chiefs wouldn't join him. And this was one of the loyal chiefs, and this Chakijana was sent to kill Dhlomo, he was a chief. And to kill my dad, and to kill Sitshitshili. Well, he managed to kill Sitshitshili, but the other two he never got.

He and another boy, they were on horseback, and they saw the kitchen boy. They went round to the kitchen, and said that they wanted to buy something—because my dad was then running a native store at Nsuze which is called Ndigwe—but it was called Nsuze in those days, because at the back of it you have the big Nsuze River.

So Dad said, "All right."

So the kitchen boy slipped in, and he said, "Nkosi, be careful, there's some trouble here."

So Dad said, "Yes?"

He said, "I don't know his name, but," he says, "this is a trouble-maker." He says, "Be careful."

So Dad said, "Right!"

So Dad took his revolver, put it in his pocket. Now, in the Nsuze store, there's a front door to the store. Then there's the storeroom. So Dad opened the storeroom, and he slipped in. Then he opened the store door from the *inside*. And this man got such a surprise when the door opened! So he saluted.

So Dad said, "Yes, what do you want?"

And he recognized him straightaway as Chakijana! Then he knew that there was trouble. And so he watched him very carefully.

So Chakijana said, "Nkos', I want a couple of tins of beef, and some bully-biscuits, and some sugar."

He said, "Yes."

He had a big overcoat on.

So he served him, and all of a sudden Dad jumped over the counter and grabbed him by the throat.

He said, "Chakijana, what do you want?"

So he said, "Hhh! hh! Oh, Nkos'!"

So Dad said, "No, no, it's all right. Just calm yourself down. What is it you're after?"

"No," he says, "I'm just going through, and I want to buy a little bit of food, that's all."

So Dad said, "Right."

So he gave him a shove, and let him go. But that put the fear into him straightaway, you see.

So he said to his kitchen boy, he said, "Mbuzi, just watch this fellow *clean* off! *right* a mile away! Then come back and tell me where you last saw them."

"Yes!"

Then Dad, the following morning, sent word to Dhlomo. His name was Luzimbela Dhlomo, he was the chief of the Dhlomo tribe.

So he said, "Be careful! Chakijana is on the way to shoot you!"

So he looked after himself, and Chakijana couldn't get in anywhere.

So he went over to the next loyal chief, which was on top of the Tala. And he went there and the chief talked to him, and he said he had a message from the great king, Dinuzulu, and all the rest of it. And he sat, then the chief gave him a small pot of beer, and he drank it.

And he said, "Well, just take—" He got in a position where the chief was sitting against the wall of the hut—you know, those grass huts. And he said he was going outside to relieve himself, got the gun, and he put a bullet slap through the chief and killed him, stone dead. The chief was Sitshitshili Sibisi, his clan name. Sitshitshili Sibisi. So he shot him, and then they got on their horses, and away they went.

Oh, I can tell you! Chakijana had committed many murders, sent of course by Dinuzulu. And the government wanted him, dead or alive. And they'd give a hundred pounds for the first man that produced Chakijana, dead or alive. So everybody was after Chakijana.

So then he had some relatives at Mahlabatini. So the sergeant at Mahlabatini heard of this, so he called up a hundred policemen. And at a certain hour at night, they knew that Chakijana would be in a certain kraal. So after that hour, when they knew that Chakijana was in the kraal, they surrounded it during the night, then they took the occupants one by one.

He was in the hut, he said to a young woman who had a baby, he said, "Now," to the old woman, his mother. He said, "You lend me all your kit!" So he put all her kit on. Then he took the little baby and pinched it. And the police were all around, and he went right up against the sergeant!

So the sergeant: "Eh!"

He pretended he was the old woman, you see—the grandmother! And he kept on pinching this kid, who was screaming!

So the sergeant: "Hey! Get away, you old fool! What do you want here? We want all these— We're inspecting all these people!"

And they kept on pushing this old woman away. And she kept on pinching the kid.

And then she said, "You see that big tree behind the kraal?"

"Yes!"

"I'll put the baby there, and I'll pinch it. When everything's over, and the police have gone, then you go and collect your baby."

So that was agreed upon.

So they took every inmate of the kraal—and there was no Chakijana! Chakijana had been pushed out. And he had just wound his way, until he got out of the circle of the police. And there he sat, waiting. And when everything was over, they said it was a false alarm, there was no Chakijana there. He pinched the kid, and it howled, and the mother went and picked the kid up.

That's how he got away from those people.

Well, my dad eventually got him to give himself up in Maritzburg. My dad sat down and wrote a letter to Chakijana, got two natives. And he lived—you know the Bhekamuzi Valley? You go from Mahlabatini, straight down—a long ridge, and a bit of a flat. Then you get to where they hold sales. That's called the Bhekamuzi Sale Yard. It's on the top side of the road. They use it a lot. And he used to live somewhere in that locality, yes. Because the niggers reckoned he was a great witch, and the chief put him there with another great witchdoctor. So they could doctor themselves.

So Dad said, "Now look, Chakijana, you're a wanted man. And the best plan for you—" This letter was written as if from Miss [Harriette] Colenso, who was a great friend of the Zulus, you see. And he signed it, So-and-so Colenso. There were two girls Colenso,[8] and there was Bishop Colenso. You know about him. Now, he wrote and said, "Now Chakijana, you're a wanted man, and they'll get you sooner or later. The best plan now is to go and give yourself up in Maritzburg. I'll take you to the authorities and hand you over, and plead for you." So he said, "All right." He signed it, "Miss Colenso."

Chakijana's mother used to live at the kraal, and he used to get up early in the morning, about two o'clock, go into the bush, and hide there. And then at night, he used to come, and she used to give him a feed, and he used to sleep there. And every day he repeated this hiding business. He'd get up at two o'clock in the morning, and go and hide in the veld, in the bush. And he'd come back, and his mother would give him a feed, and he'd sleep there in his kraal.

So these two messengers took the letter, and they said, "Is Chakijana here?"

They said, "No, he's not here. He's gone away. He's gone to interview somebody."

You know, they never said he was hiding.

And so they said, "All right, here's the letter. When he comes back, give it to him. Let him take it, because he's illiterate, let him have it to read. It's got some very good news for him."

So that night he came back, and the old woman gave him the letter and told him all about these messengers who had come with a letter from Miss Colenso.

And he said, "Oh, I must get it read tomorrow."

So he went and found somebody that had been taught, and they read it to him. So he killed a beast, and they had a good feed. And he was engaged to a girl at Qudeni. Qudeni is on the way to Maritzburg.

So Dad thought, "I will catch him going through the Thukela River. Then I'll hand him over to the government."

And he told Mother about the plan. Mother didn't like it, because Chakijana was a dangerous man, and he always had four or five armed people with him.

So, then they watched Chakijana, and he left his kraal. And he was going to stop a day or two with this girl, this girlfriend of his at Qudeni, and then proceed to Maritzburg, because they didn't smell a rat—that it was written by my father. They thought that Miss Colenso—it was quite authentic. And so Dad got a horse, saddled, everything, getting ready to go and waylay him at Thukela. He had him watched at Qudeni as well, and he knew exactly when he left there, and knew exactly when he would be crossing the river. You see, there's only one crossing, because it's a deep river. Otherwise, horses would have to swim across, you see.

So Mother said, "No!" She concocted a yarn: "One of the children is sick!" Because my dad had eight, in the end he had eight children. So he must have had three or four children by that time. And one of the children was sick, there was no doctor. And Mom pleaded with him not to go. And afterwards, she said it was a dangerous mission, and she was afraid for his life, because they could have turned round and shot him, you see.

And so he rang up from Melmoth in the days when Mr. Dean was postmaster. He got on his horse, and he came down here. About eleven o'clock at night he got here. And he rang up.

And Dean said, "You can't ring up at eleven o'clock, Calverley, at night!"

"Oh yes!" he said. So Dad put his hand in his pocket, pulled out the government authority, you see, because he was on the Government Intelligence. So he said, "Just read that, Dean."

So: "Oh yes, certainly, Calverley!" he said. Dean was a very grumpy old chap. So he said, "Yes, I'll put you through to Maritzburg. What number do you want?"

"So-and-so."

"Right!"

And he got the man that he wanted, a sergeant at Maritzburg, and he said to him, "Now listen carefully!" He said, "Tomorrow morning, there's a distinguished native by the name of Chakijana. . . ."

"Yes," he says, "I know him."

He said, "Now you go to the outskirts on a certain road, the Greytown Road, and wait there. And you'll find three or four natives." Dad told him how many natives. He said, "Just handcuff the whole lot, and put them inside the prison. And I will come along, and then we'll put the case in immediately. And tell the government who this man is."

So he said, "You know, Calverley, I don't believe you!"

Dad said, "Look here, I don't care whether you believe me or not!" He said, "Please do as I instruct you!" Because Dad was an officer—over him, you see.

And so he said, "Certainly, I will do so."

He got there ten minutes too late. Miss Colenso had already collected him, put him in the buckboard. Now she was taking him to Government House, and that man rang up afterwards, and he said, "Calverley, you were perfectly correct! I was ten minutes too late. Miss Colenso had already gone."

So that was the end of that story. Miss Colenso pleaded for him, and told them that he had surrendered. And they jailed him for three or four years, then they let him go again. After that, he was very quiet. He had gone through quite a lot, you see, and they had given him a big fright.

P. W. van Niekerk

THE WHITES WERE TO BE KILLED

(ENGLISH)

P. W. Van Niekerk, a government administrator for many years in Zululand, was the magistrate in Mahlabatini District in 1968. He spoke to me about Chakijana in his office in Mahlabatini on February 19 of that year. (3891, tape 76, side 1)

At the time of the Bambatha Rebellion, which was a rebellion that was initiated by one Bambatha Zondi [Bambatha, chief of the Zondi people] in the Greytown Magistracy, to go and murder the whites because they [Bambatha and his followers] didn't want to pay taxes. And, of course, the English government at that stage retaliated. And a war ensued between Bambatha and the English government there. It spread to Maphololo, and it came over to Nkandla and eventually came up here [to Mahlabatini]. And in 1906, I think it was December, there were rumors that the Mahlabatini magistracy was to be attacked and the whites were to be killed. So the then magistrate, Mr. [H. M.] Stainbank, led the white people out of Mahlabatini, came to Nolele Drift on the banks of the White Mfolozi where they decided to spend the night. While there, he tried to phone Melmoth by means of a field telephone. Actually, he had a British soldier on either side of him, but somebody—some Bantu burst out of the bush a couple of yards from him, and at more or less point-blank range shot him with a shotgun.[1] The man was later arrested, a man by the name of Chakijana Sithole, and he stood trial. He stood trial, and he was eventually acquitted. Obviously, there was no evidence lacking him. It was proved that he was in that area, that he was seen on that day with a shotgun, but there just was not the proof to connect him to the actual murder. And he was acquitted. He played a very active role in furthering Bambatha's cause in Zululand, he tried—he was moving around, he tried to get people to join and to rebel. And after the Zulu War, I'm not sure, he might have been tried then too, I don't know. But I know that he eventually came and settled just below Nkonjeni Mountain here near Ngoqo. And he drew a government pension then. In fact, in 1957, '58, I still paid him his pension.

SEIZERS OF THE INHERITANCE

"THE STORY IS PAINFUL"

> A child, when he is born,
> Looks up to his father,
> So that there should be honor
> Here on earth.
> —*Magagamela Koko*[1]

INTRODUCTION

Nomusa Makhoba's Zulu tale, "Jabulani Alone," comes from the same oral tradition as the stories performed by Noplani Gxavu and Emily Ntsobane. Like Ntsobane, Makhoba weaves fear and uncertainty into a tale about the movement into adulthood of a boy. The various "seizers of the inheritance" of Jabulani were, Makhoba argued in discussions about her story, characters who were encoded: this, she asserted, was the effect of the whites' influence on African lives and traditions in South Africa.

It is that melancholy note that Magagamela Koko, a Xhosa poet, catches in his two autobiographical poems, "When You Are Grey" and "Now I Am Spent." Something has happened to his land and its institutions, the aging poet says in the latter poem: "The *men* are absent." The world of his past is ebbing:

> I see but a dim blurred figure.
> It is deeply painful.

The poet uses images of his old age as metaphors for the Xhosa people. In "When You Are Grey," he recounts the great change:

> It is painful
> To start life with wealth,
> Then, when physical strength ebbs,
> To lose everything.

ONE

Like Emily Ntsobane in her story "The Deadly Pumpkin," the Zulu story-teller Nomusa Makhoba constructed a story in which hope was undermined by reality. For her, the seizers of the inheritance were the aliens, the whites. This is also a puberty ritual story, about a boy, Jabulani, coming of age. But there is the danger here that all of his institutions, all that he has inherited from the past, will be lost because of the seizers of the inheritance, the outsiders who sought to rob him of his connections with his forebears.

Nomusa Makhoba was clearly fascinated by Jabulani, a youth fraught with uncertainties as he moved to maturity and manhood. She wove into Jabulani's movement to adulthood themes having to do with women. She described the indecision and qualms as Jabulani experienced the betwixt-and-between stage of his movement between childhood and adulthood,

361

and she was also interested in studying the reasons for those qualms and that indecision, the disruption of the relationship between the present generation and "the ancients." She made it plain in discussions regarding her story that she was referring to the Europeans, though she felt it dangerous to bring them precisely into her tale. So it is that they take the form of those outside the Zulu tradition, those who would damage the relationship between present and past.

TWO

If, in the tale, imagination dominates and the obvious facts of history are obscured, the truth of history is more clearly delineated and experienced. The storyteller works the emotions of the members of the audience into the images of tale and history, and so engages the audience wholly in meaning.

A poet has written, "The body is poetry's door; the sound of words —throbbing in legs and arms—lets us into the house." He continues, "Readers who enjoy this small poem don't think about its balances and variations; we *feel* them, the way we feel a musical theme that returns slightly altered: expectation fulfilled and denied."[2]

The manipulation of patterns, sensations of expectation and predictability, and the alteration of such sensations owe as much to music and dance as they do to narrative. Lévi-Strauss has noted, for example, that "Aesthetic enjoyment is made up of this multiplicity of excitements and moments of respite, of expectations disappointed or fulfilled beyond anticipation—a multiplicity resulting from the challenges made by the work and from the contradictory feeling it arouses that the tests it is subjecting us to are impossible, at the same time as it prepares to provide us with the marvelously unpredictable means of coping with them."[3] Somewhat earlier, E. M. Forster saw an analogy between narrative and music also, Forster's concern being literature rather than oral forms. He argued that rhythm in the novel "may be defined as repetition plus variation," and added, "Music, though it does not employ human beings, though it is governed by intricate laws, nevertheless does offer in its final expression a type of beauty which fiction might achieve in its own way."[4] Arthur Dart Bissell, writing of music, states that "repetition is basic and not incidental, a psychological necessity as postulate for all later development [of music]. . . . [R]epetition is the basis for all that side of musical art known as form. . . ."[5] And on the subject of patterns in music,

> [I]t has remained the rule for good psychological reasons to start out with a simple pattern for theme, simple too in rhythm, melody and harmony, no matter how elaborately they enlarged upon it and

"The body is poetry's door." A Zulu storyteller.

even stretched it to almost unrecognizable dimensions. Moreover the variations begin with one that makes comparatively slight demands on the attention as if the composer wishes to lead the hearer by gradual steps to more intricate modifications of the theme, so that he would not then be bewildered as if wandering in a labyrinth but could still follow the general clue furnished by the original pattern, which underlies even the most complex variation. The hearer is further aided by the composer in that the several parts of a variation are repeated just as those of the theme were, and this permits of better grasping and following the intent of the variation the second time, its relation to the original.[6]

Musical meanings, Leonard Bernstein comments, include transformations, metaphorical renderings. He argues that "variation cannot exist without the previously assumed idea of repetition." And "even when the repetition itself is not there at all," the *idea* of repetition is, since it is "inherent in music."[7]

Poetry also provides an appropriate analogy. I. A. Richards writes, "Rhythm and its specialized form, metre, depend upon repetition, and expectancy. Equally where what is expected recurs and where it fails, all rhythmical and metrical effects spring from anticipation. As a rule this anticipation is unconscious. . . ." And he concludes, "This texture of expectations, satisfactions, disappointments, surprisals, which the sequence of syllables [in a poem] brings about, is rhythm. And the sound of words comes to its full power only through rhythm. Evidently there can be no surprise and no disappointment unless there is expectation and most rhythms perhaps are made up as much of disappointments and postponements and surprises and betrayals as of simple, straightforward satisfactions."[8] Henry David Aiken suggests that Richards is shifting a major emphasis:

> By showing how meagre is the cognitive content of so much great poetry, he indirectly but none the less effectually succeeds in discouraging its informative uses, while at the same time by skillfully demonstrating the powerful emotive effects of poetry which seems lacking in any significant cognitive content, he reinforces our willingness to accept a poem for what it can provide as an embodiment of feeling without regard to the beliefs that enabled the artist himself, perhaps, to focus and articulate the feelings he sought to express.[9]

Members of audiences of oral narrative performance experience identical relationships organizing like images, and unlike images. Repetition establishes anticipation in the aesthetic experience of the members of the audience, and that anticipation is purposefully interfered with: friction is introduced.[10] As to the introduction of friction into the regular patterning of a work of art, Leonard B. Meyer writes, "Affect or emotion-felt is aroused when an expectation—a tendency to respond—activated by the musical stimulus situation, is temporarily inhibited or permanently blocked."[11]

The body plays its full part in this process. "Another aspect of variation flows from the manner in which the categories (and subcategories) function in controlled anticipation," writes John Paul Spiegel. "Each category contains a program which the viewer expects to be unfolded as the performance moves along. The elements of the program—the subcategories—are usually unconscious. The programs specify what should be happening. A surprise or novelty is something not in the viewer's cognitive program for that particular category."[12] The body reveals the patterning: "[T]he regular movement of the artist's body and the resulting harmonizing of the body movements of the members of the audience (sometimes physical, always an emotional harmonizing). In some if not all narrative performances, the completely nonverbal movements of the artist—those which are not simply complementary to the verbal elements (as is mime, for example) but which supplement the verbal—are involved in the experiencing of the narrative message."[13]

In Nomusa Makhoba's haunting story of the increasingly isolated Jabulani can be found the strains of music of the storytelling tradition, the music that moves through and connects the images, in turn providing linkages with the emotions of the members of the audience, thereby assuring that they are thoroughly involved in the unfolding story—more significantly, providing resonating connections with the past.

THREE

For Nomusa Makhoba, the narrative of Jabulani becomes a metaphor for the treatment of Africans by the Europeans, the seizers of the inheritance.[14] The story begins on a disturbing note, an incident that remains unresolved but which sets the tone for the remainder of this bleak tale. The new roof on the house being built for the father of Jabulani is being eerily destroyed. Something hangs in the ceiling, knocking against it. "Has it ever happened that a house just tears apart like this?" wonders Jabulani's father. Something, lurking just under the surface, is wrong. The puzzle deepens as the audience learns about the philandering of Jabulani's father. As his house is being constructed, he becomes ill, and, when he finally confesses to the "filthy things" that he has done, he dies. After the burial, another strange event occurs. They find that two head of cattle in the fold have mysteriously died.

So begins a terrible pattern, as the inheritance of Jabulani is progressively seized by relatives of his father. His mother warns him that these envious relatives and acquaintances will claim his livestock and property. They begin to arrive and, as Jabulani grows up, the pattern having to do with his declining inheritance continues. Though he struggles against the interlopers, his birthright, the storyteller says, begins to diminish. His cattle are taken from him, others die, even his uncle turns against him, and the boy and his mother are reduced to eating locusts. And "So Jabulani grew."

Eventually, though, he becomes a man, establishing his own homestead. "Today," he says, "I have come of age. I am a man occupying the place of my father." His homestead built, he invites his relatives to come for a house-warming celebration. But he insists that he will not marry: "When one is married," he explains, "one becomes forlorn. All the stock he has disappears." He reminds the people of the source of his strength, that his "abilities have been given to [him] by the ancient of ancients," and he defiantly insists that he will remain faithful to Zulu ways until he dies.

His father is dead, his stock and property dwindling. The seizers of the inheritance are getting their way. Now his mother dies, and Jabulani is left on his own. Typically in oral tales having to do with the puberty ritual, this is the proper movement: parents die or are left behind, and the youth, alone and often in a state of nature, is on his own, as he moves into adulthood. He is convinced that his mother "was done in, bewitched by [his] uncle," destroyed by those who robbed him of his inheritance. As the young man develops his own resources, his uncle becomes progressively more covetous. Jabulani warns him of the consequences of his envy, that if his uncle persists he "will fall out with the ancient man called God."

The youth decides to leave but he first builds his own kraal. To avoid further resentment, he does this without anyone's help. As he goes to seek employment, he heeds the voice of wisdom, of the Zulu past, the advice of an old man who instructs him as to how he can secure his cattle from mishaps while he is gone.

Jabulani works a long time, and returns a changed person. The old man, not recognizing this stranger, teases him: "You are wedded to the machines of the white man, these harmonicas that you play when you walk." Jabulani, the old man suggests, is losing his ties with his customs, and that break with the past is complete when Jabulani refuses to participate in the traditional Zulu marriage ceremony, thereby cutting himself off from his ancestral and institutional origins. This rupture with convention is coupled, for the old man, the representative of that past, with the harmonica, the instrument of the whites.

To protect the inheritance, Jabulani is prepared to sell his livestock so that no one else will get it. He will take the money and depart. The old man argues that "a legacy does have a rightful heir. When you are dead, you will have done what all the ancients do, Jabulani. You will preserve the dead, you will remember your grandmother. . . ." And the grandfather prepares to give over the legacy to Jabulani, the legitimate heir.

Having learned the decisive relationship between present and past, Jabulani is at last prepared to marry. He decides to wed because, in his own estimation, he has matured. Both the old man and the old woman have died, and Jabulani finds himself alone. To assure the continuity between present and past, the youth resolves to marry. But he remains uncertain if he should have a child.

Jabulani's quandary and the uncertainty of his world reveal the condition of a human being who trusts in his institutions and traditions, but who learns that they are not necessarily proof against the exigencies of reality. Storytellers are regularly afflicted by these reservations. Their stories celebration tradition, but in the interstices of the narratives are the qualms and misgivings, the ambiguities, the tragedies, the weight of reality. The genealogies of Ndumiso Bhotomane and Mdukiswa Tyabashe are only the most obvious of the storytellers' means of providing conduits to the past. The fictional stories, like those of Nomusa Makhoba, Noplani Gxavu, and Emily Ntsobane, the narrative histories, like those of Tyabashe and Sondoda Ngcobo, and the poems, like those of Mtshophane Mamba and Ashton Ngcama, all depend conclusively on the ancient motifs, deeply embedded in the people's past experiences. Storytellers of whatever genre depend on the past for the essential components of their art, as they require contemporary images that will accordingly be shaped by those defining images of the past. Humans achieve their identities and the contours of their destiny from their histories, and it is up to the storyteller to discern the nature and the shape of those histories and their effects on present reality. History never exists for its own sake; it is always the means whereby a people find the requisite qualities of their culture, whereby they sketch in the outlines of their future. Apartheid, so traumatic a human experience, so disruptive of tradition, so entrenched in South African life for such a lengthy span of years, should, one might conclude, have overwhelmed and annihilated tradition, making of it a set of disjointed, plaintive historical echoes. But this is not so, protest the storytellers, and they produce the eternal verities of their stories to reveal how it is that the past continues to influence the present, regardless of the ordeals and stresses precipitated by apartheid.

The storytellers of South Africa struggle with such contemporary events as apartheid in two ways. They address it in a direct way, as Tyabashe and Ngcobo did, or they tacitly place it into larger historical contexts, as Gxavu, Makhoba, Ntsobane, and Zenani did. For those who, like the youths in Soweto, object that some of the stories of the people, some of the stories in this collection, do not confront apartheid in a clear and obvious way, storytellers have some advice: Master the language of storytelling, and you will understand.

This anthology of stories, and this includes the histories and poems, are at once defiant, hopeful, and realistic. Nomusa Makhoba's story of Jabulani gives tentative support to tradition, but it occurs within the brutal context of reality, represented by the brief image of the harmonica, undermining confidence. But before the coming of the whites to South Africa, there were elements that also had the effect of causing apprehension: The seizers of the inheritance are found both within the society and without. Humans cling to their traditions, as Jabulani does, hoping that they will withstand any corrosive influences. But there is never certainty of this, and that is why aloneness and sadness pervade this story.

It is this sense of aloneness and sadness that Magagamela Koko reproduces in the poems that appropriately end this collection of oral traditions.

Memories casts long shadows. Never easily grasped, they are the stuff of our elusive past, the shapers of our bewildering present. It is to the storytellers, with the tongues of fire, to divine the shadows, then work those phantoms of the past into definitions of our reality.

Nomusa Makhoba

JABULANI ALONE

(ZULU)

The performer of this story of Jabulani was Nomusa Makhoba, about forty-five years old, a Zulu woman. The performance occurred on February 10, 1968, in a home in Mahlabatini District, Zululand, in the Dlamini area. The audience consisted of six men, six women, and three children. (3749; tape 73, side 1)

DEATH OF THE FATHER

"I KNOW THAT YOU'RE RATHER SHARP WITH WOMEN. . . ."

There was a woman, the mother of Jabulani. Now, Jabulani's father died, and these are the circumstances of his death.

They were living in a land in which Zulu-style houses were customary. They had eleven such houses, and Jabulani's mother was thatching them. During the period that she was thatching these houses, she would get up early in the morning and cook. She would cook, she would dish out the food for Jabulani's father, then they would sit down and eat. When they finished eating, she would take a pot and go to the river to dip water for moistening grass that she would plait into ropes. She would plait until the sun set, then she would tie up the ropes, she would roll them and put them away. Having done that, she would return home, and she would cook.

One day, she was thatching these houses. She had begun with the great house of her homestead, the one built for the father of Jabulani, where the important men would live, and she was now thatching that house.

Before bedtime, one of the children said, "Mother, something is hanging up there."

"It's knocking against the ceiling!" another said.

Jabulani's mother said, "Don't talk like that! There's no such thing! What are you saying?"

One of the children said, "I'm sure of it, Mother! Something's touching the rungs of the roof frame!"

Jabulani's mother was quiet, and everyone went to sleep.

At dawn the next morning, they discovered that the roof of the house had been ripped open on one side. The ropes that Jabulani's mother had plaited had come apart.

369

She went to tell Jabulani's father about this. "Father of Jabulani, the house has fallen apart. I don't know what has ripped it to pieces."

Jabulani's father said, "Has it ever happened that a house just tears apart like this? The cattle didn't leave the kraal, they couldn't have done it. So I wonder how this happened, Child of my home."

She said, "It's very strange, Father. I've turned it over in my mind: I can see nothing out of the ordinary as far as the cattle are concerned. What could possibly have caused these houses to be torn apart like this?"

They went to the house, and time passed.

The next morning, Jabulani's mother woke up. She took the grass and began again to plait it for these houses. As she made ropes for the houses, she said, "It's time I brewed some beer, so that I can invite some other women to come and help me. If I don't do that, my grass will soon start to rot." She said to Jabulani's father, "There will be a lot of rain soon. If I work by myself, I'll not be able to finish in time."

Jabulani's father said, "All right, go on building, prepare the beer. Ask other women to help you to build, because I don't have the strength to pull the thatching needle anymore. I'm getting old, my arms are paining me, I'm no longer able to pull the needle. My limbs have lost their suppleness, they've become stiff because of the work I've done on the other houses."

Jabulani's mother brewed the beer.

The thatching bundles were spread out on a cleared area.

She invited the women, and they came and helped her to climb up on one of the houses. This house was erected and brought into shape.

Then they drank the beer. They drank the beer, and the women began to dance, they had become a little intoxicated. They danced on and on.

Jabulani's father came out, and said, "I didn't realize that these women could dance so well! But one thing baffles me about the women—their garments begin to smell after a time, the entire house fills up with the stench of their clothes. These women dance well.[1] Even their sweat fills the house." He peered through the door, and said, "Please give me a sip of beer, I'm dry too."

By now, his wife was also dancing. He said that she should face the other way, because, he said, "My youthful blood is welling up inside me. If this continues, I'll be rounding up the cattle. This takes me back to the time when I was courting this wife of mine." He said, "My brother, did you think that I would have paid so much money[2] for nothing? Why shouldn't I gloat when my wife is dancing in a way that distinguishes her from other women? I would be wrong if I didn't praise her."

Soon, the dance came to a stop. Then another portion of beer was produced.

Dancing at dusk

Jabulani's mother said, "My friends, please help me thatch this little house."

The thatch was sewn on the next morning.

"I want it to be bound loosely, temporarily at first, all along the way. Let it be loosely bound."

Everyone got up early that next morning.

"I'll strain the beer and get it ready quickly, that won't be much trouble. We'll drink fresh beer."

Jabulani's mother did that. She worked at it, she strained the beer in the evening.

Jabulani's father said, "I'm getting a headache."

Jabulani's mother said, "Don't you think that you just have a hangover, Father?"

He said, "No, I hardly touched the beer. I sipped only once, from a little vessel, Child of my home. I couldn't have become sick from that."

She said, "Is it possible that I am under a spell because I have a task on my hands? Now you fall sick, which means that I won't be able to work. How can I build the homestead when you're ill? And what if you were to die? I'd be unprotected, in shame, because I wouldn't have a person who could help me to build a fine homestead."

He said, "Warm up some water, so that I can go and dip a little and recover. I shall not die."

Jabulani's mother warmed some water. She said, "The water is warm now, Father."

He said, "Take my dipper."

She took this ladle—it was a dipper used in olden times, it was in the form of a small vessel. She went there, she bent over and dipped.

He called out and said, "Please give me some porridge, I'm dry."

Jabulani's mother took porridge to him. He took several sips, then said, "I can't take anymore. Now my stomach aches, it's very sore."

Jabulani's mother said, "Drink some more of the porridge, Father. Drink a lot of it."

The father took more of the porridge.

She said, "Hurry, Jabulani! Go and call your father's older brother! Father is fainting! He might die right now, he might simply pass out and die! Hurry! What have the women done to me? What have they done to my husband?"

Jabulani said, "Mother, don't talk like that! If Father should die, whom will I be left with?"

She said, "I know, I'm not a child. Hurry!"

Jabulani ran some distance beyond his home. His uncle had built his homestead at another place. He arrived there and said, "Father, Mother says that I should come and get you, she wants you to look at Father. He is fainting!"

His uncle said, "He's fainting? What is he doing? Tell me exactly what is happening, Jabulani!"

He said, "I don't know, I'm only reporting what my mother said."

Jabulani's father's brother hurried, and when he got there he said, "Brother! Brother!"

"What?"

"What has happened?"

"It's in my stomach!"

"What is paining you in the stomach?"

"Something is cutting up my stomach. It's hitting me hard. It's as if it's moving around on foot inside me, tearing me up. It's slashing me!"

"Let's go, Brother. Limp along. When we get home, I'll find something in my bag that might help. Nxumalo's son will bring me my bag, it contains certain potions that I sometimes use. Before we give up, let's try those. We'll try various things, even if they turn out to be of little value to us. I know that you're rather sharp with women,[3] and it's just possible that you might have committed an offense of some kind. This is your usual practice. You drink a little beer, you sneak out of the house, and you turn up in the company of someone's wife. Then the people miss you, they become incensed. Let's go now."

They got up to go to his home. When they reached that place, the brother of Jabulani's father threw the divining bones.⁴ The bones began to speak: "Take a dipper with a white lid," they said, "and have him smoke by means of it, have him lick it."

The bones spoke.

Jabulani's uncle said, "My brother, my brother."

He said, "Yes?"

"Look at me. Do you hear what has been going on here?"

"Yes, I hear."

"Did you not chase someone else's wife?"

"Oh, my brother! No!"

He consulted the bones again: "You⁵ are not moving along the right path. You are not yet speaking the truth that goes into my heart. You are still missing the mark."

He threw the bones again; he cast them repeatedly, and each time they reported the same thing.

He said, "No, Brother, stop struggling. Concede. Otherwise, your wife is going to be left alone, and you won't be able to build the homestead that you've been thinking of building. You must realize that, if you insist on keeping this secret, you'll die."

He said, "Get away, Brother! You persist in talking nonsense! Just because *you*'re sharp with women, must you insist that I am as well? I'm not that sharp! This is all that happens: A woman offers herself to me, and I follow her. She lifts her skirts, so I go after her. You must know what a cow and bull are like, the way they do things. The cow tends to go to the bull, they follow each other. It's as if the cattle are heading home, and the bull hurries along, following a cow. Don't say that I've been committing an offense, I have not been misbehaving! It was offered to me."

His brother said, "Because I told you that you're about to die, you're confessing."

He said, "Treat me, Brother. Bring your medicine bags so that I can lick them."

He caused him to lick the medicine bags, then he said to Jabulani, "Go and get some milk, Jabulani."

Jabulani brought the milk. His uncle boiled it. Then he took the medicine⁶ and poured it onto the milk.

He said, "Drink some of it with a spoon. Take it twice with the spoon." Then he said, "Sleep."

When his brother was sleeping, he told the others, "Cover him with blankets."

They put three blankets over him.

He said, "Watch him." And he added, "Make a fire in the hearth."

Jabulani's mother made a fire.

When she had done that, the brother of Jabulani's father said, "Sit down."

The mother sat.

He said, "Sit down next to him." He added, "Do you see how he sleeps? He will speak while he is under the blankets. He will sneeze three times. You must keep saying, 'Spirits of the departed, Spirits, Spirits.' Say that ten times. Every time this brother of mine sneezes, say it ten times. When he has sneezed, he will sit up and say, 'Bring the dish.' "

When Jabulani's uncle took the blankets off, Jabulani's father was wet with perspiration. Then he gave him a dish, and he vomited. When Jabulani's father had finished vomiting, the uncle said, "Bring a cup, a big white cup." He brought the cup near to his brother, and said, "Vomit into this. I'll tell you what will come out. Blood will come out from the upper part of your body. This is the blood you have gotten from this female person."

So he vomited this blood, it came out in clots. Some came out from the lower part of his body, some from the upper part.

Jabulani's mother began to cry. She said, "If Jabulani's father does die, we have quite a large inheritance. We have our own homestead. But, my lord, who will rear Jabulani for me?"

The brother of Jabulani's father said, "Don't be distressed. When I apply my medicines, no one should cry. If someone cries, the medicines will also weep, will weep tears. So don't cry. Just keep quiet, wait, see what happens at sunset."

Jabulani's mother was quiet. She brought a container, she churned, and a foam formed and rose.

He said, "Drink it."

Jabulani's father drank it, he drank the foam that was in this vessel.

He said, "Don't drink the liquid, just drink the foam. Only the foam." He belched. After he had belched, he said, "I'm full, Brother."

"Sit up. Get up, sit from the waist up."

He sat up.

"When I bring this woman in, you'll see where you went wrong."

Jabulani's father said, "I shall see where I went wrong."

By magic, then, the uncle brought the woman in, he brought in two women. The women came in and sat there. They took a vessel of beer, they brought it in and put it down.

He said, "When I have seen your reaction to her, I shall know that you have definitely identified the woman you have done this to. I shall know this when you get up from the ground, take the vessel, and offer it to her."

The women came in, they took this vessel of beer, singling it out. Soon the foam formed and rose up, and when that had happened, the sick man got up and took the vessel; he took a sip. His brother was watching him. When he had taken another drink, he looked at his brother. When he tried to put the vessel down, he could not do so. He could not put it down.

He took it, and offered it to this woman.

His brother was saying, "Hear, Doctor! Hear, Doctor! What have I been saying all this time? I have been telling you all this time, I have been saying that my medicine bags are effective, that they move to the heart of the matter. Are they not now touching the heart of the matter? Are you not saved now that I have found the woman with whom you have misbehaved? When I asked you, you denied it. You denied it, you said that you never in any way did anything wrong. How is it then?"

Then he said, "Child of my home, you have indeed helped me. I almost died, the sun was setting for me."

His brother departed, and the others returned to their own home. They had been at the mountain, on the brow of the hill. Jabulani's father also went home, together with his wife. When it was night, they went into the house and sat down. A meal was eaten.

He said, "Please give me a lot of food, Child of my home. I have become so hungry that I have difficulty understanding that food is something that is eaten on earth. I didn't know that I would see food anymore."

She gave him food, and he said, "Come close, put the food into my mouth."

Jabulani's mother began to debate within herself: "He's never asked me to feed him like a baby before. What has happened today that he should say that I should feed him?"

"Take my wooden ladle, and feed me with it. I want my traditional wooden ladle, not a spoon. And bring that pot of mine, the one that my mother made for me before she died."

She took this pot and prepared food with milk. She prepared it, then took it to him. He ate this milk-food.

Then he said, "I'm leaving behind my father's cattle.[7] I'm leaving behind my father's inheritance, which is considerable." Then he said, "Bring me my goats. Don't bring all of the goats from the pasture, just bring my three favorite ones."

The three goats were brought.

When they had been brought, he pointed to one of them and said, "Slaughter this one for me. I want its meat. I want to have it for dinner now, I want to sleep having eaten it."

Jabulani said, "Father, why do this in the middle of the night?"

But he said, "Prepare it quickly. Hurry! Cut its throat, put some wood near here. Your mother will boil some water."

They did that. The goat was flayed, then brought into the house. And he ate that goat, he ate it.

He said, "I want its liver."

He ate the liver, he took three mouthfuls.

He said, "My lord, now I cannot even swallow! I can swallow nothing." He said, "Jabulani."

Jabulani responded, "Father."

He said, "Jabulani, you must help to build this homestead. I am departing now, I can stay no longer. You'll remain behind, building this homestead." He added, "I can see my father who died long ago. He tells me that I am not running my home well here. It is necessary therefore that he take me away. I must go, because I have done only filthy things here at home. 'Now your homestead has a stench in it,' he says. 'It reeks of filth.' So I am departing. Now, my child, please be good enough to continue to look after this homestead of mine. Manage it wisely, treat your mother well. But if you behave scandalously, if you act as I did, Jabulani, all of the cattle will die and be finished. And your mother will not have the wherewithal to raise you."

His father died as he said those words.

Jabulani was then five years old.

His mother began to cry. She cried, Jabulani also cried. He was distressed, and he went outside, saying that he was going to watch over his father. But he found that his father was not there.

It was said, "He is not here. He has departed. He is not here."

His mother said, "My God, what shall I do?"

Jabulani again appeared, he said, "Mother, let us take Father into Grandmother's house. I do not want the smell of a dead person inside Father's house. Let us take him out of his own house, let us take him to Grandmother's house."

His mother said, "My child, the smell will not be that of just any person, it will be your father's. It is proper that he remain inside his own house."

Jabulani said, "No, Mother, Father must be taken to Grandmother's house, to the great house. He should die there."

Just then, his father's younger brother arrived. He took Jabulani's father to die at his grandmother's house.

His uncle[8] said, "Jabulani, tomorrow morning everyone will get up and go and bury your father. When your father has been buried, I want you to observe the event in this way: brew some beer. When the people return from the graveyard, they will eat meat and drink this beer. This will all be dedicated to your father now that he has died—because when it comes time to make a ritual sacrifice for your father, I shall be gone, I shall no longer be here. I have many things to do, I don't want my medicine bags to remain idle, to be adversely affected because I am not working. Someone might even die."

When these people had finished the burial, they were given food. When they had finished eating the food, it was already the following morning. On this morning, Jabulani's mother's hair would be shaved off at the river, and she would put on other clothes.

Then they discovered that two head of cattle in the fold were dead. A large ox had died; it was a favorite, an ox that Jabulani's father had loved and with which he had ploughed. It was this large ox that had died, and a red one too.

Jabulani said, "Mother, things are already being damaged: my father's cattle are beginning to be diminished. I have been left behind to eat what, Mother?"

His mother said, "My child, I don't know. Grandmother used to say, 'The favorite ends up eating locusts.' I don't know if that applies to me, if I shall end up eating those locusts, if locusts are to be the things with which I shall rear you, Jabulani. The ancients say, 'A person raised by means of locusts grows to eat locusts like grasshoppers.'"

Jabulani said, "Mother, what does that mean?"

His mother said, "My child, don't ask. Your father has now died. You see these cattle here at home. You will find that others will become jealous of you. They will come here, claiming portions of this livestock."

Jabulani said, "No one will dare come here, Mother! I shall stab all such people with my spear!" Then he said, "Mother, remain quiet. You'll see what happens at sunrise. Not one person will enter the homestead of my father with the intention of seizing the inheritance. My father left the inheritance to me. He said that I should handle it wisely."

So Jabulani grew up.

DESTITUTE

"WE'LL EAT LOCUSTS, MY CHILD."

He grew up, always looking after his inheritance. But this birthright of his began to diminish; the cattle were dying, one by one, despite the fact that his mother provided some protective medicine, and even though he got people to help him to preserve the cattle.

Even his uncle turned against him. He no longer wished to come and perform obligations here at this home because he was envious of the inheritance that had fallen to Jabulani. The legacy included everything, the goats as well. But now, these goats began to disappear. Jabulani went to ask for advice from his uncle. "Father, I'm missing goats at home."

His uncle said, "I'll not talk with a fool who wastes his time roaming all over the place, going to concerts, and who doesn't know what he's doing."

"Uncle, all I did was to courteously ask a question. My father's stock is diminishing."

"Jabulani, get away from here! If you're not careful, I'll stab you with my spear. Don't come here and talk such nonsense to me."

Jabulani told his mother, "Mother, when I went to ask my uncle about my father's stock, whether he had seen it at all at his home, he threatened to stab me."

His mother said, "My child, let's just build this homestead and keep quiet. God will look after us. We'll eat locusts, my child, I'll just go out and look for locusts. No matter what happens—even if the cattle should die, even if they are wiped out—I shall never take one ox of your father to barter for a sack of maize, because if I were to do that, you would have nothing when you are older, Jabulani."

His mother went out, and Jabulani said, "Mother, let's go then. Show me how these locusts are hunted, the edible ones."

They went out, and his mother said, "Take a cup and put some water into it. Put the water into a billycan."

They hunted for locusts.

His mother said, "Dig up some earthworms, Jabulani." There was one billycan for the worms, another for the locusts. She said, "With both of us destitute, Jabulani, what shall I raise you with now that your father is dead?" She had no one to help her. There were only Jabulani and his uncle here at home.

Jabulani said, "Mother, I'm hungry."

His mother said, "Heat the water, my child. There's nothing else we can do."

He put the water on the fire. Then he took some locusts and put them into the pot and boiled them. When the locusts were cooked, his mother took them off the fire and said, "Eat these, my child."

Jabulani said, "Mother, how are these things eaten? I don't know how to handle them, Mother."

She said, "Just eat them, my child. Once, a blind old woman craved meat, so the children of her child went out to dig earthworms. They said, 'Grandmother, eat! Here's some meat.' Yes, Jabulani, that's meat. It's all we have these days."

Jabulani ate.

His mother said, "Please leave some for me too—leave just two of them for me, so that I might wipe my mouth."[9]

Jabulani left some of the locusts for her. His mother ate. They both ate, they finished. That was it.

And time passed.

SEIZERS OF THE INHERITANCE

"ALL WE KNOW IS THAT THE LIVESTOCK BELONGS TO US. . . ."

Jabulani became tired. He said, "Mama, I feel very sleepy, because I haven't had enough to eat. Let's go, Mother, and chop."

His mother said, "Go and chop what, my child? I don't have strength anymore."

"Mother, my father's homestead will not die! Let's go and cut grass. We shall build these houses again."

They went out to cut grass. Jabulani carried three bundles. His mother carried a large one; he accompanied her when she went back to pick up that Zulu-style bundle for building the houses.

Jabulani said, "These bundles of grass are here, Mother. Now, where shall we get people to help us to build?"

His mother said, "My child, you have not yet seen how a widow works. Just watch and see, my child. You'll see how the sickle performs."

They chopped and chopped, she and Jabulani. They finished chopping. When they had finished, Jabulani's mother said, "My child, take the digging tool and come outside. I'll show you how to dig."

"Mother, how will you do it? You're not a man."

His mother said, "My child, for a woman, the testicles are inside. They're not on the outside."

His mother dug, and made a circle[10] around the homestead. Then she said, "Jabulani, dig here."

Jabulani said, "I don't know how, Mother. Show me."

She took a tool and dug, demonstrating for him. She said, "Do you see now? This is how we'll put up the posts. Like this. Like this, Jabulani. This house that I'm building is for you, Jabulani, because among these houses none belongs to you. Other people will come when they hear that your father is dead. When they get here, they'll demand all of these houses of their brother. They'll say that we don't have a homestead, that we should get our own. When they do this, when they insist on having these houses, to divide them up among themselves and stake a claim on the great house of their brother, we can't do a thing to them, Jabulani. It would be wise, therefore, that by the time they come we should have our own homestead."

So they built this house, the two of them—she and Jabulani built it, he and his mother helping each other to hold things and to chop.

The ones who wanted to swallow the inheritance came. A man and his wife came.

They said, "Mother, we've arrived. We understand that our brother has died. But you never told us."

Going to the market

His mother said, "Oh, go and talk with him in the grave! It's in the grave where he is! There's nothing I can possibly talk to you about. As this person's sickness progressed, I wrote to you and you did not reply, you seemed not to understand what I said. You were just waiting to seize the inheritance. Go and seek the inheritance from your kinsman. I am not your kinsman, I belong to another clan. As for Jabulani, there's nothing belonging to your kin that you can deprive him of, because all these things are Jabulani's. They were given to him by his father."

Jabulani said, "Mother, I'll go and confront them, I'll kill them."

His mother said, "Don't kill them, my child. If you do that, you'll just cause yourself to lose what your father gave to you along with all the strength that you have."

Jabulani said, "Mother, if you say so, I'll give way to them and allow them to take all these cattle. Only mine will remain, those that I have earned by herding."

His relatives came, and they said, "We shall take this one and that one," referring to those remaining stock that had not died. "We shall take those cattle, and go away with them."

The brother of Jabulani's father said, "You can't take cattle away from this home, because you don't know the herder. You don't know who takes them to pasture in the morning, who it is who takes these beasts to the dipping tank. Have you attempted to discover who has been doing all these chores here at home now that the owner of the homestead has died?"

These seizers of the inheritance said, "Well, who can tell us? We didn't come here to shepherd this stock. All we know is that the livestock belongs to us. No one informed us when our kinsman was sick, telling us to 'Please come and watch over the inheritance, it needs taking care of.' "[11]

Jabulani said, "Fathers, wait a little! Take the stock away. No one will suck my blood. My blood will be sucked only by lice, because a louse feeds on the blood of its host. Take away these cattle of yours, I have my own strength. I shall grow up and go to work for myself. And I shall also look after my mother. I don't want you to remove my mother from this homestead. Don't take her away with you—it's clear that if you do take her away, all you'll do when you get back there is have her courted by someone so that you can marry her off. I don't want my mother to marry and leave home. There were just three of us here at home—Mother and Father and me. And when Father died, he left me with Mother. I was five years old when Father died. I was not yet a child who had attained full consciousness. Now I have grown up, and I have built a homestead, a very beautiful homestead in the Zulu style. My father detested a rondavel, he argued that a stone wall is not proper. Zulu-style houses, he said, are comfortable. My father used to say that Zulu-style houses were warm even when the weather was cold. They would keep one warm, one would even sweat in them. When Father sat on his stool, it was hard to get him out of it. So I want to build my father's homestead in a grand manner, a homestead in the Zulu style."

So Jabulani grew.

COMING OF AGE

"I HAVE COME OF AGE TODAY. I AM A MAN."

He went to seek work. Jabulani worked, and the money that he earned he gave to relatives to preserve for him. He continued to do this, to give the money to his relatives for safekeeping. The money yielded dividends: it became a lot of money, it bought cattle and goats, it bought everything.

When Jabulani returned from work, he went to his uncle, and said, "Uncle, I have grown up, I want my own site on which to build, so that I can leave my father's tract."

His uncle said, "Do you know how one goes about establishing a homestead, my child?"

Jabulani said, "I do know a little, Uncle, but I don't know everything about it. Tell me what I ought to do to establish my own homestead. My mother and I are indigent, we have only each other. We live on locusts, no one looks after us. I want to vomit up these locusts that I've been eating all this time. I now have strength of my own."

His uncle said, "All right, my child, go and petition for a new site from the headman. I'll meet you there early in the morning."

So Jabulani went. When he got to the headman, he said, "I have come to petition for a site, Father. I want a place on which to build a homestead. I'm tired of living on nothing. My mother and I have been eating grass like cattle who know only grass. Even the dry cow dung is enclosed in the kraal, so they don't eat dung, they eat grass."

"No! Well."

The headman gave the youth a plot of ground, and Jabulani expressed his thanks.

He said, "Mother, I've obtained a site. Our state of depression will end today. Jabulani has grown up. He's a young man, he's no longer a little boy. I've become a big boy today, no longer a mere herder of calves." Then he said, "Mother, soak the grain tomorrow morning. While you're doing that, I'll go and chop wood, so that we can build our homestead."

The grain was soaked, and it germinated. Sprouts appeared. When the sprouts had appeared, the preparation of beer went ahead. Beer was brewed.

Jabulani said, "Mother, I want the first cow that I bought, the first of the beasts that I bought with my first pay, Mother. It was a cow, and it bore six calves, it was the seventh."

Jabulani was asking for this seventh cow from his mother, so that she should call together all the family of his father, to show them that "Today, I have come of age. I am a man occupying the place of my father. I have even built a homestead for my father today."

The beer was brewed, the beer mellowed, it was ready to drink. All of his fathers came, along with their sisters, aunts, his cousins, Jabulani's uncles. The mother of his mother was also there; she was very proud. She said, "Let me see Jabulani's homestead, because today Jabulani has emerged from childhood. He is a man. Jabulani has his own place."

The cow was roasted, the beast was eaten. The meat of the cow was eaten.

Jabulani said to his relatives, "My people, I have called you together because I want everyone to eat of this beast, my 'first fruits' which have laid the foundation of this homestead of my father. When I received my first pay, I gave the money to my uncle, saying, 'Uncle, buy these cattle for me, because I know that there is a time that will, as the ancients say, burst forth like a trap.' The ancients of long ago said, 'The time of your death will come like a thief. You will be caught by surprise, you do not know the time when you will die. You might be on the road, on a journey. Death may catch up with you while you're rejoicing over some great expectation, and you'll not be able to fulfill it.' Now, I rejoice, my people, that today I have built this homestead of my father. I have come of age today, I am a man. When people beg and plead with me from now on, they will say, 'We pray and plead with you of the Ntungwa clan.' "

Jabulani belonged to the Ntungwa clan—"Ntungwa" was the clan praise-name of his people.[12]

Jabulani was happy, as his name indicates.[13]

His uncle said, "I shall proceed in the appropriate way. I offer you, my kin, ten shillings.[14] I place Jabulani in his rightful place today, as if he were my brother. When I go into the house, I shall find Jabulani presiding with dignity here at home, because he is now a man."

The others said, "We give thanks, Household of the Ntungwa, that you are honoring Jabulani. Today, Jabulani has left grief behind. For a long time, he has been living on locusts."

His uncle said, "I am offering a red ox, with which I express thanks for the successful way in which Jabulani has worked—and also for the sharpness of his brain, for his drive. I ask that the ancients, the ancestors below, our people who have gone to sleep, I ask them that Jabulani not lose this faculty of mind, that Jabulani not forsake this mother of his, because his father left Jabulani by himself."

Jabulani's response was, "My fathers, I do not want to marry, because I know what marriage is like. When one is married, one becomes forlorn. All the stock he has disappears. The money that one might have is finished when one has a wife, because a woman wants this and that and that over there. Sickness also accompanies a woman. Everything requires money. Starvation is pursuing me. Children become my responsibility. Perhaps I shall have many children because I was the only child of my father. It is possible that I shall have many children. I am thankful, my extended family, that I have not married, because if I had already married, it is possible that I might neglect this mother of mine. Were I to marry, I might just marry a woman without a head,[15] who would not want me to give my mother food, who would not want me to clothe my mother, who would say, 'Your father who looked after your mother died long ago. This money is mine, it will not go to your mother!' My heart would ache then, because I would think that perhaps I should murder my wife. If I do not marry, it will be much better. I shall remain just as I am, in peace with my mother. I have seen the sorrow that my mother has borne because of my father, and I have observed that marriage is sorrowful in that way. My father lived well with my mother. But he died in the midst of all sorts of scandal associated with Zulu marriage. If this father of mine had never married, he would still be alive.

"I choose not to marry, because if I should get married, I can see that I'll be hurt, and my father's name will be blotted out. Moreover I don't want to combine this inheritance of my father with the fruits of my own efforts. My abilities—bestowed on me by whom? My abilities have been given to me by the ancient of ancients, so I should be able to procure this stock, and, with this alert mind, this drive, I should be able to work this homestead of mine which I have this day erected. It is said that, long ago, thanksgiving for a homestead would take place on an ox. All the people would come and celebrate in the cattle-fold, and songs would be sung while the meat was being eaten in praise of this person."

Jabulani's uncle said, "I thank you, my child, for all that you have said, and for conducting yourself so well. But, my child, I want you to know that, as you are a man, a human being is offered food. Yes, a human being, even when he is sleeping overnight at a home, is treated well. He is put to bed well. As a youth who does not want to get married, will you be able to do all these things? Will you be able to keep all these things in order?"

Jabulani said, "I shall be able to do so, Father, because when I lack something, I shall take my bag and look for work. And when my mother's time comes to an end, I shall take her with me, and hire a farm and live there on the farm—because I do not want to be married."

"My son, may you build this homestead of yours. Build it well, live well, even though you do not wish to marry. I understand you, when you say that you do not wish to marry."

Jabulani kept seeking work. When he had gone to work, he worked hard. Then he came back, and said, "Father, I think now of the ageing of my mother. I think that I should let this mother of mine grow old. I remember the time when my father died."

His uncle said, "Do you still remember it, my son?"

Jabulani said, "Yes, I do remember. I ask, Father, that you give me a beast so that, regarding my father's death, I may show my respects, so that I may make a memorial to him."

His uncle said, "My child, you'll get the beast, I'll give it to you. I don't want you to take a second beast from among your cattle, because—yes, I can see that your intelligence is going to exceed that of your father. You are taking the disappearance of your homestead well."

This beast was killed. When it had been killed, they brewed beer, unfermented beer as well as stamped mealies. All of these were brought to Jabulani. Loads of food were brought in, and there was a big feast.

Then his uncle said that the favorite song of the deceased should be sung. Many young men were called, they responded quickly. Their garments were beautiful, Jabulani's father had been a dandy. These young men got up as one. When the meat was being eaten, Jabulani's mother, even though she was rather old, was excited. She danced, girding her garments. Her small head was grey, but she danced with it vigorously: the turban on her head was red. She comported herself proudly. She wore a laced shawl that Jabulani had purchased for her. All the mothers, daughters, and wives of Jabulani's uncle—Jabulani had bought shawls for all his mothers. They ululated. It did not seem to be a sorrowful occasion, a time to mourn the dead.

Jabulani's uncle said, "My child, this ritual of yours is appropriate. It reminds me of the day your father went courting, the day he sang praises to your mother in the flower of his youth. We and your mothers were in agreement. Even though they are now grey-haired—and at that time they had no skirts like these, this scanty clothing; they had their own styles, they had clothing that was appropriately reverential, clothing that reflected a respectful attitude to our fathers. When a young woman met with her father-in-law, she would modestly cover herself—it would be said, 'Here comes the father-in-law of the young wife,' so that she should not actually come face to face with her father-in-law."

Jabulani said, "I am thankful, Father. In this land of the Zulu, I do not like to separate myself from tradition. My father cautioned me that I should never go to a far country that has been westernized. He wanted me to keep to Zulu ways until I die in this homestead of his. When I require people to be clothed the way they are now, I am remembering the words that were spoken by my father.

"My father lived with Ve whom he called his grandfather, who was the wooden stool, in the Zulu idiom, who used to have bugs of which my father used to say, 'Come close here, kill these creatures.' And so I would kill them, I would kill these bugs. My father would be pleased, he would laugh and laugh. It was very nice when he did this.

"So I thank you of the Ntungwa clan. Now that I have grown, now that I have reached this phase, I certainly do not want to be separated from my land of the Zulu. When I do not like this place anymore, here in the land of the Zulu where I live, since I do not want to marry, I shall go to seek a plot of ground in a certain place, still in the land of the Zulu. I won't return to Johannesburg. I just don't like Johannesburg, I don't like Johannesburg things at all. I prefer Zulu ways only. I want to cut grass like my mother. I want to help my mother build, to help her build even when she is dead. I shall go and hire someone's homestead, and live there."

DEATH OF THE MOTHER

"MY CHILD, I AM DEFEATED."

Jabulani's mother became ill. She was sick for some time. There were just the two of them in this homestead.

Jabulani said, "Now, what shall I do? If I should leave this place and go to someone else's homestead, it will look as if my mother were too heavy for me. No, I must remain here."

Jabulani remained and nursed his mother. His mother was sick, so he opened the grinding stone, ground meal, and cooked it in the hearth to make porridge. His mother drank it. He took sorghum, he took the pot, then cooked the porridge. He pleaded with his mother, and said, "Drink this please, Mother."

His mother drank, and said, "My child, I am defeated. Please take me to your uncle's place."

Jabulani said, "You are not going there. I don't want you to enter someone else's homestead. If I were to take you from here at home, Mother, if I were to have the heir of my father take me and you away, then everything that belongs to me would go to ruin. All that I have in mind to do would be totally destroyed were I to take you out of this home of my father and put you in someone else's homestead."

So Jabulani's mother's health deteriorated. It became serious.

They were by themselves on the side of the mountain. When Jabulani took the cattle to pasture, he took his mother outside to a sheltered spot, but after a time, his mother said, "My child, I am too hot. Take me inside the house." So Jabulani took her into the house. When she was inside the house, she said, "Ee, Jabulani! Ee, Jabulani!"

"Mother."

"Please come and make a fire for me, I am getting cold."

Jabulani came in and made the fire. When he had made the fire in the hearth, his mother warmed herself at the fire and was there for some time. When she had warmed herself, she said, "Oh, my child, it's getting very hot."

So Jabulani opened the door and transported his mother on a skin mat and placed her near the entrance, supporting her with blankets. He began to realize that death was near at hand, that his mother would die.

"Mother, do you want some meat?"

She said, "Yes, yes."

He said, "What kind of meat do you want, Mother? Just name it."

She said, "I crave goat meat."

Jabulani brought a goat and slaughtered it, and said, "Mother."

She said, "Yes?"

He said, "What part of the goat do you want?"

His mother said, "My child, I want the tripe. Roast it in the hearth before I eat it."

Jabulani roasted the tripe of the goat, he roasted it, he roasted and gave some of it to his mother to taste.

She said, "Feed me, my child."

Jabulani put the meat into his mother's mouth, he fed her.

She said, "Look here, Jabulani, my muscles are stiffening. Don't stop doing what you're doing with this meat. Just keep cutting pieces for me, a piece at a time. Without you, Jabulani, there would be no one to provide meat for me. You said that I should take some beasts from your stock and slaughter them. That really pleased me.

"Your father did not approve of polygamy. He said that it is vexatious, that it causes scarcity, and a person begins to lack such things as goats. When one is married to many women, one's inheritance becomes invisible, Jabulani. When I die, my child, what I want is this: I want your inheritance to increase for you until you are an old man, without ever having gotten married—as you yourself have solemnly vowed, saying that you do not want to marry."

Jabulani's mother's health deteriorated, and at length death came.

Jabulani went out to tell his people: "My mother has died. I am left alone."

They buried his mother.

Having buried her, Jabulani took two sheep and slaughtered them. The meat was eaten on that day, the day his mother was buried.

INDEPENDENCE

"YOU WILL FALL OUT WITH THE ANCIENT MAN CALLED GOD."

Jabulani said to his cousin, "Prepare some provisions for me, Cousin. My mother has died, and I'm leaving tomorrow morning. I shall not return for a long time, because I know that my mother was done in, bewitched by my uncle. He had stopped visiting our house because of this inheritance of mine which he said was too great. But this inheritance was not the result of doing anything wrong, like witchcraft. It grew so large because I used my brains, that's the way I accumulated so much stock." When Jabulani had been employed, he would send down money to buy red mealies with which to feed his cattle. So Jabulani's cattle were fed, and he planted reeds, the kind that are eaten by cattle. And the cattle of Jabulani increased greatly. Before his uncle became jealous of Jabulani's inheritance, he had visited the home of his brother frequently. Jabulani had said, "Uncle, please don't begrudge me. If you persist in being jealous of me, you will fall out with the ancient man called God. What should a person do when he seeks worldly wisdom, when he applies his brain in the world?"

"For me," Jabulani told his cousin, "this was the plan: I did not want to marry, because I knew that marrying subverts well-laid plans. If, for example, a child lacks clothing, if a wife lacks clothing, if the wife is starving, and the children are starving, I shall have to take out a beast from the cattle kraal and sell it cheaply. I must all but throw it away for ten pounds, in order to buy bags of corn. They would get no clothing, because the money would not stretch that far. So I said, 'No! Not for me!' For this reason, my uncle begrudged me because I had done this work in my father's house. Now that I am leaving, Cousin, I will seek out a person who is reliable and hard-working with the intention of leaving these goods, this stock, of mine with him, and pay him."

So Jabulani did take these cattle of his—all the stock, including sheep and goats. He took them to that homestead, and constructed a kraal. He wove wire, and made a strong fence, Jabulani built a strong fence.

Then he chopped wood. He got up while it was still dark, and took loaves of bread and put them into a bag. Then he took a bottle, put water into the bag, and departed. At the edge of a forest, he sat down, and said to those with whom he had journeyed, "Go, transport that wood!" Jabulani went along with them, he said, "Please transport the wood." He accompanied them. So it went until the sun set. By the time he got home, Jabulani was so tired he could eat no food. He went to bed, then returned to work.

Eventually, Jabulani completed the task. He built this kraal by himself.

The daughters of his cousin said, "Cousin, why don't you let us prepare some beer for you so that you can invite some people to come and work for you?"

Jabulani said, "No, I don't want anybody's help, because that might cause envy. If people become envious, they will bewitch my cattle. I don't want to be in want because I am an orphan."

Jabulani went on building the cattle-fold. Then, when the kraal had been completely built, he took these cattle of his and drove them to the homestead of the person who had agreed to help Jabulani and look after his cattle.

This person said, "My son, I thank you. When you find work, I ask that you buy a raincoat for me that will enable me to herd these cattle without catching cold. You have built a kraal for the cattle and built a fold for your goats. Nothing is ever going to bother you, Jabulani. All this stock of yours will increase and multiply, because nobody will eat it." Then this father at whose place Jabulani had come to leave his possessions said, "Since you're leaving tomorrow morning, it's necessary that you take a little calf that is still young, with horns just beginning to appear, and kill it. Then pour its bile on these cattle, Jabulani, so that they are secure from mishaps."

Jabulani did all that the senior man told him to do. He slaughtered the beast, then invited all the people to come and eat. The people, however, did not know why Jabulani was doing this. They thought he had slaughtered the animal for no particular reason. But Jabulani and the old man knew what they were doing to these cattle of his.

Jabulani departed in the morning, going to seek employment.

RETURN

"I HAVE BECOME A MAN, GRANDFATHER!"

Jabulani worked and worked, remaining employed for a long time.

Then, suddenly one day, he reappeared, now a vigorous young man, his chin covered by a massive beard. When he arrived, he removed his hat and began to speak.

"Sir."

This old father of his came outside.

"I cannot see you, my child. I cannot see at all, I'm very old."

"Have you aged that much, Father? Tell me now, is this my home?"

"But where did you think it was? Is this not the village of the Nxube clan?"

Jabulani said, "The last I remember, it was, Father."

"My child, tell me, where do you come from?"

He said, "I come from far away, from the pass of Ntunjambili, the Rock-of-two-holes."[16]

"What are you doing here, my child? What has brought you here?"

"Well, Father, it is the intestines that bring me here. I am hungry. I'm defeated. I am seeking my home. I don't know anymore in which direction it lies."

Actually, Jabulani could see that this was his home. He was playing a joke on this old man of his because the old man could not see. Jabulani knew that this was his home, the place from which he had set out. He could also see the kraal.

It was the old man who did not recognize Jabulani.

"Hunger is what made me come here, Father. I ask for a little something that goes to the intestine."

"My young man, what kind of sense does it make that you traverse so much territory without provisions?"

"Father, I am an orphan. I got off the bus, and my heart thumped as I remembered my home."

"Do you have your mother at home? Whom do you miss then?"

"Well, I do have people at home. My mother is there. However, I do not have a father anymore."

"But, my young man, why are you laughing at me?"

"Well, Sir, I laugh because we young people have become accustomed to laughing when a person is just talking."

"Oh, aren't you Jabulani? Your voice resembles Jabulani's voice even in its hoarseness."

Then Jabulani burst out laughing.

His cousin came then, and said, "Grandfather, this Jabulani is trifling with you!"

The old man got up and fumbled with his cane. He playfully hit Jabulani, feigning at hitting him. Jabulani, however, jumped, and stepped back.

The old man said, "You are a wicked boy, Jabulani! You play with me because I am very old!"

Jabulani said, "Grandfather, I too—just look at me! I have quite a chin now!"

So saying, Jabulani stroked his beard, he twirled his whiskers, and said, "Hand me that stool, Grandfather. You sit on the ground, so that I may open my provisions for you. I am not hungry. See, Grandfather, I am full. Don't you see my stomach? It has become this big, a paunch! I have become a man, Grandfather, I'm no longer thin and delicate. I told you that not getting married is desirable, Grandfather, because in that case nothing bothers one. One comes back from the place of employment, and one is untroubled, doesn't have to be accountable to anyone.

"But look at you! You are the way you are because you are married. You are reprimanded by this wife, by that one, then by another. One will offer you food without salt. The other will give you food that lacks flavor. Maybe there is no sugar. A lot of things! The porridge is perhaps not properly cooked, it is lumpy. But just look at me, Grandfather. I am a sturdy young man!"

The old man laughed and said, "Well, Jabulani, if you'll share what you eat with me, perhaps I too will have a glossy appearance."

Jabulani said to the children, "Bring water with a bowl, and place it before Grandfather. Here is bread. Here is jam."

Jabulani cooked it, and gave it to the old man, and said, "Eat it yourself, Grandfather."

When the old man called in his old wife, Jabulani said, "Don't give it to her, Grandfather. She is the one who has consumed all your food, and the result is your present condition. It is marriage that diminishes the food. I told you that I will not marry any woman."

The old man said, "Even though your ancestors say that marriage causes the household to grow robustly?"

He said, "Well, you married, Grandfather. Where is that robust homestead? Are all the grandmothers still here?"

He said, "They are no more."

"What took them away?" said Jabulani.

He said, "Death took them away. If one marries too much, poisoners begin to appear. One comes upon someone gasping for breath, crying out in a feeble voice, unable to speak because of the deadly spells that have been cast. There is a sickness caused by love spells: one person causes another to eat something,[17] and then, as time passes and the herb lodges in the stomach of a person, it is said, 'He has been caused to eat.' "

Jabulani was amused by these comments about marriage, because he really feared it. He had never come close to doing it.

He said, "Grandfather."

The old man said, "Yes?"

He said, "Are there still cattle in the kraal?"

The old man said, "I don't have cattle anymore, Child of my child. They have been wiped out, finished by your grandmothers who lacked clothing, having worn out their garments. Your grandmothers ran out of fat, and there was nothing with which to make those garments supple. They went to the river to wash, and the skin garments were not soft enough. When I approached a wife to touch her, the stiff garments were rough to the touch.

" 'But what kind of garment are you wearing, Wife,' I asked, 'it is rough to the touch!'

" 'Don't provoke me to anger! You no longer supply me with fat to soften them — I miss that! Can't you see that the weather is hard on them?'

"So there would be an argument. And there was no thread with which to sew the garments when the seams broke. 'What shall I sew this garment with?' "

"See now! I told you, Grandfather! I said that I shall never marry! My property has not been compromised, can't you see, because I never married. You have wives, they have stripped you of everything. If you should die, Grandfather, there would not even be a beast with which to pay ritual respects to you. Maybe a cat will be seized, Grandfather, and it will be killed in your honor!"

Jabulani's old grandfather laughed. He said, "It is really an incompetent person who cannot manage wives." He added, "You are wedded to the machines of the white man, these harmonicas that you play when you walk."

Jabulani said, "That's right, Grandfather. A harmonica is very nice because it does not talk back. A woman may be exceedingly warm, may even sweat, Grandfather. Then you are driven away from home by a wife, and you disappear for years, maybe six years. Here is this wife, arguing with you, taking you to task. And when you say that you want food, the wife throws a bowl at you, and says, 'Where do you think I'll get food? I told you that the sack of maize is finished! There is no salt, there is no paraffin. Where do you suggest I get it?' So a man disappears and never comes back. A child consequently forgets what his father looked like, because the man's wife drove him away. Perhaps he is not clothing his wife properly. He does not give her food when she is hungry, and she refuses to give him food. A person therefore disappears and never again comes home. In the end, he will not even recognize his children. He might disappear completely!

"If he should come across a person from that same village, the question is asked, 'Where does this person come from? You look like someone I know, my child!'

" 'Oh, Mother! Where could you have seen me?' He will look down and say, 'You have never seen me, not at all, Mother, really! It must have been someone else, it certainly was not me. He could not have been like me, it must be that you saw my brother!'

"So the young man would bury his head and look down and pass on, singing a tune or, pressing forward, whistling as he went. Then the young man would put a cigarette into his mouth and sing hoarsely."

Jabulani said, "Well, Grandfather, I have come back. However, I'm still tired. I shall see how you get along here at home."

JABULANI ALONE

" 'I CLAIM GRANDMOTHER,' DEATH SAID."

Time passed, Jabulani living here at home with his grandfather and grandmother. Then his grandmother fell ill, she was sick for some time.

Jabulani said, "I was destined to come and bury my grandmother here at home. Grandmother is about to die. I should go, it is better that I depart and never return."

Jabulani took two head of cattle and sold them. When he had sold these two cows, he tried to cure this grandmother of his.

However, death came.

"I claim Grandmother," Death said. "I shall take Grandmother away."

With this old and dying woman were two young women who had borne children[18] by two young men in the neighborhood.

Jabulani said to one of them, "Grandmother is dying. I cannot see what I shall do now. With whom will the old man live here at home? I shall take Grandfather and depart with him. No one here will look after him. You won't care for him, because you have become an immoral woman here at home, out of parental control. Having seen that Grandmother is exhausted, you have consumed her possessions. Now, because you think of yourself as a permanent resident here at this home, you have the audacity to admit all sorts of men into this home to 'eat' these cattle. Because there is no available young man here, you don't bother to marry. You play the role of a man even though you are a woman here at home." Then he spoke bluntly. "Go away from here!" said Jabulani, expelling this woman who had borne these two children by two young men. He said, "These children, where do they belong in this home? Aren't they the ones who drive people away from this home, these children of yours, because they want the inheritance?"

The old woman said, "How did you guess all this, Jabulani, my child? I'm overcome by this person. When I ask her to bring the cattle home, she refuses, telling me that she does not belong here at home. She came here as a stranger.

"She is a total stranger. She does not herd the cattle here at home. It is she who has destroyed me and told me, 'Grandmother, you deserve to be beaten with a stick and die.' However, she does not hit me with a stick. I have become ill and all my bones are cracking, my bones are cracking. When it is time to open the kraal for the cattle to go out and graze, I find that I cannot do it, I cannot even sit down or bend. I just stand up, and when someone appears I call to the person, asking him to come and open the kraal to let the cattle out, I just cannot do it myself.

"Go after her, Jabulani, expel her from this home! It is she who has brought this condition on me!"

Jabulani said, "Put your things together and leave, so that by the time Grandmother dies you will be gone from here at home."

The young woman put her things together, and she went out, departing with these two children of hers. One of them was older, the other one was still somewhat young. The other young woman also departed.

Meanwhile, Jabulani's grandmother's illness got worse. Soon enough, she was about to die. In the end, she died, and Jabulani buried her.

When Jabulani had buried his grandmother, the old man said, "Well, Jabulani, I too, my child, am exhausted. Take me away. It is preferable that you take me away."

Jabulani said, "Where shall I put you, Grandfather?"

He said, "My child, rent a place and put me there."

Jabulani said, "No, Grandfather, just be calm. I'll think of something. I don't want these possessions to go to ruin. I don't want them all to end, because, Grandfather, there is no one to acquire this inheritance of yours. Just compose yourself."

Time passed, and when those who had come to observe the death of his grandmother had departed, Jabulani said, "Grandfather, see now, all of these cattle, four hundred of them—these cattle, as well as six hundred goats. We shall take these cattle and sell them, we shall take the money and preserve it. Then, when death overtakes you, Grandfather, nothing will happen to this stock of mine, nobody will get it. I shall take my money and go to my place of employment. I do not want anyone to benefit at my expense. When I die, I shall die with all this money of mine. And your money too, I want to die with it because this child of yours will watch out for the inheritance at home. She has already set herself to be the inheritor of the legacy. Nothing else matters to her—she just wants to acquire the estate."

His grandfather said, "Jabulani, in that case, you should help me. I alone worked for this legacy. There was no second person, no third person. By the time these people die, they have already cut into the legacy because, even if some distance is involved, a legacy does have a rightful heir. When you are dead, you will have done what all the ancients do, Jabulani. You will preserve the dead, you will remember your grandmother, and not be filled with envy. I want you to do what you like about that stock of mine, as well as yours. I put them all together. They are all yours. You will do what you like with them, because you say you will not marry."

Jabulani said, "Well, Grandfather, in that case I shall get married, because I have matured. I have learned. If a wife troubles me, I'll just drive her off, because I lack nothing."

The discussion between Jabulani and this grandfather of his went on and on. After a while, death came to the grand old man. Jabulani wept and mourned when this grandfather of his died. He wondered how he would bury him.

He said, "I am now in trouble, and alone, with no one." Jabulani took money and went to hire people to help him dig a grave in which to bury his father. People came and helped him to dig the grave, and Jabulani interred this father of his.

When he had finished burying this grandfather of his, Jabulani hired a homestead from someone. He occupied it. But he found that it was all rondavels, and this bothered Jabulani. He was not accustomed to rondavels, he was used to Zulu-style houses.

Jabulani said, "This is bothersome, I really don't like this type of house. I am used to Zulu houses. My father used to build Zulu houses, and I grew up in the Zulu tradition. I want to build a house like my people's in which to live, because I am alone now."

Jabulani decided to marry because he was wondering who would inherit his estate. All of his relatives had died, and Jabulani remained alone. So he began to look for a young woman. He found one quickly. He provided a dowry for her, and the time came that they should marry. When Jabulani and this woman had married, his wife said, "I don't think we should continue to live in this homestead. I prefer that we build our own homestead."

They left and built their own homestead, she and Jabulani.

After a time, Jabulani said, "I don't want us to get a child because our estate is sizeable. Even if we don't have a child, we shall enjoy our life and property. I myself do not want any child because a child brings trouble."

The young wife said, "What kind of person is this who does not want children? Who will inherit all this property?"

Jabulani said, "You will take it with you and go to your people because we are married. I do not want an heir who will eat all this stock of mine."

Magagamela Koko

AGE AND DEATH

(XHOSA)

On August 31, 1967, the Xhosa poet, Magagamela Koko, a Mfengu, about eighty years old, performed these two poems about age and death. The performance took place in a home overlooking the Kei River valley, in Nqancule, Ngqamakhwe District, in the Transkei. The audience consisted of ten women, two men, and ten children. (451; tape 8, side 2)

WHEN YOU ARE GREY

The story is painful:
To begin by being wealthy,
Wealthy in one's youth,
Born into wealth,
And then, when you are grey,
As old as I,
To be shorn,
To have one's feathers shorn.
You recall, then, what once you were,
You look at yourself,
You see that you had been eight
And now, suddenly, you are seven.
And you are unable to understand
What it means on this earth.

It is painful
To start life with wealth,
Then, when physical strength ebbs,
To lose everything:
Strength leaves you,
Your stock diminishes,
You wonder who will care for you.

What I ask is this:
Why has God preserved me?
Perhaps I have offended him,
He must know why he has done so.

395

He does not want my protest,
He created me after all.
But I cannot help myself,
My anguish prompts me to it.

NOW I AM SPENT

Where I came from, I do not know.
But when I was born,
I learned to fight with sticks,
To fight with sticks with vigor—

There are cowards,
There are heroes.
From the time of my birth, I knew no fear;
From my birth, I have been that way.
I came to the earth to confront
Whatever came to me,
To pursue nothing that did not affect me.

I grew, I matured, I became a boy.
We fought many fights then,
And in those battles, if I was absent,
It would be said, "The *boys* are absent,"
Yet I was the only boy not there.

What made me this way?
That I cannot say.
I have only heard that I was brave,
That there was no fear.
To this day, that is the way I am.
If there is a discussion
And I am not present,
It is said, "The *men* are absent."
I did not create this view of myself,
I cannot tell you how it came about.

Now I am as you see me—
A being, because of vanishing years,
With a head full of patches
Like a bull-eagle.
Now I wait only to snap,

I have reached that age.
No peer of mine remains,
I am all alone
As if I were a bull-baboon
Barked at even by small dogs.
Now I am spent, my eyes are gone,
I cannot see.
I speak, yet cannot see you,
I see but a dim blurred figure.
It is deeply painful

When I regard my stock:
I look at my goat,
Yet do not recognize it.
I look at my ox,
Yet do not see it.
Only one ox remains at my home
That I am able to recognize.
Only one ox, a spotted one.
It is this ox that I shall slaughter.
And when I do, I shall say,
"We Xhosa people, when we transform
The things of nature,
We do it like this."
I shall slaughter it next week,
I shall slaughter it
To make things right.
Yes, to make things right
Even for those not yet born.

Notes

Sources

Index

Notes

PREFACE

1. *The Holy Bible,* James 3:8.

2. A. C. Jordan, *Tales from Southern Africa* (Berkeley: University of California Press, 1973), p. xxii.

3. Gabriel García Márquez, *One Hundred Years of Solitude,* trans. Gregory Rabassa (New York: Harper and Row, 1970), p. 16.

4. Eva Ndlovu, a forty-five-year-old Ndebele woman, made this comment in a story that she performed on November 15, 1972, in the Matopo/Gulati area of southern Zimbabwe. In the audience were five children, five teenagers, and one woman. (NS-2388; tape 46, side 2.)

5. I refer to such works as Nadine Gordimer's *July's People* (New York: Viking Press, 1981), Alan Paton's *Cry, the Beloved Country* (New York: Charles Scribner's Sons, 1948), J. M. Coetzee's *Life & Times of Michael K* (New York: Viking Press, 1984), Sipho Sepamla's *A Ride on the Whirlwind* (London: Heinemann, 1981), Es'kia Mphahlele's *Down Second Avenue* (Garden City: Doubleday, 1971), and Miriam Tlali's *Amandla* (Johannesburg: Ravan Press, 1980).

6. Jan Vansina, *Oral Tradition as History* (Madison: University of Wisconsin Press, 1985), p. 11.

7. Robert Lowell, "History," in *History* (New York: Farrar, Straus and Giroux, 1973), lines 1–2, p. 24.

8. Simon Schama, *Citizens* (New York: Alfred A. Knopf, 1989), p. xvi.

9. Hayden White, "The Value of Narrativity in the Representation of Reality," in *On Narrative,* ed. W. J. T. Mitchell (Chicago: University of Chicago Press, 1981), p. 4.

10. David Carr, "Narrative and the Real World: An Argument for Continuity," *History and Theory* 25.2 (1986): 125.

11. Immanuel Wallerstein, *The Modern World System* (New York: Academic Press, 1974), vol. 1, p. 9.

12. Paul Veyne, *Writing History: Essay on Epistemology,* trans. Mina Moore-Rinvolucri (Middletown, Conn.: Wesleyan University Press, 1984), p. 4. [Originally published as *Comment on ecrit l'histoire: Essai d'épistémologie* (Paris: Éditions Seuil, 1971).]

13. Steven Feierman, *The Shambaa Kingdom: A History* (Madison: University of Wisconsin Press, 1974), pp. 65, 66.

14. Felipe Fernández-Armesto, *Millennium: A History of the Last Thousand Years* (New York: Scribner, 1995), p. 22.

15. Jacob Burckhardt, *The Civilization of the Renaissance in Italy,* trans. S. C. C. Middlemore (London: Penguin Books, 1990 [originally published in 1860]), p. 19.

16. Fernández-Armesto, *Millennium,* p. 23.

17. Quoted in Thomas J. Cobble, *Black Testimony: The Voices of Britain's West Indians* (Philadelphia: Temple University Press, 1980), p. 156.

18. Isidore Okpewho, *African Oral Literature* (Bloomington: Indiana University Press, 1992), p. 113.

19. Philip D. Curtin, *The Image of Africa: British Ideas and Action, 1780–1850* (Madison: University of Wisconsin Press, 1964).

20. Donald Cosentino, *Defiant Maids and Stubborn Farmers* (Cambridge: Cambridge University Press, 1982), p. 1.

21. Eileen Julien, *African Novels and the Question of Orality* (Bloomington: Indiana University Press, 1992), p. 51.

22. Mircea Eliade, *Myth and Reality,* trans. Willard R. Trask (New York: Harper and Row, 1963), p. 5–6.

23. *The Holy Bible,* James 3:5, 6.

NOTE

1. See Harold Scheub, "Translation of African Oral Narrative-Performances to the Written Word," *Yearbook of Comparative and General Literature* no. 20 (1971): 28–36.

INTRODUCTION

1. This does not purport to be a history of South Africa. It is meant to be a brief survey, touching on some important events and themes, significant figures and events. For histories of South Africa, see Monica Wilson and Leonard Thompson, eds., *The Oxford History of South Africa* (Oxford: Oxford University Press, 1969, 1971); T. R. H. Davenport, *South Africa: A Modern History* (Toronto: University of Toronto Press, 1977); Leo Marquard, *The Peoples and Policies of South Africa* (London: Oxford University Press, 1962); and Leonard Thompson, *A History of South Africa* (New Haven: Yale University Press, 1990).

2. R. Raven-Hart, *Before Van Riebeeck: Callers at South Africa from 1488 to 1652* (Cape Town: C. Struik, Pty., 1967), p. 115.

3. Daniel Beeckman, quoted in Richard Elphick, *Kraal and Castle: Khoikhoi and the Founding of White South Africa* (New Haven: Yale University Press, 1977), p. 205. Elphick notes, "There was, to my knowledge, no law directed specifically at intercourse between whites and Khoikhoi: there was certainly none that was enforced in the courts. However, on December 9, 1678, a pro forma proclamation outlawed *all* types of concubinage. . . . On his expedition to Namaqualand in 1685, Simon van der Stel forbade his men to sleep with Khoikhoi women on pain of flogging and dismissal from the Company's service; this, however, was not a general law" (p. 205 footnote).

4. Jan van Riebeeck, *Précis of the Cape Archives: Letters Despatched, 1652–1662,* ed. H. C. M. Leibbrandt (Cape Town: W. A. Richards and Sons, 1900), vol. 3, p. 128.

5. *The Real Story,* ed. Dougie Oakes (Pleasantville: The Reader's Digest Association, 1988), p. 39.

6. In the early 1700s, some Dutch settlers "began openly to adopt the name

Afrikaner to distinguish themselves from the expatriate servants of the [Dutch East India] Company and subsequently the name came to apply to all white South Africans who were native speakers of Afrikaans, a language that evolved from the Dutch spoken at the Cape" (J. D. Omer-Cooper, *History of Southern Africa* [London: James Currey; Portsmouth, N.H.: Heinemann; Claremont, South Africa: David Philip, 1987], p. 21).

7. Quoted in *The Real Story,* ed. Dougie Oakes, p. 326.

8. Quoted in Robert Edgar, *Because They Chose the Plan of God* (Johannesburg: Ravan Press, 1988), p. 26.

9. Quoted in Edgar, *Because They Chose the Plan of God,* p. 1.

10. Quoted in Edgar, *Because They Chose the Plan of God,* p. 38.

11. Quoted in Edgar, *Because They Chose the Plan of God,* p. 39.

12. Quoted in Edward Roux, *Time Longer than Rope: A History of the Black Man's Struggle for Freedom in South Africa* (Madison: University of Wisconsin Press, 1964), p. 138. At about the same time, in 1922, the Bondelswart people in Namibia refused to pay taxes, and objected to the pass system and the forced servitude of males. At Smuts's order, South African aircraft bombed the homes of the Bondelswart, resulting in a massacre: one hundred of the Bondelswart people were killed. On May 23, 1923, Smuts, speaking to the House of Assembly in regard to his act of terrorism, said, "It leaves me cold." His words would have an eerie echo fifty-four years later, when the Minister of Justice, James Thomas Kruger, used the same words in reference to the death of Stephen Biko, the black consciousness leader: *"Dit laat my koud,"* "It leaves me cold."

13. See Gail M. Gerhart, *Black Power in South Africa: The Evolution of an Ideology* (Berkeley: University of California Press, 1978).

14. William Beinart, *"Amafelandawonye* (the Die-hards)," in William Beinart and Colin Bundy, *Hidden Struggles in Rural South Africa* (London: James Currey, 1987), pp. 222–269.

15. *Apartheid* is an Afrikaans word meaning apartness, separateness, distinctness. As official South African government policy after 1948, it came to mean total racial separation on all levels and in all aspects of life. "Grand apartheid" had to do with "separate development as a major political policy"; "petty apartheid" had to do with "separate entrance doors, park benches and other amenities for White and non-White" (Jean Branford, *A Dictionary of South African English* [Cape Town: Oxford University Press, 1980], p. 9).

16. See Martin Murray, *South Africa: Time of Agony, Time of Destiny* (London: Verso, 1987).

17. Quoted in Tom Hopkinson, *In the Fiery Continent* (Garden City: Doubleday, 1963), pp. 258, 260.

18. "Sharpeville and After," *Africa Today* 7.3 (May 1960): 7.

19. John Kane-Berman, *Soweto: Black Revolt, White Reaction* (Johannesburg: Ravan Press, 1978).

20. Margaret Ellsworth makes a more general observation regarding the state of education for Africans: "Expenditure on each White child averages R400-R550 a year, on an African child less than R30 a year. R30 simply cannot buy a year of education. Thus all school facilities, teachers' salaries, classroom accommodation

are totally inadequate. In the Republic 11,000 teachers are involved in teaching double sessions because there are too few classrooms and too few teachers" ("The Rejection of Bantu Education," *South African Outlook* 106 [August 1976]: 124).

21. "The Choice," *South African Outlook* 106 (August 1976): 114.

22. Steve Biko, "Black Consciousness and the Quest for True Humanity," *Reality* 4.1 (March 1972): 6.

23. Donald Woods, *Biko* (New York: Paddington Press, 1978), p. 9.

24. From a verbatim transcript of a speech given by Mr. Kruger to the Transvaal Congress of the National Party in September, 1977 (*South African Outlook* 107 (September 1977): 142. See also June Goodwin and Ben Schiff, "Who Killed Steve Biko?" *Nation* 261 (November 13, 1995): 565–568.

25. Adam Small, "Steve Biko," *Drum* (November 1977): 21.

26. John Solilo (died 1940), "Mthandi Wesizwe" ("Lover of the Nation"), *Imibengo*, ed. W. G. Bennie (Lovedale: Lovedale Press, 1935), p. 169.

27. Baroness Emmuska Orczy (1865–1947) was an English novelist and playwright, author of *The Scarlet Pimpernel* (1905), *A Son of the People* (1906), and *The Divine Folly* (1937).

28. "Mandela," said a British correspondent, "was the most impressive delegate at Addis."

29. See Allister Sparks, *Tomorrow Is Another Country: The Inside Story of South Africa's Road to Change* (New York: Hill and Wang, 1995).

30. In an address to South African business executives on May 23, 1990, Mandela said, "Many a time the . . . deprived people who we represent have posed the same bitter question that Shylock posed in Shakespeare's *Merchant of Venice:* 'Hath not a Jew eyes? Hath not a Jew hands, organs, dimensions, senses, affections, passions? Fed with the same food, hurt with the same weapons, subject to the same diseases, healed by the same means, warmed and cooled by the same winter and summer, as a Christian is? If you prick us, do we not bleed? If you tickle us, do we not laugh? If you poison us, do we not die? And if you wrong us, shall we not revenge? If we are like you in the rest, we will resemble you in that. . . .' Questions such as these . . . about . . . the universal nature of human pain and suffering, can only be posed by people who are discriminated against, in a society that condemns them to persistent deprivation of the material artifacts and the dignity that are due to them as human beings. We pose them for the same reasons."

31. John Matshikiza, "And I Watch it in Mandela," *Poets to the People: South African Freedom Poems*, ed. Barry Feinberg (London: Heinemann, 1980), lines 11–12, p. 138.

PROLOGUE: FOUNDERS OF THE INHERITANCE

1. In the Apocrypha, *Ecclesiasticus*, 44: 1, 3, 4, 7, and 8.

2. Deneys Reitz, *No Outspan* (London: Faber and Faber, 1943), p. 60.

3. Reitz, *No Outspan*, p. 66.

4. Nelson Mandela, *Long Walk to Freedom: The Autobiography of Nelson Mandela* (Boston: Little, Brown and Company, 1994), pp. 19, 20.

5. Felipe Fernández-Armesto, "Rewriting History," *Index on Censorship* 24:3 (May/June 1995): 26–27.

6. Ndaba was the great-grandson (some say the great-great grandson) of Zulu, who was the founder of the group that would one day comprise the Zulu nation. Ndaba's son was Jama, the father of Senzangakhona, who was the father of Shaka.

7. Umhle Biyela, about forty years old, a Zulu poet, performed these poems on September 12, 1972. The performance took place in an open field, in Yanguya, Zululand. In attendance were thirty men, women, and children. (NS-689; tape 19, side 2) Note that here and in all subsequent performance data, the attendance numbers do not include myself.

8. Qaphela-bazozela: literally, "Crouch-till-they-become-drowsy."

9. From an interview with Chinua Achebe, in the film *Chinua Achebe* (Princeton: Films for the Humanities and Sciences, 1995).

ORIGINS OF THE XHOSA

1. If a man, a commoner, has two wives, the woman he marries first is called the great wife, and her house, the great house. The woman he marries second is called the right-hand wife, and her house, the right-hand house. The third wife is the supporting house; such third houses may support either the great house or the right-hand house.

2. East London.

3. King William's Town.

4. San.

5. These are Rharhabe's clans, later to become the Ngqika.

6. The support of the great wife in the form of a son who will become the chief if the great wife has no son of her own. The supporting house is attached to one of the two principal houses, the great house or the right-hand house. Should there be no male progeny in the house to which the supporting house is attached, the eldest son of the senior supporting house becomes the heir.

7. A member of the audience interjects, "Tyhali's household!"

8. A member of the audience says, "We want them all!"

9. Literally, "They were smelled out"; figuratively, they were discovered by divination to have caused their father to become ill; they were suspected of witchcraft.

10. A member of the audience says, "You haven't told us anything about Tyhali!" Bhotomane laughs.

11. Later, Mr. Bhotomane added the following remarks, which he wished to be appended to this part of the history he had earlier recounted:

> I just want to make a few comments about the important councillors here—not all of them, only the important ones here in Gcalekaland and Ngqikaland. I shall name only a few of the men, I do not want to cover all of the councillors. It would take a long time to do so, the sun would set. I am just trying to explain the institution of the chieftaincy.
>
> Kingship among the Xhosa is not unlike the policy of the whites, who also have councillors who speak for them. A chief usually has a council under him, a coun-

cil that responds to business that comes from the [European] government and from other nations; he answers through that council, which deliberates and hands decisions over to him, to be the spokesman. That is how things go according to Xhosa custom among the Gcaleka.

Here are the Gcaleka Xhosa: number one is Sijako, son of Bhacela, son of Khwaza:

Sijako, son of Bhacela,
Son of Khwaza,
Son of Ngqila,
Son of Wohle.

He is an important councillor in Xhosaland; he comes after that Khwane who had earned the chieftaincy during the period when King Phalo was fighting with Mjobi. This courtier, Khwazu Sijako, comes after him in importance.

Sijako is the son of Bhacela,
Bhacela is the son of Khwaza,
Khwaza is the son of Ngqila,
Ngqila is the son of Wohle,
Wohle is the son of Thotywayo.

Other councillors include Hedeni, Hlangabeza, Maki, Ntsheco, Hena, Geqe, and Wohle. He is the eldest son of Wohle, this side of Maki in the councillorship. Madolo is the son of Khwaza, in the right-hand house. Mabala is the son of Ngqila in the supporting house. In the right-hand house, it is Magile. Those are the important councillors in Gcalekaland—those ones I have mentioned.

The lesser councillors are as follows:

Runeyi, his father is Qeqe,
Qeqe is the son of Ganya,
Ganya is the son of Mpulu.

That is another notable. After that one comes Gwatyuza, the scion of Njimbane of Mpondoland. He has a younger brother, Wolela. Another councillor, coming after these in importance, is Msasa, the scion of Tsatsi, from the Ndlintsha section. There are other councillors, but the important ones in Gcalekaland are those I have mentioned, coming after Majeki.

Now, to Ngqikaland. The foremost councillor is Tyhala:

Tyhala fathered Ntsangana,
Ntsangana fathered Mhlontlo,
Mhlontlo fathered Mmoshi,

the headman at Nxaxho. He is a notable in the Ngqikaland section, there is no greater. Second in importance is Soga:

Festile is Soga's heir,
Festile fathered Henry,
Henry fathered Joni,

and he is another prominent councillor of Ngqikaland—both of those are important councillors. After that comes

Qukwana, who fathered Mbhoyi,
Mbhoyi fathered Ndesana,
Ndesana fathered Mlawuli,

and Mlawuli is now at Msebe. He is a distinguished dignitary in Sandile's domain, and comes after those in importance.

Another notable councillor is Gaqa:

He fathered Nzima,
And he fathered Hokisi,
Hokisi fathered Kaiser,

the incumbent at Nxaxha—Kaiser, yes, he is a great councillor. Following that one in importance is Somana. He fathered Gwebinibiza, the incumbent here at Khobonqaba—at Khobe, actually.

These are the significant councillors in Sandile's realm. After that one is Vuso, who fathered Zimasile; he is at Qombolo. Another is Geza, who fathered Sifingo, over there at Qombolo. The third is Falakhe; he is here at Ngxizela. These are consequential councillors of Sandile's kingdom.

I am attempting to clarify the kingdom system of the Xhosa in making these comments. I shall stop with those. There are others, there are great ones on both sides. I have tried to explain the kingdom of the Xhosa: the king does not act alone, as if he has no councillors. The kingship of the Xhosa has councillors: it is ordered, it has a council under the king that acts as his spokesman. Even when the [European] government wants the king to make a commitment, the king will express an opinion that he has obtained from his council; he will call the council together at the appropriate time.

12. A member of the audience asks, "Where are they? In what area?"

13. The Zulu, called "Shaka" because that was the name of their leader.

14. John Ayliff (1797–1862) was a Wesleyan missionary whose first assignment was at Gcuwa with Hintsa's people. He became especially attached to the Mfengu people.

15. A member of the audience says, "At Ngqushwa."

16. I.e., to Christianity.

PART ONE: CULTIVATING THE PAST

1. Felipe Fernández-Armesto, "Rewriting History," *Index on Censorship* 24.3 (May/June 1995), p. 32.

2. Voltaire, *Works: A Contemporary Version*, trans. W. F. Fleming (London: The St. Hubert's Guild, n.d.), vol. 10, p. 61.

3. Charles G. Boyd, "Making Peace with the Guilty, The Truth about Bosnia," *Foreign Affairs* 74.5 (September/October 1995): 23.

4. See Nongenile Masithathu Zenani, *The World and the Word: Tales and Observations from the Xhosa Oral Tradition* ed. Harold Scheub (Madison: University of Wisconsin Press, 1992).

5. See Mircea Eliade, *Myth and Reality*, trans. Willard R. Trask (New York: Harper and Row, 1963), for a useful discussion of history, myth, and fiction.

6. Quoted in Archibald MacLeisch, *Poetry and Experience* (Baltimore: Penguin Books, 1964), p. 17.

7. See my articles: "The Technique of the Expansible Image in Xhosa *Ntsomi*-performances," *Research in African Literatures* 1 (1970): 119–146; "Parallel Image-Sets in African Oral Performances," *Review of National Literatures* 2 (1971): 206–223; "Translation of African Oral Narrative-Performances to the Written Word," *Yearbook of Comparative and General Literature*, no. 20 (1971): 28–36; and "Fixed and Non-Fixed Symbols in Xhosa and Zulu Oral Narrative Traditions," *Journal of American Folklore* 85 (1972): 267–273. For another view of the formal characteristics of oral stories, see Brian du Toit, *Content and Form of Zulu Folk-Narratives* (Gainesville: University Presses of Florida, 1976).

8. Compare Eric Havelock, *Preface to Plato* (New York: Grosset and Dunlap, 1967).

THE NECESSARY CLOWN

1. Until she introduces herself as the bride, Mrs. Zenani tells the story in the third person. After she identifies herself as the central character of this autobiographical sketch, she continues the story in the first person.

2. *inkazana:* a young woman who for some reason is living at her homestead by birth. She may be separated or divorced from her husband, or she may never have married. "*Inkazana* is used in a good or a bad sense," notes Albert Kropf, "as shown by the connection; in a bad sense it means a female who has lost her virginity" (*A Kafir-English Dictionary* [Alice, South Africa: Lovedale Mission Press, 1915], p. 273). I find it difficult to translate this word into a single English equivalent, so I have retained the Xhosa word throughout this section, along with its plural, *amankazana.*

3. Gomomo: It was his homestead.

4. *nka!*—an ideophone, suggesting the sound made when the pick hits the ground.

5. The master of ceremonies accompanied the bride throughout the wedding ceremony, orchestrating all aspects of the ritual.

6. Here, she uses *umnyatheli,* the *hlonipha* (reverential word) for *umntu,* person. The literal translation is "one who steps." She adds parenthetically, "An *umnyatheli* is an *umntu* in Xhosa." According to Albert Kropf, "This word [i.e., *hlonipha*] describes a custom between relations-in-law, and is generally but not exclusively applied to the female sex, who, when married, are not allowed to pronounce or use words which have for their principal syllable any part or syllable of the names of their chief's or their husband's relations, especially of their fathers-in-law; they must also keep at a distance from the latter. Hence, they have the habit of inventing new names for those persons; for instance, if one of these persons is called *uMehlo,* which is derived from *amehlo* (eyes), the women will no longer use *amehlo,* but substitute *amakangelo* (lookers)" (*A Kafir-English Dictionary* [Alice, South Africa: Lovedale Mission Press, 1915], p. 161).

7. "who eat early": literally, "who eat quickly."

8. Nciba River: the Kei River.

9. A member of the audience says, "Oh, you're *hlonipha*-ing. Is that the way you construct a tale?"

10. "Bring down from the mountains," i.e., "Bring the bridal party down from the place above the homestead where they have been sitting, bring the bridal party into the homestead."

11. *abantwenyana:* the women, especially the bride. Mrs. Zenani explained, "When they said *abantwenyana,* they meant me together with the women who were my companions, according to Xhosa custom. My groom also had companions, and two men would be taken also. My groom was treated in the same way as I was treated. One Ntlane clansman accompanied him, and the other man was a Dala clansman. For me as well, one woman was my sister, and the other was from the village. It was the same for bride and groom. This was natural [i.e., this was the proper form]."

12. That is, at the first signs of dawn.

13. The master of ceremonies was speaking to the *abantwenyana*, the women and especially the bride, urging them to oversleep so that he might get the fine-money.

14. That is, there was no sexual intercourse or wrangling.

15. That is, "Pour out the money, pay your fine!"

16. Literally, "sat quietly in his purse."

17. Literally, "that it should sleep."

18. Referring to the bride.

19. Attracted by Masithathu Zenani's beauty.

20. Literally, "became lazy."

21. The custom of leaving small amounts of money at each of the stages of the marriage custom symbolizes the network of linkages being established between the bride's home and the home of the groom.

22. That is, to show stylistically and symbolically how the hoeing was done.

23. That is, when a cow is being milked.

24. The master of ceremonies seems to be suggesting that the remainder of the dowry must be produced before the bride can do the chores that are being demonstrated by the in-laws. The master of ceremonies' pretending to milk is a not-so-subtle way of reminding them that more cattle are necessary for the dowry, that the full dowry has not yet been produced.

25. That is, with the turbans on our heads, we looked like lumpy-headed hammerheads.

26. That is, the skin of the goat that was slaughtered for the buttermilk-drinking ritual belongs to the master of ceremonies.

27. Masithathu Zenani's father, a Christian, seemed to be in a hurry to get things over with—this non-Christian custom—but he was willing to go through with the custom, willing to pay the necessary amount of money. He was at home, not at the marriage ceremony, but it seems that he wished that the entire thing be done quickly.

28. That is, the money was all apportioned, and it was distinct for each purpose—it could not be used for any other purpose.

29. The married women.

30. That is, the wife of the older brother and the wife of the younger brother. The custom of referring to the woman according to the title of the husband seems to be indulged in here.

31. The older brother, like the parents, was apparently dead.

32. Her sister-in-law took the place of the parents.

THE ENDLESS MOUNTAIN

1. *hayi bo:* The word *hayi*, in Xhosa, means "no." *bo* is an enclitic particle, expressing emphasis. The combination is a negative exclamation.

2. The storyteller is thereby equating Hayibo's behavior to that of the thing mentioned earlier.

3. Suggesting, possibly, Hayibo's universality, that every woman is his mother, every house is his home.

4. Again, perhaps suggesting Hayibo's universality.

5. Compare with "the thing" that Hayibo and his sister earlier met on their way to their grandparents' place.

6. I.e., the work of women.

PART TWO: AMBIGUOUS PROMISE

1. Gabriel García Márquez, *Of Love and Other Demons,* trans. Edith Grossman (New York: Alfred A. Knopf, 1995), p. 80.

2. Nongenile Masithathu Zenani, August 3, 1972, near her home in Nkanga, in Gatyana District in the Transkei. (NS-22; tape 2, side 2.)

3. Nongenile Masithathu Zenani, "The Art of the Storyteller," *The World and the Word: Tales and Observations from the Xhosa Oral Tradition* (Madison: University of Wisconsin Press, 1992), p. 7.

4. Images are felt actions or sets of actions, evoked in the imaginations of the members of the audience by verbal and nonverbal elements arranged by the artist, requiring a common experience by both artist and audience. See Scheub, "Oral Narrative Process and the Use of Models," *New Literary History* 6.2 (Winter 1975): 353–377.

5. Léopold Sédar Senghor, "On Negrohood: Psychology of the African-Negro," *Diogenes* 37 (1962): 6.

6. Susan Sontag, "Against Interpretation," in *Against Interpretation* (New York: Farrar, Straus and Giroux, 1965), p. 7.

7. Stuart Davis, *Stuart Davis,* ed. Diane Kelder (New York: Praeger, 1971), p. 47.

8. Paul Klee, *Notebooks* (New York: Wittenborn Art Books, 1961), vol. 1 (*The Thinking Eye*), p. 191.

9. Leonard Bernstein, *The Unanswered Question: Six Talks at Harvard* (Cambridge: Harvard University Press, 1976), pp. 154–162.

10. Doris Lessing, "The Black Madonna," *African Stories* (New York: Simon and Schuster, 1965), pp. 11–24.

11. It often happened, during my study of the oral traditions of southern Africa, that, when the storytelling sessions had come to an end, storytellers and their audiences would discuss with me in some depth the stories that had just been performed. This was the case with these two performances by Noplani Gxavu and Emily Ntsobane. I had discussions with members of their audiences, and I later played the tapes of the stories to other Xhosa audiences to elicit their responses. I provide the substance of the notes that I made of the discussions regarding these two stories.

PART THREE: THE THREATENED DREAM

1. Victor Brombert, "The Idea of the Hero," in *The Hero in Literature,* ed. Victor Brombert (Greenwich, Conn.: Fawcett, 1969), p. 11.

2. J. R. R. Tolkien, "*Beowulf:* The Monster and the Critics," in *The Beowulf Poet,* ed. Donald K. Fry (Englewood Cliffs, N.J.: Prentice-Hall, 1968), p. 23.

3. This took place on August 12, 1967, in the royal residence of King Diliza Iintaba Mditshwa at Mdibanisweni, Tshiqo, in Tsolo District in the Transkei.

4. Montgomery of Alamein led the eighth army in Egypt in 1942 and, at El Alamein, routed General Erwin Rommel's forces, driving them from northern Africa.

5. Nelson Mandela, *Long Walk to Freedom: The Autobiography of Nelson Mandela* (Boston: Little, Brown and Company, 1994), p. 21.

6. From my collection. This performance was described by a Xhosa poet in 1967 (NS-15, tape 1, side 2).

7. A. C. Jordan, *Towards an African Literature: The Emergence of Literary Form in Xhosa* (Berkeley: University of California Press, 1973), p. 21. The subject of oral poetry, he adds, may be a nation, a clan, a person, an animal, or even a lifeless object.

8. From my collection (NS-1426, tape 33, side 2).

9. From my collection. Nombhonjo Zungu of Mahlabatini performed his poem on September 13, 1972, in Yanguya, Zululand (NS-733, tape 20, side 1).

10. S. K. Lekgothoane, "Praises of Animals in Northern Sotho," *Bantu Studies* 12 (1938): 191.

11. "Izibongo zikaSibhozo Mnzabele," in W. B. Rubusana, *Zemk' Inkomo Magwalandini* (London: Butler and Tanner, 1911), pp. 239–240, lines 1–12.

12. Jordan, *Towards an African Literature*, p. 21.

13. Rubusana, *Zemk' Inkomo Magwalandini*, p. vi.

14. Edison M. Bokako, "Bo-Santagane: An Anthology of Tswana Heroic Verse" (MS, Kimberley, 1938), Appendix A, pp. 1–2. This manuscript was prepared under the direction of Professor Z. K. Matthews and is in the collection of Z. K. Matthews, Manuscripts Division, University of Cape Town. It is used with permission.

15. Benedict Wallet Vilakazi, "The Oral and Written Literature in Nguni," Ph. D. diss. University of the Witwatersrand, Johannesburg, 1945, p. 23. ("Nguni" is the generic term for the language family comprising the Swati, Xhosa, Zimbabwe Ndebele, and Zulu.)

16. Magema M. Fuze, *Abantu Abamnyama Lapha Bavela Ngakhona* [The Black People and Where They Came From] (Pietermaritzburg: City Printing Works, 1922), pp. 73–74.

17. Everitt Lechesa Segoete, *Raphepheng* [Father of the Scorpion] (Morija: Morija Sesuto Book Depot, 1913), p. 37.

18. Azariele M. Sekese, *Mekhoa Le Maele a Ba-Sotho* [Customs and Proverbs of the Sotho] (Morija: Morija Sesuto Book Depot, 1931), pp. 69–70.

19. C. L. S. Nyembezi, "The Historical Background to the Izibongo of the Zulu Military Age," *African Studies* 7.2–3 (1948): 110.

20. Bokako, "Bo-Santangane," appendix A, p. 1.

21. Bokako, "Bo-Santangane," appendix A, p. 1.

22. Nyembezi, "The Historical Background to the Izibongo of the Zulu Military Age," p. 111.

23. James Stuart, *uKulumetule* (London: Longmans, Green and Company, Ltd., 1925), pp. 106–111.

24. R. R. R. Dhlomo, *uShaka* (Pietermaritzburg: Shuter and Shooter, 1937), pp. 96–97.

25. Archie Mafeje, "The Role of a Bard in a Contemporary African Community," *Journal of African Languages* 4.3 (1967): 195.

26. Ernest Sedumeli Moloto, "The Growth and Tendencies of Tswana Poetry," Ph.D. diss. University of South Africa, Pretoria, 1970, pp. 81–82.

27. Bokako, "Bo-Santangane," appendix A, p. 1.

28. S. K. Lekgothoane, "Praises of Animals in Northern Sotho," *Bantu Studies* 12 (1938): 191–192.

29. See also P. A. W. Cook, "History and *Izibongo* of the Swazi Chiefs," *Bantu Studies* 5 (1931): 181–201; Trevor Cope, *Izibongo, Zulu Praise-Poems* (Oxford: Clarendon Press, 1968); M. Damane and P. B. Sanders, eds., *Lithoko, Sotho Praise-Poems* (Oxford: Clarendon Press, 1974); Ruth Finnegan, *Oral Poetry* (Cambridge: Cambridge University Press, 1977); Graham Furness and Elizabeth Gunner, eds., *Power, Marginality and African Oral Literature* (Cambridge: Cambridge University Press, 1995); E. W. Grant, "The *Izibongo* of the Zulu Chiefs," *Bantu Studies* 3.3 (1929): 203–244; Elizabeth Gunner, *Politics and Performance: Theatre, Poetry, and Song in Southern Africa* (Johannesburg: University of the Witwatersrand Press, 1994); Elizabeth Gunner, "Songs of Innocence and Experience: Women as Composers and Performers of *Izibongo*, Zulu Praise Poetry," *Research in African Literatures* 10 (1979): 239–267; *Musho! Zulu Popular Praises,* trans. and ed. Elizabeth Gunner and Mafika Gwala (East Lansing: Michigan State University Press, 1991); Daniel P. Kunene, *Heroic Poetry of the Basotho* (Oxford: Clarendon Press, 1971); P. Lamula, *Isabelo sikaZulu* (Pietermaritzburg: Shuter and Shooter, 1936); G. P. Lestrade, "Bantu Praise-Poems," *The Critic* 4 (1937): 1–10; G. P. Lestrade, "Traditional Literature," in: Isaac Schapera, ed., *The Bantu-Speaking Tribes of South Africa* (London: Routledge, 1937); J. S. M. Matsebula, *Izakhiwo zamaSwazi* (Johannesburg: Afrikaanse Pers-Boekhandel, 1948); S. M. Mofokeng, "Notes and Annotations of the Praise-poems of Certain Chiefs and the Structure of Praise-poems in Southern Sotho," Ph. D. diss. Bantu Studies, University of the Witwatersrand (Johannesburg), 1945; H. M. Ndawo, *Izibongo zenkosi zamaHlubi nezamaBhaca* (Mariannhill: Mariannhill Mission Press, 1928); C. L. S. Nyembezi, *Izibongo zamakhosi* (Pietermaritzburg: Shuter and Shooter, 1958); Isidore Okpewho, *African Oral Literature* (Bloomington: Indiana University Press, 1992); Jeff Opland, "*Imbongi Nezibongo:* The Xhosa Tribal Poet and the Contemporary Poetic Tradition," *PMLA* 90.2 (March 1975): 185–208; Jeff Opland, "Praise Poems as Historical Sources," in Christopher Saunders and Robin Derricourt, *Beyond the Cape Frontier: Studies in the History of the Transkei and Ciskei* (London: Longmans, 1974), pp. 1–37; Jeff Opland, "*Scop* and *Imbongi* IV: Reading Praise Poems," *Comparative Literature* 45.2 (1993): 97–120; Jeff Opland, *Xhosa Oral Poetry* (Cambridge: Cambridge University Press, 1983); Rubusana, *Zemk' Inkomo Magwalandini ;* David Rycroft, "Zulu *Izibongo:* A Survey of Documentary Sources," *African Language Studies* 15 (1974): 55–79; David Rycroft, "Zulu and Xhosa Praise-Poetry and Song," *African Music* 3 (1962): 79–85; R. C. Samuelson, *Long, Long Ago* (Durban: Knox, 1929); Harold Scheub, "Oral Poetry and History," *New Literary History* 18 (1987): 477–496; James Stuart, *uBaxoxele* (London: Longmans, Green and Company, 1924), *uHlangakula* (London: Longmans, Green and Company, 1924), *uKulumetule* (London: Longmans, Green and Company, 1925), *uTulasizwe* (London: Longmans, Green and Company, 1929), *uVusezakiti* (London: Longmans, Green and Company, 1926); Leroy Vail and Landeg White, *Capitalism and Colonialism in Mozambique* (Minneapolis: University of Minnesota Press, 1980),

pp. 321–391; Leroy Vail and Landeg White, "Forms of Resistance: Oral Poetry and Perceptions of Power in Colonial Mozambique," *American Historical Review* 88.4 (1983): 883–919; Leroy Vail and Landeg White, "Ndebele Praise Poetry, 1835–1971," in Landeg White and Tim Couzens, eds., *Literature and Society in Southern Africa* (London: Longmans, 1984); Leroy Vail and Landeg White, "Plantation Protest: The History of a Mozambican Song," *Journal of Southern African Studies* 5.1 (October, 1978): 1–25; Leroy Vail and Landeg White, *Power and the Praise Poem: Southern African Voices in History* (Charlottesville: University Press of Virginia, 1991); N. J. Van Warmelo, *History of Matiwane and the amaNgwane Tribe* (Pretoria: Government Printer, 1938); N. J. Van Warmelo, *Transvaal Ndebele Texts* (Pretoria: Government Printer, 1930); Benedict Wallet Vilakazi, "The Conception and Development of Poetry in Zulu," *Bantu Studies* 12 (1938): 105–144; D. P. Yali-Manisi, *Izibongo zeenkosi zamaXhosa* (Lovedale: Lovedale Press, 1952).

30. From my collection. The poem was performed at the royal residence of Chief Diliz' Iintaba Mditshwa in 1967, with the chief in attendance, along with about two hundred people (122, tape 3, side 2).

31. Magagamela Koko, then eighty years old, created this poem in 1967 at his home in the Transkei in South Africa. His audience consisted of thirty Xhosa men, women, and children (451, tape 8, side 2).

32. Umhle Biyela, forty years old, performed these poems in 1972 in Yanguya, Zululand. His audience consisted of about thirty Zulu men, women, and children.

33. *Praise-Poems of Tswana Chiefs*, trans. and ed. I. Schapera (Oxford: Oxford University Press, 1965), p. 71, lines. 5–6. *Masonya* ("black ants") is a nickname of Kgamanyane's generation. "A two-pointed awl," according to Schapera, was a proverbial expression for someone playing a double game, and here it implies that Kgamanyane helped the Sotho as well as the Afrikaners (p. 71, n. 3).

34. Moloto, "The Growth and Tendencies of Tswana Poetry," p. 90. Moloto notes that "a two-faced person is known as *lamao lenthla pedi* [i.e., two-pointed awl], from experience with awls in the kaross-making trade of the Tswana" (p. 91).

35. From my collection. The poem was performed in 1972 before an audience of some seven Xhosa men (NS-486, tape 15, side 2).

36. Throughout South Africa, the young learned the poetry. Vilakazi, in "The Oral and Written Literature in Nguni," tells how every Zulu boy "was expected to know something of these praises, and to recite the most important ones, dealing first of all with his own ancestors and persons of importance still living" (p. 23). S. K. Lekgothoane notes that the Sotho "are taught hundreds and even thousands of lines of praise poems . . ." ("Praises of Animals in Northern Sotho," *Bantu Studies* 5 [1931]: 191).

37. Tyabashe's comments were made during conversations in 1967 in Tsolo District in the Transkei. I taped one of these conversations (79, tape 2, side 2).

38. He uses the word *ithongo* (dream, trance, nocturnal vision) which I have translated as "the world of dreams."

39. The word he uses here, *umoya*, signifies "spirit" or "ghost," or, alternately, "breath," "wind" or "air." I have translated it as "spirit."

40. Ngcama's comments were made before and after a series of poetry performances in Mount Ayliff District in the Transkei in 1972. One of those conversations, on August 24, 1972, was taped (NS-486, tape 15, side 2).

41. See, for example, Nongenile Masithathu Zenani, "A Woman Behaves Like

a Man," *The World and the Word: Tales and Observations from the Xhosa Oral Tradition* (Madison: University of Wisconsin Press, 1992) pp. 152–158.

42. Shakespeare, *King Richard II,* Act II, scene i, lines 41, 50, 66.

ALL THE LAND OF THE MPONDOMISE

1. Cf. Nelson Mandela, *Long Walk to Freedom: The Autobiography of Nelson Mandela* (Boston: Little Brown and Company, 1994), p. 21.

2. An *intsomi* is a fantasy story. I have retained the Xhosa term here, to dramatize the injection of fantasy tale into a historical account.

3. Literally, stomach of the cat.

4. The *imfecane* (called the *difaqane* among the Sotho) was the upheaval caused by wars in southeastern Africa. The effects of these wars were felt throughout this area, including cataclysmic political and economic changes.

5. Diliza Iintaba Mditshwa.

6. In Tsolo District.

7. The "other one" is Chief Sikizi.

8. "Across the river" in Qumbu District.

9. Mhlontlo (born in Xura, in Mpondoland, in 1837, died in Qumbu in 1912) was a Mpondomise king, the son of Matiwana, son of Myeki. When Mhlontlo was still a child, Matiwana was killed in a battle, and Mhlontlo's uncle, Mbali, became the regent. Mbali had to be forced to relinquish the throne when Mhlontlo came of age.

10. The Xhosa word, *bhaca,* means to wander about in a destitute state, to be homeless. An *imbhaca* is one who wanders in search of a home or livelihood, a refugee (Albert Kropf, *A Kafir-English Dictionary* [Alice: Lovedale Mission Press, 1915], p. 18). Hence, the origin of the name of the Bhaca people of the Transkei.

11. Joseph Millerd Orpen (born in Dublin on November 5, 1828, died in East London [South Africa] on December 17, 1923) was a surveyor, farmer, and member of the volksraad of the Orange Free State. In July, 1873, he was appointed magistrate of the area that included the Mpondomise, known to the South African whites as No Man's Land (later to be called Griqualand East). His headquarters were at Tsolo, among the Mpondomise. He represented the Cape Colony there, remaining until 1875.

THE LAND WAS SEIZED

1. A member of the audience asks, "At Gobe?"

THE LAND HAS GROWN OLD

1. John Ayliff (1797–1862) was a missionary who did mission work in the Transkei.

PART FOUR: UNCERTAIN HOPE

1. Carl G. Jung, "On the Psychology of the Trickster Figure," in Paul Radin, *The Trickster* (New York: Bell, 1956), p. 200.

2. Jan Christiaan Smuts (1870–1950) was a South African soldier and statesman, and prime minister of the Union of South Africa from 1919 to 1924 and from 1939 to 1948. Louis Botha (1862–1919), also a South African soldier and statesman, fought in the Anglo-Boer War. Jan van Riebeeck (1619–1677) represented the Dutch East India company in South Africa in 1652. He was a Dutch naval surgeon. Cecil John Rhodes (1853–1902) was a British administrator in South Africa, and one of the early diamond and gold magnates.

3. The story of Nongqawuse is often called a "cargo cult" story. Cargo cults have to do with a belief that a new age is about to dawn. That age will be ushered in when a "cargo" of goods arrives. That cargo will be sent by supernatural beings, gods, heroes, or ancestors. The living make elaborate preparations for the arrival of the cargo, believing that the old order will be destroyed and a new and splendid order will begin. Cargo cults are frequently led by prophets. See Peter Worsley, *The Trumpet Shall Sound: A Study of "Cargo" Cults in Melanesia* (London: MacGibbon and Kee, 1957). Worsley writes of "a third type of social situation in which activist millenarian ideas are likely to flourish. This comes about when a society with differentiated political institutions is fighting for its existence by quite secular military-political means, but is meeting with defeat after defeat. One may cite the case of the rise of the prophet Nongqause [*sic*] at a time when the Xhosa people were beginning to realize that they were losing the long-drawn-out Kaffir Wars" (p. 230). He later notes that "there have been many religious movements led by prophets—the Mahdi in the Sudan; Joan of Arc; Makana, Nongqause and Umlanjeni in South Africa—which were not specifically millenarian, but which had a similar political function" (p. 236). See also John Beattie, "Ritual and Social Change," *Man* 1 (1966): 60–74; William Beinart and Colin Bundy, *Hidden Struggles in Rural South Africa* (London: James Currey, 1987); Kenelm O. L. Burridge, *Mambu: A Melanesian Millennium* (London: Methuen, 1960), and *New Heaven New Earth: A Study of Millenarian Activities* (Oxford: Basil Blackwell, 1969); Jean Comaroff, *Body of Power, Spirit of Resistance: The Culture and History of a South African People* (Chicago: University of Chicago Press, 1985); Robert Edgar, *Prophets with Honor* (Johannesburg: Ravan Press, n.d.); Raymond Firth, *Symbols, Public and Private* (Ithaca: Cornell University Press, 1973); George M. Fredrickson, *Black Liberation* (Oxford: Oxford University Press, 1995); Louise Kretzschmar, *The Voice of Black Theology in South Africa* (Johannesburg: Ravan Press, 1986); Vittorio Lanternari, *The Religions of the Oppressed*, trans. Lisa Sergio (New York: Alfred A. Knopf, 1963); Peter Lawrence, *Road Belong Cargo* (Manchester: University Press, 1964); André Odendaal, *Vukani Bantu! The Beginnings of Black Protest Politics in South Africa to 1912* (Cape Town: David Philip, 1984); and B. G. M. Sundkler, *Bantu Prophets in South Africa* (London: Oxford University Press, 1948). Regarding Nongqawuse specifically, see also Charles Pacalt Brownlee, *Reminscences of Kafir Life and History* (Lovedale: Lovedale Press, 1896), pp. 126–159; John A. Chalmers, *Tiyo Soga: A Page of South African Mission Work* (Edinburgh: Andrew Elliot,

1877), pp. 101–129; Herbert I. E. Dhlomo, *The Girl Who Killed to Save: Nongqawuse the Liberator* (Alice, South Africa: Lovedale Press, 1936); Noël Mostert, *Frontiers* (New York: Alfred A. Knopf, 1992), pp. 1161–1242; J. B. Peires, *The Dead Will Arise: Nongqawuse and the Great Xhosa Cattle-Killing Movement of 1856–7* (Johannesburg: Ravan Press, 1989); J. Rutherford, *Sir George Grey* (London: Cassell, 1961), pp. 340–370; John Henderson Soga, "The Cattle-killing delusion—Nongqawuse," *The Ama-Xosa: Life and Customs* (Lovedale: Lovedale Press, 1931), pp. 121–122.

4. Velaphi Mzini, an eighty-year-old Ngqika man, said these words as he took me to kwaNkonki in Centane District in the Transkei, to show me Nongqawuse country. We were sitting on the edge of the Gxarha River near the Indian Ocean on the morning of September 9, 1967. Other elderly Xhosa men were also present. (580; tape 10, side 2)

5. John A. Chalmers, *Tiyo Soga*, pp. 101–129.

6. Herbert I. E. Dhlomo, *The Girl Who Killed to Save*, pp. 9, 25–26, 40–41.

7. A. C. Jordan, *Towards an African Literature: The Emergence of Literary Form in Xhosa* (Berkeley: University of California Press, 1973), pp. 69, 77, 78.

8. James J. R. Jolobe, "Ingqawule," in *Ilitha* (Johannesburg: Bona Press, 1959), pp. 40–59. I discussed my translation of this poem in a number of conversations with Mr. Jolobe in New Brighton in 1967, and later through correspondence.

9. From the transcript of court proceedings. At Chakijana's request, the crown appointed the lawyer, A. H. Hime, as his counsel for the defense.

10. Another witness, Magwababa, described Chakijana as a "man of no importance whatever," his father being "a household officer of Dinuzulu and Chakijana his water-carrier" (*The Greytown Gazette*, November 7, 1908, p. 5).

11. James Stuart notes that he was thirty-three years old at the time of the Bambatha Rebellion (*A History of the Zulu Rebellion, 1906, and of Dinuzulu's Arrest, Trial and Expatriation* [London: Macmillan, 1913], p. 501).

12. C. T. Binns, *Dinuzulu: The Death of the House of Shaka* (London: Longmans, Green and Company, 1968), p. 214.

13. Stuart, *A History of the Zulu Rebellion*, p. 501.

14. Stuart, *A History of the Zulu Rebellion*, p. 176, footnote.

15. Stuart, *A History of the Zulu Rebellion*, p. 176, footnote.

16. The discussion took place in February, 1968, in the Yanguye section of Ntonjaneni District, the Biyela area, Zululand (4070, tape 79, side 2).

17. *chakide*: a slender mongoose; in Latin, *herpestes gracilis*. A derivation, *ubuchakide*, means "cunning."

18. *zabafu*: abbreviation of *abafukazi*.

19. The mongoose just eats the head of fowl, says Ellen Biyela, leaving the rest. It is equally at home in trees and on the ground, and it lives in burrowed-out areas under rocks.

20. Jung, "On the Psychology of the Trickster Figure," p. 200.

21. Bambatha was born in the Mpanza valley near Greytown, Natal, c. 1865. He was the son of Mancinga (Sobuza), a member of the Zondi people; his mother was the daughter of Pakade, chief of the Cunu people.

22. But questions remained about the fate of Bambatha. Some questioned that the body identified as Bambatha was in fact the body of the renowned Zulu guer-

rilla. The body had already been decomposing when William J. Calverley found it, cut the head off, then rode with the head in his saddlebag. When the head had been identified in Nkandla, it was taken back to Mome Gorge and buried with Bambatha's body. Some argued that Bambatha had escaped to Mozambique, that the body belonged to someone else, that it was identified as Bambatha's by Joseph Nzama, a Zulu, "to give Bambatha the chance to escape" (C. T. Binns, *Dinuzulu: The Death of the House of Shaka* [London: Longmans, Green and Company, 1968], p. 280).

23. Leo Kuper, "African Nationalism in South Africa, 1910–1964," in Monica Wilson and Leonard Thompson, *The Oxford History of South Africa*, vol. 2 (Oxford: Oxford University Press, 1971), p. 345.

24. J. D. Omer-Cooper, *History of Southern Africa* (London: James Currey; Portsmouth, N.H.: Heinemann; Claremont, South Africa: David Philip, 1987), p. 154.

25. See also James Bryce, *Impressions of South Africa* (New York: Century, 1897); John Buchan, *Prester John* (London: T. Nelson, 1910); R. R. R. Dhlomo, *uDinuzulu kaCetshwayo* (Pietermaritzburg: Shuter and Shooter, 1968); Shula Marks, *Reluctant Rebellion: The 1906–8 Disturbances in Natal* (Oxford: Clarendon Press, 1970); Bertram Mitford, *The White Hand and the Black* (London: J. Long, 1907), James Stuart, *A History of the Zulu Rebellion*; and Benedict Wallet Vilakazi, *Nje-nempela* (Mariannhill: Mariannhill Mission Press, 1966).

26. See Harold Scheub, *Meanings* (Dubuque: Kendall/Hunt, 1994), pp. 37–38.

SHE SPOKE ABOUT THE RESURRECTION

1. For a detailed account of this event, and for other views of the incident, see J. B. Peires, *The Dead Will Arise: Nongqawuse and the Great Xhosa Cattle-Killing Movement of 1856–7* (Johannesburg: Ravan Press, 1989).

2. A member of the audience asks, "And this girl, was she there also?"

3. A member of the audience says, "Sarhili had called a meeting."

4. That is, among the Mpondomise. A member of the audience says, "At Qumbu."

5. A member of the audience asks, "And he came?"

CHAKIJANA, ZULU FREEDOM-FIGHTER

1. That is, the trickster, Chakijana, of the Zulu oral imaginative tradition.

SO EVERYBODY WAS AFTER CHAKIJANA

1. The "Basotho Rebellion" (1880–1881) was also called the War of the Guns. The South African government's attempt to disarm the Sotho led to the uprising. From September, 1880, until April 29, 1881, the war went on. The Sotho, under Chief Lerotholi, lost the war.

2. Lesotho.

3. 1906.

4. Duncan McKenzie (1859–1932), a Natal soldier and farmer, fought in the second Anglo-Boer War. He commanded the Natal force that, in 1906, fought Bambatha and Dinuzulu. In 1908, he became commander-in-chief of the Natal forces.

5. A washed out ravine or gully.

6. Circa 1870–1913.

7. The Bambatha Rebellion.

8. Harriette Emily (1847–1932) and Francis Ellen (1849–1887) were the daughters of John William Colenso (1814–1883), Bishop of Natal.

THE WHITES WERE TO BE KILLED

1. This was on May 4th, 1906. He was murdered "not by the main body of the rebel army and a considerable distance away from the scene of operations" [p. 216]. "For most of the tribesmen in the area, Stainbank's murder probably came as a relief. He was extremely unpopular in the division, not only because of his slaughter of infected cattle during the outbreak of East Coast fever but also because he was extremely highhanded and rude to the leading chiefs of the area. In April 1906 the Commissioner for Native Affairs had actually recommended his transfer for this reason. Not only did the people of Mahlabatini not want to be involved in the processes of an alien law—they also sympathized entirely with whoever it was who killed the magistrate. . . . After four or five unsuccessful attempts to find the Africans responsible for the murder, in 1912 the Natal government prosecuted Mayatana for the crime and he was found guilty by the Natal Supreme Court, and sentenced to death. Yet again the plea was an order from Dinuzulu, whose attendant he was. Like Cakijana [Chakijana], Mayatana had been employed as a police spy in 1908: he was used to track down Cakijana. In 1911 there were reports that Cakijana had been released to find the Stainbank murderer. In neither of their cases can much reliance be placed on this plea of an order from Dinuzulu. It is impossible to be dogmatic about the murders in Zululand in 1906–7. On the whole, it seems unlikely that Dinuzulu personally hatched the plots or was a party to them, although he may have been turning a discreet blind eye, especially in connection with the murder of Gence. If there was a single master-mind between all the murders, all the clues lead to Cakijana rather than Dinuzulu, although it is impossible to assess how much Dinuzulu knew or approved of his schemes" (Shula Marks, *Reluctant Rebellion: The 1906–8 Disturbances in Natal* [Oxford: Clarendon Press, 1970], pp. 298–300).

EPILOGUE: SEIZERS OF THE INHERITANCE

1. Magagamela Koko, a Mfengu, eighty years old, performed this poem on August 31, 1967, in a home overlooking the Kei River valley in Nqancule, Ngqamakhwe District, the Transkei. In the audience were ten women, two men, and ten children. (451; tape 8, side 2.)

2. Donald Hall, *Poetry: The Unsayable Said* (Port Townsend, Washington: Cooper Canyon Press, 1993), pp. 2, 3. The "small poem" of which he writes is "A Farm Picture," by Walt Whitman.

3. Claude Lévi-Strauss, *The Raw and the Cooked*, trans. John and Doreen Weightman (New York: Harper and Row, 1969), p. 17.

4. E. M. Forster, *Aspects of the Novel* (London: E. Arnold, 1927), pp. 169, 170. Cf. E. K. Brown, *Rhythm in the Novel* (Toronto: University of Toronto Press, 1950), and Bruce F. Kawin, *Telling It Again and Again* (Ithaca: Cornell University Press, 1972).

5. Arthur Dart Bissell, *The Role of Expectation in Music* (New Haven: Yale University Press, 1921), p. xii.

6. Bissell, *The Role of Expectation in Music*, p. 53.

7. Leonard Bernstein, *The Unanswered Question: Six Talks at Harvard* (Cambridge: Harvard University Press, 1976) p. 162.

8. I. A. Richards, *Principles of Literary Criticism* (New York: Harcourt, Brace and Company, 1925), pp. 134, 137–138.

9. Henry David Aiken, "The Aesthetic Relevance of Belief," *Journal of Aesthetics and Art Criticism* 9 (1951): 301.

10. See Harold Scheub, "Narrative Patterning in Oral Performance," *Ba Shiru* 7.2 (1976): 29. See also Scheub, "Body and Image in Oral Narrative Performance," *New Literary History* 8 (1976–1977): 345–367. These conclusions were derived from my conversations with southern African storytellers, and especially with Nongenile Masithathu Zenani. See reports of her commentaries in Nongenile Masithathu Zenani, *The World and the Word: Tales and Observations from the Xhosa Oral Tradition* (Madison: University of Wisconsin Press, 1992), pp. 19–20, 81–87, 269–271, 373–375.

11. Leonard B. Meyer, *Emotion and Meaning in Music* (Chicago: University of Chicago Press, 1956), p. 31. See also Leonard B. Meyer, *Music, the Arts and Ideas* (Chicago: University of Chicago Press, 1967).

12. John Paul Spiegel and Pavel Machotka, *Messages of the Body* (New York: The Free Press, 1974), p. 38.

13. Scheub, "Body and Image in Oral Narrative Performance," pp. 345–367. See also Jonathan Benthall and Ted Polhemus, eds., *The Body as a Medium of Expression* (London: Allen Lane, 1975), especially Donald G. MacRae, "The Body and Social Metaphor," pp. 59–73, and David Crystal, "Paralinguistics," pp. 162–174.

14. The analytical comments that follow are based on discussions that I had with Nomusa Makhoba regarding Jabulani's growth into manhood.

JABULANI ALONE

1. Literally, badly.

2. I. e., dowry.

3. That is, he is a philanderer.

4. Makhoba notes, parenthetically, "It was believed that these bones were used for divining in the beginning."

5. He is addressing the divining bones.

6. An herb.

7. That is, I am dying.

8. The storyteller frequently refers to Jabulani's father's younger brother as his "father." To avoid confusion, I have consistently translated it as "uncle."

9. That is, just for the sake of token eating.

10. Perhaps a drain furrow.

11. That is, that it is spoiling.

12. *umNtungwa* is the praise name for a group of clans, which includes the Khumalo people.

13. *Jabula* means "rejoice, be happy."

14. This symbolic offering is a part of the ritual having to do with the consecration of the new home site.

15. That is, a foolish woman.

16. Ntunjambili, the Rock-of-two-holes, is a site in many Zulu tales.

17. That is, poisons a person.

18. The suggestion is that the children were illegitimate.

Sources

Achebe, Chinua. *Chinua Achebe* (film). Princeton: Films for the Humanities and Sciences, 1995.

Aiken, Henry David. "The Aesthetic Relevance of Belief." *Journal of Aesthetics and Art Criticism* 9 (1951): 301–315.

Beattie, John. "Ritual and Social Change." *Man* 1 (1966): 60–74.

Beinart, William, and Colin Bundy. *Hidden Struggles in Rural South Africa.* London: James Currey, 1987.

Benthall, Jonathan, and Ted Polhemus, eds. *The Body as a Medium of Expression.* London: Allen Lane, 1975.

Bernstein, Leonard. *The Unanswered Question: Six Talks at Harvard.* Cambridge: Harvard University Press, 1976.

Bhotomane, Ndumiso England. Xhosa historian.

Biko, Steve. "Black Consciousness and the Quest for True Humanity." *Reality,* 4.1 (March 1972): 4–10.

Binns, C. T. *Dinuzulu: The Death of the House of Shaka.* London: Longmans, Green and Company, 1968.

Bissell, Arthur Dart. *The Role of Expectation in Music.* New Haven: Yale University Press, 1921.

Biyela, Ellen. Zulu storyteller.

Biyela, Umhle. Zulu poet.

Bokako, Edison M. "Bo-Santagane: An Anthology of Tswana Heroic Verse." In manuscript, Kimberley, 1938. Collection of Z. K. Matthews, Manuscripts Division, University of Cape Town.

Boyd, Charles G. "Making Peace with the Guilty: The Truth about Bosnia." *Foreign Affairs* 74.5 (September/October, 1995): 22–38.

Branford, Jean. *A Dictionary of South African English.* Cape Town: Oxford University Press, 1980.

Brombert, Victor. "The Idea of the Hero." In *The Hero in Literature,* edited by Victor Brombert, pp. 11–21. Greenwich, Conn.: Fawcett, 1969.

Brown, E. K. *Rhythm in the Novel.* Toronto: University of Toronto Press, 1950.

Brownlee, Charles Pacalt. *Reminiscences of Kafir Life and History.* Lovedale: Lovedale Press, 1896.

Bryce, James. *Impressions of South Africa.* New York: Century, 1897.

Buchan, John. *Prester John.* London: T. Nelson, 1910.

Burckhardt, Jacob. *The Civilization of the Renaissance in Italy.* Translated by S. C. C. Middlemore. London: Penguin Books, 1990.

Burridge, Kenelm O. L. *Mambu: A Melanesian Millennium.* London: Methuen, 1960.

Burridge, Kenelm O. L. *New Heaven New Earth: A Study of Millenarian Activities.* Oxford: Basil Blackwell, 1969.

Calverley, Frederick William. Resident of Zululand.

Carr, David. "Narrative and the Real World: An Argument for Continuity." *History and Theory*, 25.2 (1986): 117–131.

Chalmers, John A. *Tiyo Soga: A Page of South African Mission Work*. Edinburgh: Andrew Elliot, 1877.

"Choice, The." *South African Outlook*. 106 (August 1976): 114.

Cobble, Thomas J. *Black Testimony: The Voices of Britain's West Indians*. Philadelphia: Temple University Press, 1980.

Coetzee, J. M. *Life & Times of Michael K*. New York: Viking Press, 1984.

Comaroff, Jean. *Body of Power, Spirit of Resistance: The Culture and History of a South African People*. Chicago: University of Chicago Press, 1985.

Cook, P. A. W. "History and *Izibongo* of the Swazi Chiefs." *Bantu Studies*, 5 (1931): 181–201.

Cope, Trevor. *Izibongo, Zulu Praise-Poems*. Oxford: Clarendon Press, 1968.

Cosentino, Donald. *Defiant Maids and Stubborn Farmers*. Cambridge: Cambridge University Press, 1982.

Crystal, David. "Paralinguistics." In *The Body as a Medium of Expression*, edited by Jonathan Benthall and Ted Polhemus, pp. 162–174. London: Allen Lane, 1975.

Curtin, Philip D. *The Image of Africa: British Ideas and Action, 1780–1850*. Madison: University of Wisconsin Press, 1964.

Damane, M., and P. B. Sanders, eds. *Lithoko, Sotho Praise-Poems*. Oxford: Clarendon Press, 1974.

Davenport, T. R. H. *South Africa: A Modern History*. Toronto: University of Toronto Press, 1977.

Davis, Stuart. *Stuart Davis*. Edited by Diane Kelder. New York: Praeger, 1971.

Dhlomo, Herbert I. E. *The Girl Who Killed to Save: Nongqawuse the Liberator*. Alice, South Africa: Lovedale Press, 1936.

Dhlomo, R. R. R. *uDinuzulu kaCetshwayo*. Pietermaritzburg: Shuter and Shooter, 1968.

Dhlomo, R. R. R. *uShaka*. Pietermaritzburg: Shuter and Shooter, 1937.

Du Toit, Brian. *Content and Form of Zulu Folk-narratives*. Gainesville: University Presses of Florida, 1976.

Ecclesiasticus. In: The Apochrypha.

Edgar, Robert. *Because They Chose the Plan of God*. Johannesburg: Ravan Press, 1988.

Edgar, Robert. *Prophets with Honor*. Johannesburg: Ravan Press, n.d.

Eliade, Mircea. *Myth and Reality*. Translated by Willard R. Trask. New York: Harper and Row, 1963.

Ellsworth, Margaret. "The Rejection of Bantu Education." *South African Outlook* 106 (August 1976): 124–125.

Elphick, Richard. *Kraal and Castle: Khoikhoi and the Founding of White South Africa*. New Haven: Yale University Press, 1977.

Feierman, Steven. *The Shambaa Kingdom: A History*. Madison: University of Wisconsin Press, 1974.

Fernández-Armesto, Felipe. *Millennium: A History of the Last Thousand Years*. New York: Scribner, 1995.

Fernández-Armesto, Felipe. "Rewriting History." *Index on Censorship*, 24.3 (May/June 1995): 25–32.

Finnegan, Ruth. *Oral Poetry*. Cambridge: Cambridge University Press, 1977.

Firth, Raymond. *Symbols, Public and Private.* Ithaca: Cornell University Press, 1973.

Forster, E. M. *Aspects of the Novel.* London: E. Arnold, 1927.

Fredrickson, George M. *Black Liberation.* Oxford: Oxford University Press, 1995.

Furness, Graham, and Elizabeth Gunner, eds. *Power, Marginality and African Oral Literature.* Cambridge: Cambridge University Press, 1995.

Fuze, Magema M. *Abantu Abamnyama Lapha Bavela Ngakhona.* Pietermaritzburg: City Printing Works, 1922.

Gerhart, Gail M. *Black Power in South Africa: The Evolution of an Ideology.* Berkeley: University of California Press, 1978.

Goodwin, June, and Benn Schiff. "Who Killed Steve Biko?" *Nation* 261 (November 13, 1995): 565–568.

Gordimer, Nadine. *July's People.* New York: Viking Press, 1981.

Grant, E. W. "The *Izibongo* of the Zulu Chiefs." *Bantu Studies* 3.3 (1929): 203–244.

Greytown Gazette, The (Greytown, South Africa), November 7, 1908.

Gunner, Elizabeth. *Musho! Zulu Popular Praises.* Translated and edited by Elizabeth Gunner and Mafika Gwala. East Lansing: Michigan State University Press, 1991.

Gunner, Elizabeth. *Politics and Performance: Theatre, Poetry, and Song in Southern Africa.* Johannesburg: University of the Witwatersrand Press, 1994.

Gunner, Elizabeth. "Songs of Innocence and Experience: Women as Composers and Performers of *Izibongo,* Zulu Praise Poetry." *Research in African Literatures* 10 (1979): 239–267.

Gxavu, Noplani. Xhosa storyteller.

Hall, Donald. *Poetry: The Unsayable Said.* Port Townsend, Washington: Cooper Canyon Press, 1993.

Havelock, Eric. *Preface to Plato.* New York: Grosset and Dunlap, 1967.

Hopkinson, Tom. *In the Fiery Continent.* Garden City: Doubleday, 1963.

Jolobe, James J. R. "Ingqawule." In *Ilitha,* pp. 40–59. Johannesburg: Bona Press, 1959.

Jordan, A. C. *Tales from Southern Africa.* Berkeley: University of California Press, 1973.

Jordan, A. C. *Towards an African Literature: The Emergence of Literary Form in Xhosa.* Berkeley: University of California Press, 1973.

Julien, Eileen. *African Novels and the Question of Orality.* Bloomington: Indiana University Press, 1992.

Jung, Carl G. "On the Psychology of the Trickster Figure." In *The Trickster,* edited by Paul Radin, pp. 195–211. New York: Bell, 1956.

Kane-Berman, John. *Soweto: Black Revolt, White Reaction.* Johannesburg: Ravan Press, 1978.

Kawin, Bruce F. *Telling It Again and Again.* Ithaca: Cornell University Press, 1972.

Klee, Paul. *Notebooks,* volume I (*The Thinking Eye*). New York: Wittenborn Art Books, 1961.

Koko, Magagamela. Xhosa poet.

Kretzschmar, Louise. *The Voice of Black Theology in South Africa.* Johannesburg: Ravan Press, 1986.

Kropf, Albert. *A Kafir-English Dictionary.* Alice, South Africa: Lovedale Mission Press, 1915.

Kruger, James. Speech to the Transvaal Congress of the National Party, September, 1977. *South African Outlook* 107 (September 1977): 142.

Kunene, Daniel P. *Heroic Poetry of the Basotho.* Oxford: Clarendon Press, 1971.

Kuper, Leo. "African Nationalism in South Africa, 1910–1964." In *The Oxford History of South Africa,* edited by Monica Wilson and Leonard Thompson, vol. 2, pp. 424–476. Oxford: Oxford University Press, 1971.

Lamula, P. *Isabelo sikaZulu.* Pietermaritzburg: Shuter and Shooter, 1936.

Lanternari, Vittorio. *The Religions of the Oppressed.* Translated by Lisa Sergio. New York: Alfred A. Knopf, 1963.

Lawrence, Peter. *Road Belong Cargo.* Manchester: University Press, 1964.

Lekgothoane, S. K. "Praises of Animals in Northern Sotho," *Bantu Studies* 12 (1938): 189–213.

Lessing, Doris. "The Black Madonna." In *African Stories,* pp. 11–24. New York: Simon and Schuster, 1965.

Lestrade, G. P. "Bantu Praise-Poems." *The Critic,* 4 (1937): 1–10.

Lestrade, G. P. "Traditional Literature." In *The Bantu-speaking Tribes of South Africa,* edited by Isaac Schapera, pp. 291–308. London: Routledge, 1937.

Lévi-Strauss, Claude. *The Raw and the Cooked.* Translated by John and Doreen Weightman. New York: Harper and Row, 1969.

Lowell, Robert. "History." In *History,* p. 24. New York: Farrar, Straus and Giroux, 1973.

MacLeisch, Archibald. *Poetry and Experience.* Baltimore: Penguin Books, 1964.

MacRae, Donald G. "The Body and Social Metaphor." In *The Body as a Medium of Expression,* edited by Jonathan Benthall and Ted Polhemus, pp. 59–73. London: Allen Lane, 1975.

Mafeje, Archie. "The Role of a Bard in a Contemporary African Community," *Journal of African Languages* 4.3 (1967): 193–223.

Makhoba, Nomusa. Zulu storyteller.

Mamba, Mtshophane. Swati poet.

Mandela, Nelson. *Long Walk to Freedom: The Autobiography of Nelson Mandela.* Boston: Little, Brown and Company, 1994.

Marks, Shula. *Reluctant Rebellion: The 1906–8 Disturbances in Natal.* Oxford: Clarendon Press, 1970.

Marquard, Leo. *The Peoples and Policies of South Africa.* London: Oxford University Press, 1962.

Márquez, Gabriel García. *Of Love and Other Demons.* Translated by Edith Grossman. New York: Albert A. Knopf, 1995.

Márquez, Gabriel García. *One Hundred Years of Solitude.* Translated by Gregory Rabassa. New York: Harper and Row, 1970.

Matsebula, J. S. M. *Izakhiwo zamaSwazi.* Johannesburg: Afrikaanse Pers-Boekhandel, 1948.

Matshikiza, John. "And I Watch it in Mandela." In *Poets to the People, South African Freedom Poems,* edited by Barry Feinberg, p. 138. London: Heinemann, 1980.

Meyer, Leonard B. *Emotion and Meaning in Music.* Chicago: University of Chicago Press, 1956.

Meyer, Leonard B. *Music, the Arts and Ideas.* Chicago: University of Chicago Press, 1967.

Mitford, Bertram. *The White Hand and the Black.* London: J. Long, 1907.

Mofokeng, S. M. "Notes and Annotations of the Praise-Poems of Certain Chiefs and the Structure of Praise-poems in Southern Sotho." Ph. D. diss., Bantu Studies, University of the Witwatersrand (Johannesburg), 1945.

Moloto, Ernest Sedumeli. "The Growth and Tendencies of Tswana Poetry." Ph. D. diss., University of South Africa (Pretoria), 1970.

Mostert, Noël. *Frontiers.* New York: Alfred A. Knopf, 1992.

Mphahlele, Es'kia [Ezekiel]. *Down Second Avenue.* Garden City: Doubleday, 1971.

Murray, Martin. *South Africa: Time of Agony, Time of Destiny.* London: Verso, 1987.

Mzini, Velaphi. Xhosa historian.

Ndawo, H. M. *Izibongo zenkosi zamaHlubi nezamaBhaca.* Mariannhill: Mariannhill Mission Press, 1928.

Ndlovu, Eva. Ndebele storyteller.

Ngcama, Ashton. Xhosa poet.

Ngcobo, Sondoda. Zulu storyteller and historian.

Ntsobane, Emily. Xhosa storyteller.

Nyembezi, C. L. S. "The Historical Background to the Izibongo of the Zulu Military Age" *African Studies* 7.2–3 (1948): 110–125; 7.4 (1948): 157–174.

Nyembezi, C. L. S. *Izibongo zamakhosi.* Pietermaritzburg: Shuter and Shooter, 1958.

Oakes, Dougie, ed. *The Real Story.* Pleasantville: The Reader's Digest Association, 1988.

Odendaal, André. *Vukani Bantu! The Beginnings of Black Protest Politics in South Africa to 1912.* Cape Town: David Philip, 1984.

Okpewho, Isidore. *African Oral Literature.* Bloomington: Indiana University Press, 1992.

Omer-Cooper, J. D. *History of Southern Africa.* London: James Currey; Portsmouth, N.H.: Heinemann; and Claremont, South Africa: David Philip, 1987.

Opland, Jeff. "*Imbongi Nezibongo:* The Xhosa Tribal Poet and the Contemporary Poetic Tradition." *PMLA* 90.2 (March 1975): 185–208.

Opland, Jeff. "Praise Poems as Historical Sources." In *Beyond the Cape Frontier: Studies in the History of the Transkei and Ciskei,* edited by Christopher Saunders and Robin Derricourt, pp. 1–37. London: Longman, 1974.

Opland, Jeff. "*Scop* and *Imbongi* IV: Reading Praise Poems." *Comparative Literature* 45.2 (1993): 97–120.

Opland, Jeff. *Xhosa Oral Poetry.* Cambridge: Cambridge University Press, 1983.

Paton, Alan. *Cry, the Beloved Country.* New York: Charles Scribner's Sons, 1948.

Peires, J. B. *The Dead Will Arise: Nongqawuse and the Great Xhosa Cattle-Killing Movement of 1856–7.* Johannesburg: Ravan Press, 1989.

Peires, J. B. *The House of Phalo.* Berkeley: University of California Press, 1982.

Raven-Hart, R. *Before Van Riebeeck: Callers at South Africa from 1488 to 1652.* Cape Town: C. Struik, Pty., 1967.

Reitz, Deneys. *No Outspan.* London: Faber and Faber, 1943.

Richards, I. A. *Principles of Literary Criticism.* New York: Harcourt, Brace and Co., 1925.

Romero, Patricia W., ed. *Life Histories of African Women.* London: Ashfield Press, 1988.

Roux, Edward. *Time Longer than Rope: A History of the Black Man's Struggle for Freedom in South Africa.* Madison: University of Wisconsin Press, 1964.

Rubusana, W. B. *Zemk' Inkomo Magwalandini.* London: Butler and Tanner, 1911.

Rutherford, J. *Sir George Grey.* London: Cassell, 1961.

Rycroft, David. "Zulu and Xhosa Praise-Poetry and Song." *African Music* 3 (1962): 79–85.

Rycroft, David. "Zulu *Izibongo:* A Survey of Documentary Sources." *African Language Studies* 15 (1974): 55–79.

Samuelson, R. C. *Long, Long Ago.* Durban: Knox, 1929.

Schama, Simon. *Citizens.* New York: Alfred A. Knopf, 1989.

Schapera, I. *Praise-Poems of Tswana Chiefs.* Oxford: Oxford University Press, 1965.

Scheub, Harold. "Body and Image in Oral Narrative Performance" *New Literary History* 8 (1976–1977): 345–367.

Scheub, Harold. "Fixed and Non-Fixed Symbols in Xhosa and Zulu Oral Narrative Traditions" *Journal of American Folklore* 85 (1972): 267–273.

Scheub, Harold. *Meanings.* Dubuque: Kendall/Hunt, 1994.

Scheub, Harold. "Narrative Patterning in Oral Performance" *Ba Shiru,* 7.2 (1976): 10–30.

Scheub, Harold. "Oral Poetry and History" *New Literary History* 18 (1986–1987): 477–496.

Scheub, Harold. "Oral Narrative Process and the Use of Models" *New Literary History* 6.2 (Winter 1975): 353–377.

Scheub, Harold. "Parallel Image-Sets in African Oral Performances" *Review of National Literatures* 2 (1971): 206–223.

Scheub, Harold. "The Technique of the Expansible Image in Xhosa *Ntsomi-*performances" *Research in African Literatures,* 1 (1970): 119–146.

Scheub, Harold. "Translation of African Oral Narrative-Performances to the Written Word" *Yearbook of Comparative and General Literature,* no. 20 (1971): 28–36.

Scheub, Harold. "Xhosa Oral and Literary Traditions," *Literatures in African Languages, Theoretical Issues and Sample Surveys,* edited by B. W. Andrzejewski, S. Pilaszewicz, and W. Tyloch, pp. 529–609. Cambridge: Cambridge University Press, 1985.

Scheub, Harold. *The Xhosa Ntsomi.* Oxford: Clarendon Press, 1975.

Scheub, Harold. "Zulu Oral Tradition and Literature." *Literatures in African Languages, Theoretical Issues and Sample Surveys,* edited by B. W. Andrzejewski, S. Pilaszewicz, and W. Tyloch, pp. 493–528. Cambridge: Cambridge University Press, 1985.

Segoete, Everitt Lechesa. *Raphepheng.* Morija: Morija Sesuto Book Depot, 1913.

Sekese, Azariele M. *Mekhoa Le Maele a Ba-Sotho.* Morija: Morija Sesuto Book Depot, 1931.

Senghor, Léopold Sédar. "On Negrohood: Psychology of the African-Negro," *Diogenes,* no. 37 (1962): 1–15.

Sepamla, Sipho. *A Ride on the Whirlwind.* London: Heinemann, 1981.

Small, Adam. "Steve Biko." *Drum* (November 1977): 21.

Soga, John Henderson. *The Ama-Xosa: Life and Customs.* Lovedale: Lovedale Press, 1931.

Solilo, John. "Mthandi Wesizwe." In *Imibengo,* edited by W. G. Bennie, pp. 169–170. Lovedale: Lovedale Press, 1935.

Sontag, Susan. "Against Interpretation." In *Against Interpretation,* pp. 3–14. New York: Farrar, Straus and Giroux, 1965.

Sparks, Allister. *Tomorrow Is Another Country: The Inside Story of South Africa's Road to Change.* New York: Hill and Wang, 1995.

Spiegel, John Paul, and Pavel Machotka. *Messages of the Body.* New York: The Free Press, 1974.

Stuart, James. *A History of the Zulu Rebellion, 1906, and of Dinuzulu's Arrest, Trial and Expatriation.* London: Macmillan, 1913.

Stuart, James. *uBaxoxele.* London: Longmans, Green and Company, 1924.

Stuart, James. *uHlangakula.* London: Longmans, Green and Company, 1924.

Stuart, James. *uKulumetule.* London: Longmans, Green and Company, 1925.

Stuart, James. *uTulasizwe.* London: Longmans, Green and Company, 1929.

Stuart, James. *uVusezakiti.* London: Longmans, Green and Company, 1926.

Sundkler, B. G. M. *Bantu Prophets in South Africa.* London: Oxford University Press, 1948.

Thompson, Leonard. *A History of South Africa.* New Haven: Yale University Press, 1990.

Tlali, Miriam. *Amandla.* Johannesburg: Ravan Press, 1980.

Tolkien, J. R. R. "*Beowulf:* The Monster and the Critics." In *The Beowulf Poet,* edited by Donald K. Fry, pp. 8–56. Englewood Cliffs, N.J.: Prentice-Hall, 1968.

Tyabashe, Mdukiswa. Xhosa poet and historian.

Tyler, Humphrey, et al. "Sharpeville and After." *Africa Today.* 7.3 (1960): 5–8.

Vail, Leroy, and Landeg White. *Capitalism and Colonialism in Mozambique.* Minneapolis: University of Minnesota Press, 1980.

Vail, Leroy, and Landeg White. "Forms of Resistance: Oral Poetry and Perceptions of Power in Colonial Mozambique." *American Historical Review* 88.4 (1983): 883–919.

Vail, Leroy, and Landeg White. "Ndebele Praise Poetry, 1835–1971." In *Literature and Society in Southern Africa,* edited by Landeg White and Tim Couzens. London: Longmans, 1984.

Vail, Leroy, and Landeg White. "Plantation Protest: The History of a Mozambican Song." *Journal of Southern African Studies* 5.1 (October 1978): 1–25.

Vail, Leroy, and Landeg White. *Power and the Praise Poem: Southern African Voices in History.* Charlottesville: University Press of Virginia, 1991.

Van Niekerk, P. W. Magistrate in Zululand.

Van Riebeeck, Jan. *Précis of the Cape Archives: Letters Despatched, 1652–1662.* Edited by H. C. M. Leibbrandt. Cape Town: W. A. Richards and Sons, 1900.

Vansina, Jan. *Oral Tradition as History.* Madison: University of Wisconsin Press, 1985.

Van Warmelo, N. J. *History of Matiwane and the amaNgwane Tribe.* Pretoria: Government Printer, 1938.

Van Warmelo, N. J. *Transvaal Ndebele Texts.* Pretoria: Government Printer, 1930.

Veyne, Paul. *Writing History: Essay on Epistemology.* Translated by Mina Moore-Rinvolucri. Middletown, Conn.: Wesleyan University Press, 1984.

Vilakazi, Benedict Wallet. "The Conception and Development of Poetry in Zulu." *Bantu Studies* 12 (1938): 105–144.

Vilakazi, Benedict Wallet. *Nje-nempela*. Mariannhill: Mariannhill Mission Press, 1966.

Vilakazi, Benedict Wallet. "The Oral and Written Literature in Nguni." Ph. D. diss., University of the Witwatersrand, Johannesburg, 1945.

Voltaire. *Works: A Contemporary Version*. Translated by By W. F. Fleming. London: The St. Hubert's Guild, n.d.

Wallerstein, Immanuel. *The Modern World System*, vol. 1. New York: Academic Press, 1974.

White, Hayden. "The Value of Narrativity in the Representation of Reality." In *On Narrative*, edited by W. J. T. Mitchell, pp. 1–23. Chicago: University of Chicago Press, 1981.

Wilson, Monica, and Leonard Thompson, eds. 2 volumes. *The Oxford History of South Africa*. Oxford: Oxford University Press, 1969, 1971.

Woods, Donald. *Biko*. New York: Paddington Press, 1978.

Worsley, Peter. *The Trumpet Shall Sound: A Study of "Cargo" Cults in Melanesia*. London: MacGibbon and Kee, 1957.

Yali-Manisi, D. P. *Izibongo zeenkosi zamaXhosa*. Lovedale: Lovedale Press, 1952.

Zenani, Nongenile Masithathu. Xhosa storyteller.

Zenani, Nongenile Masithathu. "'And So I Grew Up': The Autobiography of Nongenile Masithathu Zenani," translated and edited by Harold Scheub. In *Life Histories of African Women*, edited by Patricia W. Romero, pp. 7–46. Atlantic Highlands: The Ashfield Press, 1988.

Zenani, Nongenile Masithathu. *The World and the Word: Tales and Observations from the Xhosa Oral Tradition*. Edited by Harold Scheub. Madison: University of Wisconsin Press, 1992.

Index

Abyssinia, 277
Achebe, Chinua, 28, 405*n9*
Addis Ababa, 16, 404*n28*
Aesop's fables, xviii
Aesthetic experience, 365; aesthetics of performance, 150, 151, 210; aesthetic tension, 150–58
African National Congress, 9, 13, 15, 16; banning of, 13
Africans: disparity in education funds, 403–4*n20*; education, 403–4*n20*; and Europeans, xxi, 9, 10, 13–14, 205, 206, 293–301, 304–13, 362, 365, 369–94; resistance, 12; rights, 11; unity, 11
Afrikaans, 13
Afrikaner: origin of the name, 403*n6*; nationalism, 8; Afrikaner Party, 12
Afrikaners, 6, 7, 8, 9, 11, 12, 13, 217, 293, 300, 334–45, 346–57, 358, 413*n33*; Boer army, 271; Boer republics, 8; support of Germany, 12. *See also* Dutch
Aiken, Henry David: "The Aesthetic Relevance of Belief," 364, 419*n9*
Amafelandawonye (the Die-hards) movement, 11
Amankazana, 408*n2*
Amanzimtoti, 346
American blacks, 11–12
Ancestors, 219, 289, 311
Anglo-Boer War, 9, 299–300, 334, 347, 415*n2*
Anta, 39
Anti-white ideology, 11
Apartheid, xv, xvi, xvii, xviii, xxii, xxiii, xxiv, xxv, 9, 12, 13, 21, 24, 28, 52, 57, 162, 205, 293, 301, 367–68; definition, 403*n15*; grand apartheid, 403*n15*; laws, 12; petty apartheid, 403*n15*
Apocrypha, 404*n1*
Archie, 33, 38, 41, 42
Audience of oral performance, 28, 53, 54, 55, 57, 150–58, 209, 213, 219, 362, 365, 410*nn4, 11*
Ayliff, John, 46, 284, 407*n14*, 414*n1*
Ayliff Memorial Church, 46

Badzir, 43
Bala, 229
Bamba, 279, 306
Bambatha, xxvi, 6, 8, 10, 301, 303, 334–45, 346–57, 358, 418*n4*; beheading of, 10, 351–52; birth, 416*n21*, 417*n22*
Bambatha Rebellion, 10, 293, 300–301, 334–45, 346–57, 358, 416*n11*, 418*nn1, 7*
Banning of Pan Africanist Congress and African National Congress, 13
Bantu education act, 12
Bards. *See* poets
Barnato, Barney, 8–9
Basotho Rebellion, 347–48, 417*n1*
Battle of Blood River, 7
Bawa, 279
Bazindlovu, 42
Beattie, John: "Ritual and Social Change," 415*n3*
Beeckman, Daniel, 402*n3*
Beinart, William: "*Amafelandawonye* (the Die-hards)," 403*n14*
Beinart, William, and Colin Bundy: *Hidden Struggles in Rural South Africa*, 403*n14*, 415*n3*
Bennie, W. G., ed.: *Imibengo*, 404*n26*
Benthall, Jonathan, and Ted Polhemus, eds.: *The Body as a Medium of Expression*, 419*n13*
Beowulf, 203
Bernstein, Leonard: *The Unanswered Question*, 157, 364, 410*n9*, 419*n7*
Bethany, 276
Bhaca, 253, 254, 255, 256, 270, 412*n29*, 414*n10*; defined, 414*n10*; and the Mpondomise, 253–57, 270
Bhacela, 406*n11*
Bhayi, 43
Bhekamuzi Valley, 355
Bhengele, 215
Bhisa River, 230, 231, 232
Bhobhozayo, 39
Bhobhu, 284, 285
Bhodi, 250
Bhojini, 35

Bhokleni, 257

Bholo, 41, 42

Bhota, 35

Bhotomane, 36, 280, 281, 304, 306

Bhotomane, Ndumiso England, xvii, xviii, xxiv, xxv, 21, 24, 25, 27, 31–47, 51, 52, 150, 221, 222, 293, 367, 405nn10, 11; "The Land Was Seized," 205, 279–81; "Origins of the Xhosa," 31–47; "She Spoke about the Resurrection," 297–98, 304–6

Bhukwana, 240

Bhulekane, 272

Bhungane, 223

Bhuru, 35, 279, 280, 305, 306

Bika, 280, 281

Biko, Bantu Stephen, 6, 14–15; "Black Consciousness and the Quest for True Humanity," 404n22

Binns, C. T.: Dinuzulu: The Death of the House of Shaka, 416n12, 417n22

Bissell, Arthur Dart: The Role of Expectation in Music, 362, 364, 419n5, 6

Biyela, Ellen, 299

Biyela, Umhle, 25–27, 217, 218, 405n7, 413n32

Biyela (people), 25–27, 416n16

Black Consciousness Movement, 13, 14

Black Pimpernel, 15

Blaudin, Ben, 62

Bobe Ridge, 349

Body: in performance, 28, 30, 53, 150–58, 365

Boers. See Afrikaners; Dutch

Bokako, Edison M.: "Bo-Santagane . . . ," 213, 214, 215, 411nn14, 20, 21, 412n27

Bomvana, 5, 44, 45, 305, 306

Bomvu, 42

Bondelswart massacre, 403n12

Bonisani, 41, 42

Botha, Louis, 293, 415n2

Botha, P. W., 16

Boya, 215

Boyd, Charles G.: "Making Peace with the Guilty," 49, 407n3

Branford, Jean: A Dictionary of South African English, 403n15

Bridal attire: Xhosa, 70–71, 73–74

Bridal party: Mpondomise, 246; Xhosa, 61–77

Bride: Xhosa, 61–77, 408n11, 409n18

British, 5, 6, 7, 8, 9, 10, 11, 293, 300, 415n2; Commonwealth, 12; forces, 303, 347–57; language: English versus Dutch, 7; government, 355, 358

Brombert, Victor: "The Idea of the Hero," 203, 410n1

Brombert, Victor, ed.: The Hero in Literature, 410n1

Brown, E. K.: Rhythm in the Novel, 419n4

Brownlee, Charles Pacalt: Reminiscences of Kafir Life and History, 415n3

Bryce, James: Impressions of South Africa, 417n25

Buchan, John: Prester John, 417n25

Bulembu, 33, 39

Bulhoek, 6

Bulhoek Massacre, 10–11

Bundy, Colin. See Beinart, William, and Colin Bundy

Burckhardt, Jacob: The Civilization of the Renaissance in Italy, xx, 401n15

Burial places of the kings, 24, 43–44; of Mpondomise kings, 229–30, 232, 241, 242, 243, 244–45, 249, 250, 273; of Ngqika, 305

Burridge, Kenelm O. L.: Mambu: A Melanesian Millennium, 415n3; New Heaven New Earth: A Study of Millenarian Activities, 415n3

Bushula, 223

Buthelezi, Wellington, 11, 274

Cabe, 229

Calverley, Frederick William: "So Everybody Was After Chakijana," 293, 303, 346–57

Calverley, Louis, 351

Calverley, William James, 303, 346–57, 417n22

Cape Colony, 6, 7, 8, 9, 11, 293, 295, 296, 414n14

Cape Colored, 6

Cape Native Convention, 9

Cape Province, 15

Cape Town, 6, 7, 16, 42

Cape Town: University of, 411n14

Cargo cult: defined, 415n3

Carr, David: "Narrative and the Real World," xix, 401n10

Cattle: favorite, of the kings, 24

Cattle-killing, 304–313. See Nongqawuse

Cebo, 33, 38
Cende, 36
Centane, 281, 304, 306
Centane District, 31, 279, 294, 304, 416n4
Cetshwayo, 22
Chafutweni, 37
Chakide (mongoose), 299
Chakijana, 293
Chakijana: fictional, 293, 301–2, 303, 314–
   33, 417n1; historical, xxv, xxvi, 10, 293,
   294, 298–301, 302–3, 334–45, 346–57, 358,
   416nn9, 10, 11, 418n1; mongoose, 298–99;
   praise names, 298–99; trial, 298
Chalmers, John A.: *Tiyo Soga: A Page of
   South African Mission Work*, 415n3, 416n5
Charles (son of Mhlontlo), 272, 273, 274
Charlie, 45
Charter of Justice, 7
Charter of the United Nations, 12
Chebe, 281
Chithwayo, 229
Chizela River, 231
Christian converts, 10, 46, 76, 296; Mhlontlo,
   271–72
Christianity, 407n14, 409n27
Churches: independent, 11
Cinderella, 59
Cingco, 252
Cira (Gcaleka person), 241, 242
Cira (Mpondomise person), 222, 236–42
Cira (people), 207, 208
Ciskei, 306
Citizen Force, 14
Civil disobedience, 13
Clothing: Xhosa, 307, 308
Clown, 57, 58, 61–77
Coal mine, 346–47
Cobble, Thomas J.: *Black Testimony*, 402n17
Coetzee, J. M.: *Life & Times of Michael K*,
   xviii, 401n5
Cofimvaba, 306
Colenso, Bishop John William, 355, 418n8
Colenso, Francis Ellen, 355, 418n8
Colenso, Harriette Emily, 355–57, 418n8
Color bar, 8, 9
Comaroff, Jean: *Body of Power, Spirit of
   Resistance*, 415n3
Commissioner for Native Affairs, 418n1
Communism, 11
Concentration camps, 9

Cook, P. A. W.: "History and *Izibongo* of the
   Swazi Chiefs," 412n29
Cope, Trevor: *Izibongo, Zulu Praise-Poems*,
   412n29
Cosentino, Donald: *Defiant Maids and
   Stubborn Farmers*, xxi, 402n20
Cosmic time and historical time, 51, 52
Councillors: Gcaleka and Ngqika, 405–7n11
Couzens, Tim. *See* White, Landeg, and Tim
   Couzens, eds.
Crystal, David: "Paralinguistics," 419n13
Cumakala, 305
Cumngce, 43
Cunu (people), 416n21
Curtin, Philip: *The Image of Africa*, xxi,
   402n19
Cwede, 281
Cwera, 231

Dakwaukwesuta, 298
Dala, 408n11
Dalasile, 34, 306
Daluhlanga, 34
Damane, M., and P. B. Sanders, eds.: *Lithoko,
   Sotho Praise-Poems*, 412n29
Dance, 30, 53, 150; dancing, 236, 242, 371
Dange, 32
Davenport, T. H. R.: *South Africa: A Modern
   History*, 402n1
Davis, Stuart: *Stuart Davis*, 157, 410n7
De Klerk, F. W., 16
Debeza, 231
Dedisa, 229
Derricourt, Robin. *See* Saunders, Christo-
   pher, and Robin Derricourt
Dhlomo, Herbert I. E.: *The Girl Who Killed
   to Save: Nongqawuse the Liberator*, 296,
   416nn3, 6
Dhlomo, Luzimbela, 353
Dhlomo (people), 353
Dhlomo, R. R. R., 215; *uDinuzulu
   kaCetshwayo*, 417n25; *uShaka*, 411n24
Diamonds, 8, 415n2
Didi, 25, 26
Dike, 42
Diko, 254, 255, 257, 258
Diliz' [Diliza] Iintaba Mditshwa, 205, 216–
   17, 222–26, 253, 274, 410n3, 413n30, 414n5
Dimanda, 36, 304
Dingana, 306

Dingane, 251, 252, 253
Dinuzulu, 7, 10, 22, 228, 301, 303, 340, 352, 354, 416n10, 418nn1, 4; arrest and imprisonment, 301
Diviners, 261
Dlambulo, 46
Dlamini, 46, 369
Dlungwana, 26
Dobsonville, 14
Doctors, 53, 307, 312
Dogs, 230
Dom, 33, 39
Dosini, 222, 236–41
Dowry, 234–35, 246
Drakensberg Mountains, 7, 222, 223, 228, 231, 232, 241, 245, 249, 259, 261, 262, 274
Drommedaris, 5
Drought, 10
Drum magazine, 13, 15
Dublin, 414n11
Dukuza Regiment, 251
Dumalisile, 35
Dundee, 350
Dunn, John, 346
Durban, 7, 205, 277, 346
Dushane, 33
Dutch, 5, 6, 293; language, 403n6; settlers, 403n6; trekboere, 6. See also Afrikaners
Dutch East India Company, 5, 403n6, 415n2
Du Toit, Brian, Content and Form of Zulu Folk-Narratives, 407n7
Dutywa, 306
Dwayi, 35
Dyamfu, 231
Dyan, 38
Dyosini, 43

East Africa, 206
East London, 405n2, 414n11
East London Daily Dispatch, 14
Ecclesiasticus, 19, 404n1
Edgar, Robert: Because They Chose the Plan of God, 403nn8, 9, 10, 11; Prophets with Honor, 415n3
Educational system, 54, 55
Edward, 266
Egypt, 411n4
El Alamein, 411n4
Elections, 16
Eliade, Mircea: Myth and Reality, xxiii, 402n22, 407n5

Ellsworth, Margaret: "The Rejection of Bantu Education," 403–4n20
Elphick, Richard: Kraal and Castle: Khoikhoi and the Founding of White South Africa, 402n3
Emotions in storytelling, xxiv, 28, 30, 53, 55, 150, 151–58, 209–16, 220–21, 362, 364, 365
England, 274
English. See British
Entfonjeni, 210, 275
Epic, xxiii, 27, 28, 51, 52, 53, 58–60, 150; "The Endless Mountain," by Nongenile Masithathu Zenani, xvii, xxiv, 58–60, 78–145
Epidemics, typhoid fever, 9
Ethiopian religious movement, 300
Europe, 6
Europeans, xxvi, 11, 205, 211, 262, 296; and Africans, xxi, 293–301, 304–13, 362, 365, 369–94; and Africans, disparity in education funds, 403–4n20; and Mpondomise, 260–74; army, 260, 265, 267, 268, 269, 271, 272, 280, 281, 301; government, 42, 44, 46, 47, 260–68, 280, 281, 306, 406n11, 407n11, 418n1; government, oaths, 46–47; government's determination to possess the land, 305; murder of three Europeans, by Mahlangeni, 264; white armed forces, 301; white farmers, 10; white government, 222; white political unity, 301; whites and Khoi, 402n3; white suburbs, 14; white supremacy, 301
Expectation and predictability in narratives, 362, 364, 365

Fable, 49
Fadane, Titus, 272
Faku, 33, 36, 38, 41, 42, 43, 229, 248, 251, 254, 304
Falakhe, 407n11
Falase, 225
Fantasy, 28, 51, 54, 57, 150, 155, 158, 160, 162, 208, 210, 217, 222, 302, 414n2
Farming, 10, 300
Fees, cattle-dipping, 11
Feierman, Steven: The Shambaa Kingdom: A History, xx, 401n13
Feinberg, Barry: Poets to the People, 404n31
Feni, 42
Fernández-Armesto, Felipe: Millennium: A History of the Last Thousand Years, xx,

401*nn14, 16;* "Rewriting History," 24, 49, 405*n5*, 407*n1*
Fesi, 32
Festile, 406*n11*
Fiction, 52; and history, 293, 295, 299
Fikeni, 283
Finnegan, Ruth: *Oral Poetry,* 412*n29*
First World War, 11
Firth, Raymond: *Symbols, Public and Private,* 415*n3*
Fitoyi, 41
Form: artistic, xviii, xx, xxi, 53, 150–58, 211
Formulas in oral poetry, 210
Forster, E. M.: *Aspects of the Novel,* 419*n4*
Fort Hare, 15
Fort of Good Hope, 5
Foster, E. M., 362
Fredrickson, George M.: *Black Liberation,* 415*n3*
Freedom, xxv; struggle for, 293; and tradition, xxi, xxii, xxiii, xxiv
Freedom-fighter: Chakijana, 334–45
Free press, 7
French Huguenots, 5, 6
Frontier wars, 40
Fry, Donald K., ed.: *The Beowulf Poet,* 410*n2*
Fundakubi, 36
Furness, Graham, and Elizabeth Gunner, eds.: *Power, Marginality, and African Oral Literature,* 412*n29*
Fuze, Magema M.: *Abantu Abamnyama Lapha Bavela Ngakhona,* 213, 411*n16*

Gabushe, 45
Gangata, 229
Ganya, 406*n11*
Gaqa, 406*n11*
Garvey, Marcus, 11
Gasa, 258
Gasela, 32, 33, 38
Gatyana, 36, 44, 45, 280, 306, 307
Gatyana District, 61, 78, 150, 163, 410*n2*
Gawusha, 35
Gcaleka (people), 5, 31, 44, 45, 58, 150, 207, 241, 245, 247, 252, 273, 279, 295, 304, 306, 406*n11*
Gcaleka (person), 32, 33, 34, 35, 36, 37, 43, 245, 247, 304; councillors, 405–7*n11*; and the Mpondomise, 245
Gcalekaland, 38, 247, 249, 297, 305, 405*n11*, 406*n11*

Gcara, 45
Gcazimbana (Mhlontlo's horse), 267–68, 269–71
Gcina, 32
Gcuwa, 32, 45, 46, 306, 407*n14*
Genealogies, xxiv, 21, 24, 25, 27, 31–47, 51, 52, 57, 205, 210, 221, 367; genealogist, 52
Geqe, 406*n11*
Gerhart, Gail M.: *Black Power in South Africa,* 403*n13*
Germans, 11, 12
Gesture, 53; movement during performance, 209
Geza, 407*n11*
Giqwa, 45, 46
Goat, ritual, 76, 186
Goba River, 279
Gobe, 279, 414*n1*
Godidi, 42
Gojela (ox), 43
Gold, 9, 415*n2*
Gold mines, xvi, 346
Golizulu, 253
Gomomo, 62, 63, 408*n3*
Gonya, 33, 38, 41, 42
Goodwin, June, and Ben Schiff: "Who Killed Steve Biko?" 404*n24*
Gordimer, Nadine: *July's People,* xviii, 401*n5*
Government House (Natal), 356
Government Intelligence, 348, 356
Gqili River, 306
Gqirana, 216, 225
Gqongqo, 32
Gqubushe, 32
Gqubushe-mpulomsini, 31
Gqungqe, 40
Grand Parade, Cape Town, 16
Grant, E. W.: "The *Izibongo* of the Zulu Chiefs," 412*n29*
Great Fish River, 6
Great house, 32, 33, 38, 41, 405*nn1, 6. See also* Royal houses
Great Trek, 7, 8
Great wife, 405*n6*
Greytown, 356, 416*n21*
Greytown Gazette, The, 416*n10*
Greytown Magistracy, 358
Griffiths, 36, 304
Griqua, 8
Griqualand East, 414*n11*
Groom: Xhosa, 408*n11*

Group areas act, 12
Guerrilla warfare, 301, 303, 334–45, 346–57, 358; Zulu guerrilla, 417*n22*
Gulati, 401*n4*
Gumna, 33
Gungululu, 250
Gunner, Elizabeth, and Mafika Gwala, eds., *Musho! Zulu Popular Praises,* 412*n29*; *Politics and Performance: Theatre, Poetry, and Song in Southern Africa,* 412*n29*; "Songs of Innocence and Experience: Women as Composers and Performers of *Izibongo,* Zulu Praise Poetry," 412*n29. See also* Furness, Graham, and Elizabeth Gunner, eds.
Gushiphela, 33, 38, 39
Guze, 281
Gwadane, 280, 281
Gwala, Mafika. *See* Gunner, Elizabeth, and Mafika Gwala, eds.
Gwashu, 40
Gwatyuza, 406*n11*
Gwazakanjani, 298
Gwebinibiza, 407*n11*
Gweb'indlala, 45
Gwebinkumbi, 34, 43, 44
Gxaba, 34, 35
Gxahra, 304
Gxarha River, 294, 416*n4*
Gxavu, Noplani, xvii, 150, 361, 367, 368, 410*n11*; "Malikophu's Daughter," xxiv, 149, 158–60, 161, 163–86
Gxumisa, 264, 265

Haga (people), 242
Hala, 211
Hall, Donald: *Poetry: The Unsayable Said,* 362, 418*n2*
Hamilton Hope versus Mhlontlo, 262–64
Harmony with nature, 217
Havelock, Eric: *Preface to Plato,* 407*n8*
Hedeni, 406*n11*
Hedges, Jack, 348–49, 351
Hegebe, 44
Hena, 406*n11*
Henry, 406*n11*
Herbalist-diviner, 254
Hero, xxi, xxii, xxiii, xxiv, xxv, 6, 24, 59, 60, 203, 205–22, 225, 232, 252, 298, 299, 303, 396
Herschel District, 11

Hime, A. H., 298, 416*n9*
Hintsa, 33, 34, 35, 37, 43, 44, 45, 46, 47, 206, 208, 304, 407*n14*
Historian, xvii, xxi, xxiii, xxiv, 21, 24, 25, 27, 51, 52, 58, 205, 209, 213, 307, 367, 368; and the past, xv; art of, xix; as a poet, xx, xxi
Historical intent, xx
Historical narrative, xx
Historical time and cosmic time, 51, 52
History, xx, xxi, xxiii, xxiv, xxv, 24, 25, 27, 28, 49, 51, 52, 53, 55, 57, 60, 149, 150, 208, 209, 210, 213, 215, 216, 221, 295, 299, 362, 367, 368; as cultural memory, xxi; definition, xviii; and fantasy, 210; and fiction, xviii, xix, 49, 205, 221–22, 228, 230–31, 293, 295, 299; as folkloric motif, xxi; and memory, xix, xxi; and metaphor, 209; and poetry, 209; South Africa, 402*n1*; and story, 51, 52, 53, 221–22, 295
Hlamandana, 228
Hlambangobubende, 228
Hlangabeza, 406*n11*
Hlathikhulu, 39
Hlayizeni, 25, 26
Hleke, 32
Hlonipha (word of reverence), 408*nn6, 9*
Hlubi, 45, 46, 150, 187, 254, 261, 272, 412*n29*
Hohela, 306
Hohita, 304
Hokisi, 406*n11*
Holela, 280, 281
Holela (ox), 43
Homelands, 16
Hope, Hamilton, 263, 264, 266, 272, 273
Hopkinson, Tom: *In the Fiery Continent,* 403*n17*
House, supporting, 279
House of Assembly, 403*n12*

Idutywa, 36, 39
Image, xxi, 27, 28, 51, 53, 54, 55, 57, 59, 150–58, 205, 209, 210, 211, 213, 221, 365, 367; definition, 410*n4*; folkloric, xx; historical, xx, 209; and reality, 49
Imagination, 49, 53, 55, 57, 60, 150, 203; imaginative story, 299
Imfecane, 250; defined, 414*n4*
Immorality act, 5, 12
India, 277
Indian Ocean, 5, 6, 294, 416*n4*
Indians, 15

Inkazana, 408*n2*
Intsomi: defined, 414*n2*
Isandlwana, 298
Israel, 277
Israelites, 10, 11
Italy, 278

Jama, 405*n6*
Jamangile, 40
Jengca, 225, 252, 253, 259
Jingqi, 35, 40
Joan of Arc, 415*n3*
Jobe, 276
Johannesburg, xvi, 13, 14, 346, 385
John of Gaunt, 222
John Wesley missionaries, 46
Jojo (Gcaleka), 36
Jojo (Xesibe), 218–19, 255, 282–86
Jolobe, James J. R.: "Ingqawule," 297, 416*n8*
Jongizulu, 40
Joni, 406*n11*
Jordan, A. C.: *Tales from Southern Africa*, xv, 401*n2; Towards an African Literature*, 209, 213, 296–97, 411*nn7*, *12*, 416*n7*
Jordan, Z. Pallo, xv
Joyi, 258, 281
Joyi, Zwelibhangile, 22, 206
Julien, Eileen: *African Novels and the Question of Orality*, xxi, 402*n21*
Jumba, 259
Jung, Carl G.: "On the Psychology of the Trickster Figure," 291, 300, 415*n1*, 416*n20*
Juxu, 254

Kadalie, Clements, 11
Kadeni, 33, 39
Kaiser, 406*n11*
Kane-Berman, John: *Soweto: Black Revolt, White Reaction*, 403*n19*
Kawin, Bruce F.: *Telling It Again and Again*, 419*n4*
Kei River, 8, 294, 395, 408*n8*, 418*n1*
Key, Bishop Bransby Lewis, 260, 266
Kgamanyane, 217, 413*n33*
Kgatla, 217
Khabeni, 26
Khama, 305
Khawuta, 33, 34, 35, 36, 37, 40, 43, 44, 279, 305
Khewuthi, 279
Khobe, 407*n11*

Khobonqaba, 42, 279, 280, 407*n11*
Khohlombeni, 265
Khoi, 3, 5, 6, 283, 289, 402*n3;* and whites, 402*n3*
Khwabakazi, 281
Khwane, 406*n11*
Khwangane, 304
Khwaza, 406*n11*
Khwazu Sijako, 406*n11*
Khwenxura, 32
Khwetshube, 238
Kimberley, 8
King William's Town, 14, 405*n3*
King-lists, 24, 25, 27, 31–47, 51, 52
Kingship, 209; among the Xhosa, 405–7*n11*
Klee, Paul: *Notebooks*, 157, 410*n8*
Kliptown, 14
Koko, Magagamela, xvii, xxvi, 217, 359, 368, 413*n31*, 418*n1;* "Now I Am Spent," 361, 396–97; "When You Are Grey," 361, 395–96
Kokstad, 271
Kokstad District, 243, 245, 250, 262
Kona, 40
Krazukile, 35
Kretzschmar, Louise: *The Voice of Black Theology in South Africa*, 415*n3*
Kropf, Albert: *A Kafir-English Dictionary*, 408*nn2*, *6*, 414*n10*
Kruger, James Thomas (minister of justice), 15, 403*n12*, 404*n24*
Kunene, Daniel P.: *Heroic Poetry of the Basotho*, 412*n29*
Kuper, Leo: "African Nationalism in South Africa . . . ," 417*n23*
Kwayi, 35, 211

Labor, 9, 10, 300
Labor Party, 11
Lady Frere, 304
Lake Nyasa, 227
Lake Tanganyika, 227
Lamula, P.: *Isabelo sikaZulu*, 412*n29*
Langalibalele, 261, 262
Langwane, 276
Lanternari, Vittorio: *The Religions of the Oppressed*, 415*n3*
Larry, 267
Lathana River, 241
Lawrence, Peter: *Road Belong Cargo*, 415*n3*

Lejaha, 214
Lekgothoane, S. K.: "Praises of Animals in Northern Sotho," 211, 215–16, 411*n10*, 412*n28*, 413*n36*
Leopards, 230–31
Lerotholi, 268, 417*n1*
Lesotho, 262, 266, 268, 269, 270, 271, 347, 417*n2*
Lessing, Doris: "The Black Madonna," 157, 410*n10*
Lestrade, G. P.: "Bantu Praise-Poems," 412*n29*; "Traditional Literature," 412*n29*
Letsie (people), 268
Lévi-Strauss, Claude: *The Raw and the Cooked*, 362, 419*n3*
Liberalism, 12
Libode, 259
Libya, 278
Lindile, 42
Lipina, 256
Literature, 362; Xhosa, 297
Lothana River, 242, 243
Lowell, Robert: "History," xix, 401*n7*
Lu Chi, 53
Lubenye, 259, 262
Ludidi, 261
Ludidi Hintsa, 37
Ludwanga, 279
Luhane, 259, 262
Lusikisiki District, 150, 187
Lutshaba, 37, 38
Lutshoto, 223, 274
Lyric, 209, 213

Mabala, 61, 406*n11*
Mabilokazi, 226
Mabobothi, 35
McClear District, 262
Machotka, Pavel. *See* Spiegel, John Paul, and Pavel Machotka
Macingwane, 26, 250
McKenzie, Colonel Duncan, 9, 301, 349, 350, 351, 352, 418*n4*
MacLeish, Archibald: *Poetry and Experience*, 407*n6*
MacRae, Donald G.: "The Body and Social Metaphor," 419*n13*
Madikane, 250, 253
Madlala, Mandla, xvi, xvii, xxiii
Madodendlini, 35

Madolo, 406*n11*
Madongci, 211
Madubedube, 226
Mafeje, Archie: "The Role of a Bard in a Contemporary African Community," 215, 412*n25*
Mageba, 26
Magic, 230–31, 248
Magile, 406*n11*
Magistrates, 260, 261, 262, 264, 265, 272, 300, 358, 418*n1*
Magolwana, 214–15
Magwababa, 10, 301, 416*n10*
Magwayi, 259, 262, 264, 265
Mahatyini, 352
Mahdi (Sudan), 415*n3*
Mahlabatini, 355, 411*n9*, 418*n1*
Mahlabatini District, xvi, 314, 334, 358, 369
Mahlangeni, xxvi, 264–68; death of, 268; murders Hamilton Hope, 264
Mahlokohla, 210, 275
Majeke, 31
Majeki, 406*n11*
Majola: person, 243–45, 258; snake, 222, 243–44
Makana, 415*n3*
Makhamba, 226
Makhandezinyoni, 225
Makhawula, 255, 256
Makhoba, Nomusa, xvii, xxvi; "Jabulani Alone," 361–62, 365–68, 369–94, 419*n14*, 419*n4*
Maki, 406*n11*
Makinana, 39, 253
Malandela, 31, 34
Malangana, 24, 31, 34, 222, 229–31, 232
Malawi, 11
Malaysians, 6
Malephe River, 216, 225
Mali (ox), 43
Mamani, 222, 245–47
Mamba, Mtshophane: "Snapping at the Water's Foam," xvii, xxv, 205, 210, 275–78, 367
Mancinga, 416*n21*
Mandamela, 27
Mandela (Mpondomise), 254, 257
Mandela, Rolilahlahla Nelson Dalibhunga, xv, 6, 11, 15–17, 22, 206, 404*nn28, 30, 31*; elected president, 16; *Long Walk to Freedom*, 404*n4*, 411*n5*, 414*n1*

Mandela, Winnie, 16
Mandlakazi, 342
Mangutyana, 233
Mankulumane, 21, 22
Manqophu, 266, 267
Manxangashe, 233–35, 236
Manxiwa, 37
Manzini, 276
Map of South Africa, 4
Mapasa, 35
Maphasa, 279, 280, 305, 306
Maphololo, 358
Maphonya, 306
Maqoma, 33, 40, 42
Market, 380
Marks, Shula: *Reluctant Rebellion: The 1906–8 Disturbances in Natal*, 417n25, 418n1
Marquard, Leo: *The Peoples and Policies of South Africa*, 402n1
Márquez, Gabriel García: *Of Love and Other Demons*, 147, 410n1; *One Hundred Years of Solitude*, xvii, 401n3
Marriage, 31, 59, 60, 61–77, 246, 279; dowry, 75–77; master of ceremonies, 51, 53, 57–58; of Thwa and Mpondomise, 232–35; Xhosa marriage ceremony, 51, 57–58, 61–77, 408nn1, 10, 11, 409nn21, 27; Zulu marriage ceremony, 366
Mask, xxiv
Masonya, 218
Mass political action, 11
Massacre: of the Bondelswart, 403n12
Master of ceremonies: Xhosa, 51, 53, 57–58, 60, 61–77, 408n5, 409nn13, 24, 26
Matatiele, 262
Matatiele District, 187, 232, 241, 262
Mathanzima, 41, 42
Matheguda, 226
Matiwana, 414n9
Matiwane, 223
Matopo, 401n4
Matsebula, J. S. M.: *Izakhiwo zamaSwazi*, 412n29
Matshezi, Manto, 30
Matshikiza, John: "And I Watch it in Mandela," 16, 404n31
Matshiliba, 225
Matthews, Z. K., 11, 411n14
Mavu Mabandla, 249
Maya, 45
Mayatana, 418n1

Mayiwane, 224
Maziyane, 26
Mbali, 254, 255, 256, 414n9
Mbalu, 32
Mbangcolo, 44
Mbashe River, 44, 45, 65, 252
Mbelembele, 26
Mbhoyi, 406n11
Mbiko, 43
Mbizana District, 230, 232
Mbo, 46, 227, 228, 229
Mbola, 258
Mboland, 45, 228
Mbombo (people), 281
Mbubhuzile, 44
Mbulu, 244
Mbune, 27, 279
Mbutho, 252
Mbuyazwe, 45
Mbuyeni, 26
Mcothama, 35
Mdabuka, 34
Mdibanisweni, 223, 410n3
Mditshwa, 222, 257, 258, 259, 261, 265, 266, 267, 271, 274
Mdlabela, 36
Mdlalose, 340, 341, 342
Mdlangazi, 40
Mdushane, 33, 36, 38, 39
Meaning in storytelling, 28, 30, 51, 52, 53, 55, 150–58, 210
Medicine, 53
Meerkat, 299
Melele, 298
Melmoth, 346, 356, 358
Memory, 27, 211, 368
Menzi, 211
Menziwa, 25, 26, 33, 38, 39
Metaphor, xviii, xxi, xxiv, xxv, 24, 25, 30, 51, 205, 208, 209; and history, 209
Methodist Church, Gcuwa, 46
Methodist missionaries, 46
Methula, 278
Meyer, Leonard B.: *Emotion and Meaning in Music*, 365, 419n11; *Music, the Arts and Ideas*, 419n11
Mfengu, xxv, 5, 45, 46–47, 258, 280, 306, 407n14, 418n1; oaths, 46–47
Mfolozi River, 342
Mgabisa, 247, 248, 249
Mgengo, 36

Mgijima, Charles, 10
Mgijima, Enoch, 6, 8, 10, 11
Mgodeli, 42
Mgqatsa, 270
Mgudlwa, 45
Mgugwani, 150, 187
Mgungundlovu, 276
Mgwebi, 37, 207
Mhaga, 242
Mhala, 39
Mhlabathi, 241
Mhlabeni, 40
Mhlakaza, 294, 295, 296, 304, 313
Mhlathuze River, 228, 229
Mhlawuli, 406n11
Mhle, 242, 243
Mhlontlo (Mpondomise), 207, 254, 255, 256,
    257, 259, 260, 261, 262, 263, 264, 265, 266,
    268, 269, 270, 271, 272, 273, 306, 414n9
Mhlontlo (Ngqika), 406n11
Mhosheni, 276
Migrant workers, 301
Millenarian ideas, 415n3
Mime, 30
Mining, 9, 293, 300; coal, 346–47; diamond,
    9; gold, 346; mine owners, 10
Minister of justice, 14
Minor house, 24, 32, 37–38, 41, 42
Missionaries, 216, 219, 224, 256, 260, 264,
    274, 296, 407n14; Roman Catholic, 271–72
Mission station, 260
Mitford, Bertram: The White Hand and the
    Black, 417n25
Mityi: hero of Xhosa epic, xxiv, 53, 59, 60,
    78–145
Mityo, 211
Miyeki, Nohatyula, 151
Mjika River, 216, 225
Mjingane, 205, 277
Mjobi, 406n11
Mjoli, 283, 284
Mkamkam, 211
Mkhalana, 259
Mkhondwane, 228
Mkhubiso, 305
Mkreqo, 272, 273
Mlawu, 32, 33, 38, 39, 40, 305
Mlotshwa, 276
Mmoshi, 406n11
Mncotsho, 39
Mneke, 36, 43

Mngazana, 44
Mngazi, 254
Mngcambe, 247, 248, 249, 250, 251, 253
Mngcayi, 258
Mngcele, 336
Mngcothane, 265
Mngqalasi, 32, 37
Mnqalazi (ox), 42, 43
Mntalana, 211
Mnyaluza, 42
Mnyameni, 43
Mofokeng, S. M.: "Notes and Annotations
    of the Praise-Poems of Certain Chiefs
    and the Structure of Praise-poems in
    Southern Sotho," 412n29
Moloto, Ernest Sedumeli: "The Growth and
    Tendencies of Tswana Poetry," 215, 218,
    412n26, 413n34
Mome Gorge, 10, 301, 303, 349, 351, 417n22
Monakali, 32
Mongoose, 298–99, 416nn17, 19
Moni, 45, 306
Montgomery of Alamein, 205, 278, 411n4
Monti, 32
Montshiwa, 215
Moses, 277
Moshweshwe, 217
Mostert, Noël: Frontiers, 416n3
Motif, xxii, 216
Mount Ayliff, 232, 233
Mount Ayliff District, 262, 282, 287, 414n40
Mount Frere, 254
Mount Frere District, 250, 255, 262
Mozambique, 417n22
Mpande, 214
Mpanza, 416n21
Mpethu, 305
Mphahlele, Es'kia: Down Second Avenue,
    xviii, 401n5
Mphame, 281
Mphanda, 276
Mpinga, 231
Mpisekhaya, 34, 44
Mpondo, 5, 40, 41, 150; army, 265; people,
    228–83 passim; person, 228
Mpondoland, 42, 222, 240–69 passim,
    406n11, 414n9
Mpondomise, xviii, xxv, 5, 24, 205, 206,
    216–74 passim, 414n11, 414n9, 417n4; and
    the Bhaca, 253–57, 270; custom, 263;
    the destruction by the Zulu, 250–53;

the division of the kingdom, 253; emergence as a nation, 227–29; ethos, 266; and Europeans, 260–74; fighting among themselves, 257–60; and the Gcaleka, 245; kings, 227–74; Mpondomise and Mpondo (twins), 228; person, 228, 229; and the Thwa, 232–35; under the protection of the European government, 261; War of Phakana, 259–60
Mpondomiseland, 242–70 *passim*
Mpukane River, 249
Mpulu, 406*n11*
Mqanduli, 44, 45
Mqhayi, 38
Mqhikela, 269
Mqhwashu, 46, 47
Mqikela, 229
Mqoloza, 44
Mqulakazi, 25
Mrawuzeli, 38
Msamo, 279
Msasa, 406*n11*
Msebe, 406*n11*
Msinga, 352
Msingaphantsi, 256
Msintsana, 281
Msiza, 229
Msuze, 43
Mthatha, 257, 265, 267, 272, 273, 283, 289
Mthatha District, 259
Mthatha River, 222, 231, 241, 243, 245, 249, 259, 261, 262, 274
Mthini, 36
Mthirara, 37
Mthulu, 43
Mthweli, 27
Mtika, 258
Mtoto, 37
Mtshayelo (ox), 43
Mtshayelweni, 37
Mtshazi, 274
Murray, Martin: *South Africa: Time of Agony, Time of Destiny*, 403*n16*
Music, 30, 152, 157, 362, 364, 365; intonation, 53; sound, in oral performance, 54, 209, 210, 211; and words, 54. *See also* Rhythm
Mussolini, 278
Mvelelo, 45
Mveli, 300
Mvenyane, 232, 233, 234, 235, 241
Mxhoxho, 254

Mxoli, 27, 279, 280
Mxolisi, 42
Myeki, 250, 251, 252, 253, 254, 414*n9*
Myth, xx, xxiii, xxiv, xxv, 3, 22, 24, 27, 28, 51, 52, 205, 218, 291, 300, 303
Mze, 260
Mzilikazi, 215
Mzimkhulu, 40, 241, 250, 283
Mzimkhulu River, 222, 230, 231, 243, 244, 245, 249, 250, 251, 252, 256, 259, 261, 262, 274
Mzini, Velaphi, 294–95, 416*n4*
Mzintlavu River, 249, 250

Namaqualand, 402*n3*
Namba, 40
Namibia, 403*n12*
Nandi, 26
Natal, 7, 21, 229, 230, 301, 346, 416*n21*, 418*n4*; colonial troops, 300, 418*n4*
Natal Province, 300
Natal Supreme Court, 418*n1*
Nationalism, xv, xxii; Zulu, 301
Nationalist Party, 8, 11, 12
National Party, 404*n24*
Native Affairs: Commissioner for, 418*n1*
Natives' Land Act of 1913, 10
Native Trust, 351
Nature, 217
Nature: harmony with, 159
Nazo, 279
Ncamba, 35
Ncaphayi (son of Madikane), 253–54, 255
Nciba River, 65, 306, 408*n8*
Ncindise, 229
Ncitha, 279
Ndaba, 25, 26, 211, 214, 217, 276, 405*n6*
Ndaba of Chakijana, 334
Ndabakazi, 43
Ndamase, 40, 257, 258
Ndawo, H. M.: *Izibongo zenkosi zamaHlubi nezamaBhaca*, 412*n29*
Ndayeni, 31, 32, 229
Ndebele, xvii, 401*n4*; language, 411*n15*; oral traditions, xvii
Ndesana, 406*n11*
Ndigwe, 353
Ndima, 37
Ndiyalwa, 44
Ndlambe, 32, 33, 38, 39, 67
Ndlebe, 258, 300

Ndlintsha, 406*n11*
Ndlovu, Eva, xvii, 401*n4*
Ndluntsha (people), 281
Ndonga, 27
Ndosina, 236. *See also* Dosini
Ndunu, 229, 230
Ndwandwe, 26
Ndwe, 304, 306
New Brighton, 416*n8*
Newcastle, 346–47
New York, 16
Ngangana, 62
Ngangelizwe, 273
Ngangolwande, 37
Ngazindaka, 298
Ngcama, Ashton, xvii, xxv, 205, 218, 219–21, 282–89, 367, 413–14*n40*; "The Land Has Grown Old," 206, 218–19, 282–86; on the creation of oral poetry, 220–21; "Tears in Your Stomach," 206, 287–89
Ngcaphayi, 35
Ngcayechibi, 222, 279
Ngcayechibi War, xxv, 27, 37, 42, 222, 273, 279–81
Ngcengcezi, 25
Ngcobo District, 253
Ngcobo, Sondoda, xvii, xviii, xxvi, 293, 299, 301, 303, 367; "Chakijana, the Trickster," 301–3, 314–33; "Chakijana, Zulu Freedom-Fighter," 301–3, 334–45
Ngcolosi, 227
Ngconde, 31, 34, 36, 42, 43, 44
Ngcwangu, 230, 242
Ngcwanguba, 43, 44
Ngcweleshe, 36
Ngcwina, 222, 232, 233–35, 236–41
Ngele, 230, 232, 233
Ngodwana, 64
Ngonyama, 26, 42, 45
Ngoqo, 358
Ngozi, 250
Ngqamakhwe, 46, 306
Ngqamakhwe District, 395, 418*n1*
Ngqaqini, 61
Ngqaqini (ox), 43
Ngqelenga, 306
Ngqeleni District, 254
Ngqeleni, 43, 257, 259
Ngqika: councillors, 405–7*n11*; grave of Ngqika, 305; people, 41, 42, 294, 297,

405*n5*; person, 33, 38, 39, 40, 42, 304, 305, 416*n4*
Ngqikaland, 38, 42, 305, 405*n11*, 406*n11*
Ngqila, 406*n11*
Ngqongongqongo, 36
Ngqosini, 41, 42, 304
Ngqungqushe, 229
Ngqushwa, 46, 407*n14*
Ngubenani, 225
Ngubencuka, 45
Ngubezulu, 35, 42, 45
Ngubo, 281
Ngunduza, 281
Nguni, 5, 7, 215, 283; defined, 411*n15*
Ngutyana, 236
Ngwabalanda, 25
Ngwane, 277
Ngwanya, 245, 258
Ngwenyenyathi, 39
Ngxabane: people, 249, 250, 268; person, 243, 249
Ngxala, 45
Ngxito, 35, 37
Ngxizela, 407*n11*
Nhlazatsha Mountain, 300
Nigeria, 28
Niphazi, 258
Njanye, 230, 231
Njimbane, 406*n11*
Njoli, 253, 254, 255
Nkabana, 31
Nkandla, 349, 352, 358, 417*n22*
Nkandla District, 351
Nkandla Forest, 301, 303, 346, 348, 349, 352
Nkandla Mountains, 301
Nkanga, 61, 62, 64, 67, 78, 150, 163, 307, 410*n2*
Nkani, 36
Nkatha, 45
Nkayishana, 27
Nkheshengu, 336
Nkombi, 211
Nkondwane, 306
Nkonjeni Mountain, 358
Nkonki, 294, 416*n4*
Nkosiyamntu, 31, 34, 43
Nkulu, 248
Nkunzana, 346
Nkuzana, 27, 279
Nkweleni, 26

Nokhaka, 266
Nolangeni Mountain, 250, 285, 287–89
Nolele Drift, 358
Nolenti, 41
Nomantyane, 271
Nombanjana, 42
Nomkholokhotha Mountains, 223
Nomlala, 266
Nompita, 284
Nomse, 44, 45
Nomvula, 26
Nongawuza, 231
Nongoma, 22
Nongqawuse, xxv, 6, 8, 293, 294–98, 303,
    304–13, 415n3, 416n4
Noposi, 40, 41
Noqingatha, 258
North Africa, 411n4
Nothembu, 211
Nothonto, 42
Novel, xx
Noziyongwane, 265
Nqabana, 283
Nqabara, 46
Nqabe, 44
Nqadu, 35, 44, 45
Nqancule, 395, 418n1
Nqanda, 231
Nqangqeni, 225
Nqaqa, 27
Nqenqa, 279
Nqoko, 37
Nqwiliso, 257
Nsintsana, 40
Nsuze, 353
Nsuze River, 353
Ntabankulu, 43, 268; person, 273
Ntabankulu District, 268
Ntabelanga, 10
Ntibana, 225
Ntimbo, 33, 39
Ntinde, 32, 36
Ntingwe, 349
Ntlakomzi, 37
Ntlambe, 304, 306
Ntlane, 64, 65, 67, 70, 71, 408n11
Ntlangwini, 255–56
Ntlazatshe, 342
Ntlazatshe Mountains, 337, 338
Ntlikithi, 42

Ntombose, 227
Ntonjaneni District, 416n16
Ntose, 231, 232
Ntsangana, 406n11
Ntsheco, 406n11
Ntshunqe, 44, 45
Ntsibatha, 246, 247, 248, 249
Ntsobane, Emily: "The Deadly Pumpkin,"
    xvii, xxiv, 149, 150, 160–62, 187–201, 361,
    367, 368, 410n11
Ntsusa, 32, 33, 38
Ntsuzi River, 349
Ntungwa, 383, 385, 420n12
Ntunjambili, 389, 420n16
Nukwa, 32, 33, 39
Nxarini, 305
Nxaruni, 43
Nxaxha, 407n11
Nxaxho, 406n11
Nxokazi, 250
Nxotwe, 240
Nxuba River, 46
Nyanda, 243, 254
Nyandeni, 250
Nyandube, 238, 240
Nyasaland. See Malawi
Nyawuza, 229, 246, 247, 248
Nyembezi, C. L. S.: "The Historical Back-
    ground to the Izibongo of the Zulu
    Military Age," 214, 411nn19, 22; Izibongo
    zamakhosi, 412n29
Nyila, 32, 45
Nzabela, 304
Nzama, Joseph, 417n22
Nzima, 46, 406n11
Nzotshwa, 279
Nzuza, 26

Oakes, Dougie: The Real Story, 402n5, 403n7
Odendaal, André: Vukani Bantu! 415n3
Okpewho, Isidore: African Oral Literature,
    xxi, 402n18, 412n29
Omer-Cooper, J. D.: History of Southern
    Africa, 403n6, 417n24
Opland, Jeff: "Imibongo Nezibongo: The
    Xhosa Tribal Poet and the Contemporary
    Poetic Tradition," 412n29; "Praise Poems
    as Historical Sources," 412n29; "Scop
    and Imbongi IV: Reading Praise Poems,"
    412n29; Xhosa Oral Poetry, 412n29

Oral tradition, xix, xx, xxi, 303; oral poetry, xx, 411nn7, 9, 11, 13, 412n29; as prayer, 215–16; learning, 413n36

Orange Free State, 7, 8, 9, 224, 414n11

Orange River Sovereignty, 7

Orczy, Emmuska: *The Scarlet Pimpernel*, 15, 404n27

Origins, 59, 60

Orpen, Joseph Millerd, 260, 261, 262, 414n11

Osborne, 256

Ox, 59, 60, 61–62, 66–67, 75–76, 104–45 *passim*; as dowry, 234–35; of the kings, 42–43

Painting, and oral narrative performance, 157

Pakade, 416n21

Palestine, 277, 278

Pan Africanist Congress, 12, 13, 15; banning of, 13

Pan-African Freedom Movement of East and Central Africa, 16

Pass laws, 6, 7, 10, 12

Past and present, xv, xviii, xix, xxiv, xxv, 51, 52, 149, 203, 205, 211, 213, 218, 367, 368

Paton, Alan: *Cry, the Beloved Country*, xviii, 401n5

Patterning of images, 28, 51, 53, 58, 150–58, 160, 209, 210, 211, 213, 222, 301–2, 362–64

Peires, J. B.: *The Dead Will Arise: Nongqawuse and the Great Xhosa Cattle-Killing Movement of 1856-7*, 416n3, 417n1

Performance, xviii, 24, 28, 30, 53, 54, 57, 59, 60, 61, 149, 150–58, 209, 213, 219–20; aesthetic experience, 365; aesthetics of performance, 150, 151, 210; aesthetic tension, 150–58; audience, 28, 53, 54, 55, 57, 150–58, 209, 213, 219, 362, 365, 410nn4, 11; body, in performance, 28, 30, 53, 150–58, 365; dance, 30, 53, 150; emotions in storytelling, xxiv, 28, 30, 53, 55, 150, 151–58, 209–16, 220–21, 362, 364, 365; fantasy, 28, 51, 54, 57, 150, 155, 158, 160, 162, 208, 210, 217, 222, 302, 414n2; form, artistic, xviii, xx, xxi, 53, 150–58, 211; formulas in oral poetry, 210; gesture, 53, 209; image, xxi, 27, 28, 51, 53, 54, 55, 57, 59, 150–58, 205, 209, 210, 211, 213, 221, 365, 367; image, definition, 410n4; image, folkloric, xx; image, historical, xx, 209; image and

reality, 49; imagination, 49, 53, 55, 57, 60, 203; imaginative story, 299; intonation, 53; *intsomi*, defined, 414n2; lyric, 209, 213; meaning in storytelling, 28, 30, 51, 52, 53, 55, 150–58, 210; memory, 27, 211, 368; memory and history, 209; metaphor, xviii, xxi, xxiv, xxv, 24, 25, 30, 51, 205, 207, 209; motif, xxii, 216; music, 30, 152, 157, 362, 364, 365; music and words, 54; myth, xx, xxiii, xxiv, xxv, 3, 22, 24, 27, 28, 51, 52, 205, 218, 291, 300, 303; oral poetry, xx, 411nn7, 9, 11, 13, 412n29; oral poetry, learning, 413n36; oral poetry as prayer, 215–16; oral tradition, xix, xx, xxi, 303; painting, and oral narrative performance, 157; panegyric, 214; patterning of images, 28, 51, 53, 58, 150–58, 160, 209, 210, 211, 213, 222, 301–2, 362–64; plot clichés, 54; poetic line, 211, 213–16; praise poetry, 214, 215, 220–21; rhythm, 53, 150–58, 209, 211, 213, 364; sound, 54, 209, 210, 211; suspense, 55; symbol, 57; tragedy, 203. *See also* poet, poetry, story, storyteller, tradition

Performer, 54, 55, 151

Phahle, 222

Phahlo, 245, 247, 249

Phakana, 259–60

Phakana, War of, 273

Phalo (Gcaleka), 31, 32, 33, 34, 38, 43, 44, 247, 249, 406n11

Phalo (Mpondomise), 249

Phatho, Abeli, 272, 273

Phunga, 26

Pietermaritzburg, 16, 354, 355, 356

Pinga, 306

Poet, xxi, xxiii, xxiv, xxv, 27, 51, 58, 205, 206, 207–8, 209, 210, 211, 212, 214, 216, 217, 218, 219, 288; as a loving critic, 215; and the past, xv; Xhosa, 411n6; Zulu, 405n7

Poetry, 51, 60, 152, 216, 219, 220, 223–26; creating, 220–21; heroic, xxi, xxiii; and history, 209; learning, 413n36; oral, xviii, 205–22, 364, 411nn7, 9, 11, 13, 412n29; poetic line, 211, 213–16; praise poetry, 214, 215, 220–21

Poets, 21, 22, 24, 25, 252

Polhemus, Ted. *See* Benthall, Jonathan, and Ted Polhemus

Police, 342; security, 16; spy, 418n1

Poll tax, 300
Polsmoor Prison, 16
Population registration act, 12
Port Elizabeth, 14, 15
Poto, 42, 229, 243, 257
Poverty, 11
Press, 14
Pretoria, xvii, xxv, 15, 205, 218
Pretoria Central Prison, 16
Prince of Wales, 274
Prison, 300
Prophet, 295
Protest march, 13
Puberty rite of passage, 149, 158–86, 187–201, 255–56, 361, 365–94
Purification rituals, 59

Qakaza, 258
Qala-indawo, 42
Qamatha, 297
Qaphela-bazozela, 25
Qengebe, 243
Qeqe, 406n11
Qhashe's Nek, 271
Qhokama, 43
Qocwa, 42
Qolora, 304
Qombolo, 40, 407n11
Qonce, 32, 33, 36, 38, 39, 42, 305
Qudeni, 355, 356
Queenstown, 10
Qukwana, 406n11
Qumbu, 417n4
Qumbu District, 241, 243, 253, 254, 256, 262, 263, 265, 273, 306, 414nn8, 9
Qwambi, 62
Qwaninga, 37
Qwaninga River, 61, 66

Raba, 36, 304
Racial segregation. See Apartheid
Racism, 52
Radebe, 46
Radin, Paul: The Trickster, 415n1, 416n20
Rain-making: the Thwa and the Mpondomise, 235
Rambatotshile, 225
Rand Daily Mail, 14
Randlords, 9
Raven-Hart, R.: Before Van Riebeeck: Callers at South Africa from 1488 to 1652, 402n2
Reality and story, 53, 54, 55, 57, 150
Rebel: Chakijana, 334–45, 346–57, 358
Rebellion, 300–301; Zulu, 334–45, 346–57, 358
Rebirth, 158–60, 163–86
Red Sea, 277
Refugees, 253, 254
Regiments, Swati, 276, 277
Reitz, Deneys: No Outspan, 21, 22, 404nn2, 3
Reneyi, 406n11
Repetition. See Patterning of images
Resistance, 11, 13, 14
Reverential words in Xhosa (hlonipha), 408nn6, 9
Revolution, 16, 293
Rharhabe, 32, 33, 34, 38, 39, 305, 405n5
Rhini, 272
Rhinoceros, 232
Rhodes, Cecil John, 8, 293, 415n2
Rhodesia, 22; See also Zimbabwe
Rhythm, 53, 150–58, 209, 211, 213, 364. See also Music
Richards, I. A.: Principles of Literary Criticism, 364, 419n8
Right-hand house, 32, 33, 34–35, 38, 39, 40, 42, 405nn1, 6, 406n11
Rinderpest, 10
Riotous Assemblies Act, 14
Riots, 14
Rites of passage, 149, 150; puberty, 158–86, 187–201, 255–56, 361, 365–94
Ritual, xx, 51, 57, 59, 186; wedding, 51, 75–76
Robben Island, 16, 271
Rode, 254
Roman Catholic missionaries, 271–72
Rommel, General Erwin, 411n4
Roux, Edward: Time Longer Than Rope, 403n12
Royal houses, 24, 42, 249
Rubusana, W. B.: Zemk' Inkomo Magwalandini, 213, 411nn11, 13, 412n29
Rudulu: people, 242; person, 230, 231, 242
Rutherford, J.: Sir George Grey, 416n3
Rwantsana, 31, 279, 304, 306
Rycroft, David: "Zulu and Xhosa Praise-Poetry and Song," 412n29; "Zulu Izibongo: A Survey of Documentary Sources," 412n29

Ryunosuke, Akutagawa, *Rashomon*, xx

Sabatha, 45
Sabe, 241, 242
St. Augustine's, 260
St. James, xxiii, xv, 401*n1*, 402*n23*
Samuelson, R. C.: *Long, Long Ago*, 412*n29*
San Francisco Conference, 12
San, 5, 6, 222, 405*n4*; paintings, 3, 6. *See also* Thwa
Sanders, P. B. *See* Damane, M., and P. B. Sanders
Sandile, 33, 38, 40, 41, 305, 406–7*n11*
Saracen armored cars, 13
Sarhili, 8, 34, 35, 37, 43, 44, 45, 263, 273, 279, 280, 281, 304, 305, 306, 417*n3*
Saunders, Christopher, and Robin Derricourt: *Beyond the Cape Frontier*, 412*n29*
Schama, Simon: *Citizens*, xix, 401*n8*
Schapera, Isaac, ed.: *The Bantu-Speaking Tribes of South Africa*, 412*n29*; ed., *Praise-Poems of Tswana Chiefs*, 413*n33*
Scheub, Harold: "Body and Image in Oral Narrative Performance," 365, 419*nn10, 13*; "Fixed and Non-Fixed Symbols in Xhosa and Zulu Oral Narrative Traditions," 407*n7*; *Meanings*, 417*n26*; "Narrative Patterning in Oral Performance," 419*n10*; "Oral Narrative Process and the Use of Models," 410*n4*; "Oral Poetry and History," 412*n29*; "Parallel Image Sets in African Oral Performances," 407*n7*; "The Technique of the Expansible Image in Xhosa *Ntsomi* Performances," 407*n7*; "Translation of African Oral Narrative-Performances to the Written Word," 402*n1*, 407*n7*
Schiff, Ben. *See* Goodwin, June, and Ben Schiff
Schools, 403–4*n20*
Sculpture, 54
Sebeni, 36, 281
Second World War, 12, 205
Segoete, Everitt Lechesa: "Mokorotlo," 214; *Raphepheng*, 411*n17*
Sekese, Azariele M.: *Mekhoa Le Maele a Ba-Sotho*, 214, 411*n18*
Selani (ox), 61–62, 66–67
Selele, 35
Senghor, Léopold Sédar: "On Negrohood:

Psychology of the African-Negro," 150, 410*n5*
Senzangakhona, 6, 7, 405*n6*
Sepamla, Sipho, xviii; *A Ride on the Whirlwind*, 401*n5*
Shaka, xxv, 6, 7, 24, 46, 210, 213, 214, 222, 227, 228, 250, 251, 252, 253, 405*n6*; as a name for the Zulu people, 45, 407*n13*. *See also* Zulu
Shaka Zulu. *See* Shaka
Shakespeare: *King Richard II*, 222, 414*n42*; *Merchant of Venice* (quoted by Nelson Mandela), 404*n30*
Sharecroppers, African, 10
Sharpeville, 6, 12
Sharpeville Massacre, xv, 12–13, 15, 293
Shawbury, 264
Sibango, 42
Sibhalala, 266–67
Sibhozo Mnzabele, 411*nn11, 13*
Sibhozo, 36, 304
Sibini, Nololo, 295
Sibisi, 352, 354
Sibiside, 227, 228, 229
Sidoyi, 255, 259
Sifingo, 407*n11*
Sigananda, 301, 348
Sigcawu, 34, 35, 43, 44, 229, 273
Sigidi, 273, 274, 305
Sigilamikuba, 298
Sihula, 228
Sijako, 406*n11*
Sikhakha, 26
Sikhomo (Gcaleka), 31, 34, 43, 44, 230, 242
Sikhomo (Mpondomise), 230, 242
Sikizi, 253, 414*n7*
Silimela, 39
Silothile, 265
Sirunyana, 256
Sisulu, Walter, 15
Sisusempaka, 238
Sitata, 35
Sitokwe, 36
Sitshitshili, 352, 354
Siwabese, 39
Siwani, 33, 38, 39
Slavery, 6, 7
Small, Adam: "Steve Biko," 15, 404*n25*
Smith, 39
Smuts, Jan, 11, 12, 21, 22, 293, 403*n12*, 415*n2*

Sobhini, 45
Sobhuza II, xxv, 205, 210, 275–78
Sobuza, 416*n21*
Sodidi, Manyawusa, 28, 30
Soga, John Henderson: "The Cattle-killing delusion—Nongqawuse," 416*n3*
Soga, 406*n11*
Soga, Freddie, 279
Soga, Tiyo. *See* Chalmers, John A.
Solilo, John: "Mthandi Wesizwe," 15, 404*n26*
Solomon, 22
Somana, 407*n11*
Somerville, 260, 262, 264, 265
Somhlahlo, 266
Somyalo, 270, 271
Song, 53, 55, 155, 213, 214
Sontag, Susan: *Against Interpretation*, 150, 410*n6*
Sontlo, 246, 247, 248, 249
Sonyangwe, 256
Sotho, 5, 214, 217, 256, 260, 262, 347–48, 412*n29*, 413*n33*, 417*n1*
Sotshangane, 252
South African: army, 16; government, 403*n15*; history, 402*n1*; "native policy," 11; police, 12–13, 14, 15, 16; republic, 12
South African Native Convention, 9
South African Native National Congress, 9
South African Outlook, 14
South African Republic (Transvaal), 8
South African Students' Organization, 14
Soweto, xv, xvii, 6, 12, 13, 14, 368
Soweto Students' Representative Council, 13
Soweto uprising, xv, 13–14, 293
Soya, 35
Sparks, Allister: *Tomorrow Is Another Country*, 404*n29*
Spiegel, John Paul, and Pavel Machotka: *Messages of the Body*, 365, 419*n12*
Spirits, 295
Stainbank, H. M., 358, 418*n1*
Stay-at-home strike, 13, 15
Stemela, 279
Stokwe, 45
story, xviii, xix, xx, 52, 60, 149, 150–58; and history, 241; as medium of protest, xv; and memory, xxiii; plot clichés, 54
storyteller, xxi, xxiii, xxiv, xxv, 21, 23, 24, 25, 27, 28, 29, 51, 52, 53, 56, 57, 58, 60, 79,

149, 150, 154, 164, 188, 205, 299, 307, 362, 363, 367, 368; as clown, 57; as creator, 57; and emotion, xxii; and history, xix; as master of ceremonies, 57; and memory, xxi; as moralizer, 55–56; as orchestrator, 55; ordering past and present, xix; and the past, xv; as performer, 57; as shaper, 55; as teacher, 55–56
Stuart, James: *A History of the Zulu Rebellion, 1906, and of Dinuzulu's Arrest, Trial and Expatriation*, 416*nn11, 13, 14, 15*, 417*n25*; *uBaxoxele*, 412*n29*; *uHlangakula*, 412*n29*; *uKulumetule*, 411*n23*, 412*n29*; *uTulasizwe*, 412*n29*; *uVusezakiti*, 412*n29*
Stutterheim, 305
Sudan, 415*n3*
Sukabekuluma (Chakijana), 298, 299
Sukude, 228
Sundkler, B. G. M.: *Bantu Prophets in South Africa*, 415*n3*
Sunduza, 264
Supernatural, 203
Supporting house, 24, 36–37, 41, 43, 279, 405*nn1, 6*, 406*n11*
Swati, xxv, 24, 205, 210, 211, 228, 229, 275–78, 339, 412*n29*; language, 411*n15*; oral traditions, xvii; regiments, 276, 277; storytellers and poets, xvii
Swazi. *See* Swati
Swaziland, 210, 227, 275–78, 339
Symbol, 57

Table Mountain, 5
Tahle, 229
Tala Hill, 352, 354
Taxes, 10, 11, 261, 262, 263, 264; dog licences, 11; dog tax, 9; "hut" tax, 9; laws, 10; poll tax, 9
Teachers, 403–4*n20*
Thabathile, 35
Thandela, 245, 247, 248
Thembani, 266, 267
Thembu, xxv, 5, 32, 35, 40, 44, 45, 222, 250, 252, 253, 257, 258, 259, 266, 271, 273, 283, 304, 305, 306
Thembuland, 35, 231, 253, 257
Thethani, 264
Thethwa, 227, 228
Thina River, 245, 256
Thiso (ox), 43

Thithiya, 238
Thixo, 297
Thompson, Leonard: *A History of South Africa*, 402*n1*. *See also* Wilson, Monica, and Leonard Thompson
Thongwana, 43
Thotywayo, 406*n11*
Thukela River, 349, 355, 356
Thulura, 304
Thulura River, 279
Thuthura, 306
Thwa, 32, 222, 231–35, 236, 241; and Mpondomise, 232–35
Thwana, 279
Tikita, 266
Time, 213; time line, 57, 205
Titlestad, Elias, 348–49, 351
Tlali, Miriam: *Amandla*, xviii, 401*n5*
Tobe, 228
Togu, 31, 34, 43, 44
Tolkien, J. R. R.: "*Beowulf:* The Monster and the Critics," 203, 410*n2*
Tolo, 258
Toyise, 33, 38, 39
Trade unions, 11
Tradition, xvii, xxiv, xxv, xxvi, 162, 218, 219, 284–86, 367, 369–94, 397; and apartheid, xvi, 162; and freedom, xxi, xxii, xxiii, xxiv; Zulu, 365–68, 369–94
Tragedy, 203
Transitions, xxv, 149
Transkei, 11, 15, 28, 31, 61, 78, 150, 163, 187, 206, 223, 227, 273, 279, 282, 287, 289, 294, 304, 307, 395, 410*nn2, 3*, 413*nn31, 37*, 414*nn10, 40*, 414*n1*, 416*n4*, 418*n1*
Transvaal, 7, 8, 9, 217, 300
Transvaal Congress of the National Party, 404*n24*
Treason trial, 16
Treaty of Amiens, 6
Treaty of Vereeniging, 9
Trial of Chakijana, 298
Trickster, 10, 291, 298–303, 417*n1*; as a boundary character, 302; as a transitional force, 302; Zulu, 301, 314–333. *See also* Chakijana
Truter, Colonel Theo, 10
Tsatsi, 406*n11*
Tshali, 252
Tshatshu, 35, 40
Tshawe, 31, 34, 241, 242

Tshayeni, 268, 269
Tshezi, 44
Tshiqo, 410*n3*
Tshiwo, 31, 34, 37, 42, 43, 44
Tshomane, 44
Tshungwane, 256
Tsitsa River, 249, 252
Tsolo, 414*n11*
Tsolo District, 223, 227, 241, 249, 250, 253, 262, 264, 274, 410*n3*, 413*n37*, 414*n6*
Tsolo Mountain, 265
Tsomo, 46, 76, 306
Tsonga, 5
Tsonyana, 211, 279, 280
Tswana, 214, 215, 217, 413*n34*; heroic verse, 411*nn14, 20, 21*
Tyabashe, Mdukiswa, xvii, xviii, xix, xx, xxi, xxv, xxvi, 24, 205, 206, 216–17, 218, 219–21, 224, 367, 413*n37*; "All the Land of the Mpondomise," 221–22, 227–74; on the creation of oral poetry, 220; "So Tall He Touched the Heavens," 205, 216–17, 223–26
Tyhala, 406*n11*
Tyhali, 42, 305, 405*nn7, 10*
Tyholora, 44
Tyindye, 306
Tyler, Humphrey, 13

Umkhonto weSizwe, 16
Umlanjeni, 415*n3*
Union of South Africa, 9, 12, 415*n2*
Unity in performance, 153
Universal Negro Improvement Association, 11
University students, 14
University of Cape Town, 411*n14*
University of Natal, 14
University of Turfloop, 14
University of Zululand, 14

Vaal River, 8
Vail, Leroy, and Landeg White: *Capitalism and Colonialism in Mozambique*, 412–13*n29*; "Forms of Resistance: Oral Poetry and Perceptions of Power in Colonial Mozambique," 413*n29*; "Ndebele Praise Poetry, 1835–1971," 413*n29*; "Plantation Protest: The History of a Mozambican Song," 413*n29*; *Power and the Praise Poem: Southern African Voices in History*, 413*n29*

Van der Stel, Simon, 402*n3*
Van Niekerk, P. W., 293, 358
Van Riebeeck, Jan, 293, 415*n2*; *Précis of the Cape Archives*, 5, 402*n4*
Vansina, Jan: *Oral Tradition as History*, xviii, 401*n6*
Van Warmelo, N. J.: *History of Matiwane and the amaNgwane Tribe*, 413*n29*; *Transvaal Ndebele Texts*, 413*n29*
Vatshile, 253
Velaphi, 39
Veldtman, 36
Veldtman Bhikitshi, 45
Velelo, 34, 45, 248, 250, 251, 252, 253, 254, 257; people, 281
Velenzima, 40
Vena, 36
Venda, 5
Vereeniging, 12
Verwoerd, Hendrik, 12
Veyne, Paul: *Writing History: Essay on Epistemology*, xix, 401*n12*
Vilakazi, Benedict Wallet: "The Conception and Development of Poetry in Zulu," 413*n29*; *Nje-nempela*, 417*n25*; "The Oral and Written Literature in Nguni," 213, 411*n15*, 413*n36*
Volksraad, 414*n11*
Voltaire: *Works: A Contemporary Version*, 49, 407*n2*
Voortrekkers, 7, 293
Voting, 9
Vukela, 37
Vundle, 306
Vuso, 407*n11*
Vuthela, 254

Wallerstein, Immanuel: *The Modern World System*, xix, 401*n11*
War, 214; Anglo-Boer War, 9, 299–300; Basotho Rebellion (War of the Guns), 347–48, 417*n1*; Bhaca and Mpondomise, 253–57; of Dispossession, 297; Dutch and the Xhosa, 6, 7; frontier, 8, 293; guerrilla, 301; *imfecane*, 7; "Kaffir Wars," 7; of Khohlombeni, 265; Khoi and the Dutch, 5; of Langalibalele, 261–62; Mpondomise and the Zulu, 250–53; Mpondomise versus Thembu and Mpondo, 257–60; Ngcayechibi War, 279–81; of Phakana, 259–60; Xhosa and the Thwa, 32

Wellington Movement, 11
Welsh, Alexander R., 264–65
Wesleyan missionary, 407*n14*
White, Landeg. *See also* Vail, Leroy, and Landeg White
White, Landeg, and Tim Couzens, eds.: *Literature and Society in Southern Africa*, 413*n29*
White, Hayden, xix; "The Value of Narrativity in the Representation of Reality," 401*n9*
White Mfolozi River, 358
Whites, 22, 51, 218, 219, 222, 277, 284–86, 287–89, 298, 300, 303, 308, 334–45, 346–57, 358, 403*n6*, 405*n11*. *See also* Europeans
Whitman, Walt: "A Farm Picture," 418*n2*
Wilson, Monica, and Leonard Thompson: *The Oxford History of South Africa*, 402*n1*, 417*n23*
Witchcraft, 247, 405*n9*
Witwatersrand, 9
Wohle, 406*n11*
Wolela, 406*n11*
Woods, Donald: *Biko*, 14–15, 404*n23*
Worsley, Peter: *The Trumpet Shall Sound*, 415*n3*

Xesi, 305
Xesibe, 5, 28, 205, 245, 246, 282–89
Xhelinkunzi, 35
Xhelo, 211
Xhobane River, 279
Xhoko, 25, 26
Xhokonxa, 252
Xholoxholo Mountain, 285
Xhonxa, 38
Xhora, 306
Xhosa, mentioned *passim*; bridal attire, 70–71, 73–74; bride, 408*n11*, 409*n18*; chiefs, 304; children, 237; civilization, 60; clothing, 307; custom, 60, 61–77, 219, 406*n11*; epic, xxiv, 78–145; ethos, 295; girl, 106; groom, 61–77, 408*n11*; herdboys, 274; historians, xviii; history and tale, xviii; homes, 206; kingship, 31–47, 405–7*n11*; language, 411*n15*; literature, 297; marriage ceremony, xxiv, 51, 57–58, 408*nn1*, *10*, *11*, 409*nn21*, *27*; master of ceremonies (at a wedding), 61–77, 408*n5*, 409*nn13*, *24*, *26*; oral traditions, xvii, xxiv, 222; person, 24, 31, 34; poet, 411*n6*; storytellers and

Xhosa (*continued*)
  poets, xvii, 150; woman, 127; youth, 255
Xhosaland, 295, 406*n11*
Xhoxho, 35
Xhwangu, 225, 238
Xolilizwe, 34
Xuka, 305
Xura, 414*n9*

Yali-Manisi, D. P.: *Izibongo zeenkosi zama-Xhosa*, 413*n29*
Yanguya, 405*n7*, 411*n9*, 413*n32*
Yanguye, 416*n16*

Zambezi River, 227
Zana Forest, 230, 231
Zanelanga, 35
Zebangweni, 226
Zelenqaba, 45
Zenani, Nongenile Masithathu, xvii, xxiv, 51, 52, 53, 58–60, 61, 78–145, 221, 222, 293, 368, 408*n1*, 409*nn19, 27*, 410*n2*, 419*n10*; autobiography, 61–77; as a bride, 61–77; "The Endless Mountain," 78–145, 222; "The Necessary Clown," pp. 61–77; "No Person Arose," 298, 307–13; on performing stories, 149; *The World and the Word*, 407*n4*, 410*n3*, 414*n41*, 419*n10*
Zenzile, 39

Zimasile, 407*n11*
Zimbabwe, xvii, 401*n4*
Zimlindile, 33, 38, 39
Zingqayi, 45
Zondi, 301, 358, 416*n21*
Zozi, 251, 252
Zulu, mentioned *passim;* boys, 327; chiefs, 300; executions, 300; guerrillas, 303, 417*n22*; historians, xviii, 21, 24; history, 22; language, 346, 411*n15*; marriage, 366, 369–94; novel, 214, 215; oral traditions, xvii, 293, 417*n1*, 420*n16*; person, 405*n6*; poets, xvii, 21, 214, 215, 405*n7*; rebellion, 334–45, 346–57, 358; resistance, 301; storytellers, xvii, xviii, 56, 299, 363; struggle for freedom, 303; tradition, 362, 365–68, 369–94. *See also* Shaka
Zulu (name of an ox), 43
Zululand, 22, 25, 43, 46, 227, 228, 250, 252, 253, 276, 298, 299, 301, 314, 334–45, 346–57, 358, 365–68, 369–94, 405*n7*, 411*n9*, 413*n32*, 416*n16*, 418*n1*
Zululand Mounted Rifles, 348, 350
Zumbe, 240
Zungu, Nombhonjo, 210, 212, 218, 411*n9*
Zwelidumile, 34, 35, 43, 44
Zwelinzima, 37, 207
Zwide, 62